Michael Billington

One Night Stands

A Critic's View of
Modern British Theatre

Nick Hern Books

A Nick Hern Book

One Night Stands first published in 1993 by
Nick Hern Books Limited, 14 Larden Road, London W3 7ST

This revised paperback edition published in 2001

A CIP catalogue record for this book
is available from the British Library

ISBN 1-85459-660-8

Typeset in Britain by
Raven Typesetters, Ellesmere Port, South Wirral

Printed and bound in Great Britain by
LSL Press, Bedford, MK41 0TY

Contents

Foreword

'Anybody can write dramatic criticism; it takes a very clever fellow indeed to get it reprinted.'

So wrote James Agate in 1939 and, in his case, that outrageous brag was justified. He managed to get the bulk of his weekly *Sunday Times* columns from 1923 to 1947 into hardback. This volume is a more modest selection culled from over two million words of dramatic criticism written for *The Guardian* between October 1971 – the date I joined the paper – and December 1991.

Why do it? Obviously there is a touch of personal vanity: a desire to retrieve something of one's journalistic past. But the book also springs from an urge to pin down, more or less permanently, some of the momentous events and life-enhancing personalities of the past two decades. I am a great collector of dramatic criticism and it struck me as odd that one could piece together the history of British theatre this century from the collections of Beerbohm, Walkley, Agate, Worsley, Trewin and Tynan, but that then the record peters out. It is true that two highly-esteemed colleagues, Sheridan Morley and B.A. Young, have collected their criticism and that the magazine *Theatre Record*, Ian Herbert's invaluable brainchild, has reprinted all reviews published since 1981. But there is still a big gap on the bookshelves. Where are the collections of Hobson, Wardle, Ratcliffe, Coveney? One aim of this volume is to restore a vanishing tradition.

This selection also gives me a chance to answer some of the questions I am constantly asked: either at the end of lectures or in letters on ruled-line paper from harassed A-Level students. How does one become a critic? What gives one the right to pass judgement on others? What is one's relationship with the theatre? And what actually is the function of the newspaper critic?

On the whole, I believe critics are born, not made: possibly because of some temperamental deficiency or innate shyness, many of us discover at an early age that we prefer to be among the watchers than the watched. In my own case, geographical accident also played its part. Brought up in the Midlands within easy reach of Stratford, Birmingham and Coventry (where you could see everything from Olivier to the D'Oyly Carte Opera to Jewel and Warriss), I soon found I was relieving the frustrations of small-town adolescent life not only by haunting theatres but by making notes on performances I had seen. At Oxford I also discovered I got more of a buzz from writing reviews for *Cherwell* even than I did from acting and directing: lacking the self-confidence, and talent to be a tyro Brook, I found I was at ease only behind a typewriter. Critics are always accused of being failed actors, dramatists or directors: it's nearer the truth to say that we find our emotional energies released by appraising the work of others.

Cutting a long story short, I left Oxford in 1961 hungry to be a critic and heavily influenced, like all my generation, by the glamour and style Tynan brought to the job at *The Observer*. After six traumatic months as a trainee journalist in Liverpool – where a colleague dubbed me 'the Lucky Jim of provincial journalism' – and two instructive years helping to run a rep company in Lincoln, I came to London in 1964 with pen poised but no prospects. I discovered that the best route into criticism is via specialist magazines. Peter Roberts gave me a vital kick-start at *Plays And Players*, dispatching me to review Ken Campbell's first play at RADA for a fiver. Armed with a clutch of cuttings from *P & P*, I then wrote to John Lawrence, Arts Editor of *The Times* and the patron saint of fledgling critics. He took a flier, sent me to see *Saint Joan* at Bristol Old Vic and, happily, kept employing me through the Sixties. Having shadowed Irving Wardle for six years, I wrote to *The Guardian* in 1971 and was given a crack at the main job by the then Features Editor, Peter Preston.

Enlightened patronage and bull-headed persistence are the prerequisites for a young critic: plus, of course, the ability to string a sentence together and an obsessive fascination with theatre. The charge I most frequently encounter today is that London critics are all cut from the same cloth: that they are predominantly white, male, middle-aged, middle-class and Oxbridge-educated. It's basically true. But the ground is palpably shifting, at least where sex is concerned. *The Guardian* employs a number of female theatre critics (Claire Armitstead, Joyce McMillan, Clare Bayley) and women have also made their mark at *The Observer, The Independent, Time Out* and *City Limits*. If middle-classness is still prevalent, that is a direct reflection both of the educational system and the theatregoing constituency in Britain: regrettable but a fact. Though I'd like to see critics drawn from a wider catchment area, there is a limit to what legislation can do. Critics are haunted, solitary theatre-nuts who cannot be willed into existence by editorial magic.

What exactly gives one the right to criticise? The short answer is: absolutely nothing. You can get a degree in Drama at various universities and the City Lit at the Barbican currently offers a course in Drama Criticism, but there are no diplomas licensing you to practise. Rightly so: criticism is not comparable to computing or dentistry. In the end, you earn the right to be a critic by the passion, commitment, moral zeal and verbal felicity you bring to the job. In my experience, the charlatan, the show-off or the con-artist is quickly detected. What is more, the daily and weekly critic soon discovers that every word he or she writes is monitored by editors, readers and theatre folk looking for factual inaccuracies, irrational prejudices or unproven assertions: this is one reason for including several retaliatory letters in this book. Criticism, to me, is not the last word: simply part of a permanent debate about the nature of the ideal theatre.

That, in turn, raises the question of how much, or how little, a critic should be part of the theatre scene. Just how close should we get to the practitioners? I recall once giving a talk at Nottingham Playhouse where a member of the public unnervingly asked me: 'Whose side are you on – ours or theirs?' I suppose there are two extreme answers to the question. One is to see the critic as the public's champion, who should refuse to be contaminated by contact with the profession he or she is writing about. The other is to say that we're all in the same business and that it's therefore OK to mingle freely with theatre people outside office hours. My own course is to steer a prudent middle way. I've no wish, even if I were asked, to attend theatre parties, frequent rehearsals (I did it once) or sup late night with the stars at Joe Allens. Bedding down with the people you write about is the shortest way to professional castration. On the other hand, it's useful occasionally to talk to directors of theatres about artistic policy or theatrical economics. Indeed Max Stafford-Clark at the Royal Court instituted a series of Christmas lunches for critics, invariably rounded off by practical party games. At one we were all asked to devise a programme for the Court within existing budgets: at another we debated the point at which sponsorship becomes politically unwise. All of which is instructive.

I also, as I reveal later, gladly accepted an invitation from a group of RSC actors to direct a Marivaux play: that seemed to me a far better way of putting one's theories into practice than snooping on rehearsals. I am often asked what I learned from the experience. The paramount lesson was that the outsider can never finally know just who contributed what to a production. But I don't infer from that that the critic should be privy to the creative process: simply that he or she has to make informed estimates on the evidence available. In short, I see the critic neither as totally detached outsider nor as hob-nobbing insider, neither as man from Mars nor stage-door Johnny: more as a permanent occupant of a Pinteresque no-man's-land always in danger of getting caught in enemy cross-fire.

Which brings us straight to the role of the critic. The danger is that one starts peddling lofty abstractions. The blunt truth, as any critic will tell you, is that one's role is partly defined by a set of pragmatic circumstances: the paper one writes for, the amount of space, the length of one's deadline. There is all the difference in the world between a brisk overnight review for a popular tabloid and a three thousand word analysis of Bond or Barker for an academic quarterly. I speak from some experience since I can see my own method and style subtly changing in the course of twenty years on *The Guardian*. When I began in 1971, it was the age of overnight reviewing when all copy – sometimes banged out on an office typewriter, sometimes scribbled on a pad and phoned in – had to be in the sub's hands by 11 p.m. Then in the mid-1980s the pattern changed, initially because of distribution problems. The deadline moved to lunchtime the morning after the first night: thus the review appeared in print two days after the event. What started as pragmatism eventually became policy. Today the *Daily Telegraph* and *Independent* both follow suit, though the approach remains flexible. If a first night is held to have important news value (ie. if it's a musical), it will generally be covered by the national press – sometimes with a shroud – the next day.

Within the trade there is much hair-splitting theological debate – akin to how many angels you can get on the head of a pin – about the merits of the overnight versus the morning-after review. C.E. Montague, a towering *Manchester Guardian* figure and a personal hero, put the case for overnight reviewing in *Dramatic Values* in 1910 saying 'below yourself in certain ways, you hope you were above yourself in others.' Arnold Bennett put the contrary case in 1923 writing: 'No critic, however expert, can do justice either to himself or to a play in the time placed at the disposal of critics in morning papers. The conditions ought to be altered and could be altered.' On the whole, I'm with Bennett. The overnight review can pin down the exhilaration or the outrage of the moment, but it can also lead to a flushed excitability and often militates against innovation. Lilian Baylis once cheekily complained of critics that 'they form too quick an impression of work it has taken my dear producer and his boys and girls a whole week to prepare.' More seriously, the overnight reaction of critics to plays such as *Waiting For Godot, The Birthday Party, Saved* and *Serjeant Musgrave's Dance* doesn't exactly encourage one's faith in the wisdom of instant judgement. Looking through my own work, I pause to reflect on my call to banish *The Taming Of The Shrew* from the British stage or my brutal put-down of Pinter's *Betrayal* on its first appearance. I include these pieces because they are an honest record of how I felt at the time; but the problem with one night stands is that things often look different by the sober light of dawn.

All I am saying is that form dictates function: a 900-word review written the morning after is likely to be saner, shrewder and more full of interesting contradiction than a 400-word piece written to meet a pressing deadline. Hence the old Tom Stoppard joke that any play that ends after ten o'clock is automatically self-indulgent. But whatever the circumstances, the first duty of the critic is to engage with the living event with total concentration and to present his or her uncensored reactions with maximum dash and fire. Which is not as easy as it sounds. You have to shut out your partner's reaction, preliminary hype, the muttering of cliques and the hysteria of claques to provide a rational justification of an emotional reaction. The important thing is to be match-fit for the occasion. If you are tired, liverish, sluggish or drunk you may be able to write but you won't be able to react. Advice, therefore, to a young critic: lay off the lunchtime booze and take an afternoon rest.

Criticism does, however, have a vital secondary function: to deal, as Tynan said, with what is *not* happening as well as with what is. That explains the hortatory note that consistently enters into these columns. Arriving on the scene in 1971, at a time of rising unemployment, social unrest and a Northern Irish crisis, I was constantly urging the theatre towards a greater engagement with political realities. The more I travelled in Europe in the seventies, the more I also realised how cut off we were from the great French, German, Italian, Spanish and Russian classics. The situation has now radically improved, thanks largely to the existence of theatres like the Glasgow Citizens and the Gate, but internationalism still seems to me a cause worth fighting for. In the Thatcherite eighties I then found, to my horror, one was having to defend the very principle of subsidy itself, and even the existence of a national company like the RSC, from the barbarians and philistines. I offer no apology for being a prescriptive, as well as a reactive critic. We should all have a Platonic ideal of the perfect theatre for which we should passionately fight.

As I write, my main fear is that the art of criticism is under threat from two specific quarters. One is the well-oiled PR machine. By the time any play or musical opens these days, we have been so bombarded by interviews in the dailies and Sundays, colour magazine profiles, titbits on the TV arts programmes that criticism is in danger of being reduced to a marginal postscript. Since almost everything comes surrounded with ballyhoo, it is also becoming harder for the critic to 'discover' a genuine work of art: a rare and pleasant exception was Ariel Dorfman's *Death And The Maiden* which opened in the Theatre Upstairs on a Friday night in the summer of 1991 to a total absence of drum-beating. The other enemy of criticism is the insidious cultural relativism which argues that value-judgements are suspect, the canon of acknowledged masterpieces is an elitist conspiracy and that everything is as interesting as everything else. It is, I suspect, the by-product of academic cravenness, sloppy Sixties thinking and the flattening effect of television which finds genius an imponderable concept. David Hare had a good go at it on *The Late Show*, and I share his hunger for artistic standards, however subject to debate and revision.

On that theme, I should perhaps say something about the criteria governing the selection of pieces for this book. The greatest challenge to a critic is responding to new writing and I wanted to reflect the stimulus of confronting new work by dramatists as varied as Osborne, Pinter, Bond, Storey, Stoppard, Griffiths, Ayckbourn, Hare, Brenton, Barker and Churchill. If some of their major work is excluded, it is often for personal reasons: I feel I had nothing startling to say, for instance, about Stoppard's *Jumpers* on its first appearance and Caryl Churchill's *Cloud Nine* left me intellectually bemused. I hope I am not afraid of appearing, in the light of posterity, to be wrong; but where a review is simply fence-sitting or obtuse, it has been excluded.

With classic plays, the intention was to reflect the growing variety of work on view in the last twenty years. It would be perfectly easy, for instance, to construct a book out of nothing but Shakespeare reviews, showing how we moved from communal celebration and exploration of studio spaces in the Seventies (reaching a peak in Trevor Nunn's Other Place *Macbeth*) to the eccentric individualism of the Eighties. But I also wanted to reflect attitudes to Ibsen and Chekhov – two of the strongest cards in the British theatre's suit – and the fact that we have a new generation of internationally-minded directors, people like Declan Donnellan, David Freeman and Stephen Daldry who have broken through the cultural tariff-barriers.

On top of that, I wanted to say something about the populist tradition in British theatre: to show that a critic's life is not all *Hamlet* and *Hedda Gabler*, but that it includes Ken Dodd and Ken Campbell, Andrew Lloyd Webber and Stephen Sondheim (whom we do very well), Ray Cooney and Agatha Christie. I particularly believe in the vitality of the music-hall tradition which fed and nourished a whole range of dramatists including Osborne, Pinter, Arden and Nichols. If anything worries me about the period under review, it is not the growth of populism but the deeply Thatcherite equation between commercial viability and quality: the assumption that what makes the most money is automatically the best and the identification of British theatre the world over with a legendary string of hit musicals. Only an arrant snob would deny that the musical has an important place in our culture. Yet if any one theme emerges from the ensuing pages, I hope it is that the theatre is not just a money-making business: it is also a public service to be interpreted, evaluated and fought for with whatever critical passion one can muster. In the last, and sometimes the first, resort, I believe in the critic as daily moralist.

I must thank *The Guardian*, and most especially its editor, Peter Preston, for generously giving me my head for over twenty years and for kindly permitting me to reprint my reviews. A succession of Arts Editors have also shown unswerving support, loyalty and forbearance over two decades: Mike McNay, Stuart Wavell, Tim Radford, Patrick Ensor, Roger Alton and Helen Oldfield. My gratitude to everyone, as to Nick Hern who commissioned the book in the first place, to Siân Owen for steering it into print, and to my wife, Jeanine, who sat through many of the shows and then had the onerous task of photocopying the reviews. Without all this support the book, which aims to convey the peculiar resilience of the British theatre, would have remained the dream of an idle hour.

January 1993

Postscript

It is nearly a decade since I assembled this breathless collection of theatre reviews. But some things remain constant. Attritional funding continued for much of the 90s. The West End more than ever came to resemble Broadway: i.e. a few token straight plays (of which *Art* is the most durable symbol) were lonely oases in a desert of musicals. And criticism itself was increasingly pre-empted in a culture dominated by hype, puffery and what Robert Hughes calls 'the psychotic cult of celebrity': a process that reached its apogee with the appearance of an ex-model, Jerry Hall, in a tame version of *The Graduate*. Bernhardt at her prime could not have generated more column inches.

And yet I remain perversely sanguine about the future of the theatre. Easily the most striking feature of the decade was the emergence of a new generation of writers largely, though not exclusively, through the Royal Court and the National Theatre Studio. Sarah Kane's *Blasted* achieved the same iconic status as Edward Bond's *Saved*. Mark Ravenhill's *Shopping and Fucking* toured nationwide and even made it into the Gielgud Theatre. England's Patrick Marber and Joe Penhall, Ireland's Conor McPherson and Martin McDonagh, Scotland's David Greig and David Harrower were also leaders of a creative pack united only by its belief that, in an age of bland television and blockbuster cinema, theatre offered a vital platform for the writer with a distinctive vision.

The 90s was also a decade which eroded the former dominance of the twin national companies. The National, as Trevor Nunn succeeded Richard Eyre, re-positioned itself in the populist centre-ground. The RSC, under Adrian Noble, did much good work but seemed to be restlessly searching for a new identity. In London the success-story of the decade was the Almeida: it presented an international repertory while maintaining a permanent hotline to the best actors. Cheek by Jowl and Complicite moved from the margins to become the most sought-after British troupes on the international circuit. And in the regions, which in 2001 were promised a life-saving transfusion of new money, Yorkshire became a theatrical Mecca with Jude Kelly in Leeds, Alan Ayckbourn in Scarborough and, latterly, Michael Grandage in Sheffield all proving there was life beyond London: indeed it was often *in* London, especially in the seedy environs of the West End, that the real problems lay.

So I look to the future in a spirit of modest hope tempered by cautious realism: the critic's perennially schizoid condition and one that you will find all too clearly reflected in the following pages.

Michael Billington, June 2001

1971

I only graduated from Moon *to* Birdboot, *from deputy critic to full-time aisle-squatter in October so it would be arrogant to offer Olympian judgements. But it was a year in which the National Theatre got a lot of stick both for its Old Vic programme and for an ill-fated season at the New:* Amphitryon 38, Tyger, Danton's Death, *and* The Rules Of The Game *pleased neither critics nor the million, and it was only the last-minute triumph of* Long Day's Journey Into Night *that saved the season from disaster. Even so, the National had to go cap-in-hand to the Arts Council asking for a top-up to its annual subsidy of £295,000.*

The RSC, on the other hand, could do little wrong. Its greatest-ever Aldwych season included Pinter's Old Times, *Peter Brook's production of* A Midsummer Night's Dream, *Gorky's* Enemies, *Etherege's* The Man Of Mode, *Joyce's* Exiles *and Genet's* The Balcony. *It also launched a supplementary season at The Place including Trevor Griffiths's* Occupations *and Robin Phillips's hyper-realistic production of* Miss Julie. *(One critic, in a fit of indignation, rang round his colleagues to check if a live canary really had been strangled.)*

In retrospect, it also looks like a good year for new plays: not just the Pinter, but Bond's Lear, *Storey's* The Changing Room, *Osborne's* West Of Suez, *Nichols's* Forget-Me-Not-Lane, *Gray's* Butley *and E.A. Whitehead's* The Foursome. *From posterity's vantage-point, positively mouth-watering. Jean-Louis Barrault's* Rabelais *and Ariane Mnouchkine's* 1789 *came in from Paris. The new Birmingham Rep and the Sheffield Crucible opened their doors, pushed seat prices above the £1 level for the first time in the regions and then fell flat on their face with, respectively, a musical* Pride And Prejudice *and a mediocre* Peer Gynt. *On the Fringe, simulated copulation thrived and a cuddly Christ arrived at the Young Vic with* Godspell. *Still, a good year to start out on the great adventure of criticism . . .*

West Of Suez

Cambridge Theatre: 13 October 1971

John Osborne's *West Of Suez*, which has just transferred to the Cambridge Theatre, is a work that has been chronically misinterpreted. Osborne, we have been told, has forfeited the right to speak for his own generation, has written a play that would appeal to the white minorities in South Africa or Rhodesia, has adopted the mantle of N.C. Hunter in penning a piece of Anglicised Chekhov with a fat star part and has generally swung so far to the Right as to be almost out of sight. However, instead of being a lament for the loss of Empire, the play is really about the fate of Western civilisation. It is not a hymn to times past but a prophetic warning about times to come; not a piece of Tory nostalgia but a cry of liberal despair.

It is true, of course, that Osborne sets the action in a former British colony that has recently gained its independence and that there is a good deal of talk about the vanished life-style of Empire. In one densely-written passage the author-hero and his daughters simply catalogue some of the things they remember from their own family past: the fading photographs of amateur theatricals, the timetable of the South India railway, books scented with curry-powder. But this is no more than Osborne's own Proustian acknowledgement of the evocative power of insignificant objects (in *Time Present* old theatrical posters and bills spark off a similar total recall) and is even a mark of the characters' slightly self-indulgent sentimentality. For a genuine parallel to Osborne's attitude to our colonial past, one should look to James Ivory's film *Shakespeare Wallah*, which shows a tumbledown theatrical troupe touring a changing, post-imperial India: like Ivory, Osborne admits the necessity of change but has a profound sympathy for people left stranded by the tide of history.

West Of Suez however is not really about Empire. It is about the break-up of any civilisation that no longer puts its trust in reason, in respect for other people's values and above all, in language. As has been pointed out, the play is built round a preoccupation with words. Three of the characters are writers; people are constantly commenting on the quality of each other's verbal style; and Jed, the American hippie who finally savages the bourgeois-decadents, is shown to have a pathetically limited capacity for invective. As a writer, Osborne clearly has a vested interest in language and its careful preservation; but what he says in the play is that if you don't believe in language you are not only sacrificing something of your own essential selfhood but you are also destroying a bridge between human beings and hastening the day when the law of the jungle prevails. Osborne obviously believes that the barbarians and philistines are at the gates; and that is why the hippie tirade leads so quickly to an act of utterly pointless violence. From the breakdown of verbal contact, all else will follow.

On a second hearing, the play seems much more carefully constructed than at first appeared; built on Chekhovian principles, it is as full of echoes as a whispering gallery. Thus it opens with a spiky, edgy duologue between Frederica, one of the hero's four daughters, and her pathologist husband, Edward. Most critics have taken Edward's subsequent disappearance from the action as a sign of inept craftsmanship and wondered why there should be so much stress on his off-stage friendship with the hippie; but surely the point is that both stand outside the charmed circle of this literary family and therefore feel an immediate tug of sympathy. Edward constantly describes himself as 'a blood-and-shit man'; and it can be no accident that 'blood' and 'shit' are the two words that throb through Jed's final speech like a refrain. Similarly Frederica condemns the islanders for their blend of 'apathy and hysteria, brutality and sentimentality': and her father uses exactly the same words later, unconsciously revealing the bond between himself and his most pugnacious daughter. Seemingly rather off-hand in his attitude to structure, Osborne quietly knits the play together through reiterated words and phrases.

The weakness in *West Of Suez* is that the dissolution of civilised values is over-literally presented: what Chekhov could suggest with a breaking string or Shaw with a sound of distant gunfire Osborne presents rather nakedly with an on-stage killing. But, viewed in the context of Osborne's whole career, the play is endlessly fascinating. Despite its climax, it marks another stage in his attempt to withdraw physical action from his work; it shows him achieving greater objectivity in his delineation of character; and it also shows him eliminating the chain of theatrical and showbiz metaphor that fuelled so much of his earlier work.

This last point is highly significant: Osborne, Pinter, Wood, Livings, Owen, Dyer are just some of the modern dramatists whose writing has grown directly out of their acting career and I believe you can detect the influence of this in most of their work. Certainly in Osborne's case both his style and content have been deeply influenced by his understanding of the actor's temperament. In *Epitaph For George Dillon* the actor-hero's embattled, complex and turbulent relationship with his audience ('I attract hostility. I seem to be on heat for it.') uncannily foreshadows Osborne's own volatile relationship with his public. *Look Back In Anger* strikes a chord in most young people equipped with an energy, passion and concern that can find no proper social outlet; but to narrow the focus, it also reflects the problems of an actor stuck in the rut of Midlands weekly rep in the fifties knowing that he has a talent that has so far gone unremarked.

The Entertainer obviously exploits all Osborne's knowledge of the theatrical scene: indeed the music-hall idiom is built so strongly into the fabric of the play that even the domestic scenes retain the bantering, button-holing tone of Archie's front-cloth numbers. Even in *Luther* there is a resort to green-room language ('Men like you just don't forget their words' Luther's father tell him as he prepares for his gruelling first communion) and the use of the old vaudeville trick of repeating something that has just been said to one brings an unwonted touch of Max Miller into the Middle Ages. And Laurie in *The Hotel In Amsterdam* may be a successful writer but he is still loaded with an actorish delight in slightly camp conversational fantasies.

This reliance on theatrical metaphor and backstage egoism has in no way undermined the works concerned: instead it has nourished and sustained them. But I don't think it's fanciful to see Osborne in *West Of Suez* standing further outside his characters than before and banishing something of his normally intuitive identification with his hero. Obviously the Osborne trademarks are all there: the hostility to critics, the attacks on fake sociology, the sometimes whimsical animal references. But you really believe his hero might have sat at a typewriter; and you can imagine the kind of books he would have written.

Someone remarks of a character in an earlier Osborne play that she has her ear to the ground of the wrong building; and if I had to sum up Osborne's special quality as a writer it would be that he normally has his ear to the ground of the right building. His plays catch and interpret the mood of a time; and in *West Of Suez* he is (I believe) alerting us to the fact that there is a strong Fascist instinct currently abroad. It is rather like Gorky's *Enemies* seen from another angle: the difference here is that the beleaguered bourgeoisie are threatened not by rising social and political progress but by a spirit of fanatical intolerance. 'My God, they've shot the fox' is the resonant final line as the hero lies slumped on the lawn; and clearly what this signifies is that although much of the old order may have to go, its removal can at least be accomplished with dignity and propriety. That sounds to me more like the attitude of an old-fashioned liberal humanist than of a tweedy Loamshire squirearch.

The Changing Room

Royal Court: 10 November 1971

David Storey is a writer who genuinely extends the territory of drama. In *The Contractor* he used the erection of a tent to give us a vivid portrait of a feudal working society and a wretchedly divided family. And in his stunning new play, *The Changing Room*, the elaborate rituals surrounding a Rugby League game provide a microcosm of another deeply hierarchical society with its fixed traditions and inflexible code of behaviour.

As always Storey (from whom it becomes increasingly difficult to disentangle his director, Lindsay Anderson) pays enormous attention to naturalistic surface. Thus he meticulously shows us the spartan, pre-match preparations: the daubing of frozen bodies in oils and embrocations, the masseur's ceaseless manipulations, the routine frisking of the players by a stonily humourless referee. But although creating a powerful sense of community activity, he also swiftly delineates individual characters, so that the fading, accident-prone forward who gets a broken nose during the match becomes much more than an arbitrary symbol of the game's casual cruelty. And the victorious post-match atmosphere, supposedly euphoric, is also touched with deep sadness as these muscle-bound heroes reluctantly re-enter the outside world.

Despite the bawdy shower-room banter, this is a deeply moralistic society in which all personal desires are subordinated to the need to win; and it is also one in which everyone has his fixed place, from the Commie-hating cleaner who never gets to see the game to the paunchy Chairman offering banal encouragements to men he doesn't really know or understand. As in *The Contractor*, Storey concentrates on detail and leaves you to supply the larger meaning but it's not difficult to see the Rugby League world as a metaphor for a mechanised industrial society in which prodigious energy is expended for the profit of the few.

Needless to say, Mr Anderson's production is perfectly choreographed, keeping an exact balance between individual characters and group endeavours: most importantly, it gives one the feeling one is watching yet another Saturday in the life of a constantly changing group rather than a gang of actors togging up for a theatrical occasion. It's unfair to seize on individuals but I can't resist saluting John Barrett's sad, soured cleaner, Edward Judd's flash, cigar-smoking forward and David Hill's taciturn, remote centre three. But the real triumph lies in the seamless blend of acting, writing and direction.

Godspell

Roundhouse: 18 November 1971

Acting on the belief that the devil need not have all the worst tunes, Broadway and its environs have recently started turning out rock versions of the Christian message. The first to hit us is *Godspell* which takes St Matthew's gospel and turns it into an unnerving combination of a Ralph Reader Gang Show, a sterilised version of *Hair* and some thing a trendy Kingsley Amis vicar might have dreamed up given limitless resources. I can't say I warm to it but judging by the number of people leaping ecstatically to their feet at the end, I presume its message got through.

Conceived and directed by John-Michael Tebelak, the show boils down to an attempt to retell the gospel story in terms of vaudeville, circus and pop. Initially appearing as the great philosophers down the ages (from Socrates to Sartre) the cast quickly dispose of them and their apparently outworn ideas only to reappear as a gang of gawky clowns receiving a simplified version of the gospel from a baby-faced, baggy-trousered Christ. Everything is reduced to a set of relentlessly illustrated slogans; 'Consider the lilies of the field,' says Christ whimsically producing a conjuror's collapsible bouquet from his pocket, 'they don't work, they don't spin.' Beautiful poetic parables are rendered into nursery English; every showbiz cliché, even down to the Rockettes-type line-up, is untiringly exploited; and the word 'love' is bandied around without anyone pausing to define it.

Let me say at once that Stephen Schwartz's music is often superbly exhilarating and that Marti Webb, Julie Covington and Neil Fitz-william in particular put across their numbers with enormous élan. But what disturbs me about the show is the assumption that in order to propagate the Christian message you have to insult people's intelligence. Most of us are capable of understanding the parable of the sower without having actors jokily imitating fruit and tares; and the Sermon on the Mount is not much improved by being given the full Sesame Street treatment.

There is all the difference in the world between honest simplicity (such as you movingly find in the medieval Mystery cycles) and faux-naïvété (such as you get when adult actors archly pretend to be children). Admittedly in a non-religious age it's difficult to find popular ways of projecting gospel truths; but I would say there is more real Christianity in any five minutes of *Hair* than in the whole of this self-contratulatory uneloquent cartoon-like musical. God, I muttered wanly as I emerged, is not rocked.

1972

It was a year in which the split between the subsidised and commercial sectors widened into a chasm. Virtually all the good new plays came from the former: Stoppard's Jumpers, *dealing wittily with the death of God and the collapse of absolutist belief, at the Old Vic, Wood's* Veterans, *Whitehead's* Alpha Beta, *Wesker's* The Old Ones *and Osborne's much-abused* A Sense Of Detachment *at the Royal Court; Griffiths's* Sam Sam *at the Open Space.*

In contrast, the commercial theatre seemed to have given up the ghost, pumping out second-rate bedroom farces like The Mating Game *and mediocre musicals like* Gone With The Wind *and* I And Albert. *The only bright features in a dismal West End year were Sondheim's* Company, *Gielgud's classy revival of* Private Lives, *with a wildly semaphoring Maggie Smith, and bits of Frank Marcus's* Notes On A Love Affair *and Alan Ayckbourn's* Time And Time Again.

Perhaps the best feature of the year was the theatre's recognition that we were engulfed by a major political crisis in Northern Ireland. The multi-authored England's Ireland, *which was turned down by over fifty theatres, finally achieved a brief London showing at the Royal Court. John Arden and Margaretta D'Arcy's* The Ballygombeen Bequest, *dealing with an absentee English landlord's attempt to evict a tenant family from his inherited Irish estate, was seen in Belfast, Edinburgh and at the Bush before being stopped by a writ for libel and slander. Wilson John Haire's* Within Two Shadows, *which used a Belfast working-class family as a symbol of a divided nation, proceeded without interruption at the Theatre Upstairs. And O'Casey's* The Shadow Of A Gunman, *showing Irish Republicans fighting a guerilla war against detested British troops, was thrillingly revived at the Young Vic. Politics at last were firmly on the agenda.*

Oddest item of the year was the English Stage Company's announcement of plans to take over the Old Vic once the National Theatre company moved into its new home. I was dead against it at the time. But, given the subsequent, chequered history of that great playhouse, I begin to wonder what might have happened if it had become a permanent home for new drama. Alas, we shall never know . . .

Three Great Performances

Olivier, Scofield and Richardson: 7 January 1972

Before 1971 sinks irretrievably out of sight, I should like to affirm as loudly as possible something that got overlooked in all those end-of-the-year surveys: namely, that we have just witnessed an annus mirabilis for English acting. In the course of the year I saw three indisputably great performances: Olivier's in *Long Day's Journey Into Night*, Richardson's in *West Of Suez* and Scofield's in *The Captain Of Köpenick*. Anthony Hopkins at the National and John Wood at the RSC also proved that they are poised to attack the great classic roles. And there was work of enormous distinction from Ashcroft, Guinness, and McKellen, whose Hamlet was miserably under-rated.

Of course the moment one starts talking about 'great acting' one is in trouble. We all recognise it when we see it but who on earth can define it? Agate, the best modern critic of acting, argued that it was something incalculable that took you by surprise and left you no liberty to reason. 'Whoever has seen a great actor,' he wrote, 'knows that he is not an animal to be stalked in its lair but a tiger leaping out on the spectator from the bush of mediocrity and the brake of competence.' And Tynan, writing about Olivier's Othello, got down to brass tacks by listing what he considered the seven essential attributes of greatness. These were 'complete physical relaxation, powerful physical magnetism, commanding eyes visible at the back of the gallery, a commanding voice audible without effort at the back of the gallery, superb timing which includes the ability to make verse swing, chutzpah – the untranslatable Jewish word that means cool nerve and outrageous effrontery combined and the ability to communicate a sense of danger.'

But the emphasis on physical qualities leaves out one, to me, essential attribute: acute interpretative intelligence. Gordon Craig hit it when he said that the ideal actor should possess both a rich nature and a powerful brain; and while I don't believe anyone can work his way towards greatness purely by rational means, I do believe intellectual vigour is an essential component of the best acting. Olivier's Othello was great not merely because of its extraordinary emotional dynamic but because he went further than any modern actor in showing Othello as self-regarding, arrogant, and vengeful; Kean's Iago was championed by Hazlitt and Leigh Hunt not merely for its hair-raising audacity but because of its interpretative novelty, 'because instead of the Saracenic grimness usually adopted, he had personated it with the familiar air of a man of the world.'

The fascinating thing about Olivier is that his work always reveals an instinctive creative intelligence. I saw his Shylock again last week and two things about it struck me more forcibly than ever. First, the way he highlights the social and racial outsider's reversion to role-playing. As James Baldwin says in *Notes Of A Native Son* a Negro 'learns to gauge precisely what reaction the alien person facing him desires and he produces it with disarming artlessness'; and likewise Olivier's Shylock conceals an icy racial fury under a bland surface even falling into Jewish folkloristic tricks (like recounting the story of Laban's sheep) when occasion demands. Also, more than any other actor in my experience, he makes it clear that Shylock has the city by the short and curlies. Dishonouring his bond would bring the law into disrepute and thus affect Venice's credibility as a trading area. So, in the trial scene, 'If you deny me . . . there is no force in the decrees of Venice' is driven in with a series of hammer-blows just in case the court hasn't got the message. This is great acting not merely because it breathes danger but because it also illuminates the play.

The same is true of *Long Day's Journey Into Night*. I was astonished to hear Ronald Harwood describe Olivier's performance on the radio the other day as 'lightweight'. In fact, it is arguably his finest assumption since *Macbeth* in 1955. And, significantly, it builds on a totally convincing picture of O'Neill's father as he must have been. A 1915 photograph shows him with just the same lion-profile, thinning hair, and decorous dressiness. As an actor, he was also admired for his quick mind and strong, graceful body while being attacked for his 'superfluity'; seen in this context, things like Olivier's ginger-footed descent from a table top (much criticised) become immediately comprehensible.

But, again, where the greatness comes in is in the use of what Bertie Wooster called 'the old grey matter'; for Olivier creates for us a man who has placed a protective wall of mannerism round himself and the tension comes from seeing it eroded by high-pressure feeling. He is rightly actorish when, sniffing a bottle of whisky to see if it has been diluted, he holds it up to each nostril in turn; but moments later real feeling erupts when the sagging frame suggests a monumental fatigue at facing up to his wife's drug-addiction and when he utters a strangulated cry of 'Mary' that seems to come from the roots of his being.

Even his ability to find a strain of ironic comedy in the role (as in *Coriolanus*) seems proof of native shrewdness since it counterpoints the play's soul-baring intensity. It also fits in perfectly with the character of James O'Neill who, when he played Jesus Christ in *The Passion*, wanly remarked: 'My wife likes to associate me with the character'.

Like Olivier, Scofield is also an actor who combines mimetic vigour with acute intelligence; and what made his performance in *Köpenick* remarkable was his seamless blending of the two. Like Olivier also he started with a strong naturalistic foundation creating a totally credible picture of a worn-out ex-convict every line of whose body seemed to slope downwards. The shredded moustache was like a feeble parody of Kaiser Bill's; the shoulders conspicuously failed to fill a jacket several sizes too large; the fingers constantly probed the pockets of a stained fawn waistcoat adding to the downward line. But the cunning of the performance lay in the way it embodied Zuckmayer's theme: the mystic, transforming power of the German uniform. Once in the uniform, Scofield's leaden shuffle was translated into the delicate prancing of a circus liberty-horse, the shoulders became board-stiff, the eyes pin-bright and alert. Technical guile and physical daring were again at the command of interpretative intelligence.

And to clinch my thesis there was Richardson as the writer in *West Of Suez*. The great Agate was incredibly wrong about Richardson when he said that he could never play Solness in *The Master Builder* because 'Solness is as mad as a hatter whereas Ralph is as sane as all the hatters in London.' In fact Richardson's uniqueness lies in his ability to invest earthbound solidity with an aura of devilish eccentricity (the nodding head, the twitching cane, the spring-heeled walk on apparently electrified soles all testify to this). And Osborne's play seemed tailor-made for his talents: for he repeatedly showed us that under the façade of the role-playing writer was an apprehensive, alert, troubled human being.

Of course any discussion of actors' interpretative originality must make allowance for the directors' and writers' contribution; but the fact remains that acting and intelligence are more closely allied than most people ever admit. I've met stupid actors who weren't much good; but I've never met a really good actor who was dull-witted or uninteresting as a human being. Stanislavsky once wrote that intuition and emotion are helmsmen of the ship of acting; but I would argue that it is intellect that does most of the navigation.

Company

Her Majesty's: 19 January 1972

How good is *Company*? When I saw Stephen Sondheim's musical 18 months ago in New York, I thought it a marvellously tart, wry, original show that got away from all the lumbering clichés of the formula-bound Broadway musical. Second time round I admire it even more; partly because its surface exuberance seems to conceal a great sadness, partly because it has the whiplash precision of the best Broadway shows plus a good deal of intellectual resonance.

For a start it's a musical that touches on serious themes; commitment, friendship, the counter-claims of solitude and togetherness. But that makes it sound dry which it certainly isn't. With a sharp, acidulous *New Yorker*ish wit, it dissects the relationship between a perennial 35-year-old Manhattan bachelor and six married couples. They exploit him, entertain him, patronise him, feed him and in general bear out the truth of Wilde's assertion that in married life three's company, two's none. He meanwhile drifts from relationship to relationship, feigns a cool contemporaneity but ultimately yearns for some rooted personal commitment.

What I like about George Furth's book is its ambivalence: you take out of the show what you put into it. Either you can see it as an endorsement of marriage, with all its miseries, or a plea for everyone to be allowed to live his own life. It even flickered across my mind that it could be seen as a defence of the homosexual in a heterosexual society. But whatever you take the show to be about, there is no denying the brilliance of Sondheim's music and lyrics. The songs show enormous command of a variety of idioms from the Andrews Sisters pastiche of 'You Could Drive A Person Crazy' to the old-fashioned vaudeville attack of 'Side By Side', to the gentle melancholy of 'The Ladies Who Lunch'. And the lyrics, with their triple internal rhymes and spot-on social precision, put Sondheim up into the Cole Porter class.

Company is also that rare thing: a genuine ensemble musical. True, Larry Kert endows the hero with just the right vague, anonymous niceness, Elaine Stritch makes marvellous use of those stiletto legs and that dry martini voice, Beth Howland is very funny as a wound-up bride on her wedding day and Donna McKechnie does a show-stopping erotic dance. But ultimately it's a group achievement masterminded by Harold Prince and much aided by Boris Aronson's geometric set with its sleekly sliding lifts.

Shall We Join The Gentlemen?

The dearth of good women playwrights: 4 February 1972

I often think British actresses have a raw deal. No country in the world has a richer supply of living dramatists; yet the number of them capable of projecting themselves fully into the female imagination can be counted on the fingers of one badly-maimed hand. Our older writers, hovering round the male menopause, often seem preoccupied with the exploration of their own egos; and many of our young dramatists, with the possible exception of David Hare, possess an attitude to women so chillingly hostile that it makes Strindberg look like Enid Blyton. Though I don't subscribe to everything about Women's Lib (do I really have to give up watching Raquel Welch movies and the Miss World contest?) I'd be the first to admit that in the modern theatre women get singularly shabby treatment.

Two plays brought home to me last week the kind of problems they're up against. One was E.A. Whitehead's *Alpha Beta* which is much more than the harrowing study of holy deadlock it's been portrayed as: it's really about two people still caught in the tenacious grip of an old-fashioned puritanism but aware that it's no longer adequate to deal with their needs.

Whitehead pins down with great accuracy the hypocrisy of traditional working-class morality (where fidelity to the wife is combined with blue movies and dirty jokes on the side) and the sheer desperation that comes from feeling one has bankrupted the vocabulary of insult. As the husband points out, the nocturnal rows are 'the dance of a dead language'; and it's a dance conducted around a dying morality.

I thought it a fine play precisely because it related private anguish to public issues. But it would have been finer still if Whitehead could have given the wife some interior life, some non-domestic existence, some richer pre-marital history: as it was, I felt Rachel Roberts was working time-and-a-half to fill out the character. To some extent David Mercer's *Ride A Cock-Horse* up at Hampstead suffers from the same flaw. Admittedly this has a cast of 3f and 1m, and the women aren't badly drawn: indeed the pot-smoking computer-programmer who sees through the writer-hero's lies and evasions is a lovely part, played with devastating common sense by Angela Richards. But the fact remains that the three women in the play have no other dramatic function than to shed light on the male-hero's exquisitely tortured sensibility.

Of course, there are writers around capable of exploring mysterious woman. Frank Marcus's plays, for instance are all built around heroines for reasons that might not appeal much to Germaine Greer: namely that he finds it easier to write comedy when projecting himself into the opposite sex. John Osborne, consistently told by critics that he couldn't write for women, picked up the gauntlet in *Time Present* though I thought he pasted on to his heroine many of the verbal mannerisms of his earlier heroes: Frederica in *West Of Suez*, caustic, aggressive, sharp and vulnerable, is much the best female character he's yet created. Bolt in *Vivat, Vivat Regina* gave us a notable pair of Queens, though the interest in historical pattern-making precluded any deep exploration of either Mary or Elizabeth. But for a really nourishing, muscle-stretching female role in a new play you probably have to go back as far as Beatie Bryant in *Roots*.

However, if our actresses are desperately starved of good parts and have to turn either to American writers (like Albee and Williams) or to Ibsen, Shaw and Shakespeare for anything that will widen their range, then most of the blame must be laid at the feet of one particular section of society: women themselves. For the sad fact is that women writers have shown a dismal lack of interest in exploring the possibilities of theatre: in fact, there doesn't seem to have been an outstanding female dramatist (and while Duras may be Hobson's choice, she certainly isn't mine) since the Abbess of Hroswitha penned her merry little tenth century Latin plays.

Obviously there are sound historical and social reasons for the shortage of women dramatists in previous centuries: the subordinate position of women in society, the alleged licentiousness of the playhouse, the masculine domination of the medium. But none of these arguments today can wholly explain the scarcity of female dramatists. For one thing the theatre is no longer an exclusive male preserve: indeed there's a book to be written about the debt it owes internationally to a string of pioneering women such as Miss Horniman, Lilian Baylis, Joan Littlewood, Helene Weigel, Nuria Espert, Ellen Stewart, Caryl Jenner. And even though many women would still claim they're socially oppressed, it hasn't stopped their sex making sizeable contributions to other media.

So why is it that women, without whom the modern novel would be seriously impoverished, still seem reluctant to write for the theatre? Like Philip Hope-Wallace with *Giselle*, I don't want to be torn to death by howling bacchantes, but let me offer a few tentative theories. One is that the process of writing a play constitutes, consciously or otherwise, an act of self-revelation: that every choice made by the dramatist, in terms of dialogue, setting, disposition of the characters, tells us more about the writer's personality than he or she realises. Now you could argue the same is true of the novel; but there is all the difference in the world between the intimate, one-to-one relationship of novelist and reader and the noisily public relationship of the dramatist and his audience. I suspect that women may be slightly less inclined than men to bare their breasts (metaphorically speaking) before a thousand anonymous spectators a night.

Then again there is something implicitly sexual about the relationship between stage and audience. Kenneth Tynan (even before *Oh! Calcutta!*) pointed out that most plays follow the pattern of the sexual act: they begin evenly, work up to a climax of emotion and then subside. If that is so then it is less strange that drama still tends to be created by men and that audiences still tend to be dominated by women. A third possibility is that writing for the stage requires a willingness to compromise one's initial vision (in that it's modified by the director and the actors) that women may find even less appealing than men.

These are, I insist, only theories; and I shall doubtless be besieged by women up and down the land who will tell me that their plays have been rejected simply because our major theatrical institutions are run by men. But I know enough about the theatre to assert with confidence that hunger for good material takes precedence over residual masculine prejudice; and that if there are very few good women dramatists around (incidentally, whatever did happen to Shelagh Delaney and Ann Jellicoe?), then it's not because of any rooted sexual conspiracy.

However, it's a situation I should like to see altered for both aesthetic and social reasons. I don't hold the reactionary view that it takes a woman to write about a woman. But I still think it sad that the British theatre has so many talented actresses and so few plays that exploit their ability. Sadder still that the theatre has yet to find equivalents to say, Mary McCarthy and Elizabeth Bowen in the novel or Julia Jones and Fay Weldon in television: that is to say authors not myopically concerned with the problems of being a woman but simply talented writers who can deal convincingly with the whole spectrum of human relationships from a feminine standpoint. Any takers?

Napoli Milionaria

Aldwych: 9 May 1972

The face is thin, age-lined but richly-contoured; the hooded eyes have a look of weary resignation; the body constantly looks too small for the clothes that hang baggily from it. Like all remarkable performers, Eduardo De Filippo (who brings to the World Theatre Season his own company in his own production of his own play, *Napoli Milionaria*) leaves behind an ineradicable physical imprint: moreover he has what Balzac once called 'that instant responsive sympathy which distinguishes the great actor'.

De Filippo is, of course, a legendary figure in Italian theatre: the country's most important playwright since Pirandello and a prolific actor-director as old as the century itself. But although everyone stresses his work's dependence on the seething anthill vitality of Naples itself, what strikes one about *Napoli Milionaria* is its broad-based, tragi-comic humanity. Somewhat in the style of O'Casey, it shows how a working-class family is ruined and divided by wartime black-marketeering: father returns dazedly home from battle to find that his house has been unrecognisably transformed, that his own recollections of horror are submerged under the family's delight in its new-won affluence, that even the sickness of his youngest daughter is blithely disregarded. One could argue it's too conveniently ironic for the daughter's fate to hinge on drugs rendered unobtainable by the black-market; but what strikes one more is De Filippo's stern defence of family piety and his attack on the dehumanising influence of war.

It is, however, his own performance one will remember more than the play. Like all fine comic actors, he's what Mae West called 'a guy who takes his time': even when going through the farcical routine of feigning death to hide from the police the black-market loot stashed under the bed, he obstinately refuses to be rushed as if this is an act he knows inside out. He also achieves maximum emotional impact with minimum physical means: trying to interest his guzzling relatives in the fact that in battle he starved for three days and nights, his voice rarely rises above a ferocious whisper. What Thornton Wilder called his 'powerful quiet' proves infinitely more eloquent than any amount of vocal thunder. Pupella Maggio is also admirable as his profiteering wife, spraying her breasts and the furniture with air-freshener before the arrival of her lover. But what makes this production memorable is the quiet artistry of De Filippo and a performance that seems to embody all the still, sad music of humanity.

The School For Scandal

Old Vic: 12 May 1972

Jonathan Miller's National Theatre production of *The School For Scandal* is a great delight. It treats Sheridan's masterpiece not as high polite comedy but as a work rooted in the rough, tangy, eighteenth-century world of Hogarth, Smollett and Fielding. No artshop prettiness, no false posturing, no suave wristwork with fans: instead a joyous comedy about life as it was actually lived and a production that maintains an unusual degree of moral neutrality.

Sheridan's theme, as Shaw said, is the superiority of the good-natured libertine to the ill-natured hypocrite: and most productions instantly let you know where they stand by portraying Charles Surface as a saintly undergraduate prankster and his brother, Joseph, as an all-too-manifest double-dealer. Dr Miller, however, shrewdly evens up the contest by giving us a Charles straight out of *The Rake's Progress*, half-canned in a dingy, smoky cellar littered with prostrate, blood-stained topers: likewise Joseph becomes not the usual Machiavellian smoothie but someone whose spotless reputation stems chiefly from a lack of personality. For once, therefore, there is genuine theatrical tension in their rivalry; and Dr Miller gives the comedy new life by re-thinking the precise social function of every character. Thus Sir Peter Teazle becomes a tetchy, clubbable grouser with a taste for bad portraiture, his wife a wilful rural cocquette straight out of *Marriage à la Mode* and Sir Oliver Surface the kind of Evelyn Waugh colonialist who goes native, returning from the Indies with a bejewelled turban and a black fly-whisk.

Occasionally in the first half the sense of life-going-on-in-the-background dominates the interplay of character; but in the second half the comedy really takes wing. The screen scene is brilliantly handled, a marriage lying momentarily in ruins as Lady Teazle cowers in a corner like a frightened rabbit caught in a car's headlights and a stricken Sir Peter pulls his wig over his brows; at the same time the arch bitchery of the tattle-sessions is beautifully caught in Denis Quilley's Crabtree, constantly trumping his partner's conversational ace. Unlike some directors, Miller also makes the National actors look like a real company so that praise belongs equally to Ronald Pickup's thin-blooded Joseph, John Shrapnel's Hogarthian Charles, Paul Curran's dyspeptic Sir Peter and Benjamin Whitrow's quietly insidious Snake. Patrick Robertson's mouldering sets also have the merit of looking thoroughly lived in. In short, an evening that zestfully confirms the National's return to form.

An Othello

Open Space: 9 June 1972

'She was all set to marry a nice lawyer,' laments Desdemona's dad, sounding just like Walter Matthau in *Plaza Suite*. 'And what has she got? A jealous epileptic who goes crazy from hankies.' Whatever one says about Charles Marowitz's rejigged *Othello* at the Open Space, it certainly yields a fruitful line in ironic comedy; but the acid test is whether Mr Marowitz's 'total overhaul' of the tragedy actually makes it more relevant to contemporary racial attitudes. And the answer is a reluctant No.

Mr Marowitz's boldest innovatory stroke is to make Othello and Iago represent contrasting black stereotypes: what Malcolm X called the House Negro, who totally accepts his master's system of values, and the Field Negro who is a congenital revolutionary. Theatrically this yields any number of effective moments, such as Iago's running scatalogical commentary on Othello's Uncle Tomist speech to the Venetian senate or the Moor's belated refusal to fulfil a white audience's expectations by committing spectacular suicide. The crucial weakness is that many of the points Marowitz seeks to illustrate by a collage technique are inherent in the original text: for instance Othello's racial compromise in accepting an alien political system, whitey's own paranoid fantasies in which the Negro appears as both less capable of self-control and more sexually potent than himself, even Desdemona's equivocal sexiness and conceivable infidelity. I'm all for Marowitz using Shakespeare's text as a springboard; but here he's not exactly diving into totally uncharted waters.

That aside, I admire his constant directorial inventiveness. The nervy, impressionistic opening plunges one straight into a fragmented, dream-like world; in the stormy crossing to Cyprus Othello becomes like a ship's mast held firm by ropes extending from all his limbs; a giant strawberry-covered handkerchief billows down from the flies and becomes a vast bed on which Desdemona copulates with the whole camp; and there's a chilling final image in which the play's white survivors smile conspiratorially at each other having disposed of the troublesome blacks. Rudolph Walker's dignified, white-robed Othello, Anton Phillips's sardonic Black Power Iago and Judy Geeson's frail, tantalising Desdemona are also excellent. But, though the production is visually deft and theatrically captivating, it still doesn't yield any insights into black political attitudes or the Shakespearean sub-text that you couldn't get from an imaginative staging of the original play.

Long Day's Journey Into Night

Old Vic: 1 September 1972

On a second viewing the National Theatre's production of Eugene O'Neill's *Long Day's Journey Into Night* looks as commanding as ever. It has, if anything, deepened and strengthened with time, since the cast now look even more like members of a real family chained together by guilt, recrimination, jealousy and a strange, self-torturing love.

Indeed, it is this emotional ambivalence that makes the play so moving. Not simply the fact that O'Neill compresses his whole traumatic family history into a single New England day thus giving the play an Aristotelian unity; nor merely that we know the play to be written 'in tears and blood'. But the fact that, however appalling the accusations one character may fling at another, the love that binds them together can never be entirely killed. The dreadful James Tyrone (miserly as Balzac's Grandet) may consign his tubercular son to a cheap sanitorium; the sottish Jamie may warn brother Edmund that the dead part of him rejoices in the sickness; the mother may degrade and humiliate them all with her morphine injections. But, paradoxically, the deeper they sink their teeth into each other's necks, the greater their love seems to grow.

Love and waste; these are the play's two enduring themes. Olivier's James Tyrone is still a massive performance moving from an initial nervy jocularity to a throttled, brick-red despair at his wife's relapse to a thrilling, soul-baring intensity in his cups. But the lynchpin of the interpretation is Tyrone's inescapable feeling that he is a great actor manqué and when Olivier sweetly croons 'We are such stuff as dreams are made on' he magnificently evokes a vanished acting style and makes you believe this old matinée idol had the makings of an American Kean. For a genuinely great actor to play a nearly-great actor is the hardest technical feat of all: Olivier does it to perfection.

Constance Cummings's wife, bent white arms clinging tenaciously to her sides, gives one a similar feeling of wasted life and also plots more carefully than before the woman's collapse into fogbound reverie. Ronald Pickup's Edmund, uncorking his bottled intensity with terrifying power during his colloquy with his father, and Denis Quilley's Jamie, full of fake Fifth Avenue charm, compound the feeling of energy fatally misdirected. Michael Blakemore's production also does O'Neill the great service of disregarding many of his stage directions and only allowing the cracks and fissures under the surface to emerge as the day grinds on. Such, in fact, is the quality of acting and direction we seem to be not merely watching great drama but to be eavesdropping on life itself.

England's Ireland

Royal Court: 2 October 1972

I have for so long pleaded for a theatre plugged into the contemporary political scene that I feel bound to raise two and a half cheers for Portable Theatre's multi-author show, *England's Ireland*, which touched down briefly at the Royal Court yesterday. It doesn't give one anything like a complete picture of the Irish tragedy and has some fatal errors of tone; but it asks the right questions, is solidly researched and comes down on the side of common humanity rather than any one cause.

Its basic thesis is that the present crisis must be seen in the context of long-standing social injustice as well as religious bigotry. How, it asks, can one hope for a return to normal in Northern Ireland when 'normality' means an unemployment rate in some areas of 43 per cent, a weekly wage of £11 and an overall situation in which 5 per cent of the population owns 47 per cent of the wealth?

It also accuses all British parties of a criminally negligent attitude towards Ulster before the eruption of violence, and argues that the current refusal to negotiate with terrorists is inconsistent with our whole historical record.

All these (and many other) points are made in a series of terse, effectively staged scenes set against a functional metal-grey background. I have, though, two basic reservations. One is that it's a tactical mistake to treat certain individuals (such as Ian Paisley) and certain practices (such as the Masonic rites of the Orange Orders) as inherently absurd rather than as potent forces within the community. The second is that, while the authors unequivocally condemn the violence perpetrated by the IRA, they don't show it in anything like the same detail as, for instance, the brutalities of the Long Kesh internment camp: I can't help feeling that if they indicated what it really meant to tar and feather a pregnant woman, the balance of horror would be more honestly maintained.

But, to its credit, the show avoids simple agitprop and at its most effective lets the appalling statistics speak for themselves: the 400 people who have been killed in the Ulster crisis, the 2,389 civilians injured, the fact that many under-fours are on tranquillisers. It also makes clear that the only hope for Ulster lies in political negotiation rather than in a renewed attempt to meet violence with violence. And although in this context aesthetic judgements are irrelevant, the seven authors (A.M. Bicât, Howard Brenton, Brian Clark, David Edgar, Francis Fuchs, David Hare and Snoo Wilson) have produced a seamless dramatic blend whose merit is that it sends one out of the theatre even more painfully alert to the Irish tragedy than when one went in.

I And Albert

Piccadilly: 7 November 1972

A vehemently tugged forelock is rapidly becoming the symbol of the West End theatre. After the Tussaud-Royals of *Crown Matrimonial* we now have a giant PR job for Queen Victoria in the shape of an American musical called *I And Albert* at the Piccadilly. Its one positive achievement is in fact to convince me that the Lord Chamberlain can't have been all bad; for it was a holder of that office who many years ago banned a revue sketch between Disraeli and the Queen on the grounds that 'we can't have the old girl singing and dancing on the stage.' I think he had a point.

What the show offers us (via Charles Strouse's music, Lee Adams's lyrics and John Schlesinger's production) is no coherent historical vision but a series of random, sporadically ingenious effects. Thus the show bares its social conscience round about 9.22 pm in a marvellous staging of a typically ambiguous Kipling poem about the men who died fighting abroad for 'the widow at Windsor': yet ten minutes later it offers a wholly facetious production number in which Disraeli captivates the Queen with a sequence of Jasper Maskeleyne conjuring tricks. Everything by starts and nothing long, *I And Albert* tries to disguise the fact it has absolutely nothing to say under layers of theatrical artifice.

Unfortunately only a couple of the numbers rise above the humdrum and Mr Schlesinger's production has plenty of movement but no visible destination. However, Polly James as Victoria excellently makes the transition from a frail, diminutive 18-year-old, weighed down by a crown three times her size to a tetchy matriarch threatening to abdicate rather than endure another Gladstone premiership; and Lewis Fiander (Melbourne and Disraeli) and Aubrey Woods (Palmerston and

Gladstone) both bring off notable autumn doubles. But Sven-Bertil Taube as Albert, who speaks not so good the English, has little chance to do more than make the original historical point that the Prince Consort died from a bad attack of stereophonic sound. Admittedly the show has fleeting moments of vitality; but basically I was not amused.

A Sense Of Detachment

Royal Court: 5 December 1972

How to describe John Osborne's *A Sense Of Detachment* at the Royal Court? A thinking-man's 'Hellzapoppin'? A spiky, satirical, inconsequential collage? An attack on our own heartless, loveless, profiteering society in which language is corrupted daily? A moving threnody for a dying civilisation? The paradox of this (to me) provocative, innovatory and exciting work is that it manages to be all of these things, moving outwards from purely theatrical satire to an eloquent examination of the world at large.

The form of the play is bizarre to say the least: five actors, guided by a nervy chairman, occupy the stage initially sending up all the conventions of the modern theatre. Snooks are deftly cocked at elliptical, poignant chat in front of an empty cyclorama; at inconsequential Littlewoodian bursts into song-and-dance; at audience participation (symbolised by a jeering football fan in a box and Sanderstead man in the front row); at pseudo-documentary (filmic shots of Edward Heath going into Europe to the strains of the Choral Symphony); and at first person singular theatrical autobiography.

But what at first seems like a kaleidoscopic cabaret gradually turns into something sharper and sourer as Osborne counterpoints readings from a pornographic book catalogue (likely to offend all but the shock-proof) with moving protestations of love through the ages. And, as a pulpit is wheeled onto the stage, each character mounts it to offer some kind of personal credo: Rachel Kempson poignantly states the Women's Lib case before asking to be helped down from the podium: John Standing eloquently defends the pain and joy of love against all the unthinking sexual militants; and Denise Coffey attacks the corruption of language and the fact that 'we no longer love, eat or cherish: we exchange.'

Bravos and boos greeted this strange hypnotic pot-pourri at the end but I would defend it on several grounds. It is, at the very least, sustainedly entertaining. It uses an apparently inconsequential form to defend timeless human values. It is full of Osborne's characteristic rancid eloquence. And it goads, provokes and agitates its audience as only a truly vital theatrical work can. One might object to the porn-extracts (on a technical rather than a moral level) for their repetitiveness: but the work shows Osborne defiantly enlarging his stylistic territory without diluting his message.

Frank Dunlop's production is also a marvel of theatrical dexterity and apart from those mentioned, there are splendid performances from Ralph Michael as an animated traditionalist, Terence Frisby as a protesting spectator and Nigel Hawthorne as the much abused chairman.

1973

In response to the national energy crisis, the West End was forced to dim its lights and ration its neon. An apt symbol for a year that, as John Barber noted at the time, felt like the end of an era. Noël Coward and Binkie Beaumont died, Laurence Olivier handed over to Peter Hall at the National (just how grudgingly we only learned later), John Clements was rather unceremoniously bundled off the scene at Chichester, Sir Peter Daubeny proclaimed he had done his last World Theatre Season and Danny La Rue, less momentously, announced that, after his show at the Prince of Wales, he would hang up his tits: Mr La Rue then astonished us all by saying that he hoped Harold Pinter might write something for him.

As the old guard departed, the newer gang increasingly made its presence felt. Richard Eyre took over at Nottingham Playhouse and, in the wake of the Poulson scandal, launched the year's most exciting play in Brassneck. *Christopher Hampton's* Savages *(surely worth revival?) moved from the Royal Court to the West End, thanks partly to the presence of Paul Scofield. Edward Bond scored a notable double with his East Coast comedy,* The Sea, *and his moving study of artistic impotence,* Bingo, *which cast Gielgud as Shakespeare and Arthur Lowe as Ben Jonson asking combatively, 'What was the* The Winter's Tale *about?'. The Half Moon in a dingy Whitechapel synagogue established itself as London's liveliest political theatre with Brecht's* The Mother, *Steve Gooch's* Female Transport *and shows about docklands redevelopment and the children's strike of 1911.*

The West End, as usual, was pretty dim except for the Styne-Sondheim Gypsy, *Bennett's* Habeas Corpus *and Ayckbourn's* Absent Friends. *But the National was on song with* Equus *and* Saturday, Sunday, Monday, *the RSC's four-part* The Romans *acquired a new cohesiveness, and a sparky young dramatist called Tina Brown made her debut at the Bush. But, to evoke a year when the lights were going out all over London, it seems appropriate to start with a dramatist who illuminated the darkness.*

Not I *and* Krapp's Last Tape

Royal Court: 17 January 1973

Samuel Beckett, Cyril Connolly once said, is the poet of terminal stages who steps in to catechise the dying when doctors and relatives have left. And in *Not I* and *Krapp's Last Tape* at the Royal Court we get an extraordinarily powerful, concentrated double bill in which two ancients, hovering on the verge of extinction, recapture fragments of past experience with piercing nightmarish clarity.

Not I (Beckett's latest work) is the more compelling because it leaves behind an ineradicable image: an endlessly mobile mouth, rimmed by white clown-like make-up, pouring out words of agony in Stygian darkness while downstage a silent, cowled figure impassively listens. Along with two tattered tramps in a barren landscape, a blind patriarch enthroned in a wheelchair or three heads protruding out of funeral urns, this is one of those haunting, Beckettian images that takes instant root in the imagination exactly like the open-mouthed scream of a Francis Bacon cardinal.

But if Beckett has a painter's eye, he also has a poet's ear. The mouth belongs to a 70-year-old woman whose past life flashes before her like that of someone drowning but who transfers her experiences to someone else: the impression is of a buzzing skull, a mouth on fire helplessly attached to a body incapable of feeling. In fact if I had to sum up the play's theme in a phrase, it would be the anguish of memory at a time when all physical sentience had departed.

But, although the words stream out with scalding intensity, the text works on one like a poem in which certain phrases insistently recur: 'God is Love, Tender Mercies, New Every Morning,' the woman helplessly intones as if weighed down by fragments of a remembered catechism. What differentiates *Not I* from earlier Beckett monologues is that in the past there was usually reference to moments of happiness irretrievably lost: here the first impression is of a brief, stark, terrifying sojourn in hell. Billie Whitelaw's performance is, needless to say, an astonishing tour de force combining frenetic verbal speed with total sensitivity to the musical rhythm of the piece.

Anthony Page's production of *Krapp's Last Tape* wisely offers a tonal contrast: here every phrase is savoured, every nuance explored. I wouldn't put Albert Finney's Krapp in the same class as that of Martin Held who, as the old banana-munching wreck alone with his tape-recorded memories, hinted at the character's earlier fire. But Finney, with his red-rimmed eyes, chalk-white complexion and jutting jaw that looks as if it contains a boxer's gumshield, offers a meticulous study in senility.

He gets across the crucial point that Krapp once knew the possibility of happiness: indeed as he recalls the afternoon when Krapp made love to a girl in a punt, his white-knuckled hand crawls involuntarily across the table, his head sinks into the crook of his arm and he emits animal-like mews and sobs. Taken together, these two plays offer a comfortless comment on the pain of the moment before death: but, such is the paradox of art, one comes out of the theatre feeling strangely braced by Beckett's vision of despair.

A Change Of Direction At The National

22 March 1973

So Peter Hall is to join Laurence Olivier at the National Theatre on April 1. To an outsider, it looks like an eminently rational arrangement providing both change and continuity. And there's a certain historic neatness about the fact that Olivier will be handing over the baton in November, almost exactly a decade after the National began its Old Vic career with Peter O'Toole's Hamlet.

It would be ungracious not to pay tribute to the amount the company has achieved under Olivier. It has, for a start, broadened and deepened the English repertoire: glance down the regional repertory programme and you now find O'Neill in Bristol, Hecht and MacArthur surfacing in Coventry and Tom Stoppard almost everywhere. The National has also yielded many individually brilliant productions with Gaskill's *Recruiting Officer*, Brook's *Oedipus*, Blakemore's *Long Day's Journey* and the Dexter-Blakemore *Tyger* topping my own private list of favourites. And it has also produced many of the finest single performances of the decade.

It hasn't toured enough. And it hasn't built up the projected bank of productions (in an *Encore* interview in 1963 its literary manager estimated there would be 49 productions to call on after five or six years). But for the moment I should like to outline what one expects from it in the future because obviously all theatrical institutions must change depending on the temperaments of the people running them and the pressure of the times; and it is no reflection on Olivier's enormous personal achievement to suggest it may be time for the National to alter course. Critics are always accused of being wise after the event: let me risk being constructive.

And first let me expand a point I made in my notice of *The Misanthrope* where I suggested the failure to grasp the nettle of that prickly tragi-comedy was partly due to the company's lack of any 'sustained social vision'. The drama critic of *The Spectator* (whose name escapes me for the moment) pounced on this and said it could only have been written by a born Alceste; and it seems to me a fair index of the production's inability to project the turbulent idealism of its hero that this should be intended as a withering insult.

What I meant about social vision was this: that any permanent company of actors and directors must, I believe, have some shared idea of the kind of society they believe in if their work is to have any identity. Style, in short, is not something you impose on a company: it grows out of an attitude to life and work. Harold Clurman in that invaluable theatrical bible, *The Fervent Years* which charts the fortunes of the American Group Theatre, put it this way: 'The unity of theatrical production does not spring out of an abstract sense of taste or vision but out of a unity that is antecedent to the formation of a group as such . . . *A technique of the theatre has to be founded on life-values.*' And history I think bears this out: witness the development of the Moscow Art Theatre, the Berliner Ensemble, Planchon's Théâtre de la Cité, Joan Littlewood's Theatre Workshop. I hope, in future, to learn precisely what the National's life-values are.

The argument always used, of course, is that its repertoire is much too broad to accommodate any one theatrical style. And from this stems my second great hope: that Peter Hall will reform – indeed revolutionise – the whole concept of repertory planning in this country. For both the National and the RSC, in spite of their many brilliant achievements, have disappointed in one respect: in planning their seasons they have striven as desperately for a mythical sense of 'balance' as any TV current affairs producer. By this I mean they have succumbed to the long-cherished English assumption that for every tragedy you must do a comedy, for every *Lear* a *Twelfth Night*, for every Strindberg a Feydeau. What they have failed to do is build up a repertoire in which each play casts new stimulating light on those around it.

There have been exceptions. At Stratford the RSC, with Shakespeare as its staple diet, can obviously think in cyclical terms. And indeed I would say that the most exciting Stratford seasons in recent years have been 1964 when Peter Hall gave us the full English History cycle and 1972 when Trevor Nunn presented the Roman plays: in each case one saw the development of ideas, themes and characters from play to play. And, carp though one might at certain details of the Roman season, you still set out for Stratford last year knowing precisely why each play was in the repertoire.

What I'm saying is that any repertory programme should be unified by something stronger than the presence of the same group of actors: that there should be cross-currents going from play to play. Let me give a concrete instance. Last autumn I saw *The Misanthrope* at Oxford followed a couple of days later by Ibsen's *Brand* at Nottingham. Suddenly one saw the most extraordinary parallels between the two plays. Both are about uncompromising idealists who reject the society around them; yet what is fascinating is that in both cases a great dramatist shows his hero driven to extremes by other people.

Molière's Alceste does everything possible to avoid judging Oronte's lousy verses and is always trying to escape the salon to avoid giving offence; Brand's first reaction on hearing his child is dying is to fly South to save it and it is only when he is rebuked by the doctor ('So merciless towards the flock, so lenient towards yourself') that he questions his actions. Seeing the plays in proximity gave one a fascinating insight into the way a great writer complicates the stereotype of 'the misanthrope' or 'the fanatic'. And I suddenly thought what a marvellous season could be built round the idea of the uncompromising hero: *The Misanthrope, Brand, Timon of Athens, Look Back In Anger, Galileo* (though admittedly he recants).

Even as I write this, I can imagine the objections people will make: too heavy for the public to take, too difficult in practice to cast. To which, let me say that I'd be delighted to see a season showing changing styles in farce from Plautus to Ben Travers. And anyway the idea that you have to woo the public by doing a season blending heavy and light is outdated nonsense stemming from the quaint notion that people do nothing else but go to the theatre.

We are constantly bombarded by light entertainment from all sources: therefore I don't think one has to worry any more about the public's fear of too sombre a tone (has no one noticed the queues for

Wagner?). As for the practical arguments (casting problems, varying size of company and so forth) these are precisely the things a subsidised company exists to conquer.

At the moment we still plan our seasons after the fashion of that vilified Fanfare for Europe exhibition at the V & A in which one great work of art was taken from each country. Scorn was rightly heaped on such woolly eclecticism in the gallery. Yet that's exactly how the subsidised theatre still operates, ignoring the practice in other media. The National Film Theatre offers us seasons of single artists or themes like 'Women Directors'; television hooks us with the exploration of a civilisation; galleries like the Tate and Hayward offer us giant retrospectives; the opera houses offer more cycles than a Raleigh factory. Why should it only be the drama that still obstinately clings to the patchwork quilt approach to art?

Admittedly the National Theatre sticks loyally to the blueprint laid down by Granville Barker and Archer in 1903. Perhaps, after 70 years, the time has come to re-write the constitution.

Ken Dodd

Liverpool Playhouse: 17 April 1973

I have a confession to make: I have a passion for stand-up comedy. As an adolescent I haunted the halls and even now carry round pin-bright memories of the incomparable Maxes (Miller and Wall), of the lugubrious Jimmy Wheeler, of Tommy Trinder, Jewel and Warriss (best of all double acts) and of a little-remembered duo called Morris and Cowley. I'm particularly glad I caught the fag-end of the music-hall since today we are breeding a new race of mini-comics who either spend all their time imitating other people (without making any impression) or who dance a bit, sing a bit, gag a bit and who have all the pungent flavour of processed cellophane-wrapped cheese.

Exceptions exist; and to me incomparably the finest is Ken Dodd who this week opened a one-man celebration of humour at the Liverpool Playhouse called *Ha Ha*. Let me say instantly that this is the funniest evening I have spent inside a theatre since I saw *Beyond The Fringe* at the Edinburgh Lyceum in 1960. And partly for the same reason: that its sole aim is it make us laugh. There are no dancing girls in laddered fishnet, or dancing boys in bum-clinging trousers, no garish starlit backcloths, no tonsil-baring vocalists, no tumblers, trapeze artists or vent acts. All we have is Mr Dodd colonising the stage for over three hours, as if qualifying for the Guinness Book of Records with the longest comedy act ever.

Ostensibly the intention is to explore the nature of laughter: in reality what we get is a king-sized Dodd-fest. It begins with those wayward teeth spotlit in what looks like a conscious parody of Billie Whitelaw in Beckett: and it goes on to run the gamut of Doddy jokes. There are old jokes ('Tonight we have the famous lady from Belgium, Ann Twerp, the well-known contortionist Willie Snapit, the fearless lion-tamer Claud Bottom'), blue jokes ('King Midas. Everything he touched turned to gold – it could be very embarrassing'), literary jokes ('Malvolio – the sort of man who used to stand up in a strip club and shout "What time do the jugglers come on?")', surrealist jokes ('Men's legs have a terribly lonely life – standing in the dark in your trousers all day'), even topical jokes ('I saw a sign in an undertaker's window yesterday. Die now and avoid VAT').

Wisely perhaps Dodd avoids too much theorising. He quotes Freud's opinions that a laugh is a conservation of psychic energy; but, as he says, the trouble with Freud is that he never played Glasgow second house on a Friday night. Yet, in spite of its non-academic nature, the show tells us a great deal about the nature of comedy.

For a start Dodd confirms something all the great theorists assert: that comedy appeals to the head and never to the heart. Bergson refers to 'The absence of feeling which usually accompanies laughter' and says that in a society composed of pure intelligences there would be no tears, whereas one made up of highly emotional souls would neither know nor understand laughter. And Meredith takes the same line in his famous 'Essay on Comedy': that laughter depends on quickness of perception. And if you listen to Dodd carefully you realise that even at his most rude, crude and basic, he is bombarding us with images and ideas that keep us in a state of frenzied mental alertness.

Accept the idea that laughter depends on absence of feeling; and it's a short step to acknowledging that it derives largely from other people's pain. Again Dodd proves this through illustration. He points out that in the last century people went to Bedlam in order to laugh at the lunatics. Of course, he says, we are now much more civilised: an idea which he then demolishes by donning brown mob-cap, pebble glasses and twisted expression to sing a number called 'I'm not all there' at which the audience falls about. I suspect nowadays we are, in fact, more heartless (or saner?) than ever in that we believe all human activity is fit subject for comedy; Monty Python bulges with gags about madness, sick jokes became a smart Sixties cult and I shall never forget hearing a famous poet and novelist say (in the late Fifties) that the Campaign for Nuclear Disarmament was full of middle-aged women who didn't believe two heads were better than one. What price Bedlam now?

I wish Dodd had taken the cruelty theory further and examined the rich American tradition of verbal insult (an inevitable by-product of a society that puts a high premium on gregarious affability). Think of W.C. Fields greeting a monstrous fat man on a plane with 'Do you travel as one person or do you get a party rate of ten?'; or vehemently reproaching a fly-swatting bartender with 'It's killers like you that give the West a bad name.' Or remember Groucho assaulting Margaret Dumont with 'I hear they're going to tear you down and put up an office building where you're standing'; or telling her that her eyes are like the pants of a blue serge suit and adding, when she complains of insult, that it's not a reflection on her but on the suit. Why do we laugh? Chiefly, I think, because the comic unmasks an aggression that lives in all of us but that social conventions and good manners normally conceal.

I sound, however, as if I wish *Ha Ha* had been a lantern lecture: I'm glad it's not for the practice of comedy is much more fascinating than the theory. And, as it is, the show provides a brilliant demonstration of comic technique. It reminds us, for instance, how much mileage can be got out of props and costumes. One of my favourite moments comes when Dodd brings on a giant Sally Ally drum and proceeds to beat out 'Come and Join Us', 'Go to Sleep My Baby' and 'Silent Night' before asking the audience 'Give in?' And his wardrobe is like something dreamed up by a colour-blind tailor on a weekend bender: a black cape with a lining striped like a liquorice allsort, a maroon maxie allegedly made out of 28 moggies, a mustard yellow coat and a titfer that is eminently phallacious.

He also shows one how a gag should be structured to illustrate the effect of surprise. He interrupts a story about a country walk with a thunderous explosion which we think is the main joke: he then fires a pistol in the air and a life-size cow drops out of the flies. And by relentlessly piling gag on gag instead of waiting for a round of applause (the fatal Cleopatra of the modern telly-comic) Dodd keeps laughter going till it resembles Bergson's 'successive rumblings like thunder in a mountain'.

But perhaps the key fact about him and his show is that it places him squarely in the great line of English music-hall comics with their reliance on grotesque fantasy. Read Leno's monologues and you realise that the world of Lear and Carroll invaded the popular Victorian stage. Dodd himself quotes large chunks of Billy Bennett monologues with titles like 'A sailor's farewell to his horse' and containing fantastic Milliganesque lines like 'Digging for grapes with a bicycle lamp on a freezing tropical night.' But today that kind of imaginative vitality survives only in someone like Dodd whose act admits one to a baroque world full of jam-butty mines, hairy Danes with bacon sandwiches strapped to their legs and men with a third eye on the end of their finger. As he himself says: 'It's ten years since I went out of my mind. I'd never go back.'

The Wild Duck

Aldwych: 29 May 1973

Ingmar Bergman's production of *The Wild Duck* for the Royal Dramatic Theatre of Sweden is a stunner. It gives you the exhilarating sensation of seeing a classic text re-thought and re-felt from start to finish. What's more it's been done without any serious violation of Ibsen's delicate Swiss-watch structure and without any diminution of his central theme: that if you deprive a man of his life-lie you rob him of happiness and peace of mind.

Bergman's one major innovation is that he puts Hedvig's loft downstage right in front of the audience. This has the double advantage of keeping the complex, poetic symbol of the wild duck itself in the forefront of our imagination and of allowing us (as in his *Hedda Gabler*) to see what is going on in two rooms simultaneously. Thus while the blinkered, emotionally crippled idealist, Gregers Werle, is triumphantly reassuring the wretched Hjalmar Ekdal that his daughter will never leave him, we twice see her venture downstage and quiveringly aim to shoot the wild duck before turning the pistol upon herself. Some will see this as a gratuitous underlining of Ibsenite irony: to me it emphasises Ibsen's seamless blend of realism and symbolism and shows how an imaginative director can bring to the stage the geographical freedom of the cinema.

The pivot of the production, however is Max von Sydow's performance as Gregers Werle. Instead of playing him as the usual impassioned, proselytising figure whom any sane man would have turned out of the house in two minutes, he presents us with a shy, gawky, repressed fellow blatantly nervous of any human contact. He prowls warily round the edge of conversational groups watching other people's reactions, makes his point about the moral stench in Ekdal's household while staring fixedly at the table and (ironically) is at ease only when listening to Hedvig talking about the wild duck. It's a superb performance in that it shows that Gregers's destructive effect is out of all proportion to his harmless physical presence and that idealism need not be equated with fanaticism.

Jack Benny

London Palladium: 19 June 1973

Jack Benny is stand-up comedy's answer to the Noh Theatre: a great and venerable institution that makes most other forms of entertainment seem criminally energetic. Some comics tell jokes: Benny bypasses them. Some clowns knock themselves out to make us laugh: he lets us knock ourselves out to get a response from him.

Watching him at the Palladium on Sunday (before a national tour), I realised that the legendary timing is only part of his skill. Incredible as it may seem for a man in his late-seventies, he leans heavily on sex-appeal. He wanly tries to convince us that his days as a wolf are over ('though sometimes I glance through the African section of the National Geographic'). But the lazy, crooked-leg stance, the limply flapping wrist, the sharply cut attire remind us that all comedy rests on sexual ambiguity: the suspicion that inside every red-blooded male there is an ageing spinster struggling to get out.

Admittedly Benny's range of subjects is narrow: money, sex, age and money. What matters is the baffled feminine outrage with which he confronts unforeseen hazards. The best moment comes when he is interrupted in mid-joke by a clangorous pop-group who render a song called 'Cecilia' while he gazes at them with the stricken fascination of a man suddenly hit by lightning before resuming his story, as if nothing had happened.

I have seen few greater comics than Benny: certainly none who teased more life out of their material.

Magnificence in rehearsal

29 June 1973

A diary of a day spent at the Royal Court watching Howard Brenton's *Magnificence* in preparation.

10.15 am. Arrive at Court in torrential downpour. Worried that I'll be sitting there all day in quietly steaming trousers. But if I take them off on arrival, will my gesture be mis-interpreted? Should I even be here at all? 'Critics, like clergymen,' Gielgud once wrote, 'are out of place behind the scenes.' But Max Stafford-Clark, directing Howard Brenton's *Magnificence* (a wide-ranging critical study of a young bomb-throwing anarchist), generously invited me to look in on rehearsals any time. And one school of thought argues critics should understand intention before judging achievement. Sceptical; but no harm in giving it a try.

Hover inconspicuously at back of the stalls. Max S-C, barefoot, bejeaned and moustached like Brando in *Viva Zapata*, invites me to sit close to the stage. Works all morning on opening scene in which a group of squatters occupy a derelict building: a piece of almost Weskerian realism. Director concentrates on tricky passage where squatters unpack crates of food, rolling baked-bean tins across floor. 'Looks a bit carefully rehearsed and premeditated at the moment,' says M. They start throwing tins about, miss one now and then. In a flash looks less like choreographed toil, more like life. How many work-plays, in fact, resemble genuine work?

Impressed by the relaxed democratic atmosphere. Director is chairman of the group but everyone free to toss in ideas, question others. 'Like to make it a bit more sexy,' says M. of relationship between pregnant girl and protagonist Jed. 'What do you suggest, congress on the Lilo?' someone retorts. Notice how actors switch from intense concentration to bantering ebullience between sessions. 'How much do you make a year?' one squatter asks another. 'About £500,' the actress replies, out of character. Fussy, 'acted' detail gradually stripped off scene. 'Keep it clean,' says M. 'Knock off those little bits you're adding and make the script work.' Clearly the old laws still apply. As Edith Evans once said, acting is largely a matter of cutting away the dead wood.

12.15 pm. M. works on third scene where two girl squatters discuss attitudes to sex, motherhood, politics. No one seems too happy with it this morning. 'Forget the characters,' says M. at one point. 'As yourselves, just say the dialogue.' Notice he frequently uses this technique: sense and meaning always sharply heightened when there is less visible acting. 'We're getting bogged down in the dull pulse of realism,' he complains later. 'Ah, boring old realism,' echoes one actress rolling on ground and kicking legs in air. So much for realism!

1.15 pm. Beginning to get feel of Brenton's play. Obviously relies on severe dislocations of tone: straight naturalism, mock-vaudeville, elliptical expressionism in scene between two queer old Tories on the Backs at Cambridge. How will Court audiences, reared on consequential drama, take this? Brenton also deliberately equivocal in his attitudes. Squatters are shown as idealistic but muddled, failing to get local support for their action. And the bomb-throwing Jed seems part author's spokesman, part demonstration of failure of Angry Brigade-type tactics.

1.45–2.45 pm. Lunch. Return to find M. working with Kenneth Cranham as Jed on major climactic speeches when he tries (and fails) to blow up thrustful new-style Tory. One particular speech – an attack on 'the sticky mess of your English humanity' – vividly reminiscent of that passage in *US* about the wish to see a bomb exploding on an English suburban lawn. M. experiments a good deal, getting actor to deliver it devoid of all emotion: rendered with deadly cool rather than as impassioned rhetoric, the language has an almost visceral impact.

3.30 pm. Howard Brenton arrives and we retire to Nissen-hut office for a talk. (Why is so much English theatre produced in Battle of Britain buildings?) Brenton a large, genial man full of restless energy that matches his writing. Obvious question. How much does he sympathise with the anarchic Jed? 'I sympathise with him emotionally. Intellectually I think he's totally misguided. I did write a romantic piece, which was a short film, about young terrorists. But this play is meant to be a tragedy of waste. You can't have a tragedy of hubris or fate any more. But you can have a tragedy about mis-directed drive and energy. What I'm attacking is the romantic view of political action. The old Tories in the play have much the same scale of values as Jed: they too believe in fine rhetorical gestures. But that is never enough.'

How then does one change society? Through old-fashioned parliamentary democracy? 'Playwrights aren't sages. But I would say if one wanted to change things today, one would work for Shelter or the Howard League for Penal Reform or be a fellow-traveller in a Socialist group.' But why is he so invincibly hostile to the English humanist tradition? 'Because it has become so sullied. Humanist ideas always come from the Right. The humanist line, for instance, is to recognise that there is class conflict but not to accept the necessity to change it. The truth is that people are in constant pain in the way they live. Violence on the individual level is not the most horrifying thing in our society but rather the violence of a system that permits homelessness and degrading poverty.'

Brenton strikes me as a fascinating blend of opposites. He likes the proscenium arch and the moral force it contains; yet he believes it is time for a radical change in theatrical form and wishes one could invent a kind of serialism comparable to what Schoenberg achieved in music. He rejects humanism; yet, on the page, his portrait of a dying old land-owning Tory shows intuitive sympathy. He believes, like one of his characters, that you only change things through 'Work, corny work, with and for the people'; yet he feels an emotional tug towards his anarchist hero. Out of this kind of tension, of course, good writing often flows.

Does his play work? I shall only know when I've seen it on the stage. But, on the question of critics attending rehearsals, I remain mildly cautious. Our business is with the product not the process; and although one ends up knowing the play rather better and admiring the actors' and director's tireless perseverance, in rehearsals one still feels as conspicuous as a voyeur at an orgy. I think critics should occasionally direct plays (as Bentley, Clurman and Kerr have done in America) as well as write them. But, fascinatingly instructive as my day at the Court was, I still feel homework is probably best done in the confines of one's home.

Equus

Old Vic: 27 July 1973

Peter Shaffer's *Equus* is sensationally good. Like *The Royal Hunt Of The Sun* and *The Battle Of Shrivings*, it is based on a direct confrontation between reason and instinct. Like them also, it suggests that though organised faith is usually based on neurosis, a life without some form of worship or belief is ultimately barren. But it's a far better play than either if only because the intellectual argument and the poetic imagery are virtually indivisible.

It deals with the psychiatric exploration of a hideous crime. A 17-year-old boy has blinded six horses with a metal spike; and we watch as the doctor patiently pieces together the evidence that will explain this act of cruelty. Gradually we learn that the boy's mother, a religious fanatic, has filled his mind with images of Biblical cruelty; that his father, a taciturn printer, cannot communicate with him about anything; that his sexual instincts have been aroused by horseflesh and that he has come to love one particular animal as a god; that, impotent when seduced by a girl in the stables, he has wreaked a terrible revenge on the all-seeing horses around him.

A classic case-book drama then? Not at all. For, though Shaffer pieces the evidence together with an accelerating detective story tension, his real concern is with the relationship between the psychiatrist and the boy. Humane, clinical, and efficient, the doctor realises that by restoring the boy to 'normality' he is in fact killing the motivating force of his life. 'Passion,' he explains, 'can be destroyed by a doctor. It cannot be created.' And the question the play asks is whether, by rooting out the brain-sickness and abnormality of individuals, we don't ultimately deny their humanity.

What makes the play so exciting is that it presents this argument in such bold, clear, vivid theatrical terms. From the opening image of the boy nuzzling another actor clad in skeletal horse's head and hooves, we are constantly aware of his strange passion; yet the main action takes place inside a sparse rectangular room representing the orderly world of the psychiatrist. Shaffer is also shrewd enough to make the psychiatrist a complex human figure, aware that his hunger for a pagan, primitive world is scarcely fulfilled by a three-week package tour to the Peloponnese.

Intellectually, the one gap in the play is that Shaffer advocates 'worship' and passion (in a very Forsterian way) without suggesting what we do if that passion is socially destructive. To 'cure' murderers and return them to our society may be a denial of their instincts. But isn't it socially necessary? And, dramatically, he doesn't always vivify his minor characters. But this is to carp at a play of extraordinary intellectual resonance that presents us with a sequence of indelible images.

John Dexter's spare, lean production (notice the economy with which the actors, by a flick of the head, suggest equine movement) also contains two outstanding performances. Alec McCowen's psychiatrist is a brilliant study of a man of reason, soured by the need to bottle up and contain his instincts; and, as always, he articulates arguments beautifully. And Peter Firth matches him admirably as the haunted, hapless, soft-featured boy who has given rein to his fearful passion. I was much moved both by the play and its performance.

Brassneck

Nottingham Playhouse: 21 September 1973

Brassneck by Howard Brenton and David Hare is an important play. Not since John Arden's *The Workhouse Donkey* ten years ago have I seen any work that attempts to put a whole regional community on stage and to show in detail how the provincial power nexus works. Judging by the outraged huffing and puffing near me, it was courageous of Nottingham Playhouse to stage it; and, though Brenton and Hare are sometimes guilty of hasty brushwork and flimsy characterisation, it's reassuring to find two young dramatists operating on such a big canvas.

What I like about the play is the way it interweaves family, civic and national issues. In outline it traces the rise and fall of the Midlands family Bagley from 1945 to 1973. And, as in some *engagé Forsyte Saga*, we watch Bagley Senior buying his way into civic prominence via the Conservative Club, the Masonic Lodge and property speculation; his architect-nephew carrying on the family tradition by submitting artificially-low tenders for city schemes; and, even after the Bagley bubble has burst, a new generation carrying profit-without-honour to its logical conclusion by venturing into Chinese heroin. In a memorable final image the Bagleys invite the audience to join them in a toast to the last, great days of capitalism while the ground slowly swallows them up.

What lifts the play above agitprop is that it indicts left as well as right. Labour councillors and MPs are shown to be as susceptible as anyone else to the creeping magnetism of power; and, though credit is paid to the Attlee Government, we are reminded that had they carried out their promise to nationalise land the whole history of postwar Britain would have been different. Moreover, at their best, Brenton and Hare capture something of the strange texture of English provincial life: Masonic initiation rites are presented in all their black-comedy detail and there's a brilliantly bleary wedding feast, evoking the smell of stale champagne and ending with Bagley Senior's nightmare recollection of cannibalism in the First World War trenches.

In the end Brenton and Hare waste a lot of their buckshot. Why bother with expense account fiddlers and genteel housewife-poets when there are bigger targets to aim at? And by staking so much on the Bagleys they never really discuss the failures of the system they represent. But, though the play is better on illustration than argument, it's still an enormously energetic work and it's given a suitably Dionysiac production by David Hare, complete with horses, hoofers and striptease. Paul Dawkins also endows Alfred Bagley with such craggy fascination that his death leaves a sad gap in the drama and Griffith Jones oozes silvery charm as a sweet-tongued Tory manipulator. And Patrick Robertson's back-projected sets (encompassing a large slice of Britain's postwar history) contribute a lot to a rousing, provocative evening.

Jack And The Beanstalk

London Palladium: 19 December 1973

Although marginally shorter than *Götterdämmerung*, this year's Palladium pantomime, *Jack And The Beanstalk*, is a great improvement on last year's soggy pudding of a show. I still dislike the idea of a pop-star principal boy (I'm a Dorothy Ward man myself) and a female Dame (good as Dora Bryan is). And I cannot protest too much at the constant crackle and hum of the neck-mikes which sometimes makes listening to the show the theatrical equivalent of picking up a Lithuanian radio station. But all is redeemed by the luminous, unflagging presence of Frankie Howerd who, as Simple Simon, does not stint himself. Stint himself he does not.

With lips constantly pursed (silk-pursed you might say), tongue flicking out like an iguana's and a look of unspeakable affront crossing those lugubrious features, he offers us the full repertoire of his comic mannerisms. His great trick is to employ what I can only call an Argyll Street alienation-effect: that is, he often seems as much a part of the audience as of the show, sending his colleagues up rotten ('What a shocking actor,' he cries as one of the baddies noisily expires like Bully Bottom) or drawing attention to his own absurdity ('I wish I could win the pools' he mutters during 'Three Little Fishes' with its lunatic gobble-and-screech). But his best moment comes when he essays drag, looking like an elongated Mae West who's dressed in a hurry, and flashing a pair of cocoa-coloured cami-knickers that he's convinced inflame passers-by. This is Howerd in a king-sized pack; and I for one am grateful.

The rest of the show is an up-and-down affair. The plot gets abandoned more often than a Dickensian waif and the cues for song have to be heard to be disbelieved. But Dora Bryan is a spirited Dame Durden, at one point doing a marvellously inconsequential rendering of 'On The Good Ship Lollipop' in a pink tutu; Mark Wynter as Jack follows the old panto principle of standing with legs wide apart belting his songs at the audience as if defying them to belt them back; and in the transformation scene there is a particularly good dragon, bright-eyed and smoke-belching, that looks as if it's wandered in from *Beowulf*. If they can only eliminate the 2LO atmospherics, and tighten up the haunted-castle scene (which wouldn't frighten a rabbit), it should be a good panto.

The Party

Old Vic: 21 December 1973

'It is a revolutionary duty to tell the truth,' said Antonio Gramsci. And the first thing to be said about Trevor Griffiths's superb dialectical drama, *The Party* at the Old Vic, is that it does precisely that. Set in a radical telly-producer's swish SW7 home during the uprising in Paris in May, 1968, it confronts the possibility of revolution in our own society with a bleak, painful, pessimistic honesty; and it reflects the division in English society between the liberal intellectuals and the working-classes more accurately than any play I can recall.

In technique *The Party* is Shavian. The first half contains two speeches as long as the Inquisitor's summing-up in *Saint Joan*; and like Shaw, Mr Griffiths delights in setting up a seemingly impregnable argument only to have the next speaker blast it to smithereens. Thus a group of Left-wing intellectuals foregather in South Ken under the klieg lights to discuss revolution; and a Gower Street writer and lecturer lengthily argues that the Marxist idea of a proletarian dictatorship has been overtaken by history and that it is now one's function to endorse any source of militant unrest from blacks, students or wherever.

John Tagg, a granite-hard Glaswegian Trotskyite counters with a withering attack on the bourgeois intellectuals who will never sacrifice their own prestige and power in a common cause. As he says, 'You enjoy biting the hand that feeds you but you will never bite if off.' And it's a sign of Griffiths's dialectical maturity that even this argument is fractured by a drunken Wednesday Playwright who claims of the Fourth International Group that 'if reality doesn't come up to scratch, it's rejected.'

To hold in one's mind several conflicting propositions is the sign of a first-rate intellect and playwright; which, on the evidence of this and *Occupations*, Griffiths undoubtedly is. But he does not simply present us with disembodied ideas: he also shows us the intimate relation between the private and public man. Joe Shawcross, the radical telly-man, has a neurotic self-hatred and hinted impotence that explains his political ineffectualness. Tagg, however (in Laurence Olivier's rock-like performance) is a man of iron self-discipline who regards his own impending death merely as a waste for the cause. And the ribald playwright is a lovely creation, an anarchic joker who speaks as much truth as anyone in the room.

I hope to write further of this complex, gritty, intellectually fascinating play. But I must extol Olivier, phrasing his long speech like a piece of music with slow and fast movements and clarifying the argument with every gesture of his great butcher-sized hands; Frank Finlay as the grizzled mutinous toper; Ronald Pickup as the reedily helpless host; and John Shrapnel as his bull-necked, under-educated brother who simply wants privacy and independence. The minor roles are very thinly written; but John Dexter has orchestrated the arguments superbly and reminds us, through slides and film of France in '68, that while Britons endlessly talk about social uprising, other countries actually experience it.

1974

All year the talk was of crisis. Labour narrowly won two General Elections (one in February, another in October) but was confronted by a drastic rise in oil prices and the damaging effects of a world economic recession. Inevitably, this had its effect on the theatre. People began to question the whole subsidy structure at the very moment when the two major national companies were poised on the brink of expansion. Indeed fourteen artistic directors wrote a letter to The Times *warning that the new National Theatre might absorb so much government money that other theatres would be starved: amongst the signatories was, ironically enough, Peter Hall's eventual successor, Richard Eyre.*

Though still housed at the Old Vic, the National's cause wasn't much helped by the mediocre start to the Peter Hall regime: productions like The Tempest, Eden End, Next Of Kin, The Freeway *and* Grand Manoeuvres *hardly seemed to justify the gradual erection of Denys Lasdun's concrete playhouse on the South Bank. And the RSC had a very mixed year balancing spectacular hits like* Sherlock Holmes, Travesties *and Gorky's* Summerfolk *with duds like Mercer's* Duck Song, *Barnes's* The Bewitched *and Keith Hack's Stratford* Measure For Measure. *Even the Royal Court had a middling year, though* Life Class *and* Play Mas *moved to the West End.*

*In London much of the energy came from Greenwich Theatre which gave Jonathan Miller the chance to stage a season of family romances (*Ghosts, The Seagull *and* Hamlet*), brought Glenda Jackson and Susannah York back to the stage in* The Maids, *premiered Ayckbourn's* The Norman Conquests, *gave O'Neill's* More Stately Mansions *its British debut and revived* The Entertainer *with Max Wall. Nottingham also scored with* The Churchill Play, *Bill Bryden began to make waves at Edinburgh's Royal Lyceum and the*

Actors' Company hot-footed it round the country. It was a year of sporadic excitement achieved against a background of economic crisis.

Sherlock Holmes

Aldwych: 2 January 1974

Whatever terrors it may hold, at least 1974 has got off to a bright start theatrically with the RSC's ravishing production of *Sherlock Holmes* by Arthur Conan Doyle and William Gillette. Admittedly the play itself is a total betrayal of the filigree delicacy of the original stories and the messiest piece of dramatic plotting since *The Way Of The World*; but, as a piece of popular theatre it undeniably works and John Wood's performance is, quite simply, the best portrayal of Holmes I've ever seen.

The trouble with the play is that it's an attempt to combine two irreconcilable stories: *A Scandal In Bohemia* (dealing with the recovery of compromising regal documents) and *The Final Problem* (Holmes's great climactic confrontation with Professor Moriarty). Gillette's technique was basically to turn them into a ramshackle Victorian melodrama, complete with doting, maltreated heroine (no substitute for the vixen-like Irene Adler) and the capture of Moriarty by a trick that wouldn't have imposed on a child of eleven. By making the villains appear bungling incompetents, he drastically minimises Holmes's stature: and even the famous relationship with Dr Watson loses much of its testy interdependence.

But, for all its crudities, it's still a work of unabashed theatrical vigour, splendidly realised in Frank Dunlop's production and Carl Toms's sets. Take the excursion to Moriarty's underground office where the great schemer sits enthroned like some diabolical archbishop, surrounded by the Mona Lisa and the Goya Duke of Wellington, a telephone that looks as if it has a hot line to Hell and a giant grappling-hook evoking unimaginable horrors. Camp touches occasionally obtrude, such as the violin theme-music borrowed from James Bond and some outrageous noises-off suggesting we're closer to Peter Sellers's Moriarty than Conan Doyle's; but in general the cast play it commendably straight.

And John Wood's Holmes is a great performance. He gives us the sardonic humour, the biting intelligence and what Auden called the scientific curiosity raised to the status of a heroic passion. But above all, he suggests Holmes's profound melancholia, investing the tritest lines with the world-weariness of a fifth-act Macbeth. I have long regarded Mr Wood as an astonishing actor; but here he shows the great performer's ability to transmute base lead into gold. And he is finely matched by Philip Locke's Moriarty, a Napoleon of crime already half-way to St Helena.

Max Wall

28 January 1974

Byron woke up one morning and found himself famous. But he can't have been more startled than Max Wall who, after fifty years in the business, woke up one morning last December to find himself hailed by the three top Sunday drama critics as a comedian of genius. He accepts the compliment gratefully. But he adds, in that mock-anguished voice he uses as if a man has just driven over his foot, 'They call me a genius – in which case I must be the biggest underpaid genius the world has ever seen.'

Drop into a matinée of *Cockie* at the Vaudeville and you get indisputable proof of his greatness. It's a typical midweek matinée with a coach-party or two upstairs and enough room in the stalls to drive a tank through; yet by the end of Wall's abortive attempt to sing 'The Birth Of The Blues', the audience has been transformed into a unified, chuckling throng, palms smoking with applause. The act is totally different from the one I saw at the premiere; but it still has the same quality of a man keeping us amused during the last quarter of an hour before execution. 'After all,' he lugubriously remarks, 'while you're sitting there, you might just as well be entertained.'

Ingratiation is the keynote of modern comedy: desperation is the hallmark of Wall's. The band is mutinous, chorus girls scream before being touched, unseen hands goose him from behind the tabs. 'Everything happens to me,' he confides. 'If they sawed a woman in half, I'd get the half that eats.' To stave off despair he offers his impression of a totally relaxed Method actor: so relaxed that when he opens his mouth he keels over completely. He next does the splits with great aplomb, only to find his eyes widening in agony as he brings his legs together again. And finally he utters his devastating threat to his unseen assailant to turn up at his funeral with light brown boots on. On a lady's bicycle.

Between houses he amiably reminisces about his amazing switch-back career. What was it like to be acclaimed a genius at 65? 'Sheer eulogy, wasn't it,' he says, delighting as much in the word itself as in the idea. 'What's strange is that what is a romp to the comedian can be transformed into something different when it reaches the audience. I used to do exactly the same act thirty years ago, taking a number like "Sonny Boy" or "A Nightingale Sang in Berkeley Square" and using it as a peg on which to hang a lot of improvised material. Older journalists must have seen it all before, but it seems fresh, I suppose, because I respond differently to the audience each time. I remember Val Parnell used to complain about my act saying it always ran over time. 'What the bloody hell's he doing up there?' he used to shout. The answer is I was making bricks without straw: that's what my act is all about.'

But obviously there is more to it than that. Like a lot of English comics (Frankie Howerd whose flabber has never been so gasted, or Ken Dodd who radiates plumptiousness) he delights in the shape and sound of words. I notice how on his dressing-room phone he uses the word 'conducive' and then rolls it round his tongue like a mouthwash. 'I've always been fascinated,' he says 'by the oddities of the English language. I love the hard, sharp consonants in words like 'capital' and 'splendid' and I like to start a phrase like 'Standing on the stage of this exquisite theatre' playing with the rhetoric, giving it a sepulchral sound, and generally out-Wolfiting Wolfit.'

His work also has that faintly surrealist quality ('My eyeballs should drop out of their sockets if I'm telling a lie') that you find in the comic monologues of Dan Leno. He says he has often thought of himself as a reincarnation of Leno and quotes some bizarre monologues he has written, still lying around at home unperformed: 'I walked in and found him in a brown study – which is not my favourite colour. I believe he painted it himself. I could see his brain working. Since he had a cellophane panel let into his forehead, this was not difficult. Suddenly he noticed me and the shock made him turn turtle in his chair. His secretary came in but didn't recognize him with the shell on his back.'

If torturing words is one side of Wall's talent, the other side is his rubber-limbed physical plasticity. Coming from a theatrical family, he was trained from the age of twelve in the art of acrobatic comedy and was even sent to Paris to learn the art of back-benders, flip-flaps, pratfalls and somersaults. As he says, it was the tradition of Keaton, Chaplin, Stan Laurel and Fred Kitchen; and it meant he started off on the halls as a speciality dancer in what was called 'a dumb act'. The incentive to become a verbal comic was, in fact, partly financial:

dancers could only ever earn £30 a week, whereas for comedy men the sky was the limit.

What was variety like in those days? 'Very simple, naïve, child-like, with occasional touches of bawdy in the tradition of Marie Lloyd's "She sits among the cabbages and peas." But there was also genuine variety. You had turns like Owen McGiveney's Dickensian act with its trick exits and prop clothing. He would come on as Bill Sikes, do a rousing speech, go behind a curtain, literally run straight into his next costume and reappear as Vincent Crummles. Or you had things like Will Fyffe's cameo in which he'd come on in a miniature train, announcing himself as the proprietor of the "Heeland Railway", do his act and then cry, "I canna stay the noo, A tootle on the whistle and away we goo," and go chugging off into the wings. It was all curiously innocent.'

Wall's career in the twenties and thirties spanned everything: variety, revue, pantomime, cabaret. Somewhat ironically, he recalls C.B. Cochran turning him down at first, saying he was far too rough to appear in any of his shows, before putting him into *One Damn Thing After Another* at the London Pavilion in 1927. Other memories float to the surface: cabaret with Paul Whiteman at the Piccadilly Hotel and singing 'I'm mad; it's sad but it's true. I froth with wrath and bite chair-legs in two'; playing Broadway in 1932 in *Earl Carroll's Vanities* with a young Jewish comic named Milton Berle who was accompanied everywhere by his mother ('They used to say if Milton had a row with his mother she sat behind a pillar for two shows'); forming a comedy act in the Depression with two large American ladies, part of which consisted of smashing them against the proscenium arch till all the plaster fell off.

Although he is a grotesque, he still believes that delicacy, precision and simplicity are the essence of comedy. And one of his great heroes is Grock, with whom he played on a bill at the Empire, Paris, in the 1920s. 'I was finished by the first half so I used to watch him from out front every night. He would do all the famous stuff like the man going to play the violin to whom everything happens: he would throw the bow up in the air, try and catch it and miss; go behind a screen, throw it in the air again and let out a cry of triumph as he caught it; come out again, try and repeat the trick and see it fall helplessly to the ground. The point is his act was always built round a simple idea and he was a complete individual in himself. He could have done exactly the same act without funny make-up. He was just a funny man inside his soul – that's where it all comes from.'

Alas, in the fifties Wall's own career declined, partly as a result of Fleet Street suffering one of its periodic fits of morality when he was involved in a divorce case. Happily Wall has bounced right back in recent years playing in Jarry's *Ubu Roi* and Wesker's *The Old Ones* at the Royal Court, guesting on TV shows and now triumphing in the Strand. It would be good to see him given a show of his own since he still brims with comic ideas (he wants to do an act as a bassoonist whose instrument slowly falls to pieces while he plays *In The Hall Of The Mountain King*), and since he is one of the few surviving links with the great days of grotesque physical clowning. Every time he plays Professor Walloffski, in fact, you are getting a touch of Grock.

Albert Finney

23 February 1974

One autumn afternoon in 1956 I dropped into the Birmingham Repertory Theatre to see a prankish, whimsical Irish melodrama called *Happy As Larry*. The play itself has fled from my memory but I can still recall the impact made on me by a strange young man who was one of a chorus of six dancing tailors. With his round, mooncalf face, shoulders protectively hunched and centre-parted hair ironed flat across his head, he looked as if he had bounced straight out of some sepia photograph of Irish village life. His name, I noticed, was Albert Finney.

Over the next two years, I saw most of Finney's fledgling work at Birmingham. And what fascinated me was his blend of power-driven muscular authority (even at this stage Ken Tynan compared him with Spencer Tracy and Walter Huston) with a satanic impishness. He played Henry V (in a production that had Robert Chetwyn as the Earl of Cambridge and Michael Blakemore as the Duke of Exeter) not as the usual ageing boy-scout but as a hard-headed man of the people endowed with a touch of the practical joker. He also showed the born actor's capacity to leave behind an indelible physical image. I can recall to this day his death scene in John Hall's *The Lizard On The Rock*: shot in the stomach at point-blank range, he halted, stared at his killer in agonised disbelief, uttered three faint cries like a kitten mewing and keeled irrevocably over.

In the years since then Finney has often seemed like the greatest actor not on the English stage. There was of course, *Luther*, a rich year at the National Theatre and latterly, *Alpha Beta*, Beckett's *Krapp* and Storey's *Cromwell* at the Royal Court. But like Nicol Williamson and Peter O'Toole, Finney has kept his theatrical appearances strictly rationed.

Movies have helped to give today's star actors an independence and freedom of choice they rarely possessed in previous generations; and while this saves them doing rubbish, it also means their careers lack that sense of steady inexorable advance you find in the Olivier-Gielgud generation. Today actors parachute on to the summit instead of working their way rigorously from one plateau to the next.

Watching Finney in Peter Nichols's *Chez Nous*, however, one realises that his magnetic power is undiminished. For a start he demolishes one of the great journalistic myths which is that the British theatre was exclusively colonised in the Fifties by working-class actors with a flat, low-key, style: Finney is, in fact, lower middle-class in origin and like many of his contemporaries, delights in explosive effects. Last year in *Coriolanus* Nicol Williamson unforgettably showed shame, rage, and spoilt-brat petulance competing for dominance during his agonising surrender to his mother's entreaties. And Finney in *Chez Nous* memorably registers a gut-tearing anguish and remorse at the revelation he has impregnated a 14-year-old girl: he presses his palms flat against his skull as if to beat down the awful truth, the colour drains from his big, cratered face, tears prick his eyes. It's like watching a man age twenty years in three seconds.

Astonishingly, my most respected colleague sees in this moment (and the character's subsequent yearning for his child) nothing but updated Victorian melodrama. In fact, you can reduce any play ever written, from *Oedipus Rex* to Marguerite Duras's *Suzanna Andler*, to melodrama by simply outlining its plot: what counts is the detail in which it is clothed. Moreover one sure sign of melodrama is that it cannot sustain too much motivation or social accuracy in the acting: here, however, Finney's performance (and Denholm Elliott's too for that matter) confirm that we are light years away from *East Lynne*.

Finney brilliantly illuminates the architect's behaviour by showing it is not a matter of a middle-aged man seducing a minor but of two adolescents being drawn irresistibly together. As Janet Adam Smith remarked on radio, in the first act he brims over with unfocused boyish energy, as he kicks a ball about, bangs a shuttlecock around, aimlessly tinkers with a painted handcart. Only the news that he is a father shocks him into maturity; and Finney, his voice gradually thickening under the influence of bad home-made wine and his movements acquiring the slow-motion exaggeration of the half-canned, conveys that sense of heartache and longing that, far more than social satire, is the key to Nichols's plays.

Intelligence and observation are the qualities I look for in an actor; and Finney clearly has them both. The story goes that as a Salford schoolboy playing the Emperor Jones he went down to Manchester docks to study the mannerisms of Negro seamen; and in most of his work you realise that he has retained and memorised things seen. The prime instance, I suppose, was the National's *A Flea In Her Ear* where he did the famous spring double of M Chandebise, the impotent Parisian bourgeois, and Poche, the idiot hotel porter. As Chandebise he was, with his stiff-jointed walk, ramrod-straight back and arms pinned to his sides, erect in all but the most vital sense; as Poche his shoulders drooped and his knees sagged as if from a life-time of carrying insupportably heavy loads. But his masterstroke (a real sign of acting intelligence) was never to exaggerate the difference between the two men so that the confusion of one for the other became totally plausible.

The pity of it is that in recent years Finney has scarcely touched the classics. He has never, so far as I know, played Hamlet, Iago, Mercutio, Richard III; he is unknown in Ibsen, Chekhov, Shaw; and he is even a stranger to American realistic drama for which he has just the right muscle. The point is worth making because Olivier, when he had reached Finney's age of 37, had already had his first crack at most of the great Shakespearean roles as well as being internationally famous in movies. There is, I admit, no moral obligation on any actor to essay the big classic parts; yet it is only through them that he can push his talents to their furthest limits and test himself against the best work ever written for the theatre. It used to be said of our heroic actors that they spent far too little of their professional life in trousers: I am beginning to think it is high time Albert Finney, given his bull-like power and radiant sense of inner enjoyment, discarded his.

Knuckle

Comedy: 6 March 1974

I hope David Hare's *Knuckle* won't get rapped for it's the kind of play I welcome on the West End stage: an attempt to use a pop format, in this case the hard-edged Mickey Spillane thriller, as a vehicle for moral comment. In the end the form sags under the sheer weight of what it's asked to convey but the play is consistently entertaining and, with pleasing irony, uses a commercial stage to attack the degradation of the profit motive.

Mr Hare gets off to a good start by setting the brisk and brutal action in darkest Guildford: Spillane happenings, in fact, in Francis Durbridge territory. The hero is a cynical young arms-dealer who returns to the Home Counties to launch a search for his missing sister; and he crosses swords with his merchant-banker father who represents the smooth, discreetly acceptable face of capitalism, a dubious young journalist who sports a flick-knife rather than a reporter's notebook and the voluptuous hostess of a drastically under-populated local nightspot. But Mr Hare is not just out to write a Guildford *Gumshoe*: his purpose is to reveal the bubbling corruption, legitimised racketeering and institutionalised violence of life in the stockbroker belt.

I must confess at times I was reminded of the over-zealous revolutionary in Shaw's *Misalliance* who cries 'Rome fell, Babylon fell, Hindhead's turn will come.' Moreover the inherent melodrama of the pulp-thriller seriously undermines the attack on the genuine evils of property speculation. But the play is much subtler than it at first appears. For a start Mr Hare creates genuine moral uncertainty by making the exposer of corruption himself a lethal barbarian: there is little, in fact, to choose between the gun-toting hero and his city slicker of a father. In reality the work is built round a sustained, intelligent contrast between the volubility of open protest and the discretion, elegance and quietness of much British capitalism; and in that way it more seriously questions our allegedly 'civilised' values.

Moreover having chosen his style ('That's a very nice leg' – 'I got another one just like it') Mr Hare also pursues it with total consistency; and Michael Blakemore's production, with its brutal B-feature music and quicksilver fluency, skilfully matches the tone of the writing. Edward Fox is hardly my idea of a 'squat, ugly' hero but, flashing dangerous, nervy smiles, is compulsively watchable as the Guildford gun-runner and Kate Nelligan as the hostess sexily bridges the gap between Surrey and sub-Ross MacDonald. In short, this is a Hare well worth chasing.

The Tempest

Old Vic: 7 March 1974

Fourteen years ago precisely Peter Hall began his brilliant Stratford reign with an over-decorated, eccentrically-cast production of *Two Gentlemen Of Verona*. We should not therefore despair if he has begun his National Theatre career with a lethargic, vulgarly spectacular, masque-like production of *The Tempest* that almost manages to submerge the presence of the greatest living Shakespearean actor, Sir John Gielgud, in opulent excess. This, in fact, is culinary theatre with a vengeance.

It is, of course, a fallacy to argue that because *The Tempest* contains elements of Jacobean masque, the whole play is nothing but an Inigo Jones spectacular. Like all Shakespeare's late plays, it is a highly civilised debate on Nature versus Art: it is moreover a deeply political work in which Prospero is both the victim of usurpation and himself a colonial usurper. But you would never guess this from Mr Hall's production in which ideas emphatically take second place to spectacle: crucial speeches like Gonzalo's vision of a Utopian commonwealth or Prospero's magnificent access of charity pale beside Iris's descent from the rainbowed skies like Danny La Rue in *Queen Passionella* or the dance of the sunburnt sicklemen in their raffia pinnies and Oklahoma hats.

Is this literary puritanism on my part? I don't think so. For the essence of theatrical magic is not filling the stage with Jasper Maskelyne effects but creating a sense of wonder. I find little of that, however, in John Bury's jagged, mobile, mirrored sets which are the essence of primitive chic; or in the translation of Ariel into an ambisextrous, quick-change counter-tenor going up and down on a docker's pulley; or the treatment of Prospero's 'majestic vision' (greeted here with laughter) as a grotesque revel graced by a Sabrina-breasted Juno. In fact the weakness of the production is that one can discuss it only in terms of its images: not in terms of the triumph of virtue over vengeance or the ultimate superiority of life-giving Nature over artificial Nurture.

Of course Gielgud's Prospero, a bookish Renaissance Magician, is exquisitely spoken and musically phrased; but it is a typical sign of decorative philistinism that one of his greatest speeches has to compete with a whirring pulley and there is little of the contrast between the initial testiness and final benediction he got in Brook's magnificent 1957 production. Of the rest only Arthur Lowe's malevolent, tyrannical Stephano, Julian Orchard's lugubrious Trinculo and Denis Quilley's Cheyenne-like Caliban emerge with any individual clarity. I admire Mr Hall enormously; but I think he has missed the point that *The Tempest* is a play and not an oratorio or a lush visual extravaganza. There is infinitely less in this production, in fact, than meets the eye.

King John

Royal Shakespeare Theatre: 21 March 1974

This must be the first time in history the Stratford-on-Avon Festival has opened with a new play. Misleadingly billed as Shakespeare's *King John*, it in fact blends the Folio Text with lines from 'The troublesome reign of King Johan' (Shakespeare's source), from John Bale's *King John* (a Tudor Morality) and from the RSC's own John Barton's ever-active brain. The result is a complex, sprawling densely textured play that I found infinitely more fascinating than the published Shakespearean version.

Mr Barton's purpose is clearly to draw a parallel between John's waning England and our own: lands both ruled by Commodity in the sense of gain, self-interest and expediency. And the point is pushed home in a scene reminiscent of *Murder In The Cathedral* when John's six cowled barons advance to the footlights to analyse the state of England ('The price of goods soars meteor-like into the lowering heavens,' says one, obviously addressing Shirley Williams) and to plead for national harmony. Admittedly this raises the question of whether the invading Dauphin represents the EEC and the ill-advised hero, deserted by his erstwhile supporters, our own ex-PM; but, quite seriously, the strength of Barton's version is that it conveys a passionate concern for the state of the nation.

Where Mr Barton errs is in blending an attack on Commodity with a Morality play about the decline of earthly vanity and a study of medieval power politics: at times you get the feeling you're watching three different plays running concurrently. But although it's not the most coherent evening I've had at Stratford, it contains some beautiful effects: unlike Shakespeare for instance, Mr Barton lets us see the poisoning of John at Swinstead Abbey with the monks seated round him in a Last Supper grouping and with medieval carols ironically counter-pointing the killing of a king. And, as in his *Richard II*, he uses ritual and golden ceremony to expose the weakness and vulnerability of the men beneath the carapace.

Shakespearean loyalists will of course, vehemently object to the Bartonising of the Bard; but one can't, in honesty, say he has mangled a masterpiece. And the production still yields a truly affecting performance by Sheila Allen as the self-pitying Constance and good ones from Richard Pasco as the Bastard who starts off as Tony Lumpkin and ends as the voice of England, and from Emrys James as the quavering, sickly monarch. John Napier's sets, with their traverse curtains and emblematic props, combine simplicity and fluency. Trimmed and sharpened, this will become one of the best new plays we've seen this year.

Royalty Follies

Royalty: 26 March 1974

Paul Raymond's costly extravaganza *Royalty Follies*, on which no expense or taste has been spared, is certainly filled with gorgeous creatures. Slim hips, slender waists, long tapering legs – and that's only the boys. Girls too cascade on to the stage from the moment when five descend from the flies in ornamental cages in a manner unfortunately reminiscent of Katharine Hepburn in *Suddenly Last Summer*.

But although this is basically a girlie show, a kind of 'Black and White Minstrels' with breasts, it is not really a sexy one. What it is actually about is money: it invites you to thrill to the rustle of a dollar rather than a knicker and titillates you with conspicuous waste rather than inconspicuous waists. Thus we have a Genghis Khan number in which hairy gentlemen in fox furs and anklets do unspeakable things with pikes to girls with stretch-marks whilst the balding hero fiercely whips his partner (I felt, on dramatic grounds, she shouldn't look as if she enjoyed it quite so much). We have a James Bond number in which a visibly unexcited 007 writhes on a bed with hefty dames before winding up in Jamaica where a girl is incongruously ice-skating. And a large part of the evening is concerned with things going up and down – giant staircases, ornamental bridges and one's own critical eyebrows.

The trouble is it is all so damply unerotic. Admittedly we were denied the spectacle of the Miami Dolphins stripping Miss Nude International: this, we were told, was 'due to the recent industrial situation' which struck me as a tendentious attempt to blame it all on Ted Heath. But even so the show ignores the basic fact that once you've seen two, you've seen them all and that one needs more in a slap-up revue than a series of endless finales. The programme invokes the great names of Flo Ziegfeld and Earl Carroll but what Mr Raymond forgets is that Ziegfeld had Fanny Brice and Carroll had great comics: what the show lacks, in a word, is personality.

Admittedly there is an engaging magician, Luxor Gali-Gali, who produces chicks from gentleman's trouser-fronts, a ventriloquist called Georges Schlic who sings 'The cock is dead' (which has a melancholy aptness, I fear) and the Black Theatre Group stripping a willing bespectacled lady. But although the show is lavish, dressy and loud it offers minimal titillation. As Archie Rice might well have said, in fact, it is all tit and no elation.

Travesties

Aldwych: 11 June 1974

I find it difficult to write in calm, measured tones about Tom Stoppard's *Travesties*: a dazzling pyrotechnical feat that combines Wildean pastiche, political history, artistic debate, spoof-reminiscence, and song-and-dance in marvellously judicious proportions. The text itself is a dense Joycean web of literary allusions; yet it also radiates sheer intellectual joie de vivre, as if Stoppard were delightedly communicating the fruits of his own researches.

What is it actually about? Partly the fallibility of human memory in that we watch an ageing consular official, Henry Carr, recalling Zürich in 1917 when Lenin, Joyce, and the Dadaist Tristan Tzara were igniting three different revolutions; and, through an ill-remembered production of *The Importance Of Being Earnest*, Carr sees himself as a pivotal historical figure brought into frantic collision with the intellectual giants. But, on another level, the play is a running debate about the relation between politics and art in which Lenin emerges as a bourgeois traditionalist sighing over *La Dame Aux Camélias* and hating *The Lower Depths*, in which Tzara seems a dilettante cutting art off from its social roots and in which Joyce emerges as a truly great man, shaping the way future generations view reality.

What is hard to convey, however, is the sheer theatrical panache with which Stoppard juggles these, and several other themes. The Wildean pastiche is exact ('Joyce is a name which could only expose a writer to comment around the font') and funny; there are enough puns (on the lines of 'My art belongs to Dada') to make a *Guardian* sub weep for joy; Carr's reminiscences, reminding me a little of those old Henry Reed Third Programme spoofs, show the way men falsify history even to the extent of believing they could personally have stopped the Russian Revolution; and the music, such as the brisk ragtime duet for Gwendolen and Cecily, seems perfectly integrated into the text. Occasionally Stoppard becomes ensnared by his own virtuosity; but for the most part he manages the stylistic transitions with breathtaking fluency.

Meanwhile John Wood confirms that he is, after Olivier, the most exciting actor on the English stage today. Whether as the aged Carr, looking like a battered Max Miller in an outsize dressing-gown, or as his younger self, rapping out jokes with machine-like precision or hammering out key phrases in an intellectual argument, he exudes an overwhelming mental and physical zest: an astonishing performance. Tom Bell hasn't yet got the measure of Joyce but John Hurt's Tzara and Frank Windsor's Lenin are first-rate and Peter Wood's production matches Stoppards' own exuberant, freewheeling gaiety of spirit.

Alan Ayckbourn

14 August 1974

I was lunching with a film-critic friend the other day when the conversation turned to Alan Ayckbourn. 'You drama critics,' said my friend, 'haven't half made fools of yourselves over Ayckbourn. He's simply a good light comedy writer, yet you and Lambert and Nightingale talk about him as if he were some kind of social and political analyst. I went to see *Absurd Person Singular* and thought it had as much to say about life as the average 'Carry On' movie. Honestly if this is the best the theatre has to offer, then it's in an even worse state than I thought.'

I will concede that, under my colleague's attack, lay a valid general point: that critics in all media often feel the need to justify their calling by investing the ephemeral with cosmic significance. As Raymond Durgnat says in his forthcoming book on Hitchcock: 'For obvious reasons (notably the lack of prestige from which film criticism has so long suffered) film critics regularly feel obliged to rationalise their interest in a director by claiming him as a neglected master: a man who offers all the fun of the fair has to become a serious and stern moralist.' And it would be churlish to deny that drama critics often fall into the same trap, seeking the eternal verities in, say, the plays of William Douglas Home.

But I think my friend was wholly wrong about Ayckbourn: and seeing *The Norman Conquests* again confirms that impression. For a start, like all first-rate comedy, the plays are only funny because they are about serious issues: a family weekend that quickly degenerates into violent rows, physical violence and murderous hatred; a young girl wasting her life away with a bedridden mum in a gloomy Victorian house; a hero, Norman, who compensates for his own ineffectualness with a compulsive philandering; two marriages heading not so much for the rocks as for the barrier reefs. Enough material here, I'd say, to keep John Hopkins happy for years.

Now obviously serious subjects alone are no guarantee of comic success. On the other hand, I firmly believe that what distinguishes the good comedy or farce from the mediocre specimen is that the former always has a kernel of reality. Clockwork ingenuity aside, Feydeau's farces are still funny because, as Eric Bentley observed, they hinge on man's age-old desire to damage the family and desecrate the household gods. In contrast a farce like *Birds Of Paradise* fails to tickle my ribs because it is about something (a woman mistaking a Caribbean brothel for a riding-school) that has no visible contact with truth.

As for *The Norman Conquests*, I would say its real theme is the genuine human desperation that keeps breaking through stifling social forms; and that's precisely what makes it funny. Take the first play, *Table Manners*. The overwhelming desire of the bullying Sarah is that the whole family will just once sit down for a calm, 'civilised' meal. Yet what happens when they finally get round the dinner-table? Endless musical-chairs squabbles about who sits where. One guest seated at an absurdly low stool. Bickering about the merits of childless and fertile marriages. Husband insulting wife and being struck by a guest who thinks it's his girl-friend who's been vilified. Ingredients that would be funny anywhere, you may say; but the reason we laugh so loudly is that they all happen to people desperately trying to achieve an After Eight bourgeois elegance.

But I think there is a further reason for Ayckbourn's success: that he is really a regional writer exploiting a traditional metropolitan form, the farcical comedy. And into this he injects a wealth of unobtrusively accurate social detail: not the brand-name kind that in, say, John Mortimer's comedies sometimes sticks out like a sore thumb, but the kind that just gets mentioned in passing. Bit by bit, for instance, you get a total picture of orthodox middle-class Sarah with her children called Denise and Vincent gracing a weekend dancing-class, her own apparent indispensability at the Saturday bring-and-buy sale and her Whitehouseian twin-set-and-pearls public morality. 'I won't even have the television set on at all these days,' she says at one point, unconsciously speaking for a whole regiment of tight-lipped censorious women, and getting a fat laugh in the process.

Ayckbourn's problem, as he himself once said, is that he has a reputation for being a 'high-jinks and technical stuff' writer; and such is our innate puritanism we can't believe anyone that skilful has anything interesting to say. Yet all of his plays, if one thinks back, are about the precise interaction of sex and class in modern English society.

Relatively Speaking was, of course, a dazzling comedy of misunderstanding; but it was also about the territorial invasion by a weekday mistress-secretary of her boss's rural retreat, complete with Sunday lunch on the patio and rhododendron trimming before sherry (notice how many of Acykbourn's plays are set in gardens: classic status-symbol of the English middle-class). *How The Other Half Loves* was about a clandestine affair between a Lamptonish Redbrick climber and his employer's wife and their shameless joint exploitation of a mousy lower-middle-class couple. And *Absurd Person Singular* is about nothing if not the way the balance of power is shifting in provincial society with the old professional classes (e.g. bank-manager and architect) retreating before the advance of the capitalist property-developers.

As I see it, Ayckbourn is a left-wing writer using a right-wing form; and even if there is nothing strident, obvious or noisy about his socialism it is none the less apparent that he has a real detestation for the money-grubber, the status-seeker and the get-rich-quicker. Conversely, he seems instinctively drawn to the nervy, vulnerable and unsure; and *Time And Time Again* (admittedly not his best play) was very much about the intolerance of the pushy, aggressive rising middle-classes for the man with no desire or will of his own.

Of course, it's true that without his basic instinct for what 'works' in purely theatrical terms, Ayckbourn's observations and social accuracy would be unimportant. But it would be a big mistake to assume that he is just an amiable, innocuous funnyman who passes time pleasantly in the theatre for a couple of hours. Although there are moments in *The Norman Conquests* when the writing goes a bit flaccid, I defy anyone to sit through it all and not feel that he has been given a funny, serious, moving, and comprehensive account of the awfulness of middle-class family rituals un-fuelled by love or understanding; and I don't think you can say that of many 'Carry On' movies.

Timon Of Athens

Paris: 22 October 1974

'Tambours, Frappez,' Alcibiades ringingly declares at the end of Peter Brook's new Paris production of *Timon Of Athens*; and I feel like beating a few critical drums to welcome both an exhilarating achievement and Mr Brook's long-awaited return to full-scale public production.

For three years now his Centre Internationale de Recherche Théâtrale has been an itinerant experimental troupe working in Paris, Iran, Africa and America but only rarely mounting large-scale work. Now the fruits of Mr Brook's researches are there for all to see; and I believe they contain some vital lessons for our own beleagured, crisis-ridden theatre.

Not least in the very building that Brook and the CIRT have chosen to work in: the Théâtre Bouffes du Nord, a century-old, horseshoe-shaped Parisian musical house vaguely resembling the old Lyric, Hammersmith. The theatre has been dark for twenty years; but instead of tarting it up, Brook has deliberately left it in a state of dilapidated splendour. The peeling, grey walls are flecked with white stains that look like eagle-sized bird-droppings; the auditorium floor has now become the main acting area, with a sunken pit where the stage used to be and a cat-walk traversing the back wall; and the audience sits on wooden benches surrounding the actors or on three narrow tiers looking down. Everyone can see; everyone can hear; and the guts of a beautiful building have been sensibly retained.

And it is precisely this quality of relaxed, thoughtful simplicity that characterises Brook's production and the acting-style of his ensemble.

Timon. itself is, of course, a notoriously difficult play: an uneven palpably unrevised study of benevolence warped by ingratitude. The play seethes with sour, naked fury and Timon's attack on the destructive power of money is fierce enough to have won even Karl Marx's approval; but it has always been hard to believe in an ancient Athens where all friends are false and all politicians viciously corrupt and Apemantus's comment on Timon that 'the middle of humanity thou never knewest but the extremity of both ends' has often seemed like a failure in Shakespeare as well.

Brook's answer in this, however, is to treat the play as an embittered fable. He makes no more attempt to present a historical Athens than he did in *A Midsummer Night's Dream*: as he says in the published adaptation by Jean-Claude Carrière (significantly Buñuel's regular collaborator), Shakespeare's Athens is as symbolic as Ubu's Poland.

Thus the actors, who begin the evening squatting on cushions at the audience's feet, are simply people telling us a story; and their costumes are emblematic rather than literal. Timon himself wears the kind of white suit one associates with devotees of the Maharishi or even a mod Great Gatsby (another compulsive giver flawed by human contact). Alcibiades, embodying the soldierly virtues, is resplendent in black officer's uniform with white sash and red cloak. And Timon's fickle chums are adorned with rich brocade gowns that might have come (and, for all I know, did) from a Persian street-market.

Normally I distrust productions that are imprecise as to place and time: set anywhere, they often end up being placed nowhere. Büt Brook's production is held together by an absolutely clear conception of character: his Timon is not a neurotic raver (in either sense of the word) but a man who who passes from a drugged indolent dream into an appalling reality.

Surrounded everywhere he goes by applauding sycophants, Francois Marthouret who plays him looks initially like some peculiarly seraphic pop star; but in the second half, reduced to splenetic isolation in tattered rags, he is pure Beckettian man in his most aggressively terminal phase. And Brook's implication is clear: that our own civilisation is likewise being awoken from a prolonged and slumberous, fantasy. How we will react remains an open question.

But what makes the production so thrilling is Brook's ability to give such ideas exciting theatrical flesh. Let me cite one example: the first act party Timon throws for his friends. The guest squat in a semi-circle on a scarf-swathed floor. Cupidon, looking like an African medicine-man in top hat and joke-fur, heralds the arrival of the Masque of Ladies. One girl, purple-cloaked and eerily chanting, presents Timon with a golden globe encased in twine which is unravelled by the tipsily swaying guests until it binds them all. A drum beats. Cupidon cuts the golden twine and stands poised with his shears about to plunge into Timon's neck.

The moment of danger passes and fear is dissolved in laughter with the guests once more whirling like dervishes in their golden cloaks and the whorish lady idly suspending a necklace from her lascivious foot. Thus in one scene Brook embodies nearly all the key images of the play: gold and sun; bonds irrevocably severed; dreaming, careless pleasure; the retribution awaiting the over-secure man.

Brook, in fact, combines great respect for language with the knack of creating images that work in harmony with the text: the key requisite of any first-rate Shakespearean director. But not even he or M. Marthouret can conquer the problem of the second half when Timon retreats to his misanthropic wilderness. As Tynan once wrote, watching the play is rather like going to some scandalously sophisticated party at which, halfway through, the host falls down drunk and starts to rave from under the piano; and, as one figure after another comes on to be abused by the hero, one starts to feel irrevocably chained to the railings.

But when I said the production had a lot from which we could learn I was speaking nothing less than the sober truth. In the first place, the acting has a quality of relaxed skill and ensemble drive we still find only rarely in our own erratically brilliant set-up. Relaxation on stage can, of course, be a euphemism for lassitude: but an actor like Marthouret seems capable of moving from saintly gentleness to gut-tearing anguish without destroying the line of the part and it's heartening to see someone like Paul Crauchet (the lickerish father in Faraldo's movie, *Bof*) playing the relatively small role of the Poet or Maurice Benichou (dark, impassioned and intense) making Timon's servant, Flavius, seem as vital to the story as his master.

Even more instructive, however, is the economy and simplicity of the whole enterprise. Arriving back in London from Paris, it was depressing to pick up the paper and read of the building and financial crises affecting the National Theatre and the RSC.

I have no wish to knock either institution since my critical life would be infinitely poorer without them. But I couldn't help contrasting the factory-like nature of both companies with a group like Brook's in which direct, uncomplicated communication with five or six hundred people at a time is all that really matters. You may say it's unfair to compare a self-styled research-group with a big national company: but the truth is that the CIRT seems much more capable of reaching out to a cross-section of the community than either of our twin theatrical giants.

Indeed the effect of seeing *Timon of Athens* in Paris was to make one ask what the act of theatre really is: and clearly Brook has learned from his African and Iranian experience that fundamentally it has to do with the communication of a story to a group of people gathered as closely as possible round a company of actors.

It has nothing to do with hardware, hydraulic stages, scenic decoration or conspicuous displays of expenditure; but everything to do with narrative, language, ideas and physical skill. And time and again Brook's production proves that the best ideas are usually the simplest: a soldier pinned against the back wall of the theatre while Alcibiades and the Senators debate whether he lives or dies, constantly banging doors to indicate Athenian invasion-panic or the servants of Timon's creditors gradually growing more prosperous as their masters get more pressing.

But before one gets over-idealistic about this particular enterprise, it is worth adding that Brook himself told me he is anxious to come back to England again to direct. Where he did not specify; but I can think of no greater service Trevor Nunn or Peter Hall could perform than to ask this restless nomadic innovator back to either of their companies to question the path our theatre is taking.

At the moment, as his Paris *Timon* shows, he is far and away the best director the British theatre doesn't possess.

Uncle Vanya

The Other Place: 11 December 1974

Uncle Vanya has been the least revived of all Chekhov's major plays over the past decade. It is almost if Olivier's famous 1962 Chichester production had scared other directors, with the exception of Anthony Page at the Royal Court, right off. But Nicol Williamson's production at the RSC's. Other Place in Stratford-upon-Avon not only shows how perfectly Chekhov is suited to a small, intimate studio theatre but also contains an astonishing performance by Williamson himself that painfully exposes all Vanya's emotional nerve-ends.

In one crucial respect, Mr Williamson's production is bang on target; it realises that the play is about what Aristotle called 'the change from ignorance to knowledge'. In the course of the action, the main characters all discover the truth about themselves; and it is because it cottons on to this basic fact that the production acquires a greater pulse and rhythm as it continues. It suggests that the one consequence of the Professor's visit to the Serebriakov's estate is to make everyone's case that much sadder.

You see this clearly, for instance, in Jane Lapotaire's Sonya. The easy mistake with Sonya is to play her as so dowdy that no Astrov in his right mind would want to marry her. But Miss Lapotaire, bun-haired like a Victorian lady novelist, creates a sensible, practical girl so steeped in the rituals of domesticity that she cannot see a table-top without involuntarily sweeping the dust off it; and we learn that her love for Astrov is an open secret when ill-smothered giggles greet her radiant discourse on afforestation. But where Miss Lapotaire is so moving is in her discovery that she cannot stop loving Astrov even when she knows her passion is not requited: her starved-doe eyes still greedily track him round the room as he leaves, making her return to the drudgery of accounting all the more heartrending.

Jill Townsend's Elena is less technically accomplished: even in a studio, her performance seems a trifle small scale as if she's playing to an invisible camera. But with her wasp waist, hollow cheeks and cascading blonde hair, she certainly conveys Elena's languorous beauty. And, again, she gets the point that Elena only discovers herself in the course of this traumatic visit: the moment of truth comes when she faces the fact that she is 'just a minor character' forever doomed to fascinate without accomplishing anything. Miss Townsend handles this well; and her self discovery is all the more poignant for the fact that Miss Lapotaire's Sonya is just then convulsed by giggles at her own temporary happiness.

I could wish, however, the change that overtakes Astrov were more dramatically registered by Patrick Stewart. It is a performance full of intelligent detail (such as the way he vainly peers at himself in the samovar or, slumberous with drink, suddenly jerks to and carries on talking unaware he had nodded off). But what I miss is much hint of the almost old-maidish crankiness that comes from living too long alone and of the fact that the action confronts Astov with his own failure:

I have no reservations, however, about Nicol Williamson's Uncle Vanya which presents us with the extraordinary spectacle of the spirit of a child inhabiting the body of a grown man and, as with a child, emotions appear unchecked by the normal adult restraints. He pours out his scorn for the Professor with a sardonic spleen; he all the time flashes idiotic smiles at Elena while hiding from his dreaded mother behind a newspaper; and yet his lean gangling body constantly seems a dreadful encumbrance to him so that when he tries to curl up unsuccessfully on a bench you feel that his inordinate frame might snap in two.

What makes Williamson a great actor, however, is his sheer emotional candour: he has none of the small reticences and checks-and-balances of good taste that inhibit other performers. Take the famous third act scene when the Professor proposes the carving-up of the estate. At first Williamson never hears a word as he is gazing at Elena with a murderous, basilisk-stare. As the monstrousness of the scheme suddenly hits him, he goes brick-red with impotent fury, he makes short, nervous, stabbing gestures at the Professor and essays aimless kicks like a thwarted infant. As Elena tries to stop his attack, he picks up the roses he has brought her and snaps them in a gesture of magnificent futility; and when he reaches the line 'If I had had a normal life, I might have been a Schopenhauer, a Dostoyevsky' his body straightens, his eyes bulge and you feel confronted by temporary insanity. This is superb acting; and, as in all good Chekhov, the audience is caught between laughter and tears.

But what Williamson again shows is a man confronting his own tragedy; and realising that, at 47, he may have another 13 years of wretched existence to eke out. In the last act he becomes a shambling figure in a grey dressing-gown who lurches to his work-table as if seeking relief in its solidity; and as he and Sonya sit crouched over their bills huddling together for comfort like battle-survivors in the snow, I was reminded of Desmond MacCarthy's phrase about this being real tragedy, 'having in it both the flatness and poignancy of life'. Confronted by acting of this skill and emotional intensity, one's personal failures suddenly become that much easier to bear: and you feel the characters have, in an Aristotelian sense, completed their terrifying journey from ignorance to self-knowledge.

Long Running Plays

28 December 1974

I have just spent a week revisiting the four longest-running shows in London: *The Mousetrap, Pyjama Tops, Sleuth,* and *Oh! Calcutta!* which between them have clocked up a mind-boggling total of 37 years. In advance, I expected my trip to be like a prolonged incarceration in Madame Tussauds. But, to be fair, I must say the shows themselves were all in extremely good nick. What depressed me were the audiences, apparently united by nothing more than a desire to get out of the rain and to see a show that had the reassuring stamp of longevity.

It was, however, an instructive week because I realised that, by combining key elements from all four shows, I had suddenly acquired a cast-iron formula for commercial success: a nude whodunnit. I even, during longueurs, mapped out a plot line on my programme.

Tentatively entitled *Rump Stake*, the play would be set in a snowbound Berkshire guest-house with a heated swimming pool thoughtfully placed in the centre of the living room. Mine host would be a witty, games-playing aristocrat, St John Lord Stevas, and his guests a stranded nude-show company all of whom had something to hide (some, of course, more than others). Friction established, there would be a scream, a scratchy nursery-rhyme recording would issue from the piano next door, and a corpse would be discovered in the pool, sinisterly clothed.

At this point, a detective enters through the rear windows uttering a cry of pain (they happened to be closed at the time) and wearing only skis, a feather boa, and a cache-sexe. Announcing he is a private dick, he proceeds lightly to grill the naked guests. Who could have murdered the corpsed actor and with what motive? Could it have been his Italian-born understudy anxious for a bigger part? Could it have been another guest – the censorious lady JP who obviously has a grind to axe? Or could it have been the leading lady who secretly envied the slim hips, cascading hair, and rotund breasts of her co-star, Fred? These are the kind of questions best left unanswered; and, on second thoughts, best left unasked.

But, abandoning my scenario, I concede that all four shows do have certain features in common. They all revolve around sex and death; they all make use of the idea of drama as game, masquerade, and charade; and they are all, fundamentally, out to titillate (meaning 'tickle, to excite pleasantly' as Ken Tynan helpfully points out in the *Oh! Calcutta!* programme). Some people may be tickled by nude girls, others may be excited pleasantly by a murderous paranoid. But even titillation depends on a sense of vital contact between stage and audience; and in this respect *Pyjama Tops* is the least lonely of the four long-distance runners.

I must however discuss *The Mousetrap* first if only on grounds of age. It opened in 1952 when Winston Churchill was Prime Minister, Harry Truman was US President, and Harold Hobson, as the programme points out, was drama critic of the *Sunday Times*. (Some things, you see, are constant even in a changing world.) But why is the play still there?

Partly because it is genuinely titillating (in that you have to guess not only whodunnit but who's going to get it done to them next) and partly because the characterisation is so open-ended it can be adjusted to suit the needs of the time. Thus the suspects include a febrile young neurotic now played as an outrageous queen in crushed velvet, a hearty female expatriate currently seen as a butch dike doing rugger passes with her greatcoat, and a bouncy, effervescent Italian who looks like one of the Family. I can't quite believe that was what Mrs Christie had in mind in far-off 1952.

Ration books have been taken out in fact, and a touch of camp put in. But what puzzles me about Joan Knight's current production is its indeterminate period (with old-fashioned wirelesses and hemlines combining with shiny new copies of *Harper's — Queen*); and I am still wondering to what extent Agatha Christie was satirising the boredom of the English country weekend in which, after dinner, there is little to do except murder one's fellow guests.

But although the play's bones now creak a bit (why does everyone keep going off to write letters when there are five-foot snowdrifts outside somewhat impeding a visit to the post office?) it is acted by Brian McDermott, Mary Law and Brian Spink as if they believed every other word of it; and I must report that the hip young American girl next to me was quite clearly excited pleasantly.

Anthony Shaffer's *Sleuth*, of course, offers rather more sophisticated titillation. It is genuinely sending up the conventions of the classic detective story with its aristocratic, Wimseycal heroes and foreign desperadoes and fall-guys; and it does reassuringly prove that stage thrillers can be about blunt instruments without also looking as if they have been written with one. Indeed the dialogue has a smart, brittle quality full of very English place-name jokes ('Thea, the Finnish lady who runs the sauna in Swindon') suggesting conscience doth make Cowards of us all. And the highest compliment one can pay Mr Shaffer is that, even when one knows the mainspring of the plot, one is still persuasively gripped.

But when I saw it recently I felt the cast were giving their all to one of the strangest houses I have encountered outside the pages of Edgar Allen Poe. I had no quarrel with Raymond Westwell who, though lacking the faint parvenu quality Olivier brought to the film, played Andrew Wyke admirably as a sadistic, elegant bullfrog; nor with Garry Waldhorn, neat and dapper as the man who came to sherry.

Yet the audience was a wildly disparate bunch comprising an enormous party of schoolgirls mysteriously accompanied by two nuns (could this be the annual convent outing?), knowing wags whose loud laughter completely gave the plot away, and earnest Spaniards loyally explaining the story to their non-English-speaking partners. I felt this was Tower-of-London theatre in which the audience had come to see an ancient monument rather than surrender to an experience; and it says much for Shaffer's play that it survived its rubber-necking spectators.

Down at the Whitehall, however, the audience has clearly come for three things: bum and boobs. But the surprising thing about *Pyjama Tops*, lately given the John Osborne Seal of Approval, is that it's about as erotic as Richard Baker reading the news and that it has largely become a solo turn for a toothy stand-up comic, Ronnie Collis. In fact the show makes *Big Bad Mouse* look like *Britannicus* as Mr Collis chats up the audience ('Anyone from Australia? I like a little bit down under'), cracks hairy jokes ('Did you hear about the homosexual candle – it went out with a pouf'), and, with sublime inconsequentiality, launches into a Charlie Chaplin impression, someone having thoughtfully left a cane, bowler, and baggy trousers under a seat.

I dislike most of the show's assumptions: that homosexuality is some kind of disease that can be cured by a night in the sack and that women are purely mechanical sex-objects (nothing is more astonishing than the bare-toothed grins the girls manage to assume while Mr Collis plays with their spare parts). Yet the show does have a raucous, vulgar vitality and it clearly tickles its audience pleasantly. Closer to panto than to porn, it succeeds largely because it is the only show of the four to follow one of the most basic rules of theatre: that since the audience is there, it is pointless to ignore its existence.

I wish *Oh! Calcutta!* had something of the same outgoing vaudevillian attack. Admittedly Clifford Williams's production is, like the cast, in pretty good shape; but the predominantly tourist audience with whom I saw it sat through the sketches in stony, apparently uncomprehending silence. Significantly, the only two items to rouse the customers from their rash, fierce blaze of apathy were Margo Sappington's beautifully choreographed numbers (one in which the cast form and re-form alliances like figures in a dream and the famous sexual twosome in which the coital positions are given a poetic beauty). But the real trouble with the show (with the exception of one number about the perennial conflict between fashion and morals) is that it is neither elegantly playful nor stirringly erotic.

So what conclusion is one left with after a week of crowd-pulling titillation? Primarily that the polarisation of commercial and subsidised theatre is now almost total. The old argument (advanced to me the other night by a colleague) was that a thriving entertainment theatre was the soil out of which good drama grew. But this is just no longer true: I can't believe that the visible popularity of *The Mousetrap* or *Pyjama Tops* has the slightest impact on non-titillatory theatre.

A second, more daunting conclusion is that these days once a show has run for five years there is no earthly reason why it should not run for fifty: that mere staying-power is itself a box-office attraction. And a third, consequent conclusion is that managers should impose a self-denying ordinance and take a production off when they feel it (or its audience) has passed its peak. The commercial theatre can die in one of two ways: either through an endless series of short-run failures or, paradoxically, through a surfeit of long-running successes.

And while, in the current economic climate, I can understand the desire of managers like Peter Saunders, Michael White, and Paul Raymond to hang on to their hits, I think they should be aware that stagnation is in the end no less an enemy than inflation. Is your long run, in fact, really necessary?

1975

In truth, belt-tightening seemed to have quite a tonic effect on the British theatre. Subsidised companies rightly complained of being under-funded; the Arts Council's allocation to New Drama was a wretched £85,000; the Theatre Upstairs was forced into temporary closure. And yet exciting things continued to happen on stages.

New plays on view included Comedians, Fanshen, Teeth'n'Smiles, Otherwise Engaged, No Man's Land, Claw, Absent Friends, Old Flames, The Fool, Hitting Town, City Sugar, Alphabetical Order, *McGrath's* Fish In The Sea, *and Tony Harrison's Racine re-write,* Phaedra Britannica. *If we were confronted by a comparable list in the 1990s we would think we were doing rather well.*

In the commercial sector, two factors stood out. One was its increasing dependence on subsidised imports: by November, 19 out of 34 shows in the West End originated in subsidised houses. The other was the valiant attempt – the first of several over the years – to create a quasi-permanent company in Shaftesbury Avenue. Lindsay Anderson set up the Lyric Theatre Company and at least gave us a marvellous production of The Seagull, *with Helen Mirren's Nina radiating earthly sexuality, as well as an amiable Ben Travers farce,* The Bed Before Yesterday. *Against that, there were the usual* folies de grandeur *such as* Jeeves *and* Thomas And The King.

On the Fringe, the Bush and the Half Moon stood out. In the regions, the Glasgow Citizens, Nottingham Playhouse and the Liverpool Everyman continued to astonish. Peter Hall's National Theatre Company at last hit its stride with superb productions of John Gabriel Borkman, Heartbreak House *and* The Playboy of the Western World. *The RSC, despite constant threats to close down its London base, had a fine year in Stratford with Terry Hands's* Henry V *and, at the Other Place, Williamson in* Uncle Vanya *and Ian Richardson in* Richard III. *Most ominous theatrical news of the year: Mrs Thatcher became leader of the Conservative Party.*

The Troublesome Raigne of King Trevor

A Morality Play: 18 January 1975

SCENE: *The throne-room of the Royal Shakespeare Company. KING TREVOR I discovered crouched over map of world, feverishly moving toy-*

armies from one continent to another. Behind him looms a dark-cowled figure, HUGH OF WESTMINSTER, in the guise of Instant Death. DES, a member of the Commonwealth, passes by puffing vigorously. Enter a bearded scholar, JOHAN BARTON highly agitated and with an ominous bulge under his cloak.

KING: What twitches 'neath your gaberdine, old friend?
Prodigious-large, it is, if all's your own.

BARTON: A thing, it is, to which I am attached.
(*Whips out scroll*)
A play that I have doctored and rashly called King John Flagrantly flouting Trades Description Act.
Parts have I run up in my pastiche vein,
Parts have I grafted from a Tudor squib,
Parts have I copied from an antique source,
And parts in desperation taken from old Shakes himself.
Cobbled it is from sundry dust-filled tomes
Which, like the critics, slightly foxed I find.

KING: A load of cobblers I do fear indeed.
And yon same critics I see fretting in their stalls,
Flashing their torches on forgotten texts.
Hobson of Rotherham, Trewin of Plymouth.
Gay-plumèd Barber, a lean Midlands man,
Will take up quills gainst these ungodly pranks.

BARTON: Prank me no pranks and Hobson me no Hobsons.
I am no hack, Keith or otherwise,
Wantonly jigging with a masterpiece.
But Shakespeare's John has never stirred me
So I have introduced a white-faced Chorus, Death,
My old fixation with the hollow crown,
And slapstick too of the more vulgar kind:
King John I'll show with egg upon his face
Standing bare-bummed before the papal ponce
And e'en with dunce's cap upon his head
Subtly to prove he is a paltry loonish king.

KING: The hand of Tate I do espy in this.

BARTON: Nahum?

KING: Nohow. Harry I had in mind,
But I do fear the egg will be on our face too.
Wailings and howlings I do predict my friend
And pilgrims turning back en route to shrine.
How shall we answer our accusers then?

BARTON: Say this, my soverign.

When I with your forefather, politic Peter,
(He that late threw himself off Southern Bank)
To Henry Six did alteration make
Never a gripe did we encounter then.
The gods themselves did smile upon my efforts,
Showering me with trophies – and with royalties too—
Since no one, save myself, had read the play.
If true of Henry, why not then of John?
Old plays are also like a well, my lord,
Wherein the parched may dip their empty pails.
Grim-visaged Bertolt in East Germany
Did tamper with Corioli to great acclaim,
Even though fragments were beyond our Ken:
Beetle browed Planchon down in Lyons, France,
Did bend and batter Marlowe's mighty line;
And Marowitz, a malcontent, in chilly crypts,
Cuts up the Bard and calls it a collage,
What's source for goose . . .

KING: Is source for gander sure.
Yet costs perturb me, lofty-purposed man.
My state is braved, my coffers almost empty,
The best of my company is all at sea.

BARTON: So have I heard; and do in part believe.

KING: Some troops are Broadway-bound in quest of gold,
Some do anthologies in foreign parts
Whilst some in London frivol in Frank Wedekind.
And cream-bosomed Helen calls the public prints
Decrying surplus decoration.
Barely a Nicol have I left in hand.

BARTON: Stand fast, good king, all is not spent,
Brown jerkins will we use, same as in Dicky Two.
Same lords, same thrones, same Coronation robes,
Same brass, same tuckets, same lung-tickling smoke
And for the supers, same performances as well.

KING: But who shall play the feeble, flouncing King?
Wood is gone west, Howard's in the shires
And Richardson's exposed himself too oft this year.

BARTON: A Welshman, Emrys James, I have espied:
Impish, mercurial, full of Celtic quirks
And not afraid to pitch camp anywhere.
Laughs he shall give us in the early scenes
And later, to boost up an ailing plot.

A little touch of Larry in the night.
KING: No moral gravity throughout the show?
BARTON: Gravity is dead, my liege,
Irony now rules.
Sobriety's all right
For peddling Shakespeare to the schools.
But, though a Cambridge scholar,
I fain would live that down
And so, with mocking levity,
I seek to draw the town.
And if I can enough bad plays rejig
I sense through pricking of my thumb,
That Royal Shakespeare may ere long
The Royal Barton Company become. . .

Thunderclap and stage lightning. F.R. LEAVIS is suddenly glimpsed outside window mouthing fierce imprecations; an angry GEORGE RYLANDS descends from the skies mounted, precariously, on Jupiter; and the ghost of SIR ARTHUR QUILLER-COUCH flits through the room, dislodging a bust of Shakespeare which falls on JOHAN BARTON, felling him instantly. RETRIBUTION pops up through a trapdoor and addresses the cowering monarch:

RETRIBUTION: Mark, silent king, the moral of this sport:
Such is the fate of all who put themselves fore our belovèd Bard:
We punish them or make their lives unconscionably hard.
Brook we have banished, Hack we have abused,
Daniels is in an other place and Littlewood's confused.
And now we hear that Dunlop splits the Scottish king in three,
Which only goes to prove thanes ain't what they used to be.
We English never read our Will once we have left our schools
Yet we protect his memory from rash, intruding fools.
We castigate invention, sentimentally, revere his text,
So look to your Macbeth, O king, for it could be your turn next.

RETRIBUTION exits juggling with the skulls of past Shakespearean directors. DES passes by obliviously crying 'VAT's in a name?' Meanwhile, KING TREVOR, ashen in hue, starts re-reading Macbeth as the curtain slowly descends.

John Gabriel Borkman

Old Vic: 29 January 1975

Peter Hall has pulled off the impossible. He has conceived a production of *John Gabriel Borkman* that works satisfyingly on both the realistic and symbolic level and that leaps lightly over the notorious Ibsenite hurdles. After a slightly hesitant start, the play last night exerted the same iron-clad grip as that which envelops its hero.

The secret of Hall's success is that he perceives neither realism nor symbolism are ever absolute in Ibsen: that they seamlessly merge and intertwine. Thus the long opening battle between Borkman's wife and sister-in-law for possession of his son is played as a largely static duologue between two power-hungry women. And when we come to Borkman himself, the self-immured financier guilty of embezzlement, Hall presents us not with a cornered animal but with a man who bestrides his vast Empire-style drawing-room like a Colossus. Thus Hall sweeps away the pedagogic naturalism that so often mars Ibsen productions and directs him as starkly and simply as Pinter and Beckett. The result is that when Borkman and Ella Rentheim, the woman he sacrificed for dreams of industrial power, ascend the mountain in the final act there is no fatal crashing of gears but a sense that the action has reached perfect logical fulfilment.

Hall also recognises that Ibsen is an equivocal, elusive, poetic dramatist. Ostensibly the play may be about coldness of the heart, reality versus illusion and all the stock Ibsen themes. But Ibsen's attitude to Borkman himself is deeply ambiguous: on the one hand, he embodies the evils of nineteenth-century capitalism, on the other he is a mystic visionary who actually hears iron-ore singing under the surface. And it is for this reason that Sir Ralph Richardson, with his unique capacity for existing in two dimensions at once, is perfect casting.

He presents us with a man in love with his own image of himself: a Napoleon of commerce who greets visitors with a hand symbolically thrust inside his greatcoat, an ageing Peer Gynt for whom other people are simply things in his dream. When his son bids him farewell for ever, he acknowledges his departure with an airy wave of the hand that makes you wonder if he ever apprehended his existence; yet Richardson is earthy enough to produce an astonishingly realistic cry of pain when death finally claims him. Richardson's Borkman is both moral monster and self-made superman; and the performance is full of a strange, unearthly music that belongs to this actor alone.

This is not to underestimate the fine performances of Peggy

Ashcroft, suggesting a will of steel under a gracious facade as the loveless Ella Rentheim, or of Wendy Hiller whose Mrs Borkman is no cold-hearted fiend but a woman whose spirit is cankered by a fierce sense of injury. I also much admired Anna Carteret's Mrs Wilton, a sexual realist in Merry Widow clothing and Frank Grimes's Erhart, nervous, impulsive and somehow doomed to female domination. And Timothy O'Brien and Tazeena Firth have created grey-green sets that combine close-range realism with deep and shadowy perspective; which is, after all, the quintessence of Ibsen.

Entertaining Mr Sloane

Royal Court: 18 April 1975

Once the home of new English drama, the Royal Court is devoting the next five months to a Joe Orton retrospective. But who needs it? With the exception of his last under-rated farce, Orton's work has enjoyed maximum exposure in the West End, around the reps and in the cinema. And there seems little point in homage to an acclaimed stylist at a time when the Court urgently needs to regain contact with a whole new generation of English dramatists, including Brenton, Hare, Griffiths, Barker, and Poliakoff.

But although this once-dynamic theatre seems to be living in the past, I would not deny that Orton's *Entertaining Mr Sloane* is a graceful comic work in its own right. Its particular charm is that it applies a mandarin style to a seemingly sordid theme: a struggle between an ageing nymphomaniac and her homosexual brother for possession of the body and soul of a murderous young thug. And Orton gets double value out of the joke by not only contrasting the formal, stately language with the violent action but by constantly allowing the characters to slip back into the vernacular.

For the most part, however, Orton's people wear their language like a protective mask. 'Aren't the tulips glorious? What a brave show' cries the randy Kath like a duchess opening a bazaar, ignoring the fact that she has just been violently goosed. And, as in Ivy Compton-Burnett, iron decorum is the only possible reaction to the most heinous crime. After an old man's description of how he has been kicked, beaten and brutalised, his son gravely remarks, 'He's been putting in a complaint.' At times the joke is widely over-extended: and one feels that Orton had not in this early work mastered the necessity for arresting physical action. But it remains a good play in which evil is presented with the stately grace of a minuet.

Roger Croucher's production also contains a fine study of roguish seductiveness from Beryl Reid, her voracious sexual appetite contrasting neatly with her refined vowel-sounds that suggest a strange combination of Morningside spinster and Royal Christmas broadcast. But although Malcolm McDowell's Sloane has the right gay satanic charm, the sexual tension is dissipated by Ronald Fraser's blustering Ed which lacks the ambisextrous, heavyweight menace Peter Vaughan once memorably brought to the part. It's an enjoyable enough revival; but it still represents an abnegation of the Court's real function of taking the moral temperature of the age in which we live.

Letter To The Editor

Lindsay Anderson: 23 April 1975

Sir, – Michael Billington must be fully equipped to assess and interpret drama in performance – otherwise, of course, he would not be functioning as the Guardian's theatre critic. (Though his drab handling of Joe Orton – *Arts Guardian*, April 18 – dismally fails to communicate the enjoyment palpably experienced by paying audiences.)

But Michael Billington's capacity to programme and take creative responsibility for a theatre like the Royal Court is not proven. The Court, Mr Billington rules, is doing the *wrong plays*. Instead of delighting the public with Joe Orton, we should be enlightening them with 'Brenton, Hare, Griffiths, Barker and Poliakoff'. May we ask what research has gone into this glib and irrelevant reprimand?

For instance, has Michael Billington inquired how many of these playwrights had plays available when the present Royal Court season was planned? Or how many of them will shortly have plays produced at the Court? How glowingly did your critic encourage the public to support their last London-produced works – and how successfully? How much did the Royal Court lose on *Magnificence*? And how much did Michael Codron's investors make out of *Knuckle*?

Is Michael Billington prepared personally to guarantee – or can he persuade the *Guardian* to guarantee – the solvency of the Royal Court Theatre, the payment of bills and salaries, while we devote our resources exclusively to the presentation of his favoured writers?

Howard Brenton, David Hare, Trevor Griffiths, Howard Barker

and Stephen Poliakoff are not a band-wagon. They are talented and diverse writers who deserve production, and will get it. But Michael Billington should remember that the exercise of power without responsibility is the prerogative of the whore – not of the critic.

Lindsay Anderson,
Associate Director, Royal Court Theatre.

Fanshen

ICA: 22 April 1975

'What's the message?' I was asked after seeing David Hare's *Fanshen*, which the Joint Stock Company is presenting at the ICA's Terrace Theatre. The message is that there is no message: simply a masterly and intricate study, based on William Hinton's massive documentary book, of the processes of revolution in a Chinese village called Long Bow some thirty years ago. I saw a special performance in a Buckinghamshire farmhouse with the action played out on a rough stone floor and the audience perched on bales of straw; but the play has such muscle and grip I am sure it will survive the transfer to the Mall.

The first thing to stress is that *Fanshen* is not a piece of mock-oriental agitprop. Hare and the company concentrate on showing us precisely what impact the Chinese land reform movement of 1945–8 had on the day-to-day lives of Long Bow's inhabitants; and what comes across is their total unfaked respect for the people concerned. They are not utilising them for theatrical effects or to give easy comfort to our own well-heeled revolutionaries: indeed they show, with cool irony, that under communism the peasants were still manipulated by external forces and that the drive for productivity retarded the move towards complete equality.

But the play is also an enthralling blow-by-blow account of the birth of a new political system. Fanshen literally means 'to turn over'. And so we see how in 1945 the people of Long Bow, suddenly freed from Japanese occupation, acquired a voice and identity of their own. Forced into group-consciousness by the naming of collaborators, they then formed peasant associations, took over the land from their feudal bosses, and divided the soil according to past suffering and present needs. But, as always, Hare plays scrupulously fair: he shows that the seizure of the land was backed by a basic moral question ('Who depends on whom for a living?') but was also accompanied by a pent-up violence towards the owner-class.

The richest scenes, however, are those which show a Communist Party work-team arriving in the village to organise and codify a spontaneous local revolution. As the villagers sit around in groups discussing their claims to be classed as 'Poor Peasant' or 'Middle Peasant,' one sees human instinct clashing with the need for social order: thus they argue endlessly with the blacksmith's self-categorisation simply because 'they wouldn't trust him to bang a nail up an elephant's arse-hole,' and Brecht himself would not have disowned one brilliantly ironic scene in which the work-team leader, obliged to indulge in self-criticism, stoically offers his resignation. 'You always want to be the hero,' someone mutters, brutally putting him in his place.

In the end I would say *Fanshen* is a play without precedent in the history of the British theatre: one that shows in detail how a revolution actually works. And what is heartening is the way that it captures the complex, multi-faceted nature of this particular rising: it meant wholesale social reform, including sexual equality, and the activation of human intelligence; yet the national need for abundance once more turned the peasants into victims of a policy over which they had no control.

William Gaskill's and Max Stafford-Clark's crystal-clear production, like Hare's text, reports such facts without lapsing into either heroic idealism or bourgeois cynicism: and the cast (especially Philip McGough, Paul Freeman, and Pauline Melville) play Chinese peasants and revolutionaries with unpatronising truthfulness. *Fanshen*, in fact, is specific, engrossing, and unmissable.

Jeeves

Her Majesty's: 23 April 1975

Admirers of P.G. Wodehouse's work have several possibilities open to them when confronted by a musical like *Jeeves*. The more moderate among them might consider chaining themselves to Her Majesty's Theatre and hurling Cassandra-like warnings at passers-by. Hard-liners, however, should debate whether to set fire to the producer's trousers or to institute legal action under the Trade Descriptions Act. For the witless travesty that calls itself *Jeeves* is as close to the spirit of the original as Budleigh Salterton is to Timbuctoo.

What is depressing is that the disaster was so foreseeable; for anyone with the slightest feeling for Wodehouse's work would know that he created a totally innocent, fairytale world untranslatable into flesh-and-blood terms and that his humour depends on his literary style. On the page one might well chuckle over a line like 'At the mere sight of a Wooster, her fetlocks quiver'; but, as delivered by David Hemmings, the laughter dies on one's lips.

Indeed the worst thing one can say about this musical (for which Alan Ayckbourn wrote the book and lyrics and Andrew Lloyd Webber the music) is that it may convince people who have never read any Wodehouse that he was a painfully unfunny writer with an elephantine humorous style; and that I would never have thought possible.

Judged simply as an escapist musical, however, the show falls apart at the seams. For a start it lands itself with a cumbersome narrative framework that has Bertie telling his life-story in an East End club for unmanageable boys: this means that all the subsequent action takes place in commas heavily inverted.

Then again the numbers are not so much a means of advancing the complex action about Bertie's involvement with a trio of girls as a device for bringing it shuddering to a complete stop. And Eric Thompson's production has that furry imprecision that is the hallmark of British musicals with people always landing on their predestined mark a vital second after the music has stopped.

Valiantly swimming against the tide, David Hemmings (with no less than thirteen numbers to put across) puffs and sweats his way through the show but has no real chance to register Bertie's imbecilic charm; and Michael Aldridge as the titular hero is given little to do but stroll through the evening wearing a faintly superior smirk. Other good performers like Gabrielle Drake, Bill Wallis and John Turner meanwhile fall back on archly funny voices.

My only constructive suggestion is that the creators of this three-hour insult to Wodehouse go and see *A Little Night Music* two hundred times before they next lay hands on the unsuspecting musical form.

Harold Pinter

25 June 1975

I detected a certain edginess in my colleagues' initial reactions to Pinter's new play, *No Man's Land*. Here we are again, they implied, in that same old world of hidden terror, twilit menace, confused memory and Empsonian ambiguity that we have come to know as Pinterland. Like Spooner, the play's sandalled, demob-suited Bohemian whom one can imagine reminiscing of days spent with Dylan in the George, they cried: 'I have known this before.'

Well up to a point they have: for Pinter is rather like a global traveller who never sheds any luggage but simply accumulates more stuff as he goes along. But, chewing over the play it struck me we do Pinter a disservice by trying to evoke his world through abstract nouns and by talking of his plays as if they were intellectual mystery-tours for the cultural élite. At his best, he is a very concrete, precise, accessible writer (witness the popularity of his plays on television). And on one level *No Man's Land* is dealing with an experience most human beings have had and which Priestley dramatised in an Ouspensky-based Thirties play like *I Have Been Here Before*: the feeling that the strange and unknown suddenly turns out to be instantly familiar and the supposedly familiar dismayingly strange.

But, again like Priestley, Pinter expresses his ideas in concrete theatrical terms. Just as *The Birthday Party* was set very precisely in a world of seaside lodging houses, voracious landladies and damp decay and *The Caretaker,* without leaving its crumbling attic, took one on a Cook's Tour of London Transport and the North Circular, so *No Man's Land* is rivetingly specific. If it has a sense of mystery, it is counterpointed by a strong sensual appetite for cricket, women, food (buttered scones, Wiltshire cream, crumpets and strawberries, tea-and-toast) and the English countryside (weekend cottages, village churches, sunlit lawns, August rain). Pinter's theatrical poetry is not something vague and indefinable, reminiscent of Mercury Theatre apocalyptic dramas of the 1940s, but something rooted in the world around us. In that sense, he is a very basic writer.

I also suspect that Pinter is a much more autobiographical dramatist than we commonly allow. As he has moved up in the social scale, so conspicuously have his characters: and it is surely no accident that Hirst and Spooner, the twin protagonists of *No Man's Land*, are both professional literary men. Hirst, the success, lives in a rarefied world of champagne breakfasts, financial advisers, private secretaries; Spooner, the shabby poet, still inhabits a world of small magazines, stamped addressed envelopes and meetings over pubs. I am not suggesting for a moment Pinter is either character; but he did, of course, first get into print in magazines like *Poetry London* in the early Fifties and is now internationally famous. And, unless my antennae deceive me, *No Man's Land* is very much about the twin traps that face the professional scribbler: the isolation and remoteness from life imposed by success, and the demeaning chores (such as acting as a Chalk Farm pot-boy) dictated by grubbing for loot.

But if Pinter is concrete and personal, he is also (an obvious fact but one which these days goes more or less unremarked) essentially a comic writer. I don't mean an Absurdist (which is usually a way of being funny without actually getting laughs), but someone who is very aware of the English comic tradition, both on the literary and music-hall level. And seeing *No Man's Land* in the same period as Firbank's *The Princess Zoubaroff*, Ivy Compton-Burnett's *A Family And A Fortune*, and Orton's *Entertaining Mr Sloane*, I was very aware of the way Pinter's play both exploits and explodes the peculiar English comic style.

Defining that style is not easy. But it is based, I would hazard, on a silky hypocrisy: on an unspoken assumption that it is vulgar to say precisely what one means and that the most murderous impulses and insane lusts must be concealed under a mask of propriety. Obviously all the writers mentioned use this style in very different ways. Firbank often descends into impish religious camp whereas in Compton-Burnett the characters are past masters at garrotting each other with an epigram, or felling the enemy with one blow of a suave antithesis. But the essence of that style is a ruthless politeness; and one of Pinter's aims in *No Man's Land* is to blow it sky-high by exposing it to crude, direct speech.

Within five minutes of curtain-rise, in fact, you sense that the play is going to be a verbal battle: Spooner's mandarin periphrasis is contrasted with Hirst's down-to-earth briskness, and the two of them are constantly re-stating each other's viewpoints and indulging in a kind of linguistic one upmanship. 'I refer to a midsummer night,' says Spooner nostalgically 'when I shared a drink with a Hungarian émigré, lately retired from Paris.' 'The same drink?' Hirst coolly inquires. And if you want a parallel example of the retort-less-than-courteous, you have only to look at *A Family And A Fortune*, where the disgruntled Aunt Matty and her father are settling into a poky little cottage on the Gaveston's estate. 'One could almost imagine oneself anywhere.' says the father consolingly. 'But not quite,' replies Aunt Matty, as if stabbing him with a verbal hatpin.

But there is much more to Pinter's technique than the elegant putdown or the sudden clang of a four-letter word against a piece of literary rotundity. He uses a whole battery of comic effects, including one very similar to Orton's: the combination of posh words with working-class speech-rhythms. Pinter has always been fascinated by the flash arriviste, the bruiser with style, and Foster, the male secretary in *No Man's Land*, is a direct descendant of Mick in *The Caretaker*, and

Lenny in *The Homecoming*. He lovingly describes the world of flower arrangements and eighteenth century cookery books that he has rapturously entered. 'It's not rubbish,' he explains. 'We deal in originals. Nothing duff, nothing ersatz, we don't open any old bottle of brandy.' The combination of vogue words and Arthur English patter strikes me as innately comic.

It is, however, a very English joke in another sense; for it depends on the assumption that people who change their class feel obliged to change their language. And there is a whole strand of English comedy from *Twelfth Night* (I remember Olivier's Malvolio tying himself in knots over pronunciation of the word 'slough'), and *The Clandestine Marriage*, through to *Semi-detached*, and *Entertaining Mr Sloane* that plays on this kind of verbal masquerade. When Orton's businessman-homosexual responds to the murder of his father by telling Sloane: 'I can't allow you to take up abode in Dulverton Mansions now,' the gulf between what is said and what is actually felt becomes a marvellous comment on English hypocrisy.

But Pinter's comic technique is nothing if not eclectic; and it even, as I have suggested, takes in the music hall. A famous word-loving comic explained his craft to me recently by saying: 'The word is a container of meaning and if you can open the box, take the meaning out and put another meaning in, it is quite a clever little trick.' It is one that Harold Pinter uses all the time. There is a moment in his TV play, *The Basement*, when Law, the invaded hero is prattling on about an old friend's possessions while avidly studying his girl's body, exclaiming: 'What yachts, what yachts,' giving the word unexpected lascivious overtones. And when, in *No Man's Land*, Spooner announces: 'My mother remains, I have to say, a terribly attractive woman in many ways. Her buns are the best,' Pinter again gets a shock-laugh through a standard vaudeville technique.

Like all good jokes, however. Pinter's have a serious purpose; and, at bottom, I suspect he is mocking the way we use words as a barrier between ourselves and our real feelings. Like Edgar in *Lear*, Pinter's motto is 'Speak what we feel, not what we ought to say'; and this fertile, endlessly fascinating play is, among other things, about the way we all use language as an elaborate camouflage. *No Man's Land* is, in fact, everyman's land.

John Wood

12 August 1975

'Audiences always love (not merely approve or prefer) perfect articulation; a sharp, cutting voice which, though it projects a very fountain of words, leaves each one distinct, shaped and crisp; each uttered (as Olivier, as Barrault utters them) with no contortion of the face. It demonstrates command: the ability to make words perform for you, skip, leap, gyrate or, in Max Beerbohm's phrase, "tread in their precedence, like kings, gravely".'

Thus Kenneth Tynan in 1948 on Danny Kaye. But every syllable might equally well apply to John Wood who, in the past five years, has emerged as the most versatile, idiosyncratic, and imposing actor now at work on the British stage. In a sense every generation gets the great acting it deserves. And just as Olivier, since the late Thirties, has held imperious sway as the embodiment of flexible, muscular heroism, Wood epitomises perfectly the spirit of the Seventies: ironic, inquisitive, anti-heroic, and constantly aware of the absurdity under the crust of human experience.

Stoppard's *Travesties*, which tomorrow springs into the West End and which was penned with Wood in mind, shows this in abundance. Yet although one tends to think of Wood as an intellectual actor with the ability to portray mind, he visibly flinches at one's use of the term. He sees the actor as a medium or an instrument rather than a commentator on the role: and a character for him emerges through the solution of specific problems imposed by the text.

'With Henry Carr, for instance, we discussed many possible ways of achieving the change from age to youth. Peter Wood came to rehearsals with a very elaborate plan involving a baroque screen with glass panels at the top. The idea was that Carr might decide to shave and thereby change his face make-up while someone behind the screen changed his clothes. I favoured a more simple, emblematic device. The change of age is actually done by a change of hat: nothing more.

'When I come on, the dressing-gown says very old and the panama hat says uprooted English émigré probably living abroad because the gin is cheaper. I didn't want to do a pyrotechnical thing that drew attention to itself. I wanted to keep the background clear because in Tom's play the word is all. The word is beating back the silence, beating back the darkness. Thought is all we've got, says Tom, otherwise the dark, the jungle, will close in on us. I think this is what makes his plays so moving and even tragic.

'Look at those two idiots at the beginning of *Rosencrantz And Guildenstern* trying to deduce, by logical processes, with no evidence whatever, who they are, where they are, why they are. It's not manic, as you suggest: it's the only way of asserting sanity. To me it's a truthful statement about what it's like to be alive.'

Words obviously fascinate Wood; and his forte as an actor is the combination of rapid delivery with precise articulation. 'I try,' he says, speaking off-duty with the same combination of deliberation and impulse, 'to look at words vertically rather than horizontally. Take a line from a Shakespeare sonnet – 'Since brass nor earth nor stone.' In speaking that you have to experience what brass looks like, sounds like, feels like as you make the sound by which is understood the concept brass. It's not done through giving the voice a brassy timbre. It's done by a process of abdication rather than predication, by switching off rather than switching on, by allowing the idea of brass to pass through you.

'I'm not suggesting one employs a technique as esoteric as that with Henry Carr but for a character like Brutus you must in a sense surrender to the language. You must acknowledge that the words have an enormous power; yet at the same time you must never stand in their way.'

But what is fascinating as one talks to Wood about the jagged and irregular progress of his acting career is the variety of influence at work upon him: not only Stoppard but French actors of the 1940s, the comedian Jerry Lewis and the Peters, Hall and Brook. In fact, it was a chance trip to Stratford in 1949 to see Brook's *Measure For Measure* that fired him with an early ambition to be a director. But in the Oxford of the late Forties and early Fifties, where Tony Richardson and Bill Gaskill were the dominant theatrical figures, he turned to acting, starting out as Osric in a Coghill *Hamlet* and ending up as a famous, Hobson-acclaimed Richard III.

'I also had this thing about wanting to be a *French* actor. I spoke French quite well, had read a lot of French literature, and also, when I was a teenager, all the culture in the world seemed to come from Paris. Existentialism was rampant. *Les Enfants Du Paradis* had just come out, and I'd seen the Comédie Française a number of times and thought the actors technically remarkable. I even got a place as what they call an 'auditeur' at the Conservatoire in Paris but I never took it up because about that time I stumbled upon Shakespeare, realised I spoke the same language as the greatest poet who ever lived, and felt it would be foolish to encumber my mind with an alien culture. But it's now reared its ugly head again and I desperately want to play *Travesties* in Paris, though I don't know whether they will let me.'

I suspect the French connection explains Wood's ability to give a character a sharply-etched physical outline in the manner of Barrault or Hirsch and to let his lean, angular, spiky frame work for him. But the odd thing about his career is that although he emerged from Oxford an undergraduate star, he took a long time to find his professional niche.

He worked at the Old Vic ('That theatre had fallen very much into the hands of director-designers and actors were not given the time or space in which to practise their craft; one felt one was simply the cheapest way of getting the costume on stage') but was peremptorily sacked. He became a dogsbody at the Royal Court in the early Devine years, acting, reading scripts, directing a Sunday night production with Phyllis Calvert, but again got the push. 'I came in one day and gathered from the expression on people's faces I didn't work there any more. Although they were paying me nothing at all, I gathered they couldn't afford to go on paying me nothing at all.'

Up to the late Fifties, in fact, his career makes him sound like the theatrical equivalent of the hero of John Wain's *Hurry on Down*. Always hard-up ('I breathed a huge sigh of relief when I got to the point where I didn't have to wait till beyond the Final Demand before questioning the amount and then borrowing a stamp to send the letter'), more out-of-work than in, he was sustained only by a native obstinacy and a determination not to give up till he had won. Scarred by his Old Vic experience, he even turned down four separate offers from Peter Hall to join the RSC.

'There was a self-destructive thing at work. I felt I had failed to fulfil what was expected of me ten years before. I'd been left behind and a lot of important actors had arrived – Finney, O'Toole, Bates – and by the mid-1960s I had begun to establish a comfortable, seductive practice in television. I played Barnaby Rudge, Sidney Carton, a lot of Chekhov. I was *the* art actor on television for about three years. I thought sound and solid reputations are to be made on television only to discover they are not.'

The turning point came when he did two Thirty Minute Theatre Tom Stoppard plays on BBC-2: *Teeth*, about the relationship between a dentist and his patient, and *Another Moon Called Earth*, which was a remote pilot for *Jumpers*. Wood felt an immediate affinity both with the work and the man. 'His writing hit me hard, filled me with an amazing sense of elation, and gave me a sense of coming home. Our minds also seemed to click, though he's a lot cleverer than I am and I respond to things about one tenth as vibrantly as he does. Only in certain areas can I deploy any expertise such as telling him what cars to buy and that Beethoven is actually better than the Bay City Rollers.'

If Stoppard is one key influence, Jerry Lewis is another. Wood first recalls seeing him on American TV while convalescing from a cancer op after he had finished the Broadway run of *Rosencrantz And Guildenstern Are Dead*. 'My initial response to these shows of Jerry's was very much what you might expect: a fastidious shudder. Then I saw him put on that terrible physical persona which, not to put too fine a point on it, is someone who is meant to be spastic. He actually does this as a matter of laughter thereby offending us deeply.

'He showed this character appearing at a golf-club and trying to get a round with other whole human beings. Finally he got someone to play and the last minute and a half of the sketch showed him trying to get the ball on to a tee and drive it off. I suddenly found, welling up in me an incredible panic, archaic laughter. What he seems to be saying is that in the end there is only one response – and that is laughter – to the most horrific, cruel thing you can imagine. He actually does direct attention to the nightmares in your own life.

'What I encountered when I worked with him on a couple of films was an enormous intuitive talent crippled by having become vastly successful while still a teenager. He has not been allowed to grow naturally. But what he taught me was never to be afraid. His favourite story about himself is that he wanted a shot for a film in which he, the absolute novice and total innocent, puts down all the balls on a pool table in one lightning stroke. In order to get the shot he slung a camera over the pool table and did it first time. He knew that he was going to do it and did it. You can't call it risk-taking because it's not acknowledging there are any risks to take. And I think it's essential to approach every succeeding moment of a performance in precisely that spirit.'

You can see something of that intuitive abandon in Wood's astonishing body of work for the RSC in the past five years: his supine, hysterical, drunken Yakov in *Enemies*, his Saturninus in *Titus Andronicus*, greedily gnawing the ankle of a supernumerary, his definitive Brutus with its private self-regarding idealism, his Sherlock Holmes turning from ice-cold ratiocination to overpowering world-weariness.

Wood constantly suggests intellect flawed by turbulent emotion; and it therefore seems logical that after he has finished with *Travesties* he would like to have a crack at Chekhov's *Ivanov* ('The ideal mid-life crisis play'). Mention to him the possibility of Hamlet, however, and he recalls that the *New Statesman* described his Conan Doyle sleuth as the Hamlet of Baker Street. If he played the Danish Prince, he fears it might be characterised as the Lord Peter Wimsey of Elsinore. And in that remark, with its blend of self-mockery, irony, and wit, you catch some hint of what it is that makes John Wood the actor who most sharply reflects the spirit of our own times.

Comedians

Old Vic: 25 September 1975

Trevor Griffiths's *Comedians*, which began its life at Nottingham Playhouse, is the first fruit of Peter Hall's declared policy of bringing the best regional work to the National; and a fine, nourishing specimen it is. Not only does it annex new territory by putting a class for apprentice comedians on to the stage, but it has that same muscle, dialectical fairness and suppressed pain that characterised Griffiths's *The Party*. It is also very funny.

But, as with Brecht, what impresses me most about Griffiths is his ability to put conflicting attitudes, ideas and philosophies on the stage and then leave the audience to draw their own conclusions. Here, in fact, in the context of a Manchester classroom and a working men's club (where the apprentice jokers are on trial) he distinguishes three main attitudes to the art of comedy. There is that of Bert Challenor, the London talent scout, who epitomises the modern subservience to the audience ('You're there on their terms – not your own'). There is that of Gethin Price, a manic, close-cropped Celt, who believes that comedy must always be truthful, even when that involves hate, ugliness and aggression. And there is Eddie Waters, the battered old pro who runs the class, who believes that comedy must liberate the will but that there is no truth without compassion.

I think it is safe to say that Griffiths does expose the Challenor view of comedy as an ingratiating commercial-traveller craft; yet even here he plays fair by letting the comic Challenor most admires, an Ulsterman who trades on prejudice and stereotype, perform his act with professional dash and speed. But the play really boils down to a contest between two versions of comic truth; and it is fascinating to see how Griffiths's humanist sympathies lead him to present Waters as a kindly generous man in whom some vital spark is missing whilst his radical reformist side causes him to respect the wildness and bile that underpins Price's nightmare act which literally draws blood.

On top of this the play also shows a Storeyesque sense of form and a feeling for precise social detail: Griffiths locates each of his student comics in a particular professional world (lorry-driver, milkman, docker, tallyman). And one of the virtues of Richard Eyre's production is that it conveys that hollow-in-the-stomach sensation and edgy jokiness that afflicts any nervy, would-be performer. Since Nottingham, he has also toned down the hysteria of the final Waters-Gethin confrontation so that the play's climactic leap into the world of Nazism and concentration camps (is there anything Griffiths implicitly asks, which is not a fit subject for humour?) now seems less like a drastic change of gear.

Time has also increased my admiration for Jimmy Jewel's performance as Waters: his quiet despair in the club as his boys sell out to Challenor, the corrugated, seamed face that has almost forgotten how to laugh, the jaunty felt hat that is the badge of the old pro, all bring the man to life with perfect truth. And Jonathan Pryce as Gethin, with a head shaven for execution, combines mimicry of greats like Frank Randle, with a fine, disturbing sense of incipient madness. But the cast bats all the way down with Stephen Rea's hard-edged Ulsterman, Jim Norton's laconic, gently soliloquising Dubliner, and John Joyce's prosaic club secretary who can't wait for the bingo, all giving the kind of performances that make this production a living credit to the work being done at Nottingham Playhouse.

1976

It should have been a year of rejoicing. After over 130 years of lobbying, committeeing and stone-moving, the National Theatre finally opened its doors on a bleak, blustery March day with Peggy Ashcroft in Happy Days *at the Lyttelton (the Olivier kicked off in October with* Tamburlaine*). Up in Manchester the Royal Exchange – aiming to be a National Theatre of the North – also began life with lively productions of* The Rivals *and* The Prince Of Homburg*. Yet the new National was greeted, except by the public, with an astonishing chorus of backbiting and sniping, and even in Manchester there were dark mutters about bourgeois temples. Perhaps it was all part of what Peter Hall called our national nervous breakdown.*

One problem was that, at a time when housing, health, education and food subsidies were all being cut, the opening of big communal playhouses began to look like a dangerous luxury. The other problem was that it was a rather lean year artistically. Aside from Brenton's Weapons Of Happiness, *Edgar's*

Destiny *(at Stratford's Other Place), Frayn's* Clouds *and Rudkin's* Sons of Light *(in Newcastle) there were few new plays of distinction. Even more worryingly, West End audiences decisively rejected new plays from younger writers:* City Sugar, Comedians, Teeth'n'Smiles *all closed after transferring for blisteringly short runs.*

The main hope seemed to lie in the regions. Aside from Manchester, Newcastle and Stratford (John Barton's British Raj Much Ado *in the main house,* Macbeth, Hamlet *and* Bingo *in the Other Place), there was good work in Oxford (where* Dear Daddy *brought Denis Cannan back in good form), Birmingham (with Stuart Burge's revivals of* Measure For Measure *and* The Devil Is An Ass*) and Bristol (a well-cast* Duchess Of Malfi*). But the more I travelled outside Britain, the more I became aware that we were cut off from a whole strand of director-orientated European work. In 1956 Arthur Miller said the British theatre was hermetically sealed off from life. In 1976 it seemed also to be hermetically sealed off from theatre.*

Shirley MacLaine

London Palladium: 3 February 1976

Shirley MacLaine explodes on to the Palladium stage like a Fourth of July rocket. Clad in a figure-hugging, sequined, one-piece suit, she launches into that old Sweet Charity number, 'If My Friends Could See Me Now', kicks up those extravagantly long legs as if she was trying a drop kick at Twickenham and brandishes a straw-boater like a minstrel making whoopee. Showbiz rules say you should build slowly to a climax; but Ms MacLaine makes nonsense of them by starting at the top and staying there supremely for an hour and a quarter.

'Out of 34 pictures,' she confides at one point, 'I played 17 hookers.' And you can see why. She has that peculiarly American gift (Monroe had it too) of combining experience and innocence, worldly knowledge and wide-eyed wonderment. She's like a Peter Pan who's into sex, a child-like spirit at large in a grown-up world. And it's this that gives such poignancy to her rendering of 'I'm a Person Too' from *Some Came Running* ('It was made so long ago Sinatra played a Democrat') in which, with shoulder-straps wanly hanging, she starts on a note of orphaned self-pity and rises to a crescendo of self-discovery every bit as moving as Beatie Bryant's transformation at the end of *Roots*.

But it's her dancing more than her singing that lifts the audience out of its seat. And what astonishes one is her combination of energy and grace. Flashing those long legs that go up to her armpits, she demonstrates a new American dance called The Hustle in which her head violently shakes, her hips sulphurously rotate and her body seems to be operating on an invisible dynamo; yet throughout this she retains perfect fluency of line. She also has a built-in showmanship that knows exactly how to change rhythm and tempo two-thirds of the way through a number: thus her low-key rendering of the title-song from *Irma La Douce* suddenly explodes into ecstasy when she recalls 'The fireworks in the sky,' and she ends with arms exultantly outstretched.

I could live without some of the chat between numbers (Merman, after all, proved it redundant) and the obligatory hymn to the Palladium. But I don't wish to carp at a superb performer who combines high-definition skill with abundant joy, sex-appeal and bright-eyed intelligence. Most movie-stars shrink in the flesh. Ms MacLaine, backed by an excellent five-strong dance team, expands to fill the house and sends you out of the building glad to be alive.

Treats

Royal Court: 6 February 1976

With the honourable exceptions of Griffiths's *Comedians* and Stott's *Funny Peculiar*, new English drama resembles nothing so much now as a kempt herbaceous border anachronistically dumped in the midst of a jungle. And for that reason I find it dismaying that Christopher Hampton, after brilliantly tackling a large public theme in *Savages*, should have returned in *Treats* at the Royal Court to the world of hermetic middle-class relationships and small civilised ironies.

I take it *Treats* is intended partly as an ironic inversion of Ibsen's *A Doll's House*: instead of the new woman escaping from marital suffocation we have the modern beleagured male succumbing to woman's predatory inertia. The setting is a smart flat around Ladbroke Grove variously occupied by three characters. Ann, permanently resident is, like Jimmy Porter's Alison, a bruised, quiet girl with the attention-begging quality of the really vulnerable; Dave, her erstwhile lover, is a promiscuous journalist apparently hankering after marriage; and Patrick, a genial bore whom Ann temporarily sleeps with, is the buffer-state in their permanent domestic warfare. All of them apparently lead lives of quiet desperation; and, with a dapper symmetrical skill, Mr Hampton shows how the forlorn Ann, finally achieves her aim with a Nora-like slam of the door from the inside.

However the moment one invokes Ibsen (or Osborne's *Look Back In Anger*) one begins to see why the play makes such a small theatrical gesture; for whereas Mr Hampton's theatrical ancestors located their characters' agonies in a world of money, work, class, religion and culture, this trio seem curiously divorced from life. And though Mr Hampton might claim this is precisely his point, it still makes for an airless drama. Even the smart, silky dialogue reminds one of nothing so much as vintage Hugh and Margaret Williams. 'She seems to have taken up with an Australian poet – if you can imagine such a thing,' Dave remarks at one point; and although it gets the predicted Philistine laugh, it seem odd that a character who has W.H. Auden on his bookshelf should not have heard of Peter Porter. Admittedly Mr Hampton shows, with guileful sympathy, the way we love now and the mess we still make of our lives: but one looks in vain for the passion, energy and ungovernable public concern Osborne brought to precisely the same theme.

However the play could hardly be better acted than it was by James Bolam as the ravaged, crumpled journalist, by the gravely beautiful Jane Asher as the secretly manipulative Ann and by Stephen Moore as the shy, cautious Patrick who does his best to be irrational. I have no quarrel either with Robert Kidd's direction. I only wish the piercingly intelligent Mr Hampton would remember that, while the middle-classes go quietly berserk in W11, there is a world elsewhere.

Waiting For Godot

Royal Court: 23 April 1976

It's part of the English theatrical tradition that authors should rarely, if ever, direct their own work; yet the arrival of Samuel Beckett's scrupulous and beautiful production of *Waiting For Godot* from the Schiller Theatre, Berlin, shows just how myopic that approach can be. After seeing half a dozen versions of the play over the years, I would say we have tended to blunt some of its pain and substitute what Cyril Connolly called 'a hoary theatrical charm'. Beckett's production of this stoic masterpiece is, however, devoid of either easy pathos or forced fun.

Admittedly he highlights the comic physical contrast between the two tramps. Stefan Wigger's Vladimir is huge, ungainly, pigeon-toed and has knees that seem to be bound together by an invisible hoop: Horst Bollmann's Estragon meanwhile is short-legged, broad-bottomed, crab-gaited and moon-faced. Yet although they are physical and temperamental opposites, Beckett underlines their indissoluble interdependence: their clothes (which they swap after the interval) are the mis-matched halves of two suits, they react with joint exasperation to Lucky's famous tirade, frantically pummelling him to cease the verbal flow and they conduct their antiphonal exchanges with the precision born of habit. I've never seen a Didi and Gogo who belonged so irreparably to each other.

Beckett's main innovation, however, lies in the treatment of Pozzo and Lucky, normally presented as bloated rural landowner and spindle-shanked slave. Here, however, Carl Raddatz's Pozzo has the dilapidated, moth-eaten quality of a Gorkyesque ring-master, as if he too exists off memories of better days and Klaus Herm's Lucky, with a shock of ash-coloured hair that makes him look like an aged cockatoo, is no blanched hysteric but simply a man whose will has been persistently and oppressively crushed. The effect is to make the play not, as it often can become, a succession of set-pieces but a portrayal of a consistently bleak world in which the hope of salvation seems equally remote for all.

Yet this superbly-acted, German-language production also has a stoical grace. Even in their hat-swapping, trouser-dropping moments (kept well this side of vaudeville), the two tramps retain a derelict dignity and the gentleness with which Didi drapes his coat round Gogo's shoulders speaks volumes. It's part of this play's greatness that no production can ever be definitive. But at least this spare, exact, marvellously clean production shows that *Godot* is infinitely more than either slapstick tragedy or awesome cultural monument.

Macbeth

The Other Place: 10 September 1976

The simpler, the better; that is my feeling about Trevor Nunn's ceaseless quest for the ideal *Macbeth*. Two years ago he staged the play in Stratford's main house as an over elaborate religious spectacle. He then stripped away the ritual for an Aldwych version spoiled by gabbled speaking. And now at Stratford's Other Place in a production played without interval, he has hit the right balance between verbal clarity and depraved religiosity; I have never in fact seen the play come across with such throat-grabbing power.

Partly this is the result of the auditorium's intimacy. The actors perform inside a black circle and we, the audience, sit a few feet away as if sharing in an incantatory rite. But the effect is also due to Ian McKellen's overwhelming Macbeth which charts, stage by stage, the character's self-willed disintegration. If I had to pick the key to his performance I would say it lay in the line about making 'our faces vizards to our hearts'; for what we see is the gradual tearing away of Macbeth's public mask until we reach the driven psychopath beneath.

With hair swept back like Toshiro Mifune in a Samurai epic, and poker-faced stance, McKellen is at first your perfect soldier. But when he talks of his 'single state of man' being shaken, his body gives an involuntary shudder. He accomplishes the murder in a state of headlong hypnosis but, holding up his incarnadined hands thereafter, he gazes at them like a child waking from a bad dream.

He is at his best, however, when after his coronation he assumes a mask of tight-lipped diplomatic courtesy broken wide open by the vision of Banquo's ghost; the long jaw slackens and judders, the cheeks puff in and out like bellows, the mouth foams as a once whole man is reduced to epileptic frenzy. The guests gone, he turns to Lady Macbeth, who slumps stricken to the ground; picking her up and setting her features as if she were a ventriloquist's dummy, he stumbles sightlessly into the black future that awaits him.

If this is not great acting, I don't know what is; and McKellen's study of evil bursting through a mask like a clown through a paper hoop is finely complemented by Judi Dench's Lady Macbeth, which is not some painted Gorgon but a portrait of a novice dabbling in Satanic powers. Invoking evil spirits in her first scene, she suddenly darts back with a stab of fear as if having made contact; and that one gesture gives us the clue to a woman who is half-fascinated, half-terrified by the pit she has entered. Miss Dench too shows the cracking open of the mask and the cry of remorse she utters in the sleep walking scene, apparently drawn from her very soul, is guaranteed to haunt one for nights to come.

There is much else in this production one could dwell on: the extraordinary effect of a single light circling over Macbeth's head in the final scenes as if to convey a world awry; the proper attention to Duncan played by Griffith Jones as the embodiment of ruined grace; the feeling of moral and physical exhaustion as Roger Rees's Malcolm finally acquires the hollow crown: above all, perhaps, the sheer physical fluency and sustained energy Mr Nunn gives to a play that in the theatre has a habit of winding down. I have seen more bad productions of *Macbeth* than I have had hot dinners; but this one, part black ritual, part psychological study, gets closer to the play's heart than any I have known.

Light Shining In Buckinghamshire

Royal Court: 28 September 1976

What better subject for the Joint Stock Theatre Group than the attempt by the Levellers, the Diggers, and the Ranters to foment a revolution in England during and after the Civil War? And even if Caryl Churchill's *Light Shining In Buckinghamshire* doesn't have the same ferocious documentary clarity as David Hare's *Fanshen* (where, at any given moment, one knew precisely who was speaking) it remains a grippingly eloquent picture of the gulf between Cromwell and the democratic teachings of John Wildman and the communistic notions of Gerard Winstanley.

A colleague pejoratively described the play as 'committed'; but I would have said its chief commitment was to truth since it unflinchingly shows the intolerance that was the obverse side of the demand for common justice. Deftly, it sketches in the kind of social conditions (female vagrants stripped to the waist, whipped, and returned to the parish whence they came) that led to hunger for revolution. But it also shows that the primitive Christianity that fostered such revolution contained its own cruelties. And when it comes to the ideological conflict of the Putney Debates of 1647, it is scrupulously fair to both sides. It shows us Wildman and the Levellers demanding democratic government and manhood suffrage and Cromwell and Ireton standing by a franchise based on property and the rule of the virtuous.

Clearly the burden of the piece is that revolutionary idealism was betrayed by Parliament and the Army. But its great virtue is that it sets the evidence before us and makes no attempt to load the dice through presentational effects. Sydney Smith once said that he preferred the driest bread of common life to the artifice of theatre; but then he never had the good fortune to see Joint Stock who make their points through language, dialectic, the simplest of props (a bare scrubbed table), and, in this instance, the singing of unaccompanied verses from Isaiah. They remind us that these seventeenth-century revolutionaries were not so much premature Marxists as religious fundamentalists who believed passionately in the Second Coming of Christ. But they also remind us of the fanatical zeal ('Howl ye rich men for the miseries that are coming upon you' wrote Abiezer Coppe in 1649) that was part of that belief.

Beautifully directed by Max Stafford-Clark and finely acted by the whole company (Jan Chappell, Robert Hamilton, and Colin McCormack especially), the play has an austere eloquence that precisely matches its subject.

Tamburlaine The Great

Olivier: 5 October 1976

C.S. Lewis put his finger on it when he described Marlowe's *Tamburlaine The Great* as 'the story of Giant the Jack-killer.' And although Peter Hall's production at the newly-opened Olivier Theatre is in many ways very fine, it cannot get round the fact that a play in which an inordinate hero conquers everything in life but death is destined to a certain glittering monotony. If ever there were a case for editing, it is in a play like this.

But first the Olivier Theatre; and that strikes me, even in its current unfinished state, as enormously exciting. Eleven hundred and sixty spectators are gathered round a saucer-like stage dominated by a huge white circle that is echoed by the lighting-bar above. Three steps lead down from the stage to floor-level so that it is possible for an actor to come right down to the front row and still command the house. And there is a huge space behind the acting area that affords one or two magnificent vistas: as the double-doors of John Bury's set swing open one sees a smoke-wreathed Tamburlaine riding his huge chariot through what might be the corridors of hell. But basically, the Olivier is a marvellous open space in which all eyes seem directed towards a focal point.

Tamburlaine, however, is another question. In Part One, I felt Hall and Albert Finney had worked wonders in giving so much emotional variety to the Scythian shepherd's success story. There were images of flamboyant theatricality like Finney removing his hempen cloak to reveal sun-bright armour beneath (he strips to conquer). And director and actors unearthed a promising vein of ironic comedy. 'Is *this* your crown?' enquired Finney of the camp Persian king with a Lady Bracknell disdain. He also made the excellent point that much of

Tamburlaine's vaunting rhetoric is a mockery of the opposition, particularly the Turkish emperor Bajazeth who enters chairborne and red-plumed like Frank Thring in a Hollywood epic. Whether threading captured crowns on his sword like wedding-rings or inviting the audience to share the pleasure of kingship, Finney gave one a sense of a real human being.

In Part Two, however, the monotony of Marlowe's concept makes itself felt. The sub-plots involving the Kings of Buda, Natolia and Hungary are overly intricate; the barbaric cruelty grows oppressive; and Marlowe's failure to vary the poetic idiom from one character to another becomes more conspicuous. There are inventive directorial touches like making the Kings forced to draw Tamburlaine's chariot resemble Christ with a crown of thorns and fine images like the hero accompanying Zenocrate's glittering coffin with a resplendent ikon. But (and this is very much the play's fault) one feels pummelled with the monotony of conquest.

And fine though Finney is, particularly since suffering from bronchitis, one misses the shock of the hero's realisation of his own vulnerability. A crucial point since the play is about a superman who holds the mirror up to Nietzsche and finally has to face the fact that he too must die. But though Finney gives us many excellent details (such as poring over a map of the world that is upside down, which reminds me of Hemingway noticing that Mussolini at a press conference was busily reading a book which was also the wrong way up) I still felt he was all armour and no chink.

Likewise Hall's production makes good use of Harrison Birtwistle's percussive music (complete with wooden slap-stick) and David Hersey's lighting that glows a sulphurous red as one more blood-boltered victim is discovered behind the sliding Bury double-doors. But although Hall makes the effects come out of the text rather than applying them to the text, I dazedly stumbled out of the Olivier wondering if Marlowe warranted this hallowed glittering reverence.

The National Theatre

8 October 1976

Irony of ironies. In a week when the Olivier finally opened its doors and the 125-year-old dream of a properly equipped National Theatre came a little closer to reality, attacks on the institution itself seemed to intensify. What is particularly sad is that those attacks have very little to do with what appears on stage. They have much more to do with a hysterical malice, hatred, venom and envy directed by members of the theatrical profession towards Peter Hall. And we have reached the stage where, if an actor in Wrexham Rep cannot afford a new pair of tights, it is all the fault of Hall and his sybaritic cronies who spend their days lolling on beds of down puffing at opium pipes and making bonfires of public money.

I suggest it is time for the bitching to stop: time for criticism of the National to be based on its programme of work and not on the cut of Peter Hall's beard, whether he has stopped beating his wife and the size of his take-home pay. The crude, irremovable fact is that, like it or not, we have a large National Theatre with three auditoria. And that is the result of a decision taken in the early 1960s by a committee that included men of wisdom like Lord Olivier, George Devine, Peter Brook, Michael Elliott and Kenneth Tynan.

My own feeling is that they made a blunderingly wrong decision and that a large, open-stage theatre and a smaller experimental house would have been quite sufficient. But it was that committee that landed us with the industrial complex we have today and it is they, and not the Hall administration, that should be blamed for the three million or so pounds it costs to keep the National functioning annually.

But what kind of National do opponents of the present regime want? Jonathan Miller, one of the few constructive visionary enemies of the current administration, has made it abundantly clear to me and to other journalists what he would like to see: Peter Hall's head on a platter, three separate directors to run each of the existing theatres and a chain of mini national theatres up and down the country all related to the parent body. The first condition is unlikely to be met. The second is not dissimilar to what Hall himself proposes. And the problem with the third is that it would give the NT an almost monopolistic control over all the theatrical talent in this country.

Why should men like Cheeseman in Stoke, Havergal in Glasgow, Elliott in Manchester want their theatres stamped with the label NT when they have spent a lot of energy building up an individual policy? I sympathise deeply with Miller's liking for small theatres: the trouble is that the kind of low-capacity, dissenting-chapel theatre he favours is the one that demands the largest subsidy to run. Small may be beautiful. It is also bloody expensive.

But what of the National Theatre we've actually got? After seven months of operation in the Lyttelton Theatre, an experimental season at the Young Vic and one new production in the Olivier, what does the balance sheet look like? My overall impression is that Hall has played it cool and safe. Of ten productions at the Lyttelton, eight have been transfers from the Old Vic. This is pretty shrewd since it cut the cost, provided a pretty diverse programme and minimised the risk of the company falling flat on its face which might have occurred with a batch of new productions in a completely untried theatre. Audience figures of 95 per cent capacity also suggest the mix has been pretty popular.

Physically, however, the chief impression I have got from the Lyttelton is that is not well suited to naturalistic, box-set drama but is marvellous for epic, expressionist or expansive work. In *Blithe Spirit* it was a two-day route march from the centre of the living-room to the front door and the width of the auditorium made it difficult for any actor to throw a line away without it coming back to him two seconds later. Likewise in the early part of *John Gabriel Borkman* the actors looked as if they were inhabiting a living-room stuck in the middle of Madison Square Garden. Once, however, they were into the open courtyard outside the house and the snow-capped hills beyond, the stage came into its own.

The other problem with the National, in its baptismal stage, is that the turnover of actors seems unduly large. There are 126 actors on the books right now which, even allowing for a large-cast play like *Tamburlaine*, seems pretty hefty. And one doesn't currently have the exhilaration, as with the RSC at Stratford this season, of seeing the same body of overworked actors tackling a variety of plays; it has been fascinating at Stratford to watch actors like Ian McDiarmid, Bob Peck and Michael Pennington going from strength to strength as they have commuted from mainhouse Shakespeare to the Other Place. At the National, however, one man in his time seems to play very few parts.

And, while we're on the debit side of the balance sheet, it struck me that the Young Vic season of productions intended for the Cottesloe hardly set the Thames on fire. Of the three shows I saw, *Troilus And Cressida* was dismal in its bland neutrality and in its failure to use the intimate auditorium to focus on the intricacy of the language and Peter Handke's *They Are Dying Out* was equally depressing in the relentless banality of its ideas. Only Gawn Grainger's pool room play, *Four To One*, struck me as vibrantly necessary in that it gave a fledgling author a chance to see his work staged and learn what worked and what didn't.

Perhaps the moral is that Cottesloe seasons should be much rougher, readier and totally de-bureaucratised: one author told me it was very strange to be taking part in an 'experimental' season and still find the usual ring of people behind desks with notebooks night-nursing the production along.

But, on the credit side, the NT in the first seven months in its new home has done several important things. One is to establish the principle of catholicity of repertoire: along with Shakespeare, Ibsen, Synge and Coward, it has given us Travers, Beckett, Osborne, Pinter, Stoppard and Brenton. Anyone going to all ten productions thus far at the Lyttelton would have got a pretty fair cross-section of classic and contemporary drama. And such is the National's power of patronage, I would guess that more people have seen Brenton's *Weapons Of Happiness* than have probably attended all Brenton's previous plays in London.

Another feature of the National's work in its new home has been to emphasise the power of the word: it was noticeable at *Tamburlaine* on Monday night that, for all its inordinate length, the audience was raptly listening to the extent that you could have heard a pin, or an empire, drop. Unlike the Guthrie production of the play which, when it played in Canada, moved the director to remark that the notices the morning after simply put the nails in the coughing.

If the National attracts an excess of bile amongst the theatrical profession, it is I think partly because the very concept of a theatre offering 'the best of British' is properly alien to most people's thinking. In a profession where talent is spread nationwide there is no sensible way in which you can say the National is 'better' than Nottingham, Glasgow, the Other Place or the Open Space. What it can offer, which most theatres can't, is an international repertoire, the chance to do large-cast plays and the opportunity to exploit a technical sophistication that makes it possible to realise any writer's vision, I believe it right, at a time of economic crisis, for the National to be seen to be making certain sacrifices. But I hope in future the National will also be judged by the quality of its work (good or bad) and the service it offers to the public rather than backstage bitchery, starry sulks from the *ancien regime* and character-assassination dipped in the boiling oil of sour grapes.

Tartuffe

Lyttelton: 18 November 1976

We tend to play Molière's *Tartuffe* as a domestic farce: Roger Planchon's breathtaking Théâtre National Populaire production, playing at the Lyttelton this week, treats it as a cosmic tragi-comedy. From its apocalyptic thunder-peals at the beginning to its heavenly choir at the end (close on three and a half hours later), it is conceived on the grand scale; yet at the same time it gives you a rich sense of a cavernous bourgeois household in which private emotion becomes public property.

Planchon's most radical idea is to relate the confrontation of Tartuffe's religious hypocrisy and Orgon's religious zeal to a larger moral framework. In Hubert Monloup's spectacular settings the action begins on the forestage outside Orgon's house with a sword-brandishing angel poised over the actors and a mummified Christ seated alongside them. And, with each new act, scenery flies out to take us further inside the house: thus the great scene of Tartuffe's grovelling self-abasement before Orgon, after being discovered seducing his wife, is seen against a background of religious murals depicting the Slaughter of the Innocents and, I think, Abraham's sacrifice of Isaac. And this is entirely apt for a play about a man prepared to sacrifice his family to his blinkered religious idealism.

Indeed Planchon realises it is the duped Orgon rather than the hypocritical Tartuffe who is the centre of the play. And from the start he beautifully establishes both Orgon's patriarchal tyranny and penitential fervour. When he arrives home in the first scene, the family kneel before him along with the servants and, in a pure Brechtian image, Orgon divests himself of peruke, ruffs, boots, and golden finery to don a coat of sackcloth and become Tartuffe's willing slave. And as he desperately inquires after 'le pauvre homme', Tartuffe, you realise he also represents the guilt-ridden bourgeois determined to make amends for his wealth by giving it all to his pious house-guest.

But although it is a production full of stunning *coups de théâtre* (not least Tartuffe's final invasion of the house in which doors are smashed open and musket-wielding guards suddenly appear at windows), it is also rooted in domestic reality. The maidservant, Dorine, carefully closes a door before she gives her opinion of Tartuffe; Orgon's evening meal is served through a guillotine-like serving hatch; and at the end the once-divided family huddle together for comfort beating candles like figures in a Georges de la Tour painting. And it is the way Planchon holds this balance between the domestic and the cosmic that makes this TNP production so remarkable.

The performances also match the concept. Guy Tréjan's Orgon is no mere witless gull but a man of presence and silver-haired authority in the grip of a lunatic *idée fixe*. And Planchon's Tartuffe is no Gallic Uriah Heep but a figure of snake-like charm and histrionic skill who, when exposed as a lecher, crawls over the floor on all fours and flagellates himself mercilessly. But the whole household has this kind of three-dimensional reality from Arlette Gilbert's maidservant, beating table-tops in her frustration at not being able to make Orgon see sense, to Nelly Borgeaud's wife who is seduced by Tartuffe on a huge table that is part bed and part blue-clothed altar. It is a sign of a great production that it gives one a wholly new perspective on a familiar text; and, judged by that criterion, Planchon's *Tartuffe* is a superlative eye and mind-opener.

1977

The RSC struck gold. This was, in fact, the perihelion of Trevor Nunn's ten-year reign as the company's sole Artistic Director and Chief Executive (in 1978 he began to share the power with Terry Hands). In London, the company opened a new studio space at the Warehouse with plays by Barker, Taylor, Bond and Brecht. Its Aldwych repertory combined the usual Stratford transfers with Nichols's Privates On Parade, *Ibsen's* Pillars Of The Community *and Brecht's* The Days Of The Commune. *At the Royal Shakespeare Theatre, Terry Hands and Alan Howard had a marathon year working on* Henry V, *a virtually uncut, three-part* Henry VI *and* Coriolanus. *And the season at The Other Place included Jonson, Ford, Musset, Gems and Rudkin. No other company in the world could match that output for quantity or quality.*

The contrast with the new National Theatre was striking. Admittedly the place was plagued by labour disputes and financial hardship. It also put on some notable productions: Tales From The Vienna Woods, The Madras House, The Plough And The Stars, State Of Revolution. *But the Cottesloe veered uncertainly from pre-West End try-outs (Gielgud in Julian Mitchell's* Half-Life), *to mediocre 'Fringey' plays like John Mackendrick's* Lavender Blue. *One also noticed how the RSC nurtured its acting talent, like the steadily maturing Ian McDiarmid, while the National allowed a fine talent like Stephen Rea to pop in for a couple of productions and then disappear.*

*Outside London, there were ominous signs from the regional theatre: summer closures and studio cut-backs. But at Glasgow there was rare Coward and Balzac (*Vautrin*); at Nottingham a radical new version of* The Cherry Orchard *by Trevor Griffiths; a Wesker premiere (*The Wedding Feast*) in Leeds; and lively productions of* Uncle Vanya, Present Laughter *and* The Ordeal Of Gilbert Pinfold *at Manchester's Royal Exchange. In the metropolis itself one looked to the Royal Court, Hampstead Theatre and the Bush for signs of vitality. Meanwhile the West End, despite De Filippo's*

Filumena, Bennett's The Old Country *and* Bubbling Brown Sugar, *continued its sclerotic decline.*

Peter Stein

7 March 1977

Peter Stein, director of West Berlin's Schaubühne Am Halleschen Ufer, is fascinated by *No Sex Please We're British*. He hasn't actually seen it, but he loves the neon sign outside the Strand Theatre that blazes forth the Hobsonian imprimatur – 'Hysterically Funny'. He wondered if he should come before the curtain on the first night of *Summerfolk* at the Lyttelton and announce to the public: 'We have made a production that is not hysterically funny. Ours is hysterically boring.'

I am glad he didn't because it wouldn't have been true. In my opinion, Stein's production of *Summerfolk* is a masterpiece: a complete reconstruction of a particular Russian community built up from myriad detail. But Stein's point, made the morning after the first night in a populous hotel lounge, is that the English and the Germans have different expectations of theatre. He shrewdly notes that almost everything now playing in London, whether modern or classic, is a comedy. In Germany, he says, there is no great comic tradition in drama. And he is worried not merely by the way London will react to *Summerfolk* but also by the way the collective, of which he is a part, will adapt to *As You Like It* when they stage it in Berlin this summer.

Talking to this exuberant, lynx-eyed director, however, one is struck not merely by the gulf between English and German theatre but also by the vast difference in practice. Every production for the Schaubühne is a massive research project. In preparation for their first venture in Shakespeare, Stein and members of the company visited Stratford and the Shakespeare country two years ago. Then they staged in Berlin a kaleidoscopic anthology about Tudor England called *Shakespeare's Memory*.

According to Stein, 'It's an attempt to explore the world out of which Shakespeare's plays grew. And it deals not only with ideas but with physical skills. What were actors like before Shakespeare? What were the forms of entertainment? What was it like to spit fire, walk tight-ropes, dance jigs, sing ballads? Who was Tarleton? We would like to get a remembrance of the whole Shakespearean world.'

To the English, of course, the idea of such intense preparation for a particular production is hopelessly alien. Only the other day Sir Ralph Richardson was quoted in a *New Yorker* profile as asking rather warily, 'Don't you think Peter Hall has something Germanic about him?' But what makes Stein's approach particularly interesting is that it assumes there is some kind of collective folk-memory which can be resurrected through research. And I suddenly recalled an episode from a production of his I saw in Berlin, *Exercises For Actors*, in which the players led in a huge primeval beast, dismembered it and then sat in a gathering twilight softly singing over the piles of bones. It sounds pretentious, but I remarked at the time on the power of a theatrical image to reach back into one's own memory of some earlier existence.

However, Stein is not romantic or dewy-eyed about the difficulties of reaching back into the past. Although palpably left-wing, he talks unsentimentally about attracting a working-class audience to his kind of theatre. 'If you sing of the oldest things in the theatre, if you want to retain the memories of those things, you will be very lonely. In Germany, because of the kind of industrial society in which they live, the working class have lost the possibility of memory. And if you plan all your work to recapture that audience you will probably end up not doing the plays you want to do. Ten per cent of the German population perhaps go to the theatre. And probably only 4 per cent of that 10 per cent is working-class. But you can't really change the nature of the audience without also changing the society.'

What emerges in conversation with Stein is that he is that rare creature: a radical with a sense of the past. With *Summerfolk*, for instance, he and his co-adaptor, Botho Strauss, take what an English director would probably regard as unforgivable liberties with the text. Yet those liberties are based on deep scholarship.

The play was chosen, as usual, by democratic vote. Some thirty members of the collective (which gets a subsidy of £1.5 million a year) then went to Russia to visit places associated with Gorky, Chekhov, and Turgenev. Back home, there were lectures on the play and the period from members of the theatre staff. Three months or more were then spent on research by everyone involved in the production. Stein and Strauss wrote their adaptation over the next three months. Actual rehearsals lasted two months.

But how does the collective approach work in rehearsal? Who takes the decisions? 'As director,' says Stein, 'my job is really to select and edit what the actors are offering. It's not my job to invent business for actors. To take an instance when Michael König, who plays Vlass, paints his features with a clownish mask, that was entirely his idea. Since his character speaks all the time about the face as a mask, it seemed entirely legitimate. The whole point of this production is that it starts with a wide-angled shot of all the characters together instead of bringing them on two at a time like Gorky. Given that framework, it is up to the actors to devise the manner of hitting each other's nerves.'

It sounds from this as if Peter Brook is a key influence on Stein. In fact, he says he evolved his approach before he ever saw Brook's research group. The one influence he does admit to, surprisingly, is Peter Hall's production of *The Homecoming* in the mid-1960s. 'I suddenly saw the possibilities of witty, intellectual dialogue, of highly calculated and perfect actors, of a play-machine at work.'

Now Stein himself ranks with Strehler, Planchon and Ronconi as one of those directors whose every production sends out shock waves across Europe and who can dictate their own terms. In Berlin they're building a new theatre for Stein and the company and offered everyone five-year contracts. 'A one-year contract is sufficient,' says Stein. 'How can you commit yourself five years ahead when you are always putting yourselves in question? At the Schaubühne we are strong because we risk all.'

It's that element of risk, along with a belief that every classic production involves an exhausting search for *le temps perdu*, that makes the company arguably the most exciting ensemble in Europe.

Julius Caesar

Olivier: 23 March 1977

Like Mark Antony, John Schlesinger is a 'shrewd contriver'. And his production of *Julius Caesar* at the Olivier is certainly handsomely mounted. A semi-circular screen, onto which images are projected, hangs over the stage. Bas-reliefs of Caesar's head protrude from mobile, concave flats. And David Hersey's lighting is throughout coolly exact.

Why then is the overall effect so dreary? I suppose because there is little hint of the kind of tyranny that drives the conspirators into action. John Gielgud's Caesar is, as one would expect,a noble, poker-backed seemingly beneficent figure guilty, at worst, of mild caprice. Explaining why he chooses not to go to the Capitol Gielgud phrases beautifully the lines 'The cause is in my will – I *will* not come.' But although it is a real aesthetic pleasure to hear Gielgud speaking Shakespeare again, and although he dominates the action, in silent retribution, even after

Caesar's death, he is still a long way from the kind of black-leather, overweening tyrant Mark Dignam created in the last RSC production.

The result is to make the conspiracy a gratuitous attempt to kill off the best verse-speaker on the English stage. Brian Cox's Brutus suffers most in that the moral dilemma faced by the liberal intellectual in a world of *realpolitik* is here entirely absent. Lines like 'O that we could come by Caesar's spirit and not dismember Caesar' go for next to nothing because there is no sense of impending, or actual tyranny.

Similarly Ronald Pickup's Cassius is like a malevolent ferret snapping his teeth at thin air. Apart from a certain amount of thunder and lightening and Harrison Birtwistle's xylophone music, there is little evidence of disorder in the Roman world; and without that the conspirators are like men operating in a void.

The one performer who benefits is Mark McManus as Mark Antony and, if this apolitical production supports any character, it is him. McManus has a good, direct style of delivery and his speech to the crowd after Caesar's death is all the more effective for being devoid of slippery, oratorical guile. Yet there is a good, cynical touch when at the end of the scene he tears up Caesar's will. For the rest, there is a fine sardonic Casca from Gawn Grainger, some beautiful projections on John Bury's screen and an omnipresent sense of opulent, respectable dullness.

Shaw Festival

Ontario: 20 June 1977

Canada is full of surprises. A two-hour-drive away from the Stratford Festival in Ontario lies the Shaw Festival in Niagara-on-the-Lake. Here, in a beautiful little country town that resembles Chipping Camden with white clapboard houses, one discovers a summer festival devoted to Shaw and his contemporaries.

It fulfils the same kind of function as Malvern in the 1930s; and one can hardly do justice to one's astonishment at coming out of a matinée to find farmers making hay while the sun shines in the field next door to the theatre or at taking a stroll off the main street to gaze at the American coast. Like most summer festivals, this one is the product of one man's unshakable enthusiasm. Chichester has its Leslie Evershed-Martin, Stratford Ontario its Tom Patterson and Niagara-on-the-Lake a lawyer named Brian Doherty. In 1961 he conceived the idea of a Shaw

Festival beginning with *Don Juan In Hell* staged in the old ivy-covered, nineteenth-century Court House.

Year by year the project grew until in 1971 a Toronto architect designed a new Shaw Festival Theatre. From the outside it has the touching, red-brick ugliness of the Royal Shakespeare Theatre in Stratford-upon-Avon. Inside it turns out to be a spacious 833-seater with a nicely-raked auditorium, a glass-walled lobby, a stand selling Shaw mugs, T-shirts and bags and even a library. Clive Barnes has said he thinks it's the best new theatre to be built in North America and I see no reason to disagree.

That's the good news. The bad news is that a party of international journalists arrived in Niagara to see, among other things, a full-length version of *Man And* Superman (complete with *Don Juan In Hell*) only to find that Ian Richardson who plays John Tanner was in hospital with gastro-enteritis. However there was instant compensation in a production by Michael Meacham of Ben Travers's *Thark* that had the audience baying with hysteria and Shakespeare-saturated critics all but rolling in the aisles.

Written in 1927, *Thark* was the third of the nine Aldwych farces. It was written in accordance with a diktat from Tom Walls that ran 'The next one has got to be about a haunted house,' and it shows all Travers's genius for combining farcical incident with spiralling verbal absurdity. It's hard to convey in cold print why a line like 'You're Mrs Frush and you've taken Thark' (spoken to a Mayfair butterfly who hasn't the faintest idea who or what Thark is) should reduce an audience to pulp: suffice to say that it does.

Meacham's production, however, works precisely because it blends elaborate comic business with attention to language. Paxton Whitehead (the Festival's Artistic Director) plays the old Ralph Lynn part of Ronald Gamble and, with his accosting profile, giraffe-like neck and long, spidery limbs, he leaves behind a memorable physical image. Whether thrusting an unwanted amatory rival under a fringed lamp-shade or leaping on to chair-arms like a demented gazelle he has the dangerous energy of a true farce actor.

The Shaw Festival does Travers proud. Ironically, it seemed less at ease with a production of Shaw's own *Widowers' Houses* staged in the rather cramped conditions of the Court House. Paxton Whitehead's production got across the essential Shavian point that you will never destroy slum landlordism by getting rid of men like Sartorius, the devouring property-owner, but only by changing the social system. But although Ronald Bishop rightly played Sartorius from his own point of view as an efficient businessman trying to provide homes for the homeless, the production lacked much definition or drive.

The coming Shaw season, however, also includes revivals of *The Millonairess* (with Ian Richardson and Carole Shelley) and the rarely-seen *Great Catherine*. And as one wanders down the wide tree-lined main street of Niagara-on-the-Lake one can't help wondering why it is that one has to travel three thousand miles across the Atlantic to find a season devoted to the greatest British dramatist since Shakespeare. Malvern, please note.

Letter To The Editor

John Osborne: 23 June 1977

Sir, – Michael Billington cannot have read the plays of George Bernard Shaw since his Oxford days. To call him 'the greatest British dramatist since Shakespeare' (June 20) is close to having a critical brainstorm, as well as perpetulating an exam-crazy classroom myth. Having recently seen *St Joan* in London and *Caesar And Cleopatra* in Sydney, it is clearer to me than ever that Shaw is the most fraudulent, inept writer of Victorian melodramas ever to gull a timid critic or fool a dull public.

He writes like a Pakistani who has learned English when he was twelve years old in order to become a chartered accountant.

From childhood I have read these plays, watched them, indeed toured as an actor and stage manager in them on one night stands. Apart from this experience, any fair decent writer I know could put his finger on the crass, vulgar drivel in any of them.

Simply read the stage directions of *Candida* (opening this week). I had the misery of once playing Marchbanks in this ineffably feeble piece. This is Shaw's idea of a 'poet' (having no poetry in *him* at all). The Poet, a ghastly little cissy, is bullied interminably by an idiot muscular Christian Socialist who, in turn, is mothered by an insufferably patronising bully of a woman. As a 10-minute sketch on BBC2 in 1898 from South Shields it would do. But as a full-length stage play it is hard to think of anything more silly, apart from the rest of the so-called 'oeuvre'.

The one possible exception is *Pygmalion*, in which I toured the Welsh valleys in 1954 for the Arts Council. But the miners were still better than the play. I however, was very funny as Freddy Eynesford-Hill, which does go to prove that you can't make bricks entirely without straw – something play reviewers can never grasp about plays or actors.

But 'the greatest British dramatist since Shakespeare (?)'. Ben Travers could have had GBS before breakfast in Australia watching the Test.

By the time I was 25 I had been in (admittedly bad, but no matter) productions of: *Arms And The Man, Candida, You Never Can Tell, Devil's Disciple, Caesar And Cleopatra, Saint Joan, Major Barbara* and, perhaps worst of all, Chekhov-for-philistines, *Heartbreak House.*

Try *learning* them, Mr Billington; they are posturing wind and rubbish. In fact, just the sort of play you would expect a critic to write. The difference is simple: he did it.

Yours faithfully,
John Osborne.

The Madras House

Olivier: 24 June 1977

Without Harley Granville Barker, there probably wouldn't be a National Theatre. And without a National Theatre there almost certainly wouldn't be a chance to see Granville Barker's *The Madras House*: an opulent, four-act Edwardian comedy that ranges freely over the relations between men and women, parents and children, the class system, the purpose of art, British philistinism and American opportunism.

It is a fantastically rich play that illuminates everything it touches: and it is directed by William Gaskill with the sureness of a tug-boat nudging an ocean greyhound into harbour.

Like all Barker's plays, *The Madras House* (1909) is about the rejection by the individual of his society's values. In this case, Philip Madras wishes to sell off the family drapery business and all the attitudes that go with it: the chauvinist arrogance and obsessive virility of his exotic father (a Mohammedan convert), the Pooterish lifestyle and slave-owning ethos of his Denmark Hill uncle, the family-destroying atmosphere of the Peckham drapery where husbands live in, wives are locked out and young girls knocked up. The country, he declares, is a muddle; and Philip's answer is to discard his inheritance, stand for the London County Council and work towards an art and culture 'that must spring in good time from the happiness of a whole people'.

But the play is more than a study of one man's reforming zeal. Its real subject is England; and what is amazing is the amount of novelistic detail about Edwardian life Barker manages to cram into one work. The first act alone, set in South London suburbia where the head of the house cannot remember if he has five or six daughters, where Weymouth is regarded as Nirvana and where a young Major announces 'I got most of my reading done early,' is one of the funniest portraits of oppressive English philistinism in modern drama.

But Barker not only shows domesticity cramping thought. In the third act, which takes place in a Bond Street Rotunda where men solemnly sit round and discuss the role of women in society while behind them wasp-waisted models tittup and teeter under the weight of top-heavy chapeaux, he lets ideas flare up and explode like rockets in a November sky.

Plays with broad canvasses tend to be weak on individual psychology; but again Barker defies expectations. He was on the side of reform. Yet, as in *Waste*, he shows that crusading zeal often goes hand in hand with emotional barrenness. Philip Madras wants a better life for everyone; yet he admits to disliking men and despising women. And it is this tension between Philip's bright-eyed messianic fervour and his own emotional detachment that holds the play together and gives the talky final act (which Beerbohm said you could miss) a strange twilit pathos.

Gaskill's production also matches the play perfectly in that it combines sharp clarity of outline with intricacy of detail. Hayden Griffin's thrusting first act set gives you Denmark Hill down to the last rosewood cabinet, potted fern and academic portrait. But the switch to the second act Peckham office has a deliberately two-dimensional quality with four characters at loggerheads facing the audience square on as if they would be corrupted by ocular contact.

Admittedly Ronald Pickup has a tricky job playing Philip but he manages to suggest the right blend of hot gospeller, cold fish, humane employer and inhuman husband. And there is a gem of a performance from Paul Scofield as his Mohammedan father: the hair is silver, the voice blue-black, the waistcoat every colour of the rainbow and the general impression that of a thigh-smiting prophet set down incongruously in Edwardian London and looking at every minute as if he might eat the carpet or rape the parlourmaid.

From a large supporting cast one must also single out Paul Rogers as a nervy, chalk-white suburbanite, Mark McManus as a cringing Madras employee and Dinah Stabb as a sexually defiant shopgirl. All ensure that *The Madras House* has not merely been revived: it has been lovingly restored. And Barker emerges not as a second-hand Shaw but as a chronicler of English life comparable to (and often much better than) Wells, Bennett and Galsworthy.

Epsom Downs

Roundhouse: 8 August 1977

Howard Brenton's *Epsom Downs*, presented by Joint Stock at the Roundhouse, has a very respectable theatrical antecedent: Ben Jonson's *Bartholomew Fair*. For Brenton's portrait of Derby Day is, like Jonson's play, an exuberant documentary about a secular English festival. It doesn't have the old master's ability to make you care about the fate of individual eccentrics, but it gives you a sense of the two nations not quite coming together for a gaudy popular event.

The first thing to hit you is the conversion of the Roundhouse itself: in place of the old echoing Cinerama-like arena we now have an open, green-turfed stage around which eight hundred spectators are closely wrapped. And across the sward passes a gallery of Derby Day types: a drunken Socialist peer, heather-flogging Gypsies, a sacked stable-lad, a pair of lapsed evangelists, a family who blow their building society savings on Lester Piggott, bookies, buskers, cops, socialists and, not least, the ghost of the suffragette who threw herself under the king's horse. Nine actors play 47 speaking parts and at the end you feel Brenton has taken you on a sweeping panoramic tour of the Downs.

I suspect, however, that Brenton sees Derby Day as an emblem of the layer-cake English caste system in which the silver ring and the popular side never finally meet. 'England at peace on Derby Day,' cries the militant ghost. 'It's only a picture thin as paint – slash it.'

But my criticism of the play would be that in the end Brenton jabs at it rather than slashes it. He succumbs to the raucous fevered excitement of the event and to the feeling that even the shady tipsters and hard-headed bookies are weavers of dreams for an afternoon. Brenton's generosity of temperament overcomes his social criticism: and the result is his most accessible and simply enjoyable play, if not his most astringent.

It does, however, ripple with wit ('Making money?' inquires one bookie, meeting another. 'A drizzle of pennies,' comes the reply). And Max Stafford-Clark's production, with naked actors embodying the horses and swathes of litter suddenly covering the turf, has a beautiful theatrical momentum.

David Rintoul, Will Knightley, Cecily Hobbs, and Robert Hamilton are also outstanding in a cast that can clearly play anything the author throws at it. And at the end, as you see the local asylum inmates sweeping up the rubble for the price of a cup of tea, you feel that you have shared the tawdry dream and false optimism of this sweaty English pageant.

The Old Country

Queen's: 8 September 1977

A country house. Wine, talk, friends. Elgar on the turntable and light irony round the drinks table. From this bald description it sounds as if Alan Bennett's latest play, *The Old Country*, is a return to the cosy Shaftesbury Avenue world of N.C. Hunter. But the catch is (and it's a pity one has to reveal it) that the play is actually set in the spruce-backed Russian dacha of a Foreign Office defector undergoing a visit from his sister and pillar-of-the-Establishment brother-in-law.

Nominally, it is a play about exile: in reality it is, like everything Bennett has ever written, a study of England. Hilary, the hero, may have defected thirteen years ago and be working as a translator in Moscow but he still lapses into parodies of *Times* obituary notices and Buchanesque adventures and keeps people at bay with a defensive irony that is both the English disease and delight. What tension the play generates springs from his brother-in-law's request that he return home. But Bennett's point, I take it, is that he has never really left it: that, at a certain level of class and accomplishment, the English never shake off a love of books and countryside, a deadly detachment and a sense of being emotionally wounded. Home, in short, is where the hurt is.

A fair point; and Bennett makes it with his customary style and wit. There is an elegant Firbankian quality about the writing ('In England we never mean entirely what we say. Do I mean that? Not entirely') that makes most other West End stuff look tame and shoddy. And the hero's brutal dissection of Forster's famous aphorism about betraying one's country rather than one's friends is Bennett at his lethal best. If I have a cavil, it is that Bennett himself is afflicted with the disease he so expertly diagnoses: an implacable Englishness. To shrug off Solzhenitsyn with a line like: 'Which is worse – five years in a camp or three pages in *The Listener*?' is to fall into the kind of bookish parochialism one is condemning.

I am, in short, in two minds about this play: I admire its style but question its limited historical vision (all we ever learn about the Russians is that they're scrupulous about litter and avid for jeans). But I have no reservations about the acting of Clifford Williams's production. Alec Guinness's Hilary, whether brushing away a kiss, rearranging his disordered books or delivering *bon mots* with hooded eyes and curled lips, is a clinically comic study of an exiled Englishman who has taken his clubman manners with him. And there is beautiful support from John Phillips as a married, homosexual, Establishment-figure for whom life is a series of interlocking committees and from Faith Brook as his laserbeam-voiced spouse. A civilised evening; but one that might have been called, *pace* Cyril Connolly, *Lost Horizons*.

Semi-Monde

Glasgow Citizens: 12 September 1977

From the outside the Glasgow Citizens' Theatre looks none too inviting. It stands on a patch of razed Gorbals ground with only a bingo parlour and a huddle of shops for company. Yet inside it is almost voluptuously attractive. The beautiful, horseshoe-shaped, 750-seater auditorium and the front-of-house area are painted a bordello-scarlet. And for the premiere of Noël Coward's *Semi-Monde* the place was packed from floor to ceiling; not surprisingly when you learn that all seats cost 50p with half-price for students and free admission for old-age pensioners.

I wish I could say, after all that, that *Semi-Monde* was a newly discovered masterpiece. It was written in 1926 (which makes it post-*Hay Fever* and pre-*Private Lives*) but was never licensed by the Lord Chamberlain presumably because of its open references to male and female homosexuality.

Set in the lounge of the Ritz Hotel in Paris, it captures the restless kaleidoscopic glitter of the passing social scene: gay blades cavort, stuffy husbands get tromped, new marriages dissolve, old marriages come in for repair and generally the men and women come and go behaving like (rather than talking of) Michelangelo.

The problem is that Coward didn't yet have the technical address to handle with ease 28 characters. And the play contains its own depth-charge criticism. Someone remarks that people are always amusing to watch. But a suave novelist accurately replies, 'In this context they do lack variety, don't they?'

As so often with Coward, it is not so much the people themselves that grip you as his own equivocal attitude towards them. He was, by instinct, a puritan dandy with a Martini in one hand and a moral sampler in the other. And in *Semi-Monde* you can see clearly that, while he envies the rich their style, he also has the true lower-middle-class boy's belief that a life without work cannot be pure.

Even his attitude to homosexuality is not exactly encouraging: he seems to suggest it should be practised but not preached. He clearly deplores the bad manners of a Germanic lesbian chanteuse in making scenes in the middle of the Ritz and when giggling boys bounce up and down on each other's laps the observant novelist witheringly remarks: 'They're not even real of their kind.'

Significantly, the one homosexual who earns Coward's approval is a student-singer who is encouraged to devote himself to his career. This fits in with Coward's own code of constant work and sexual discretion; and it reminds one that the year after *Semi-Monde* he wrote that 'People were greedy and predatory and if you gave them the chance they would steal unscrupulously the heart and soul out of you.'

But if the play is chiefly interesting for its reminder of Coward's enthralled horror when confronted by the playboy set, Philip Prowse's production and design are a triumphant recreation of a vanished world. The stage is ringed by a wall of mirrors. A pianist (Robert David MacDonald) sits at a pink baby grand underscoring the action with Coward and Porter numbers. And leaping from table to table are men in double-breasted dinner-jackets and beautiful women in silk and chiffon, bangles and beads. It's like a vision of the damned, dressed by Erté.

More controversially, Mr Prowse has pushed the later scenes forward in time so that we get Hitler on the radio and the break-up of the glittering tribe. This strikes me as over-literal. The whole point of Coward in the mid-twenties was that he was uneasy without being prophetic. 'Cocktails and laughter. But what comes after? Nobody knows . . .' runs his most famous song. But Mr Prowse has created a retina-ravishing spectacle and from a large cast one must single out Ann Mitchell as a jealous lesbian, Mark Lewis as an adulterous novelist, Pauline Moran as an arrant spouse and Rory Edwards as a guilt-ridden homosexual. They have played Coward and won.

Britain's Theatrical Chauvinism

1 October 1977

As a London drama critic, I have much to be grateful for: our effervescent native drama, the high quality of British acting, the radical improvement in Shakespearean production over the last decade-and-a-half. But there is one thing about our theatre that makes me want to hang my head in shame: its almost total imperviousness to anything happening outside these shores.

We are still ignorant of the past riches of world drama. We see very few of the best new plays from other countries. And when some foreign company is rash enough to accept an invitation to visit London, it is usually greeted with a cold and patronising derision.

Lest this be taken as an attack on theatre workers (though, in some part, it is) let me also say that it is an attack on critics and public as well. When Roger Planchon's Théâtre National Populaire came to the Lyttelton a year ago with a sensational production of *Tartuffe* perfectly blending the domestic and the cosmic (who can forget Tartuffe's final invasion of the house in which doors were smashed open and musket-wielding guards suddenly appeared at windows?) they were greeted as if they were some middling French company tinkering with a masterpiece we knew intimately. When the National itself presented Thomas Bernhard's *The Force Of Habit*, few of my colleagues thought to attack the company for putting on a chamber play in a large theatre. Instead they vented their spleen on the Austrian poet-dramatist himself, thus ensuring we never saw any of his half-dozen other plays in England.

With a few honourable exceptions (Marcus, Levin, Barber, Young, Coveney), most drama critics actively bristle when they see a foreign name on a theatre programme. They feel more at home with Alan Ayckbourn's thirty-seventh study of suburban crisis or with some little lunchtime leftover that taxes no one's imagination.

The public is just as bad. Anything non-English, unless it be an American musical or a solo performer, is regarded as some kind of cultural letter bomb. Even Neil Simon, whose plays are popular in France, Italy, Germany, and Scandinavia, never has a run in England. Indeed, in a fascinating interview with Clive Hirschhorn in the current *Plays & Players*, he reveals that his London hotel bill has often cost him more than the royalties he was earning: for that reason we shall not see in London *The Prisoner Of Second Avenue, The Last Of The Red-Hot Lovers, God's Favourite, The Good Doctor*, or, I presume, *California Suite*.

The situation is even worse for European drama, unless it be by Ibsen or Chekhov. The Royal Exchange in Manchester has just created an admirable precedent by announcing percentage capacities for its first year's productions (something I wish all subsidised theatres were obliged to do by the Arts Council). The figures make fascinating reading. Almost every production reached 90 or 80 per cent of capacity. *Present Laughter* and *Uncle Vanya* (with Albert Finney) played to 96 and 94.5 per cent respectively. *What The Butler Saw* achieved a figure of 93.9. *The Rivals* of 91.2, *Dick Whittington* of 90.6.

The lowest figure (71.8) was, however, reserved for Heinrich von Kleist's *The Prince Of Homburg*, even though it starred Tom Courtenay and was the second production in the new building. The play is, of course, one of the acknowledged masterpieces of European theatre. Several critics, however, absented themselves from its premiere, preferring to go to see *Othello* in Nottingham; and, though the public came, they still didn't come in the same overwhelming numbers as for other productions. One can only conclude it is because Kleist is a bloody foreigner.

My impression (and it is by no means confined to theatre) is that our chauvinism is growing more intense as our international authority declines. In the post-war period, when we were still one of the four great powers, we were prepared to tolerate cultural invasion: now the shutters are going up everywhere. We don't want to know about foreign drama; we distrust the continental power of the director; we don't even want to join international organisations.

I felt constantly embarrassed, when I went to Stockholm in June to attend an International Theatre Institute congress at having to explain why the British were no longer members. The British attitude to ITI (which, ironically enough, J.B. Priestley helped to create) is one of 'What can it do for us?' The ITI's attitude to the British is one of 'Just think what you can do *to* us.' We would rather sulk from without than change from within.

But this is only a symptom of a much wider malaise: a belief that our disunited Kingdom is the hallowed centre of the universe. I remember Stephen Vizinczey writing, in a review of Balzac's *Lost Illusions*, that while it would be impossible for a child even in Red China to learn about music without so much as hearing Beethoven's name, great writers of no less universal significance are banished from the British school curriculum if they happen to be foreign.

If you want to get a comprehensive picture of what is happening around the globe, you certainly don't rely on domestic radio and TV bulletins: you tune in to the World Service. And nothing is more depressing than the resurrection, fomented by sections of the popular press and entertainment industry of a 'wogs-begin-at-Calais' attitude to all foreign residents and tourists. We are, in fact, rapidly becoming The Island That Doesn't Like To Be Visited.

But turning back to the drama, you may well ask what we are missing by our entrenched isolationism. At the very least, I would say, the anthropological pleasure that comes from discovering other civilisations and ways of living: at the highest, an enrichment of the human spirit. What is particularly staggering is our disregard of the infinite variety of world-drama.

After twenty years of fairly assiduous theatregoing, I have still seen only a fraction of the output of great masters such as Pirandello, Strindberg, Ibsen, and O'Neill. And I have seen no professional productions at all in English of Schiller, Goethe, Hauptmann, Hebbel, Grabbe, Kaiser, Toller, Grillparzer, Kotzebue, Becque, Corneille, Scribe, Brieux, Marivaux, Dumas, Augier, Poinsard, Bjornson, Holberg, Lagerkvist, Chiarelli, D'Annunzio, Antonelli, Anderson, Barry, Behrman, Kaufman, Hart, Rice, Saroyan, Calderón, De Molina, Tolstoy, Griboyedov, Pushkin or Andreyev. And that, as any student of drama will realise, is only a bare scratching of the surface.

Again, though, does it matter? Isn't the important thing that we have a living drama of our own? I think it matters precisely because we have a living drama of our own, and because that drama needs to be fertilised by an awareness of the achievement, and limitations, of the past. To take one obvious instance, there is much discussion today, as always about 'the fetters of naturalism' and the need to wrest drama free from the iron constrictions of lifelike settings and behaviour. But in England the debate is totally artificial in that we rarely see most of the landmark naturalistic plays of the late nineteenth-century.

You cannot, for instance, discuss naturalism without reference to Zola's *Thérèse Raquin* (1873) in which the author 'chose people supremely dominated by their nerves and their blood, devoid of free will, dragged along in each action of their lives by the fatalities of the flesh.'

And what about Henri Becque's *La Parisienne* (1885), which is a brutally cynical comedy about a *ménage à trois* that ends, as it began, in emotional bankruptcy, and that had a great influence on Strindberg, Wedekind and Sternheim? And when will we ever see the great forerunner of German naturalism, Gerhart Hauptmann's *Before Sunrise* (1889) in which a socialist idealist comes to stimulate reform in a morally corrupt community and ends up, like an Ibsen hero, by bringing confusion and catastrophe. Sam Wanamaker appeared in a version of *Thérèse Raquin* called *The Lovers* in 1953 and I believe *La Parisienne* had a rare outing in 1943. They are hardly, however, a standard part of the English dramatic repertory.

In fact, it would be no exaggeration to say that most of the important movements in European drama have bypassed the English theatre. We have seen next to nothing of French and German Romanticism, few of the landmarks of late nineteenth century Naturalism, and precious few of the key Expressionist works. Capek, Kaiser, and Toller, for instance, are virtual strangers to our shores. Yet, as Eric Bentley said of them, 'Alike in their passionate, nervous hedging philosophies and in their bold, loose, unfinished, messy Expressionistic forms, they will represent to history the nineteen twenties.'

I believe that some measure of Naturalism is a vital ingredient of drama. But it still seems to me absurd that we should be ignorant of the three most famous experimental playwrights of the century. I would argue further that, without some knowledge of German expressionism, one will never understand Brecht's triumphant fusion of two different traditions: the naturalist and anti-naturalist.

All very well. But who is to ransack the files of world drama and show us some of the plays we have missed? The obvious answer is the National Theatre: and I believe they have already commissioned writers to adapt and translate some of the unperformed landmarks. The problem is that the National Theatre has two large auditoria to fill. It is also operating at the moment on a knife-edge budget. For that reason, it has sacrificed thematic explorations of neglected periods (it had, in fact, planned a season of German Expressionism). But I also get the impression that the failure of Goldoni's *Il Campiello* and Bernhard's *The Force of Habit* frightened Peter Hall off little-known foreign work.

I hope that is not true: for while it's the duty of a National Theatre to explore the highways of world drama, it also has an obligation to get off the beaten track. What's the point of giving us another *Macbeth* or another *Cherry Orchard* when, with a big crowd-pulling actor rejoining the company (Albert Finney) they could give us Schiller's *Wallenstein*, Ibsen's *The Pretenders*, or Brecht's *Galileo*.

I fear, however, the rest of the theatre uses the National to excuse it's own dismal cop-out. As Henry V might have said, 'Let us our lives, our souls, our debts, our careful wives, our children and our sins lay on the National.' With the exception of Michael Elliott and his colleagues at the Royal Exchange (shortly doing a Japanese play), Giles Havergal at Glasgow (about to do Balzac's *Vautrin*), Gordon McDougall at Oxford (currently presenting *Brand*), and Peter James at the Sheffield Crucible (about to stage *The Government Inspector*), I know of few regional theatres with any wide-ranging interest in foreign drama. The most you ever get is warmed-up revivals of *Ghosts* or *The Seagull*. Yet when you think how much popular drama is still waiting to be explored (American comedies of the Twenties and Thirties for instance), you begin to wonder if most theatre directors ever get beyond reading Thursday's copy of the *Stage*.

I have so far, of course, been writing about the British theatre's neglect of the classics. But equally reprehensible is its failure to bring up the best of contemporary world drama. I was lunching last week with a Swedish broadcaster who wanted to know what I had thought of Per-Olav Enquist's *Night Of The Tribades*, a highly controversial play about Strindberg's sexism. I gently explained that I had read about it but hadn't seen it. 'But,' he said, 'it's been done in Germany and France and is shortly going to Broadway.' Politely, I explained that that didn't automatically mean we would see it in London. And when he asked if we saw much Swedish drama in London, I muttered something about having seen a play called *Seven Girls* at the Open Space a year or so back, and passed onto the next question.

Admittedly there are one or two hopeful signs around. The Mermaid is about to do a play by De Montherlant (produced in Paris ten years ago). Hampstead Theatre Club next week offers a play by a Brooklyn Franciscan, the Theatre at New End has a season of off-Broadway plays in progress. Zeffirelli is about to do a De Filippo comedy in the West End. But although that is welcome news, it still doesn't excuse the purblind parochialism of the British theatre over the last decade.

We still haven't seen, to take a sample list, Robert Wilson's astonishing peripatetic company, Eugenio Barba's Odin Theatre Group from Denmark, Goran Eriksson's *Parisian Life*, Roger Planchon's original plays, David Rabe's Vietnam trilogy, Peter Weiss's *Trotsky in Exile*. We may not be the sick man of Europe, but theatrically we are the slack men of Europe.

I am not, or course, arguing that anything foreign is automatically good: that is the snobbery of French flu. What I am saying is that we are increasingly cut off (particularly since the demise of Peter Daubeny) from world drama, and that there are movements going on in the modern theatre of which we are totally ignorant. They may be reprehensible. But we should at least know something about them. And while we have reason to be pleased with the stream of new writing talent we produce in this country, we have cause to be ashamed of our xenophobia, our insularity, our sheer ignorance.

If this applied only to the theatre, it would be bad enough. But I have an uneasy feeling that the theatre is in this respect, as in so much else, a microcosm of society at large. It is that illusory 'I'm all right, Jacques' attitude, coupled with a ferocious, current antagonism to the alien, that strikes me as the real English sickness.

Coriolanus

Royal Shakespeare Theatre: 21 October 1977

Terry Hands's production of *Coriolanus* at Stratford is staggeringly good. Played on a dark, cavernous stage over which two huge ribbed doors swing on hinges, it combines the imagistic power of Continental theatre with a very English respect for actors. True, first-night nerves caused some odd verbal slips but Hands's increasingly stylised approach to staging pays rich dividends.

The paradox of the production is that Alan Howard, one of our most likable actors, plays Coriolanus, Shakespeare's least-likable hero. But not since Olivier has anyone played the part with such complete understanding of his mental processes. From the opening scenes it is clear that in battle this man is a kind of god. And Hands emphasises the fact by, literally, elevating him. At Corioli he straddles the gap between Farrah's two huge doors like some avenging angel of death: and, as conquering hero, he is raised by the soldiers on staves like a secular idol.

Howard's interpretation thereafter is based on the impossibility of coming down to earth. Triumphant in war, he cannot ingratiate in peace. In the Senate he sullenly squats in his military jerkin like a hawk surrounded by doves. Suing for votes in the marketplace he asks the plebs for their 'voices' in a mocking sardonic singsong. And when banished, he greets Aufidius at Antium with the bright-eyed relish of a schoolboy meeting an erstwhile chum. Howard gives us not an arrogant patrician but a professional fighter with equal contempt for humbug politicians and private emotion.

What is particularly good about the production is the way emblematic imagery reinforces psychological points: thus Howard downstage reacts emotionally to the appearance of wife, mother and child outside Rome even though they enter directly behind him. And even though some of the detailed political arguments about the corn go for very little and some of the performances are a trifle strained (Graham Crowden's capering wild-eyed Menenius hardly seems like an apostle of moderation) the staging has the exciting simplicity of the TNP under Jean Vilar.

Spectacle is created with a very small cast (only seven citizens and six senators). But there are individually striking performances by Maxine Audley, caressing her son with voluptuous possessiveness as Volumnia, by Olivier Ford Davies and Tim Wylton as a pair of business-like tribunes, and by Julian Glover as a towering Aufidius, for once genuinely moved by Coriolanus's recantation. But the real surprise is that for once you come out fully understanding the hero rather than simply detesting him.

Hamlet

Paris: 23 December 1977

Paris Theatre is humming with activity this autumn. Moscow's Taganka Theatre on Saturday finishes a four-week season at the Palais de Chaillot. Three legendary French actresses – Renaud, Feuillère, Casarès – are all memorably on view. And next week Peter Brook's production of *Ubu Roi* opens at the Théâtre Bouffes du Nord. Once again London's claim to be the centre of world theatre begins to look decidedly shaky.

It is certainly a pity that we have missed out on the Taganka if only for the sake of their sensational production of *Hamlet*. The group itself was founded in 1964 by a young stage and screen actor, Yuri Lyubimov, as a retort to encrusted Soviet realism, and has since built up a repertoire that includes Gorky's *The Mother, Ten Days That Shook The World, Maiakovsky* (all on in Paris), and *Tartuffe*.

On the evidence of two productions it's hard to sum up their style except to say that it consists of bold, symbolic images that attempt to encapsulate the mood of a play and extravagantly expressive lighting. Eclecticism seems to be the name of their game, as you can deduce from the fact that the four portraits hanging on the wall of their own theatre are those of Brecht, Stanislavsky, Meyerhold and Vakhtangov.

Lyubimov's production of *Hamlet* (the most physically exciting I've ever seen) shows them, I suspect, at their best. The dominant image is of a vast mobile curtain, woven out of wool, that either swivels round from a central point, advances menacingly forwards, or traverses the stage, driving the characters before it. It can be anything: a place to hide behind, a castle wall, a protective cover. But its real power is to remind you that Elsinore is a police state and that walls have holes as well as ears.

Coldly described, it may sound like a directorial gimmick but the curtain's suggestive quality can perhaps be gauged from one particular scene: that in which Claudius and Polonius spy on Hamlet and Ophelia. Throughout the dialogue we are conscious of white-knuckled hands visible through the curtain. Hamlet and Ophelia, as they talk, then sink into the curtain so that it becomes like a swing or hammock and evokes happy days forever gone. Detecting the eavesdroppers, Hamlet then starts to beat them with his sword. Swinging round with enormous speed (the effect is of a cinematic cut) the curtain then shows us the humiliated Claudius and Polonius as they are attacked. And at the end of the scene the angry Claudius swings the curtain round with one hand and, as he does so, sweeps poor Ophelia with it into a grave at the foot of the stage. Thus the dramatic point of the scene is perfectly contained in the startling visual image.

I have some doubts about Lyubimov's other key metaphor which is, in fact, that of the ever-open grave at the front of the stage. It can be momentarily effective as when Claudius and Gertrude, discussing Elsinore's troubles, seem, literally, on the verge of walking into it. And it gives *Hamlet* himself a constant opportunity to caress discarded skulls and run his fingers through the mounds of earth on either side of it. But it is sufficiently obvious Hamlet is a play about death without our having to be incessantly reminded of the fact.

That aside, Lyubimov's staging of the play is brilliant, making rich use of strong, simple images. Along the bleached, back wall of the rough half-timbered set, for instance, stands a row of heavy swords. One assumes they are for the duel scene. But no.

At the moment when Laertes arrives back in Elsinore at the head of a rioting army (usually suggested in English productions by four or five extras poking their heads around the castle door, rhubarbing the while) the vast curtain sweeps across the stage knocking the swords clangorously over. Without a single extra being seen, one has a sense of incipient chaos and dissolution.

Time and again in fact, Lyubimov notches up intelligent points. Hamlet (Vladimir Vyssotsky: stocky, muscular, and impassioned) and Claudius, for instance, being played as roughly the same age, adding to the sense of sexual jealousy. Rosencrantz and Guildenstern being automatically frisked on arrival at Elsinore. The Players interpreted as strolling buskers led by a Ron Moody-style barnstormer in a top hat and accompanied by a café-orchestra. The panic after the play-scene itself with everyone running down a corridor, formed by the diagonally-placed curtain, and stumbling over things. The ghastly difficulty of killing Polonius as he reels around behind the huge curtain.

The grilles of underground light giving a focus to particular characters.

Scene after scene is dazzlingly alive. And even if one misses something of the play's political background (Fortinbras is gone entirely) one has an unforgettable impression of a death-fixated hero adrift in a Kafkaesque state where there is a spy behind every wall. This is a great production that, like the Kozintsev film, makes you realise the Russians have an understanding of *Hamlet* that often transcends our own.

1978

A cheering year for several reasons. One was the opening, in London, of a borough arts centre devoted to artistic excellence and literate internationalism: the Riverside Studios in Hammersmith. Under Peter Gill's direction it got off to a cracking start with his own productions of The Cherry Orchard *and* The Changeling. *It also offered some notable imports including the Japanese* Directions To Servants, *the Catalan* Mori El Merma, *McCowen doing* St Mark's Gospel *and William Gaskill's production of* The Ragged Trousered Philanthropists. *Further proof, if it were needed, of the shift of interest away from the West End.*

But it was also a varied and hopeful year for new writing. There was Hare's Plenty *and Bond's* The Woman *both at a revivified National Theatre; Stoppard's* Night And Day *at the Phoenix and* Every Good Boy Deserves Favour, *briefly at the Royal Festival Hall; Bond's* The Bundle, *Flannery's* Savage Amusement, *Barker's* The Hang Of The Gaol *at the Warehouse; and Nigel Williams's* Class Enemy, *Snoo Wilson's* The Glad Hand *and Alan Brown's* Wheelchair Willie *at the Royal Court. Admittedly Pinter's* Betrayal *disappointed on its first showing; but new British drama looked a lot healthier than the impoverished cinema and the sickly novel. Indeed I was increasingly struck by the feeling that the theatre was setting the pace for rival media: even when a play was imported from TV, as in the case of Brian Clark's* Whose Life Is It Anyway, *it was notable that it caused far more noise and discussion than when originally seen on the box.*

I still felt, partly through travelling abroad more widely, that our theatre was cut off from foreign influences. The Riverside did its bit. Oleg Tabakov directed The Government Inspector *in Sheffield. Simone Benmussa came over from Paris to do* The Singular Life Of Albert Nobbs *at Hampstead's New End.*

But one sorely missed the annual influx of shows provided by the old Peter Daubeny World Theatre Seasons. That said, it was still a year of enormous achievement: one in which, as I wrote at the time, the British theatre was out of its sickbed and capering nimbly up and down the wards.

St Mark's Gospel

Riverside Studios: 9 January 1978

Down in the smoky suburb of Hammersmith, the Riverside Studios offered a rare treat: Alec McCowen narrating St Mark's Gospel. Sporting a red open-necked shirt, fawn trousers and suede shoes and patrolling the vast spaces of a pinewood stage, McCowen related the familiar story with all the precision, irony, intelligence and faintly controlled anger that characterises all his work. It was not only a remarkable feat of memory: it was also a superb piece of acting.

McCowen prefaced his narration by reminding us that this gospel was supposedly related to Mark by Jesus's disciple, Peter; and he achieved the difficult task of transmitting it to us as if it was a story we were hearing for the first time. He expounded the parables with finicky clarity as if trying to unravel their precise meaning. He let out an astonished laugh at the way, in Capernaum, they uncovered the roof to let down the sick of the palsy. He imitated the noise of the Gaderene swine (a kind of Pshew) rushing to destruction. And, before the feeding of the multitude with loaves and fishes, he conveyed the whispered panic of the disciples hissing into Jesus's ear, 'This is a desert place,' as if to say, 'Now look what you've done.'

In short this was a performance (lasting nearly two hours with a brief interval) devoid of rhetoric and strong on humour. But if I had to single out its chief quality it would be McCowen's unerring insistence on the complex humanity of Christ. He allowed Him to show a testy impatience towards the Pharisees with their trick questions about what a man should do with an unwanted wife and even towards the disciples there was sometimes a weary resignation: having once done the miracle with the loaves and fishes, a sigh entered His voice as second time round He asked 'How many loaves have ye?'

Agnostics, atheists and believers can, in fact, all get pleasure out of this remarkable performance (to be repeated over the next three Sundays). Free from the reverend boom that often overtakes actors when they get a Bible in their hands, it handled the language of the King

James version with surgical care, abundant wit and springy intelligence.

Plenty

Lyttelton: 14 April 1978

David Hare's *Plenty* at the Lyttelton extends and enlarges themes he dealt with in his indelible TV film, *Licking Hitler*. That, set in a wartime propaganda unit was about 'the deeply corrosive national habit of lying'. *Plenty,* which has the glittering edge of a Toledo blade, shows how an ingrained wartime deceit helps to ruin the life of an individual woman; and by a superb irony she only starts to tell the truth at the moment of the Suez crisis, when England is engaged in its biggest post-war lie.

The structure of the play is complex and cinematic. It starts in 1962 with a taut, strained Englishwoman, Susan Traherne, handing over her Knightsbridge home to her friend, Alice. It then flashes back to her wartime work with SOE in France in 1943 and shows how she has been taught to camouflage emotion under a mask of impassivity. We then follow her jagged, neurotic, uncertain course through the post-war English world. She does a humdrum job in a shipping office, works for the Festival of Britain, tells professional lies for an advertising agency, marries a decent career diplomat. Gradually the bland mask of English, hypocrisy proves too much for her and she breaks wildly out, insulting a Foreign Office-chief at the time of Suez and having hysterics in Carlton Gardens. She destroys her own life and that of her husband and we last see her, in a flashback to the French high summer of 1944, crying: 'There will be days and days like this.'

Sincerity, said Somerset Maugham, is like an iron girder in a house of cards; and that basically is Mr Hare's theme. English society, he maintains, is fuelled by hypocrisy, unruffled charm and infuriating serenity: break through that and you threaten to bring the cards tumbling down. But without dissenting from his conclusion I'm not sure that he dramatically clinches his case. I feel that his heroine, Susan, has a driven duality, an incipient madness that would make her an anxious misfit in most societies. From the moment when, in the midst of a field in France she impulsively sobs into the bosom of a parachuted agent, you feel she has an unquenchable emotion. If she'd settled in Kentucky rather than Knightsbridge she would, I suspect, have gone the same way.

But for all that the play combines a marvellous thematic consistency with the shock-cuts of cinema. Susan lies to her future husband about her job in the shipping office just as much as a smooth FO official (dwarfed by a huge painting showing Britannia Colonorum Mater) lies to her with the practised edge of diplomacy. But while keeping the theme going from scene to scene, Mr Hare uses the stage with remarkable freedom, cutting, say, from a Brussels embassy to a Pimlico basement in a matter of moments. He constantly uses the dislocatory, jolting techniques of modern drama without dwindling into fragmentary bittiness.

If Mr Hare's central idea holds the play together, so too does his style which has a distinctive bilious wit. He can sum someone up in a phrase ('He was rather slow-moving and egg-stained, if you know what I mean') or he can launch into an entirely accurate parody of a BBC Third Programme announcer, circa 1947, introducing a short talk in a series on 'Musicians and Disease'. Just occasionally his period references to the one-o-one club or Bovril barrage balloons have the self-conscious air of someone who has been doing his homework in that Pelican book on *The Age of Austerity*. But scenes like the disastrous Knightsbridge dinner party where a testy FO boss puts down a couple of Burmese visitors with a silky nastiness show his sour comic sense at its best.

Blending private hells with a panoramic vista, I admit it is the kind of play I instinctively warm to. And Hare's own production takes the Lyttelton stage with commanding fluency. Kate Nelligan is also ideal casting as Susan. She has the capacity to suggest emotion welling up under a stoic surface. She also can combine a waspish irony (extending the vowel sounds mercilessly when she tells the British ambassador in Brussels that her late husband, Tony, was a doctor) with a raging self-disgust. It is a powerful performance and she is well partnered by Stephen Moore as her kindly diplomat husband whose throttled anger is all the more terrifying for being reined in. Julie Covington as her chum, Alice, a louche female Horatio, is less supplied with good lines but meticulously suggests the passage from basement-artist to above-ground do-gooder, and Basil Henson as the FO chief is the very embodiment of that cool, cufflinked English politesse that for Mr Hare, just as much as for the late Terence Rattigan, is both the national heritage and the national disease.

Henry VI

Aldwych: 17 April 1978

'We are amazed.' On Saturday some one thousand of us sat in the Aldwych Theatre from 10.30 am till 11.00 pm (with breaks for lunch and dinner) watching the gradual unfolding of the Royal Shakespeare Company's *Henry VI* trilogy. It was, in almost every sense, a staggering experience; and as one stumbled into the night air after this orgy of deceit, declamation and decapitation (Shakespearean moral: if you want to get ahead, get a head) one felt one had encountered, if not a masterpiece, then certainly a more vital and enthralling Shakespearean work than *Romeo And Juliet* or *As You Like It*.

'Not as good as *The Wars Of The Roses*,' a colleague emphatically said of Terry Hands's production half-way through the afternoon. But the judgment was both premature and irrelevant. The Hall-Barton *Wars Of The Roses* was a severely edited and partially rewritten account of the plays.

Hands's production, however, uses the full text and this has several advantages. It highlights the difference of theme and texture between the three plays. But it also brings out the young Shakespeare's continuing fascination not just with *rex* but with *res publica*. Part Two, in particular, seems to me a hitherto unreclaimed masterwork, giving one as comprehensive a vision of England as you find in *Henry IV*.

What Harold Wilson would doubtless call the governance of the land is, in fact, the abiding theme of these plays. How do you achieve stability when the nobles are all determined to, in the Duchess of Gloucester's ringing phrase, 'reach at the glorious gold' and when the commoners ape the anarchy of those higher up the ladder?

But on the private level, one other theme bursts out of these plays when you see them as a group: Shakespeare's preoccupation with the tragedy of fathers and sons. Henry is awed by the shadow cast by his father, Henry V; Talbot cradles his dead son in his arms; and, in the most heart-stirring scene of all, we see a son who has killed his father and a father who has killed his son.

If the plays gain by being seen collectively, so too do Terry Hands's productions. He hasn't found an overpowering single image for the three plays, like the diamond-shaped council-table that dominated *The Wars Of The Roses*. But he has, both here and on the Continent, evolved a style that admirably suits chronicle plays. It's based on on a minimal setting, roving spotlights and a bold, frontal style of playing that gives the actors a chance to establish direct lines of contact with the audience.

But, looking at Saturday's productions singly, the one that has improved most since Stratford is undeniably Part One, the morning's war. This is dominated by Joan of Arc and the English national hero, Talbot. At Stratford the confusing scrappiness of the battles and the constant raising and lowering of a vast bridge led me to think of it as *A Bridge Too Often*. But now the pace has been tightened, it is always possible to tell who is tactically ahead and both Charlotte Cornwell's wild-eyed, occultist Joan and David Swift's ruggedly decent Talbot have acquired something of the strong, emblematic outline they lacked before: it's as if they're now playing France and England rather than Joan and Talbot.

For me, however, the afternoon's Part Two remains the peak experience. Played on a stretch of green turf, it begins with the crowd contained behind a rope at the back of the stage and the nobles assembling in columns. And what we see is the people bursting on to the green in the Jack Cade rebellion like spectators invading the pitch at Lords and the nobles reduced to savage animalistic clusters; it's a perfect metaphor for a play which is, literally, about breaking ranks.

'Is *this* the governance of Britain's isle?' Queen Margaret asks with incredulity and you feel throughout the play Shakespeare's sorrow for this bloodstained Eden. But what is fascinating is the way he shows disorder spreading through society from the top: the Duke of Suffolk has enclosed the Commons of Melford, a Cardinal's man has appropriated someone's wife and property and, given a weak king, the way is open to a populist demagogue like Cade.

Only with Part Three do I sense a touch of creative exhaustion on Hands's part. There are fine performances from Julian Glover as the massively manipulative Warwick, Emrys James as the power-hungry York, Anton Lesser as a ferret-eyed, hump-backed Richard, and Helen Mirren's Margaret has now acquired blood-lust as well as body-lust. But Alfred Lynch's Edward IV lacks the womanising rapacity that drives this character. The climax, though, is stunning: the murder of Henry VI in what looks like a million-watt grille that rises up from the ground, and the final image of the barbarous royals trying falteringly and ineffectually to dance. The land has been riven; the crown reduced to a pass-the-parcel plaything; and what we are left with is a fragmented dance to the broken music of time.

I have, however, left out of account the performance that underpins this trilogy and that, as the day progresses, grows into a thing of beauty and wonder: Alan Howard's Henry VI. At the start he is a bewildered child, head swivelling like a Wimbledon umpire's as he listens to the barrage of arguments: perhaps a little too self-consciously simple in moments like his frightened start at the prospect of marriage. But he makes something indubitably thrilling of the discovery that he can exercise adult sway and something infinitely moving of his realisation that justice and right are merely abstract concepts.

John Wain once wrote that 'deep down every man thinks of himself as a dispossessed king.' but Howard reverses this and presents us with a king who thinks of himself as a dispossessed human being. As sons and fathers lament at mutual slaughter, Howard sits sorrowing downstage, emotion passing over his face like clouds over the sun. And when he comes to the lines 'I was anointed King at nine months old, My Father and my Grandfather were Kings,' he makes this simple statement of fact an unbearable cry of pain. This is the supreme irony of Hands's breathtaking production. Everyone is reaching at the glorious gold: only he who has it knows its real worth.

Liberace

London Palladium: 18 April 1978

Liberace at the London Palladium represents the ultimate triumph of form over content, showmanship over substance. He appears in one outlandish creation after another. He invites the front row to caress his baubles. He shows us film of his Las Vegas home. He parades his stones to the orchestra ('See what you get if you practice'). We are invited to admire him for what he is rather than what he does; and though one cannot but marvel at his jovial, self-mocking exhibitionism, one eventually begins to long for more groceries and less wrapping.

Admittedly the show itself is a skilful Las Vegas confection. It includes a juggler who does clever things with three balls. There is a brassy 23-year-old warbler, Denise Clemente, who clearly wants to enter the Streisand glass-shattering stakes. And there is a puppeteer, Barclay Shaw, who endeared himself to the audience (though not to me) by cavorting through 'Send In The Clowns' with a two-foot-high doll. Packaged kitsch is the formula and it reaches its apotheosis with 'The Dancing Waters', multi-coloured fountains that sway and swirl in harmony with the maestro's rendition of Strauss waltzes at the pianoforte.

It is impossible, of course, to send up Liberace himself: he is always there two paces ahead of you. Stripping off a black diamond mink laced with Austrian rhinestones, he cries: 'I get so horny when I do that.' And gazing wistfully at a couple of candelabra-studded concert grands he announces: 'There are only two of them in the world like that – and I've got both of them.'

But when it comes to tinkling the ivories one has to admit that what he does to Chopin is nobody's business (except possibly that of Chopin's lawyers) and that he doesn't so much caress the keyboard as launch an all-out assault on it. Only his rendering of 'Slaughter on Tenth Avenue' (along with his protégé, Vince Cardell) shows his blitzkrieg technique at its best. But, whatever one may say, his fans clearly adore him and in an age of mini-personalities he certainly takes the stage by storm rather than default.

The Taming Of The Shrew

Royal Shakespeare Theatre: 5 May 1978

A surly yobbo starts a row with an usherette in the front stalls. 'I'm not having any bloody woman telling me what to do,' he cries. He then scrambles drunkenly on to the Stratford stage, pulling down bannisters and toppling pillars like some berserk Samson. Lights explode; the stage fills with harassed backstage staff; and gullible patrons start making for the exit to call the police.

This stunning *coup de théâtre* kicks off Michael Bogdanov's production of *The Taming Of The Shrew* at Stratford-upon-Avon. But although it proves an ingenious way to pluck Christopher Sly (in the person of Jonathan Pryce) from the audience on to the stage, it also proves a hard act to follow. After all, if you start your production with what looks like the climactic scene from *A Night At The Opera*, you are in danger of making the delivery of the published text seem curiously redundant.

But the real dilemma at the heart of this modern dress production is that Bogdanov, like any intelligent man, clearly finds *The Shrew* a barbaric and disgusting play. Instead of softening its harsh edges like most recent directors, he has chosen to emphasise its moral and physical ugliness.

Chris Dyer's set, an elaborate structure of rusting iron arches, suggests a combination of the west wing at San Quentin and Paddington Station. Moreover, Jonathan Pryce, graduating from Sly to Petruchio, transforms him into a manic chauvinist pig.

'He kills her in her own humour,' one character observes of Kate's taming; but in this production the punishment seems insanely disproportionate to the offence. Paola Dionisotti's Kate emerges in the early scenes as a hot tempered, strong chinned minor Magnani. But when we see Pryce's Petruchio pinioning her wrists, hurling her to the ground, looking at his watch while wooing her and discharging his bombast through that curious scrannel-pipe voice we begin to wonder at such frenzy. And when he turns up for the wedding in a Tartan cap and filthy trousers we laugh not at his eccentricity but shudder at his thuggery.

In emphasising the play's cruelty, Mr Bogdanov underlines what is already in italics. And, for myself, I find the sheer brutality almost unbearable. Only in the final scene, set around the green baize table in a haze of cigar smoke, does Bogdanov's approach start to pay handsome dividends.

Dionisotti delivers Kate's speech of submission with a tart, stabbing irony while Pryce shame-facedly grinds his cigar butt and runs his fingers through his hair. Confronted with the logic of his own actions, he quails; and when she ventures to kiss his shoe, he instantly withdraws his foot. It is the best interpretation of this scene I remember; but one has to wade through a lot of wife-beating to get to it.

I also find much of the comic business with which Bogdanov decorates the play unfunny because it seems applied rather than organic. Some of the gags work, like Paul Brooke's admirable Baptista, enthroned behind a gilt, serpentine desk, totting up on an adding machine the competitive claims of Bianca's suitors. But no amount of oompah-pah town bands, flashlight wedding photographs and jokes with umbrellas can disguise the fact that Bogdanov, to his credit, has no temperamental affinity with the play.

I did not greatly enjoy the evening. But both Pryce and Dionisotti carry out the chosen interpretation with skill and there is good support from David Suchet as a baggy trousered Grumio and Ian Charleson as a pert, velveteen Tranio.

There is, however, a larger question at stake than the merits or otherwise of this particular production. It is whether there is any reason to revive a play that seems totally offensive to our age and our society. My own feeling is that it should be put back firmly and squarely on the shelf.

Love's Labour's Lost

Royal Shakespeare Theatre: 14 August 1978

I suspect John Barton's favourite season is the period when summer glides into autumn. In his beautiful production of *Love's Labour's Lost* at the Royal Shakespeare Theatre in Stratford-upon-Avon the leaves are just beginning to fall from the Ralph Koltai trees, there is a slight nip in the air and the evening shadows lengthen on the grass. And that idea of seasonal transition reflects Barton's vision of the play: as a corrective comedy about four young men whose lives are likewise at a turning-point.

The usual tendency is to treat the play as a high-spirited verbal romp upon which death dramatically intrudes. But Barton is much more interested in the idea of intellectual arrogance and posturing romanticism being brought down to earth. Michael Pennington's Berowne, dressed in the monkish habit of a penitent, urges his fellow-courtiers who have all withdrawn from the world to study: 'Let us once lose our oaths to find ourselves'; but Barton reminds us oaths must be kept, vows respected.

As a result, the ending of the play takes on an unusual poignancy. There is a chilling moment during the village pageant of the Nine Worthies when Berowne cruelly seizes a flag borne by Don Armado and careers around the stage with it only to find Rosaline desperately trying to wrest it off him. Thus when Rosaline later condemns Berowne to visit the 'speechless sick' and 'enforce the pained impotent to smile' she is making the punishment fit the crime. Jane Lapotaire delivers these rebukes to Berowne with gravity and weight; and the ending of the play becomes for once not a conventional dying fall but a real punishment of intellectual pride.

Within that moral framework, however, Barton still finds a lot of social accuracy and genuine fun. His productions have an almost novelistic detail: here, for instance, we are reminded that the Princess of France is of royal stock and that her ladies are expected to shine her shoes and impress pearl ornaments on her dizzy coiffure. And that attention to detail is carried over into the language. With its high-flying satire on Euphuistic conceits, this play is nothing if not verbally complicated. But I think it is indicative of the way modern RSC productions make us *listen* that the biggest laugh of the evening comes when the curate, Sir Nathaniel, is paying homage to the pedantic Holofernes and dubs him 'learned without opinion'. Any *Love's Labour's* that can raise the roof on that has clearly got its audience by the ears.

As always at Stratford, the company also seems to grow with the season. Michael Pennington's Berowne may not have the sheer verbal bravura of Ian Richardson's a few years back but it's a highly intelligent study of a man hooked on the rhetoric of love. Richard Griffiths's King of Navarre, portly and flustered, and Carmen Du Sautoy's Princess of France, a natural head-girl in granny-specs, also give you the feeling they are made for each other. And there is excellent work from Michael Hordern who turns Don Armado into a dotty Quixote full of cavernous sighs, from Paul Brooke as a slightly Celtic Holofernes (a reference to Shakespeare's grammar-school teacher, Thomas Jenkins?) skipping with ecstasy at the sight of verses and from David Suchet as a myopic curate who during the village pageant goes down with his hobby-horse like a Captain with his sinking ship.

Inadmissible Evidence

Royal Court: 13 September 1978

Judged by slide-rule methods of dramatic criticism, John Osborne's *Inadmissible Evidence* has plenty of flaws: it's static, a bit unwieldy in places and doesn't allow much breathing-space to the subsidiary characters. But so much for the slide-rule. All I can say is that seeing the play again at the Court for the first time in fourteen years, I found it an overwhelming experience in which the sense of private pain, paranoia and anguish is deeply moving.

The first key difference one notices after fourteen years is that it now seems an almost totally non-naturalistic play. True, it covers the last hours in the life of a solicitor whose business is collapsing by the minute and who is deserted by his clients, his secretary, his assistant, his telephonist, his family, his mistress. But Osborne's production is at pains to emphasise the dream-like nature of it all. One actress plays three separate clients in whom the hero, Bill Maitland, sees only an extension of his own breakdown. The lights are gradually lowered as the clients talk, giving an impression of the darkness inside Maitland's skull. And Nicol Williamson's own delivery has become much more Beckettian, full of sharp, angular phrases rather than rolling rhetorical periods.

The play does so many things so well. It gives one of the best-documented accounts of paranoia I know: witness Maitland's obsessive conviction that all over London taxi-drivers with For Hire signs showing are passing him by and that at parties people are ganging up with his wife against him. It also demolishes the old idea that tragedy is something that happens only to the elevated: Maitland is 'irredeemably mediocre' yet the intensity of his downfall is nonetheless great. It also conveys memorably the fact that Maitland's disease is a helpless longing for all the things from which his own nature excludes him: love, charity, forgiveness, effortless style.

Williamson's performance is also quite astonishing. From the first moments in the dock he is an amalgam of wheedling ingratiation, hypochondria (worrying about glands like 'broken marbles'), sneering defiance. And throughout, much like Beckett's Krapp, he seems to be possessed by some memory of lost happiness as he confronts desertion, betrayal and loss. Knocking over glasses of water, reaching nervously for non-ringing phones and staring at people as if they are figures in a dream ('Who *are* you?' he asks of a homosexual client he half recognises) he gives us a marvellous manifestation of physical breakdown.

And there is fine support from Deborah Norton as his wounded secretary, Clive Swift as his conventional assistant and Julie Peasgood as his dumbly helpless daughter. I would nit-pick at one or two details of direction (surely in a play rooted in a Sixties world of Aldermaston and CND, it is wrong for Maitland to pick up a copy of today's *Guardian*). But the play remains a piece of emotional drama of frightening, skull-battering power.

Betrayal

Lyttelton: 16 November 1978

Themes, say some critics, don't matter: what counts is the skill a dramatist brings to his chosen subject. Well the petit-point school of reviewing should have a field-night with Harold Pinter's *Betrayal* at the Lyttelton since it is full of technical resource. What distresses me is the pitifully thin strip of human experience it explores and its obsession with the tiny ripples on the stagnant pond of bourgeois-affluent life.

Its title announces its theme: the perilously loose hold we have on the lives and affections of those to whom we lay claim. Starting in 1977 with a desolate pub encounter between Jerry and Emma, quondam lovers, it tracks slowly backwards to the beginning of their affaire in 1968, marking up the intervening betrayals.

Jerry has clearly betrayed his best friend, Robert, who is Emma's husband. Robert and Emma have, more equivocally, betrayed Jerry since they have discussed the affaire in the privacy of the marital boudoir. Robert has also betrayed Emma with a variety of lovers. Meanwhile Harold Pinter has betrayed his immense talent by serving up this kind of high-class soap-opera (laced with suitable cultural brand-names like Venice, Torcello, and Yeats) instead of a real play.

I speak harshly because I am one of his admirers; in works like *The Homecoming*, *Old Times*, and *No Man's Land* he has wittily explored the racking tenacity of desire, the hazy subjectivity of memory, the use of language to disguise, instead of reveal, true feeling. But here, since nothing much seems at stake, he dwindles into mannerism.

Robert, the tromped and tromping husband, harps repeatedly on the game of squash until the very word 'squash' evokes all kinds of things: male clannishness, brute competitiveness, intimations of homosexuality. Pinter bludgeons the word into suggestiveness. In the past, however, he has been able to lend single words a magic power (such as Gielgud's reference to his mother's marvellous buns in *No Man's Land*) by the sheer inappositeness of the context.

What also dismays me about *Betrayal* is the way Pinter treats the banalities of triangular drama as if they were huge discoveries. Emma, in the course of her seven-year affaire with Robert conducted in a furnished flat in Kilburn, has borne a child called Ned. She swears it is her husband's and was conceived during her lover's absence in America. But neither man can be absolutely sure who the father is. Pinter plays amusingly with their doubts but one is less struck by the general truth (men are slaves to women's word about paternity) than by the situation's derivation from matinée comedies by John Van Druten and the like.

If the play has any interest, it is purely in the technical finesse with which Pinter starts in the present and progresses backwards. Not only do physical objects mark the various stages of the central affaire (thus a worn Venetian tablecloth in the Kilburn flat is later seen in its pristine glory at the moment of unwrapping) but we also piece together information about the characters as in one of those jigsaw-puzzles where you start with a nose or a mouth and work outwards.

But although the play would make for interesting discussion at drama-faculty level, it offers thin pleasure for the night-out playgoer. Peter Hall's production is timed as carefully as a soufflé at a cookery course, John Bury's design is as exact with Kilburn flatlets as with Soho-Italian restaurants, and Michael Gambon's Jerry (all phlegm and banked-down passion), Penelope Wilton's Emma (constantly on the verge of tears), and Daniel Massey's Robert (hinting neatly at the character's hollowness) play every nuance for all it's worth.

A Night Out With Dame Edna

Piccadilly: 15 December 1978

Any man who can keep an audience laughing for three hours on end has to be some kind of genius. But just what is it that makes Barry Humphries, whose *Night Out With Dame Edna* has just opened tumultuously at the Piccadilly, so funny? Partly it's a talent for grotesquerie, outrage and lewdness. But I think it's even more to do with a born satirist's combination of physical disgust and x-ray eye for detail. Mr Humpries is a kind of vaudeville Swift.

You can see this in the way Edna Everage has changed from the garrulous suburban ratbag of *Just A Show* ten years ago, to a privileged superstar who turns her venom on her adopted country. On this occasion she bounds on in squash gear and frizzy hair do ('I look like a Caucasian Cleo Laine') and proceeds to lay about her. Members of the audience, always female, are ruthlessly interrogated about their clothes, address and personal habits. Telly celebrities like Parkinson ('He looks as if he's stepped off a knitting pattern') are lightly trounced. And at one point Edna emits periodic cries of pain due to 'women's trouble' which turns out to be the aftermath of having her ears pierced.

So far this is all good, dirty fun. But Edna comes into her own when she describes a visit to Bruce and Joyleen, her son and daughter-in-law, who seem to have moved from Ruislip to fashionable Clapham. Humphries pins down far more ruthlessly than any modern novelist I know a certain life style which he dubs 'Contemporary South London Provincial-French-farmhouse.' He gets the detail dead right (Joyleen found her front door on an old rubbish tip). But he adds to that his own surrealist whims such as the notion of dinner mats imprinted with Edvard Munch's 'The Scream' and an extraordinary disgust with the intimate details of womanhood that reminds me of E.A. Whitehead's *The Foursome*. It will take a long time to get over the bathroom image of an old jar of Vaseline empty except for fragments of Joyleen's hair, ominously curled.

This is what makes Humphries so complex and interesting: powerful sensuous revulsion blends with an eye like a laser beam. My only cavil is that his anti-Australianism sometimes seems a bit reflex: jokes about the native film industry are a touch perverse when from over here it looks enviably flourishing. But Humphries makes up for this with a use of language that is sharp and cutting as a flint. In the first half we meet Les Patterson, the sodden Australian cultural attaché who winningly announces 'I'm as full as a fairy's phone book tonight', and the old veteran Sandy reminiscing beyond the grave about a chum who had his third coronary bang in the middle of '*The Duchess of Duke Street* and the avocado shag-pile carpet'. Humphries, one of the few entertainers equally funny in or out of skirts, can make words sing and soar.

But what is good is that he has genuinely progressed over the last decade. He has an alien's eye for the absurdities of the bourgeois life style (at times he sounds like a manic estate agent). He has transformed his disgust into a comic weapon. And by the end, with the mass gladioli-waving, he creates a sense of orgiastic delight which today only Ken Dodd can rival. As he tells us at curtain fall, 'a kind of intercourse has taken place tonight.' That presumably is why the audience was, in Aussie parlance, rooted to the spot.

The Hang Of The Gaol

Warehouse: 18 December 1978

A just anger, said Ben Jonson, puts life into a man. So sometimes does an unjust anger, as is proved by Howard Barker's new play, *The Hang Of The Gaol*, at the Warehouse. It is full of fierce, often overwrought attacks on *Guardian* liberalism, E. M. Forsterish humanism, social democracy and the malfunctioning of 'a sick and bandaged race.' But although I would challenge a lot of the play's ideas, I was constantly exhilarated by its adrenalin, its energy, its tart and venomous language.

The play takes the form of a political whodunnit. Middenhurst Gaol, run on optimistically utopian lines by a governor from the colonies, is mysteriously burned down. A government inquiry team, headed by an ex-Communist civil servant desperate for a knighthood, arrives to investigate and uncovers a crazy system and total confusion about the nature of crime and punishment.

The liberal governor defines punishment as 'sin masquerading as holiness'. The chief screw, who gives classes in language and philosophy based on *Principia Ethica*, is a traditional sadist. And Turk, a Barnadine-like prisoner who claims to be the arsonist, advocates a clear-cut division between the punisher and the punished. As he says: 'There is no reconciling E. M. Forster with a kick in the testicles.'

In the end the revelation of whodunnit matters less than the fevered, hectic debate about the English attitude to crime and about the combination of remedial platitudes with vengeful practice. But although Mr Barker's characters say some sane and sensible things

('The idea has got around that criminals are rebels – in fact they are the lowest form of speculator'), the play eventually lurches into frantic improbability.

I couldn't believe in a young civil servant so appalled by the revelation of his own inquisitorial skill that he took to running about the moors like Poor Tom. I couldn't believe in a Home Secretary who openly blackmails the senior civil servant into falsifying his report. I particularly couldn't believe in the idea of prisons burning down without the media doing their own investigative sleuthing.

Mr Barker may retort that he is not writing a realistic play. But unless there is a background of credibility I find it hard to swallow his conclusions about the corruption of civil servants, the manipulation of democracy by venal politicians and the idea (which I sniff in the air) that it would be better if we dropped our sham-liberalism and acknowledged our lust for revenge on society's enemies. Reading *Howard's End* to recidivists may have its comic side: it is none-the-less preferable to the rope, the chair and the birch.

But, for all that, I cannot stress too strongly that I found the play prickly, stimulating and written in a startlingly livid, vivid prose. And Bill Alexander, who has had a fine year as a director, gets good performances from Nicholas Le Prevost and Nigel Terry and a monumental one from Fulton MacKay as the elderly civil servant hungering for justice, sex, retirement and a knighthood roughly in that order. And never shall I forget the look of animal anger that comes into his eyes when he hears a colleague ordering the *Guardian* with his hotel breakfast. 'Know your enemies,' he thunders like Jove himself. 'Read the *Express*.' What a slogan for Victor Matthews!

1979

A turning-point year: one in which Mrs Thatcher was elected Prime Minister. I recall going on television and asking Norman St John-Stevas, then Arts Minister, what effect Mrs Thatcher's ideological opposition to the subsidy principle would have on Britain's artistic life. I was assured, in good faith, that the arts would be exempt from cuts, and I suspect the phrase 'No candle-end economies' was used. But Mr St John Stevas was eventually removed, the cuts came, and a gulf opened up between the artistic community on the one hand and government and the Arts Council on the other.

*But , passing briefly over the good things that happened in 1979 (*Amadeus, Bent, Joking Apart, Undiscovered Country, The Suicide, Chicago*), what was our theatre like in the pre-Thatcher period and how had it changed? On the plus side, a generation of writers had emerged who had shown they were ready to grapple with social and political issues. They had also written some damned good plays:* Comedians, Plenty, Destiny, Brassneck, City Sugar, Fanshen, Knuckle, Claw. *It was also cheering that, even though they had failed to capture the commercial heartland of the West End, they had increasingly taken over the commanding heights of the subsidised sector. The seventies also witnessed two contradictory phenomena. One was the opening of big public spaces like the National Theatre and the Royal Exchange which overcame initial criticism and were soon affectionately regarded by audiences. Alongside that, the clandestine intimacy of playhouses like the Other Place, the Warehouse, the Theatre Upstairs, the Open Space and the countless regional studio theatres appealed to a generation that shunned mass emotion and hungered for an almost elitist privacy.*

But there were worrying signs at the end of the decade: more and more dramatists drifting towards television; visits from foreign companies turning into occasional treats rather than regular events; rather less in the way of audacious experiment. From the mid-fifties to the late Seventies the British theatre had been endlessly productive and continually expanding. By the end of the decade, it began to look as if the party might not last that much longer.

Bob Hope

London Palladium: 28 March 1979

Very often when great showbiz veterans appear at the Palladium one is applauding the myth rather than the man, the legend rather than the reality. But with 75-year-old Bob Hope there is no call to eke out his imperfections with our thoughts. From the moment he strolls on to a storm of welcoming applause ('I'd rather have that for my finish') he is in total command of the house, himself and our attention.

Of course, he harps occasionally on his age. Once a year, he confides, he gets his whole body sand-blasted. And his make-up man, he admits, is very expensive – 'he has to come in from Lourdes.'

At one point he even does a debonair soft-shoe while seated on a pink chaise-longue. But on the whole his jokes cover the familiar, well-loved terrain. The state of London ('I haven't seen so much garbage since I played vaudeville'). Sex ('The guy next door had a pacemaker put in – every time he makes love my garage doors fly open'). The problems of modern man (He remarks of the Oregon rape case that 'It's like getting a driver's licence and not being able to drive the car').

My radical chums are, I notice, a bit sniffy about him, regarding him as the symbol of middle America. Well, Lenny Bruce he ain't. But I still unashamedly admire his dapper, quilted ease, his ability to time a joke like a perfectly-aimed dart and, above all, his capacity to capitalise even on the lines that fall flat. As one no-no hits the deck he informs us that: 'You're hearing some jokes tonight that will never be heard again,' and as a couple of American references pass us by he strolls casually over to the wings and advises an imaginary figure to delete them for tomorrow.

Hope offers us a rare pleasure: supreme expertise. One notices the way he gets the band to strike up 'Buttons and Bows' and then artfully delays the intro a dozen times to put across one more zinger. He has comic technique in spades and when he disappears a whole tradition of relaxed, unforced vaudeville will have gone with him.

Meanwhile he is with us for a week in the flesh and one can only urge those who relish the art of one man chatting intimately to 2,000 people in public to go and observe while the memory is still green.

Bent

Royal Court: 4 May 1979

With the exception of *Edward II* and *A Patriot For Me*, I can think of few good plays about homosexuality. But *Bent* by the Philadelphia-born Martin Sherman at the Royal Court, strikes me as a work of considerable dignity and passion. It opens one's eyes to a little-known aspect of the subject (the Nazi persecution of homosexuals) and it does so without indulging in special pleading or gratuitous sensationalism.

At first it looks as if we might be in for an evening of self-conscious jokiness with three guys indulging in gay banter the morning after the night before. But there are faint hints (the Klimt posters, the Art Nouveau door) that all is not quite what it seems. It soon transpires (and one cannot conceal this) that we are in Berlin in 1934 at the time of the Night of the Long Knives and of a series of Hitlerian purges directed against homosexuals. In the first half we see Max, a fugitive gay, and his lover Rudy, catapulted through a series of adventures before being despatched to Dachau. The second half is largely an extended duologue in the concentration camp between Max and a fellow-inmate, Horst, as they heave rocks from one side of the stage to the other.

As a play it works on several levels. At its most basic it is a fascinating historical document (actually I could have done with more information about Nazi repressiveness which even extended to the punishment of homosexual fantasies). But the play is also a parable about the way selfish survival gives way, under pressure, to a hunger for inter-dependence. Realising that 'it's better to be a Jew than a queer' in Nazi eyes, Max outwits the system, disowns his lover and joins those with a yellow star on their uniform. And what Mr Sherman shows, with moving simplicity, is Max gradually taking the homosexual Horst into his protective custody and succumbing to the imperatives of love.

Some scenes work better than others: in particular a splendid park-bench encounter between Max and a 'fluffy' uncle in the first part, an extraordinary piece of verbal love-making in the second part in which Max and Horst achieve orgasm purely through the exchange of erotic language. These are the highlights and they more than make up for cliché episodes like the inevitable Berlin cabaret-scene with a black-suspendered guy on a swing and the belated appearance of a mono-syllabically brutal Nazi captain surrounded by the aura of a 1948 British movie.

But I have no wish to carp at a play that deals in historical persecution without an ounce of facile self-pity. And Robert Chetwyn's very adroit production contains two complementary central performances. Ian McKellen's Max moves impeccably from a slight spoilt-boy swishiness to a survival-at-all-costs cunning (as he flashes sly ingratiating smiles at the Dachau guards) to an absorption in physical toil: even the way McKellen holds the never-ending rocks between the lower part of his thumbs suggests someone trying to minimise pain.

It is a bodily articulate performance well-matched by Tom Bell's gaunt, haggard stoicism as the much flintier Horst. There is also a neat vignette by Richard Gale as Max's dapper, voracious uncle. Admittedly the play makes its demands on its audience; but I admire the way it puts the case for the declaration of one's sexual feelings in such a sane, measured and eloquent way.

The Lady From The Sea

Roundhouse: 17 May 1979

Michael Elliott's season of plays from the Royal Exchange about obsessive protagonists who are prey to supernatural solicitings comes to a climax with Ibsen's *The Lady From The Sea*. Though I have some doubts about the extension of the play's watery images into the set itself, it makes a totally absorbing evening and boasts a performance by Vanessa Redgrave for which one has to dust down all the critical superlatives.

The play itself is a fantastically complex blend of the real and the symbolic. Dramatically it hinges on the choice confronting its strange, amphibious heroine, Ellida Wangel. On the physical plane, she is the second wife of a small-town doctor who has virtually bought her as part of a business deal. On the spiritual plane, she belongs to a long-vanished sailor with whom she once entered into a pagan compact in which they threw their rings into the sea. When the sailor arrives to reclaim her, she is torn not only between two men but between two worlds and it is only when her doctor-husband gives her the freedom to choose that she is able to accept her land-locked marriage.

As Agate used to say, Ibsen's plays exist on a ground-storey of realism and upper-storey of symbolism and the wonder of this play is that it moves so freely between the two floors. But by staging it in a set that looks a little like the lagoon scene from *Peter Pan*, I feel that Mr Elliott makes the play's symbolic content almost too explicit. The actors have to negotiate rocks and landing stages all surrounded by pools of stagnant water. But this strikes me as about as helpful as staging *Brand* in real snow. It physically slows down the action and it undercuts Ellida's feeling of physical confinement and her almost mystical hunger for the sea.

But, on the psychological level, the production works superbly. 'Can any actress,' C. E. Montague once asked, 'overcome the difficulty of making the Nereid or Venus Anadyomene side of Ellida fully effective?' Vanessa Redgrave triumphantly can. It is not only her startling first entry in bathing towel and dampened hair but her rapt inquisitiveness at all the marine references. 'You loved the sea?' she inquires of the youthful, consumptive Lynstrand, and you see her instantly fixing him with her glittering eye. She also conveys superbly the feeling of a woman who is trapped and confined on land. She constantly points an admonitory finger at her confining husband and, when he embraces her, her body goes rigid and her fists instinctively clench. It is an enthralling study of a woman who is literally out of her element.

It is also backed up by some very good supporting performances. Graham Crowden as her doctor-husband is no dry old stick but a mature man desperate to reclaim his wife and enjoy his full conjugal rights. Terence Stamp in his two brief scenes as the mysterious Stranger also supplies a gauntly handsome presence and a sense of magnetic attraction. As Bolette, the daughter who also longs to escape from small-town Norway, Sherrie Hewson cannot quite efface memories of Miss Redgrave herself in the part 18 years ago but John Franklyn-Robbins as the middle-aged tutor, who offers her marriage as her only chance of flight, has just the right desiccated desperation.

In short, an extraordinary evening. One that in seeking to free Ibsen from the supposed shackles of realism actually, in my view, limits him by over-insistence on the play's hydrophilic content. But one that also charts exactly Ellida's psychological crisis and that leaves you grateful for Miss Redgrave's overdue return to the London stage.

A Penchant For Foreign Affairs

23 June 1979

I can't believe it. Having whined incessantly about the dearth of foreign drama on the British stage, I find in successive weeks two plays as good as Nikolai Erdman's *The Suicide* at the Other Place and Arthur Schnitzler's *Undiscovered Country* at the Olivier. Can it really be true that theatrical import controls are over and that we shall no longer have to content ourselves with prettified versions of *The Seagull* and ritual revivals of *Hedda Gabler* for actresses stranded in time between Shakespeare's comic heroines and Lady Bracknell?

Already, of course, the reaction against this has started. The estimable Milton Shulman was complaining the other day about the Royal Shakespeare Company's preoccupation with things Russian in their Aldwych repertoire. By that I take it he means the production of four plays by Gorky and one by Bulgakov spread over a period of eight years. That hardly constitutes a cultural takeover; and anyway from each of the plays concerned one learns something new about Russian life. Until one has seen *The White Guard*, for instance, it is hard to appreciate the fascination the discredited values of the *ancien régime* had for Soviet audiences and for Stalin himself.

Well-written foreign drama has, in fact, a double claim on our attention: theatrical and anthropological. It can also focus attention on our own deficiencies. Watching *The Suicide* (1928) and *Undiscovered Country* (1911), I was reminded of how much easier it seems for foreign dramatists to write plays that combine a sharp, close-up portrait of an individual with a broad impression of the society that surrounds them. Twentieth-century English drama is rooted in the family. But the moment you step outside these shores you find a whole range of plays that assume it is the relation between man and the spirit of his times that it is the business of drama to explore.

Take *The Suicide*. The play was banned by the Soviet censors precisely because it asserted the claims of the individual against society. 'Our achievements, our success, our reconstructed society, you can keep it,' cries the mutinous unemployed Podsekalnikov at the end. 'I want a quiet life and a living wage.' But in order to make this point Edrman also sketches in, with the beautiful deftness of a cartoon Gogol, the bloodsuckers and parasites prepared to batten off the hero's suicidal tendencies. All claim Podsekalnikov's disposition towards death as their own: the poet believes he will sacrifice himself for ideals, the butcher for liver sausage, the beautiful temptress for romantic love. The characters are all motivated by one idea. But, taken together, they build up a rich portrait of the discontents seething under the surface of Soviet society in the late 1920s.

There is, I suspect, something deeply un-English about all this. We believe it is the business of a dramatist to give a similar degree of psychological truthfulness to all his characters. What Erdman does, quite nakedly, is to create a three-dimensional hero full of quirks and oddities (like his passion for the tuba or his sudden impulse in the middle of a party to phone the Kremlin) and then surround him with a set of semi-Expressionist figures governed by a dominant impulse. If an English dramatist did this, we would hoot and bleat about the danger of mixing styles. Erdman pulls it off triumphantly because he wants to put in a plea for the individual while satirising Soviet bureaucracy and revealing the widespread discontent with the system.

On the surface, Schnitzler's *Undiscovered Country* could hardly be more different. It occupies a bourgeois world of tennis-parties' idle chatter, casual affaires. Yet I find a very similar process at work to the one I noticed in *The Suicide*: a close-up of an individual, a long-shot of a society. Not for nothing was Sigmund Freud an admirer of Schnitzler. In the portrait of the hero, Hofreiter, you find a classic study of a manic-depressive who goes on insane jags at the prospect of seduction, company, music, escape to the Dolomites. At the same time he is obsessed by his wife's young lovers, real and imagined. There is a wonderful throwaway moment in the current production when John Wood's daemonic Hofreiter, having just killed a young lieutenant in a duel, mutters, 'I know what youth is and I can't shoot them all.' It creates a stunning image of a man who finds anyone under 25 a threat to his own virility.

Yet at the same time Schnitzler offers a panorama of a society rotten with leisure. One act takes place entirely in the lobby of a mountain hotel and through it passes a wonderful gallery of types: an affected Buddhist youth who absorbs the contents of letters by pressing them to his brow, a vague Viennese drifter who, urged to describe a play he has seen, comes up with 'Lot of Frenchmen in wigs . . . it rhymed', an obstreperous guest who turns his mislaid laundry into a public scandal. There is, of course, nothing like a hotel lobby (witness Coward's *Semi-Monde*) for creating an impression of expensive indolence. But Schnitzler goes far beyond that to describe a world of exterior respectability and inward panic. What Freud codified, he theatrically demonstrated; and the virtue of his play is that personal disaster blows apart a world of social gaiety.

Plays like *The Suicide* and *Undiscovered Country* do, of course, require the resources of a large company and I find it encouraging that some of our younger writers (notably David Hare in *Plenty*) are using the freedom of the big ensembles to create just the kind of plays I am advocating: ones that show man as both a private and a public being. We live in rooms; but we work and play in a wider context. For that reason any drama that deals only with the private self strikes me as being as artificial as one that takes place solely on public platforms. I hunger for plays about man in his totality. Consequently I very much hope *The Suicide* will be seen beyond Stratford and *Undiscovered Country* will be a bourne from which many travellers (even fellow-travellers) profitably return.

The Sickness Of London Theatreland

12 October 1979

The West End theatre, we were told yesterday, is fighting back. After the worst slump in Shaftesbury Avenue for many a long season, the Society of West End Theatre held a press conference. Its purpose? To launch a campaign to try to woo customers back into the theatre. A

Development Officer is to be appointed; an attempt is to be made to clean up the West End (the streets, not the shows); and with the help of the British Tourist Authority and the London Tourist Board, hard-sell techniques are to be employed.

Well, it's a start. It at least acknowledges that no one owes the theatre a living and that tubs have to be thumped, drums beaten and trumpets blown if the customers are going to be seduced back in. But it also begs the fundamental question as to what the West End theatre is actually for. Is it simply a shop-window for goods purchased from the subsidised sector and Broadway? Or is it a place of creative management that offers something, in the way of outsize personality or showbiz razzle-dazzle, that the subsidised theatre cannot match? At the moment, it is almost entirely a showcase; and therein, I believe, lies much of its problem.

A glance down the Entertainments Guide will confirm how much the West End is currently living off other people's initiative. The following shows were all seen first on subsidised stages: *Oliver* (a co-production between a West End management and the Leicester Haymarket), *Bodies, Chicago, The Rocky Horror Show, Bent, Songbook, Outside Edge, Whose Life Is It Anyway? The Family Reunion, Once A Catholic, Dirty Linen*. Meanwhile the following half-dozen all had their provenance on Broadway: *Hello Dolly, Deathtrap, The Crucifer Of Blood, The King and I, For Coloured Girls* and *Annie*.

That leaves a pathetically small number of shows of any artistic interest whatsoever initiated by a West End management. In fact, I can find only three: *Evita, Night And Day* (a debt of honour repaid by Tom Stoppard to Michael Codron for putting on one of his early plays), and *Can You Hear Me At The Back?* (a package deal put together by a group of people who had worked together in television).

My point is that West End managers and producers have dwindled into little more than talent-scouts: the equivalent of those figures one sees at bush-league soccer games on rainswept afternoons in the murkier shires. And the ultimate absurdity in this buy-it-up-and-whip-it-in philosophy, I should have thought, was Brian Rix nipping up to the Edinburgh Festival and plonking four of its Fringe productions into the gargantuan and in my view hugely unsuitable Shaftesbury Theatre.

I am not, obviously, against the transfer of subsidised productions – as long as they are of high quality. It is a good rather than a bad thing that a production as excellent as Michael Elliott's of *The Family Reunion* is seen by a wider audience than would have been possible either at Manchester's Royal Exchange or London's Roundhouse. Nor am I against Broadway imports – though I could wish it extended to some of the better American plays as well as the blockbuster musicals. What does worry me is that so many producers (give or take a Codron or a Gale) are apparently content to regard themselves as parasitic middlemen whose job it is to bring the latest production from Frinton-on-Sea into the West End rather than as impresarios whose function it is to bring writer, actors and director together in fruitful collusion.

Believe me, I don't underestimate the difficulties they face. One is that they are competing for talent with companies like the National and the RSC, which are both run by men who combine academic intelligence with showbiz flair: Peter Hall, for instance, well understands the box-office value of a star and always makes sure his company has a liberal supply of them. West End producers also have no cushion against spiralling costs. Ten years ago, John Gale has wistfully pointed out, a simple, small-cast play like *The Secretary Bird* was capitalised at £8,000. Today the figure would be upwards of £40,000. He also pointed out, in a Roundtable discussion last year, that the chances of getting your money back on a straight play in under 16 weeks are small. For a musical, of course, it takes even longer.

I see the problems. But what are the solutions? One would be for the theatre to be either exempt from VAT or be taxed below the standard rate (as happens in six major European countries). Another (and one perfectly consistent with the mixed-economy philosophy) would be to jack up the amount of money available to the Theatre Investment Fund. This was set up in 1976 with a quarter-of-a-million pounds of capital (£150,000 from private individuals and corporations, £100,000 from the Arts Council) to aid independent managers and to provide up to 10 per cent of the capital on a commercial show. The fund is still afloat. But it would be worth doubling the amount of money available if only to enable managements to risk something more than one-man shows in which a star's change from a mauve into a bottle-green jacket is regarded as a piece of profligate extravagance.

But even if the Theatre Investment Fund were boosted, even if the West End were as pleasant to walk in as the streets of any other West or East European capital city, even if we set up something like the TKTS scheme of New York whereby unsold tickets were available on the day at a reduced price, all this would not answer the central problem; finding the shows the customers wanted to see. By that I don't just mean letting a subsidised theatre take a risk with a play and then quickly capitalising on it. I mean creating something afresh that actually justifies splashing out a tenner or more for a couple of tickets.

Easy to say, but where do you find the product? I am not a producer but, even as an aisle-squatter, I would have thought one might find something by approaching established writers who have hitherto done nothing for the stage (which is precisely what Jonathan Lynn of the Cambridge Theatre Company did with Frederic Raphael): by ransacking English and American theatre of the past fifty years to discover some of the good plays still unrevived; by investing in a single creative talent and giving it its head (could not an English choreographer create a dance-spectacular on the lines of Bob Fosse's *Dancin'*?; by commissioning some of the more talented composers in the pop field; by countering the sanitised blandness of telly Light Entertainment with a true variety bill that blended comedians, acrobats, ballet-dancers and Shakespeare.

Of course, other things would help: a greater openness from West End managers about the true state of the theatre (in New York *Variety* publishes receipts and attendance figures every week); a greater use of theatre buildings in the day-time through the provision of food, drink and occasional entertainment (as has been tried at the Albery); more display advertising.

But my point is that the salvation of the West End theatre does not lie in simply grabbing whatever is available from other quarters. It also lies in recapturing a touch of the sheer showbiz instinct and creative flair that for the moment seems to have passed from the so-called tycoons to the ex-University graduates who run our subsidised theatres up and down the land.

Hamlet

Denmark: 1 September 1979

Hamlet at Kronborg Castle at Elsinore: it sounds like the perfect conjunction of play and setting. A bit like seeing *Macbeth* staged at Dunsinane or *Romeo And* Juliet in a square in Verona. Indeed I set out last weekend to see Derek Jacobi and the Old Vic company doing the world's most famous play in its natural setting in the spirit of a pilgrim going to Lourdes. I let slip this comparison to a member of the company, Terence Wilton, who said it was all too apt – 'In both places you get immersed in water.'

For the blunt fact is that, from the moment I arrived in Elsinore to the moment I left nearly two days later, it scarcely stopped raining. And when it wasn't raining the wind was so fierce one felt like a feather being blown about hither and yon: at one point I found myself walking backwards, like the man in the Spike Milligan song, not for Christmas but because it was the only way to withstand the wind's relentless buffeting.

But I did get to see *Hamlet* at Elsinore. Miraculously the rain stopped five minutes before the play was due to start in the courtyard of Kronborg Castle last Saturday night. Prudent members of the audience wrapped themselves in the large protective polythene sheets (rather like giant contraceptives) with which one is issued as one goes in. A chap sitting next to me generously passed the contents of a hip flask along the row. And when Hamlet's chum entered and was asked 'What, is Horatio there?' and replied (wrapping his cloak about him) 'A piece of him,' what Mr Francis Howerd would call a titter ran through the audience.

But the first half of the play worked extremely well. It was fascinating to see it played on an open stage with the audience wrapped round the action in an arc of 290 degrees, with a gallery and a curtained chamber at the back of the stage and with occasional entrances through auditorium tunnels. I felt it enabled Mr Jacobi, in particular, to make unusually close contact with the audience. When he came to the stage's edge and asked 'Who calls me villain, breaks my pate across, Plucks off my beard and blows it in my face?' it was so direct I was worried lest an aggressive Dane might get up in the third row and say 'Well, actually, I do.'

It was only after the interval the trouble started. No sooner had Hamlet said 'To be or not to be' than the heavens opened. Having watched so many Test Matches on television this summer, I naturally expected the players to run for cover (there was, in fact, a very Old Trafford moment when the whole audience rose as one man and swathed itself in sheets, rugs and mackintoshes). But no: on they went with Mr Jacobi nearly slipping up on 'Get thee to a nunnery,' with Miss Jane Wymark's Ophelia bravely playing the mad scene barefoot wearing little but a night shift and with Miss Brenda Bruce's cold-ridden Gertrude sanely choosing a dry spot in which to die.

My admiration for the Old Vic company was, by the end of the evening, unbounded. But is there any real point in playing Hamlet at Elsinore in such conditions? Debate was joined in the lobby of the Marienlyst Hotel the following night with one of the actor's wives arguing that she found the conditions turned theatre once again into an event full of risk, danger and excitement with actors and audience sharing the same hardships. It was a good, Peter Brookish line of argument: he always says, for instance, that hard seats and a touch of discomfort make you concentrate more, not less.

Against that, I would suggest that if theatre becomes a battle against the elements it turns art into a qualifying round for the Duke of Edinburgh's Award Scheme rather than something you can rationally appreciate. It also makes an audience fearfully self-conscious. So much so that Julian Glover told me that on wet nights he automatically cuts the lines when Claudius at prayer asks 'What if this cursed hand, Were thicker than itself with brother's blood, Is there not rain enough in the sweet heavens To wash it white as snow?' He knows it would get a roar of laughter but, as he says, Claudius at that point is not desperately seeking belly-laughs.

My only constructive suggestion is that the authorities at Elsinore should do what the Test panjandrums are doing this year and cover the wicket at all times. Instead of asking actors to play on bare boards where you can see their faces reflected in the puddles, why not cover the stage with matting so that they are at least secure underfoot? They could then do the duel scene at the end without fear they are inadvertently going to spear the wrong person, so that Hamlet and Laertes mysteriously outlive a peppered Osric and Horatio.

But although my trip to Elsinore (arranged by *Kaleidoscope* who will, I trust, pay for my funeral expenses when I expire of pneumonia) was not without hazard, it was in many ways instructive. It reminded me that the open-air Elizabethan audiences must often have watched plays under pretty foul conditions. It convinced me yet again that the wrap-around, open-stage with the audience close in (how else would I have detected Hamlet's final, fond glance at Horatio as of a man certain death is near?) is more exciting than the proscenium arch. It also persuaded me that the Old Vic may survive as an institution if it can engender the kind of spirit it did amongst this waterlogged company.

Richard III

Olivier: 5 October 1979

'In one who *dares* so much there is little indeed to blame.' Thus Hazlitt on Kean's *Richard III*; and that sums up my feelings about John Wood's magnetic performance at the Olivier Theatre. In the first half, when he is still Gloucester, there is a superfluity of detail. But in the second, when he is enthroned in livid scarlet, he ushers us into the presence of great acting.

I think his performance would prosper if it sometimes met weightier opposition. Christopher Morahan's production is serviceable (sometimes more) and Ralph Koltai has designed a sculpted, lead-textured set irrigated by channels and ducts that drip blood. But in the first half Wood seems to be bustling amongst blankly interchangeable characters in sub-fusc costumes that merge into the set. Once Wood is pitted against a real performance, particularly in one amazing scene with Anna Carteret's sorrowing Queen Elizabeth, his own gains immeasurably in stature.

Even the first half, however, is filled with telling detail. The arrival of Wood's Richard is announced by a monster, misshapen shadow looming upon a wall. In the wooing scene with Lady Anne he is so intrigued by the blood on her husband's corpse he dips his finger in it to lick it. And there is a chilling moment when he advances upon one of the young princes with arachnoid intensity as if about to devour him. Irony, energy, intelligence are all there. But in conveying a feverish haste for the throne he sometimes swallows the verse instead of working through it.

But in the second half both the production and performance take off into another dimension. As monarch, Wood enters as a scarlet, limping cacodemon. Assuming the throne he sits on it with a sigh as if kingship were an anti-climax to its achievement. But he tells us more and more about the character. Preparing for battle with toy ships and men on a map of England and rejected by his mother with a curse, he regresses into thumbing-sucking infantility and even curls up in a foetal position. And soliciting Queen Elizabeth for her daughter's hand (a scene full of evil eroticism) he is almost morally appalled by the ease with which she surrenders.

The essence of this Richard is, in fact, a perverse moral awareness: not pitying himself he asks no pity from others. And Richard's pre-Bosworth speech of self-analysis is spoken by Wood in a hectic whisper like a man who is simultaneously patient and psychiatrist. This, and much more, adds up to great acting. And I just wish that this performance had more animated surroundings to bounce off (contrast the particularity of every character in Hands's *Henry VI* trilogy).

There is nothing wrong with Yvonne Bryceland's chalk-faced, cursing Queen Margaret, with Jeremy Kemp's solidly devious Buckingham or with John Normington's clear-spoken Clarence. But there is nothing startlingly memorable about them either. And though the production has several imaginative touches (like the on-stage beheadings or the smithy-like clangour that surrounds the final battle) it is too often content simply to clear the stage to allow room for this Richard.

But for all one's reservations, Wood's performance will rightly draw the town and, once again as Hazlitt said of Kean, it has the singular advantage of being entirely the actor's own and of owing astonishing little to the Olivier tradition of the Satanic joker.

Amadeus

Olivier: 5 November 1979

In a year of mini-dramas Peter Shaffer's *Amadeus* at the Olivier certainly stands out as a big, bold, extravagantly theatrical play. As in *The Royal Hunt Of The Sun* and *Equus*, two male protagonists are locked in combat. One represents will and energy: the other is allegedly touched with the divine. Once again, the latter is finally crushed – though, even when death is imminent, his presence is clearly immanent.

For half its length I certainly found the play exquisitely gripping. It takes the form of a deathbed confession by Antonio Salieri, court composer to Austrian Emperor Joseph II. Salieri at the end of his life is thought to have poisoned his envied rival, Mozart, and the play transports us back to the Viennese court at the end of the 18th century to examine the truth of the claim. Salieri is seen as the man of worth and virtue who prays to God ('A candle-smoked god in a mouldering robe with dealer's eyes') for the divine inspiration that never comes: Mozart, on the other hand, is a vulgar, tactless, peacock libertine who is, unfairly, kissed with genius.

So far, so good. Shaffer sketches in the formal court background with exemplary precision (helped by John Bury's set with its translucent floor-cloth and its false proscenium arch adorned with fluting cupids) and he gets some excellent human comedy out of Salieri's teeth-gritting hostility towards his supremely gifted rival. One very funny scene shows Salieri playing a short, formal salon tune to celebrate Mozart's arrival at court which the little monster brilliantly extends and stores away for use in one of his own operas.

My doubts concern the second half when Shaffer turns Salieri and Mozart into, respectively, god-destroyer and god. Salieri talks like a Marlovian hero who, having been denied divine inspiration, will destroy and vandalise the beauty around him. What we actually see him doing is committing a series of mean and petty acts (like failing to intercede with the Emperor to come and listen to a rehearsal of *The Marriage Of Figaro*). In fact his most macabre gesture (donning a black deathmask and a grey cloak to haunt Mozart while he composed his Requiem) is pure romantic invention, as Shaffer has more or less admitted: the historical evidence suggests the messenger was one Anton von Leitgeb working on behalf of a cracked Count who used to pass off work from professional composers as his own.

I don't object to dramatic licence. What does disturb me is that Shaffer starts out with recorded fact and then tries to jack up the drama into a metaphysical confrontation between Envious Mediocrity and Harassed God. The strain shows in the writing which, having been tight and precise, becomes extremely flatulent in the scene where Mozart confronts his tormentor. And why does one have to accept the equation between Mozart and God? Why cannot one see Mozart simply as an earthly genius who found (as Charlotte Haldane says in her biography) the Viennese atmosphere poisoned against him? Shaffer has lit upon a fascinating human drama but finally tried to wrench it to fit his recurrent theme of the destruction of divinity.

He has, however, written a wonderful part in Salieri which Paul Scofield plays to perfection. His cracked-bell voice slides effortlessly between private hatred and public ingratiation: his seamed, pouched features alternate between haggard distinction and slit-eyed envy; and his hands are forever stroking and caressing the air as if only the severest effort prevented him strangling Mozart. It is a stunning performance excellently complemented, in Peter Hall's spacious and elegant production, by Simon Callow's runtish, mercurial, extravagantly coiffured Mozart and admiringly supported by John Normington's starched-vowelled Emperor and by Felicity Kendal's impishly sexy Constanze. The presentation, in short, is immaculate. But having wisely decided that Salieri was a spiritual, rather than a literal poisoner, I just wish Shaffer had not tried to elevate the play into a majestic homily on the death of a god.

1980

I doubt if we used the phrase at the time, but 'event-theatre' was the keynote of the year: the transformation of each production into a super-special occasion. The RSC, able to afford only three new shows at the Aldwych, went for broke by staging The Greeks *and* Nicholas Nickleby. *The former was regarded by many people inside the organisation as John Barton's eccentric preoccupation: the latter as a big bid for a populist audience. Yet, paradoxically, it was the former which instantly captured the public's imagination: the latter only became a box-office hit after a trumpeting piece by Bernard Levin in* The Times *told people to go. I know which I think was the more daring and innovative.*

Two other productions also became 'events' in a rather more dubious sense. One was the Old Vic Macbeth, *which got lousy notices, was publicly disowned by the theatre's artistic director and attracted vast audiences of theatrical ambulance-chasers. The other was Howard Brenton's* The Romans In Britain *at the Olivier. I remember Peter Hall saying he was a bit nervous that the play would be attacked for adopting a pro-Irish, anti-British stance. What he couldn't have foreseen was that Mrs Mary Whitehouse would eventually launch a prosecution against the play's director, Michael Bogdanov, for procuring a homosexual act on stage. After three days, the case was dropped. The furore was absurd, though it did lead to the best picture caption of the year: 'Roman Attacks Druid', as a rapacious centurion simulated buggery of an ancient Brit.*

Elsewhere, it was a good year for classic revivals: Richard Eyre's Hamlet *with Jonathan Pryce at the Royal Court, Bill Bryden's* The Crucible *at the Cottesloe, Michael Blakemore's* The Wild Duck *at the Lyric Hammersmith, John Dexter's* Galileo *at the Olivier. New plays were a bit thinner on the ground: Frayn's* Make And Break, *Ron Hutchinson's* The Irish Play *and Paul Kember's* Not Quite Jerusalem *were the best of the bunch. On the musical front* Sweeney Todd *failed to pull in the customers at Drury Lane and* Barnado *at the Royalty turned out to be the first lyric show in history based on a hero who was tone-deaf. The general mood, however, was of crisis kept at bay.*

The Greeks

Aldwych: 4 February 1980

Like Max Bygraves, John Barton wants to tell us a story. That is the central, stirring impulse behind *The Greeks*: ten plays lasting a total of nine hours that unfolded before us at the Aldwych on Saturday. Holes can (and will) be picked in both the concept and the execution. But I can only report that when the whole project came to an end on Saturday I felt I had witnessed both a marvellous narrative and a healing myth: something that exposes the running sore of human conflict but that finally resolves it in a plea for balance, harmony and order.

Though the achievement of Barton and his translator, Kenneth

Cavander, is immense, let me however start with the flaws in the crystal. The ten plays (seven of them coming from Euripides) are divided up into three sections: The War, The Murders, The Gods. They begin with an outline of the central myths (such as the mating of Peleus with the sea-nymph, Thetis, to produce the turbulent Achilles), proceed to the sacrifice of Iphigenia at Aulis, take in the fall of Troy, the murder of Agamemnon, the retribution visited upon the vengeful Orestes and his sister, Electra, and end at Tauris (in the Caucasus) with the revelation that Iphigenia was miraculously and secretly saved by Artemis.

A great story. But the problem is that to achieve a consecutive narrative Barton has had to yoke together works of uneven dramatic quality. We kick off, for instance, with a Euripidean masterpiece, *Iphigenia In Aulis,* that both states the central theme of *The Greeks* (that the gods pull people in different directions but 'It is up to us to find some kind of balance') and skilfully interweaves several different tragedies: that of Iphigenia who comes expecting a wedding and finds it's going to be a sacrifice, that of Agamemnon torn, like the Biblical Abraham, between love and duty, and that of Clytemnestra (played by Janet Suzman on a beautifully mounting arc of lamentation) who sees her daughter wrenched from her grasp. Nothing in the whole cycle is more moving than the stoicism of Iphigenia: life, she says, is brief and brutish but we who live must give it a little meaning.

An overwhelming start. But because the Greek dramatist steered clear of the Homeric subject of the wrath of Achilles, Barton then has to supply us with his own 40-minute play showing us the quarrels in the Greek camp ten years into the siege of Troy. It's a perfectly competent bit of dramatised Homer (moving even in the scene between Oliver Ford-Davies's Priam and Mike Gwilym's Achilles who sit upon the ground in exhausted union and decide that mourning requires food and drink). But the point is it marks a descent from the peak of great drama to the plateau of good dramatisation. And the whole cycle has a sierra-like effect with works of different quality juxtaposed for the sake of the story.

My only other serious cavil is with some of the visual modernisation. John Napier's basic design works very well: a steeply raked, sun-baked bowl to which bits can be emblematically added (an over-turned shrine after the murders at Mycenae, papyrus weed and pyramids for *Helen*, set in Egypt). Some of the props also have a wonderful ambiguity: the most brilliant stroke is turning the bronze chariot in which Agamemnon returns home into an engine of war, a juggernaut pulled along by a stem made up of strapped-together sten-guns.

That works because it is a superb visual pun. But when the berserk Orestes and Electra turn into gun-toting, Baader-Meinhof terrorists, that seems to me wrong because limiting. Modern urban terrorists are motivated by a frenzied political animus: Orestes and Electra by a vengeful hatred of Helen, the source of all their misery. It also seems silly for Lynn Dearth's Electra to pop into blue jeans for a spot of hi-jacking.

But though in ten plays there are bound to be irritating details, I wholeheartedly applaud the central approach: the determination to render the plays in stark, simple language and to pick out and highlight key themes (the monstrous injustice done to women, the questioning attitude towards the gods and, above all, the constant tension between a horrendous awareness of life's cruelty and a stoic acceptance of misfortune).

What I particularly like about the language is that it is always specific and concrete. Take the scene, in *Andromache*, where the ancient Peleus is re-united with the sea-nymph Thetis. In the Penguin edition Thetis urges her husband to repair to a vaulted cave 'And wait until I come out of the sea with fifty dancing nymphs to escort you home.' In this version Thetis also urges him to retire to the cave – 'Do you remember? – Where you wooed me long ago. And where you made me happy. And we will dance the wedding dance. And I will turn myself Into a thousand creatures. Fishes, sea-beasts, serpents That roll and revel and wriggle And you shall be lord of them all.' The former (I guess) is literally accurate: the latter incorporates a sense of recollected happiness and sensual invitation.

I also find Barton's ironic attitude to the gods wholly acceptable: when, for instance, John Shrapnel's Apollo comes to earth to sort out the tangled mess of human affairs in *Orestes* he turns out to be a self-regarding riddler who allows himself a vain flick of his golden curls as he whisks Helen off to Zeus's mansion. A touch campy perhaps; but it underscores Euripides's own cynicism about divine behaviour (his Apollo justifies the Trojan war on the appalling grounds that it purged the earth of superfluous mortality) and makes the crucial point that whatever confusion and contradiction there is on earth is also amply reflected in the heavens.

In the third section of the evening, The Gods, there is in fact a growing vein of absurdist comedy. When we get to the Helen play we have Janet Suzman sun-bathing on a sacred tomb in a towel and telling us, rather like a female Frankie Howerd, 'This is Egypt – by the Nile.' Sacrilege? Too close to the Offenbach of *La Belle Hélène?* But the whole point of Euripides's play was that the Helen who went to Troy was a phantom devised by the goddess Hera to pay off an old score. The real Helen, all this while, was encamped by the Nile fending off Egyptian wooers. It is, in short, a spirited black comedy proving that the Trojan war was fought for a chimera and that 'as flies to wanton boys are we to the gods . . . they kill us for their sport'. One might argue that Barton's own comic touch is a little closer to 'Carry On' movies than Giradoux; but there is no question that he is enlarging on a vein of tongue-in-mask satire to be found in the original.

For all its occasional eccentricities, *The Greeks* however is certainly never dull. It also never seems irrelevant to our concerns and preoccupations. It may deal with a vanished world of interventionist gods and goddesses but it also constantly comes back to the central question of how we are to conduct our lives. 'No man that is human ever lives his life through without pain and sorrow,' says someone in the first play. But there is a bracing stoic rigour about the notion that somehow we have to survive. It is summed up in the final speech by Athene, beautifully delivered by Billie Whitelaw, that advocates reason and balance and that tells us 'You must find a way between freedom and compulsion. You must accept that order, harmony and meaning only come to men in fragments.' I find this advent of calm very moving.

Let me also mention in despatches the cast of 24 who work like Trojans (and Greeks) and not least Judy Buxton, Lynn Dearth, Tony Church and Celia Gregory. Nick Bicât's music also wrings endless variations on a single haunting theme scored for such instruments as bouzouki, oud and Chinese membrane flute. But the final credit obviously belongs to Barton: he has created not a flawless masterpiece but he has put together, very memorably, a rich bank of myth on which future directors of Greek drama, and playgoers too, will heavily draw. Primal fluting in white bed-sheets from now on is out.

Greek

Half Moon: 15 February 1980

Last year Frederic Raphael transposed the Oedipus story, none too plausibly, to southern Arizona. Now Steven Berkoff, in *Greek* at the Half Moon, has set it in a plague-ridden modern London. Like one of the characters, I felt verballed to death (people in Berkoff plays don't exchange dialogue: they swap monologues). But Mr B knows how to hold an audience with an image and by the end even offers us his own unusual gloss on a familiar tale.

The problem with the Raphael version was that you felt the characters would have taken preventive action because they knew the original story. There seems no danger of that here since Eddie, Mr Berkoff's hero, is a flash East End bruiser with, to put it mildly, a robust turn of phrase that owes little to Sophocles. Not untypically, he describes his gran as 'looking like Mussolini in drag' and characterises his dad's face as 'hanging there like a sagging, worn-out testicle'.

The language throughout is coarse, crude and almost pathologically sexual. But it does at least impose a stylised unreality on the proceedings so that you half accept Mr Berkoff's vision of a plague-pocked London (filled with East End Fascists, rampaging hooligans and commercialised masturbation) and even such oddities as anyone's failure to call the police when Eddie bumps off a surly café-owner.

The weakness of the play lies not in the updating of the legend. It has more to do with the limitations of Mr Berkoff's sensibility : he can express violence, rage, disgust and sexual energy. But when he tries to handle love and tenderness he goes all gooey and sentimental. Indeed feminists could have a field-day analysing one speech in which Eddie expresses his passion for his new-found wife and women in general. 'I love', he says, 'the walk across to put the kettle on in that lazy, familiar way.' (He presumably has his feet up on the kitchen table.) To me this vision of women simply as obliging consorts to macho heroes undermines Eddie's final unapologetic acceptance of incest. 'I want to crawl back inside mum' he defiantly cries, 'What's wrong with that?' What's wrong is that mother may not like it.

But even if I don't subscribe to the work's values, it has (almost literally) a grinding energy and Berkoff's staging is simple and effective: four white faced players around a kitchen table conjure up everything from mealtime rituals to airport babble. They also shine individually with Barry Philips all waistcoated, cock-strutting bounce as Eddie, Linda Marlowe's black-jacketed wife-mum at least making incest understandable, and Matthew Scurfield and Janet Amsden playing the presumed parents with a teeth-baring grotesquerie for which the word 'Dickensian' would be an understatement.

Nicholas Nickleby

Aldwych: 23 June 1980

Great love and labour has clearly gone into the Royal Shakespeare Company's eight-and-a-half hour version of *Nicholas Nickleby* at the

Aldwych. David Edgar's adaptation is true to Dickens's narrative; the staging by Trevor Nunn and John Caird is darkly impressive; and the cast of 45 offer some remarkable vignettes. Yet for all that I couldn't help wondering periodically if the whole thing wasn't a waste of the RSC's amazing resources.

There seem to me two possible arguments for staging Dickens. One is that his books are so inaccessible or unread that one needs to be reminded of his prodigious vitality. The other is that people are so steeped in his work (as in Victorian England or modern Russia) that they hunger to see it made flesh. Neither argument holds good for our society where Dickens is a revered cultural object who is even occasionally read.

The other fundamental problem is the difference between drama and fiction. Drama, because it takes place in a limited time-span, concentrates on essences: a novel, because it can be dropped and picked up at will, can afford multiplying sub-plots and narrative diversions. Here Edgar has faithfully preserved the rhythm of Dickens's novel (giving us not only Dotheboys Hall and the Crummles's touring company but also the rapacity of Sir Mulberry Hawk, the philanthropy of the Cheeryble Brothers, and the miserliness of Arthur Gride). The result is less drama than acted narrative. But would anyone seriously choose to digest the whole of Dickens's rich novel at two sittings? I found it rather like being force-fed on peacock.

But although I have grave doubts about the necessity of the enterprise (are there not large-cast plays more urgently in need of the RSC's attention?) I cannot deny that it is done with gusto and invention. The Aldwych itself has been transformed by the designers, John Napier and Dermot Hayes, with a runway projecting into the stalls, a catwalk ringing the front of the dress-circle and the stage itself occupied by two sloping bridges that meet in a central pillar. The wealth of railings, grilles, and ironmongery also suggests the harshness of 1830s' England through which Nicholas and his companion, Smike, wearily travel.

Not only is the setting good, but the production is very successful at achieving complex effects through simple means. The stage in which Nicholas and Squeers set off for Yorkshire is built up out of skips and tables placed on a central rostrum. The cabriolet from which Sir Mulberry Hawk is thrown is conjured up through a press of scrum-down bodies with a velvety black cloth suggesting a rearing horse. And, most effectively, the harsh and dismal London through which the villainous Ralph Nickleby finally flees is created by a knot of actors emitting 'a windy suspiration of forced breath' or simply standing in a fixed line with their backs turned towards him.

In fact, somewhat perversely, I enjoyed the sinister-sentimental Part Two much more than the ebullient Part One. This may be because, for the first part, I was cunningly placed in a seat from which I could never get a clear view of the stage. But I also think it is because the second part captures well that dark Kafkaesque feeling that, whichever way one turns, one meets new obstacles.

The obsessive pursuit of Kate Nickleby (played by Susan Littler with demure strength) by the daemonic Hawk has the quality of living nightmare. The idea of London as a place where hands may reach out from the dark is suggested by the way the lumbering Smike (a beautiful performance from David Threlfall, all splayed feet and gaping mouth) is suddenly seized by Wackford Squeers. And the Dickens of dank rooms and death-filled garrets is well embodied by this metallic set.

Most people, however, will enjoy Part One more if only because it has the famous set-pieces. But I found the opening scenes too choppy and fragmented to make much impact (the meeting of the United Metropolitan Improved Hot Muffin Company which in the original is a wonderful piece of social satire is here simply a noisy rough-house). Dotheboys Hall, despite Ben Kingsley's hymn-singing, one-eyed Squeers running up to beat Smike like an angry fast bowler, seemed to be populated by far-from-skeletal boys. Only when we got the Vincent Crummleses, staging a hilarious, happy-ending *Romeo And Juliet* with everyone stumbling over machetes and swords, did I feel I was really connecting with the production.

Admittedly the performances are uniformly impressive. In a vast cast one can only briefly commend Roger Rees as a splendidly violent, sudden, impulsive Nicholas, Edward Petherbridge (the most Dickensian of the lot) as a Newman Noggs full of grizzled, dithering, long-ankled goodness, Suzanne Bertish for a gash-mouthed Fanny Squeers and a fluting, tootin' Mrs Snevellici, Timothy Kightley as the overweening rate-collector Mr Lillyvick, Graham Crowden and Lila Kaye as the Crummleses, full of imperious tat, Bob Peck as a saturnine Mulberry Hawk, and John Woodvine as an economically driven Ralph Nickleby who arouses unexpected reserves of sympathy.

Acting, production and design are, in short, all very fine. But I still think the RSC has come up with a perverse and needless triumph: a great deal of skill and imagination has been expended on the creation of something that gains only marginally, if at all, from being seen rather than read. Undeniably, this *Nicholas Nickleby* has been done well. My question is: should it have been done at all?

A Short Sharp Shock!

Theatre Royal Stratford East: 26 June 1980

The first thing to say about the now notorious *A Short Sharp Shock!* at the Theatre Royal, Stratford East is that all the huffing and puffing about its presentation is quite ludicrous. Certainly it is opposed to Thatcherism. But since when was that a punishable offence? And even the presentation of the ghosts of Airey Neave and Louis Mountbatten is done, for the most part, with a strange, smoke-wreathed dignity. All the scare-mongering has done is to guarantee full houses for the run.

I only wish I could say that Howard Brenton and Tony Howard had written a good play. But in truth, they leave the present government unscathed because they offer images and rhetoric rather than fact and argument. Sue Blane's surrealist design sets the tone with the nozzle of a tank protruding onto a stage full of ripped, dilapidated walls, besmirched grass and stuffed animal-heads: a metaphor for a rent, declining, antiquated Britain which, the authors argue, has been pushed nearer to the brink by present Tory policies.

A tenable line of argument. But the writers blow their case by offering us cartoon excess rather than real substance. If, as they do, you show Keith Joseph as a raving maniac, Jim Prior as a Heathite traitor and comic conjuror and Lord Carrington as a pith-helmeted caricature from *Carry On Up The Khyber*, you neutralise them by turning them into stock figures of fun: it is much easier to laugh at their personalities than analyse their policies.

Just occasionally the jokes raise a snicker as when Willie Whitelaw bravely cries 'A leader's got to have something to lead – here I am'; but even that is much cosier than discussing, say, deteriorating prison-conditions or his policy on detention centres.

But the play's real weakness shows in its treatment of the Leaderene herself, played, I must say, with just the right frosty dignity by Gwen Taylor. On the one hand, she is portrayed as the embodiment of self-interest, economic callousness and small-mindedness ('Britain is my little shop,' she cries). But, on the other hand, there is a furtive regard for the woman who has put an end to 30 years of consensus-politics and who finally brings the Left's warring factions together in common cause. I get the impression the writers, like Ian Smith, truly regard her as the only man in British politics.

It still makes for a disappointing play: one that spends much of the evening setting fire to paper targets. Even Robert Walker's bizarre production with actresses playing Cabinet leaders, seems unusually halting and unsure. One or two images – like Maggie Thatcher in blue ballgown surrounded by Tory hitmen with bulging dinner jackets – leave their mark. But the evening as a whole offers caricature instead of satire, frenetic bark instead of real bite.

Sweeney Todd

Theatre Royal Drury Lane: 3 July 1980

Sweeney Todd is the reversal of everything we traditionally expect of a musical. It has a powerful and gripping story, hardly a single extractable tune, a fierce sense of social injustice. Yet after seeing it on Broadway 18 months ago and now at the Theatre Royal, Drury Lane, I would call it sensationally effective.

Indeed, burning a boat or two, I would say it is one of the two (*My Fair Lady* being the other) durable works of popular musical theatre written in my lifetime.

The achievement rests largely with Stephen Sondheim who has written the music and lyrics (though Christopher Bond deserves more credit than he has had for penning the source-play which transformed Sweeney from a mad barber into a figure seeking revenge on a whole society). But Sondheim's gift is for composing a haunting score that, to my ear, has echoes of Britten, Copeland and Stravinsky. At the same time he has, as in earlier works, used a strong emotional counterpoint so that the scenes of greatest potential horror are constantly offset by tenderness or gaiety.

Consider the moment in which Sweeney, returning to London after 15 years in an Australian hell-hole, discovers that his wife took poison after being raped by a judge and that his daughter is now a ward of the self-same villain. Handed his old razor-case, he vows a terrible revenge. You would expect that to be the cue for a particularly tormented lyric. In fact, it becomes a romantic ballad ('Rest now my friends') addressed to the glistening blades. Sondheim even intensifies the effect by having the pie-shop owner, Mrs Lovett, serenade Sweeney while he is absorbed in his cut-throats.

Time and again, Sondheim defies cliché expectation. Thus when Judge Turpin is finally lured into Sweeney's tonsorial parlour, the natural fear is that blood will be shed. But again Sondheim counterpoints the awaited horror by having the two men join forces in a rhapsody to 'Pretty Women' that has the pristine sweetness of a tune you expect to hear on a Victorian musical-box.

Even when Sweeney and Mrs Lovett decide to make meat-pies out of human flesh, the Brechtian moral that 'The history of the world, my sweet, is who gets eaten and who gets to eat' is put over in strict waltz-time. Only Sondheim, I suspect, could yoke together Strauss and cannibalism.

But although I think the work itself is a masterpiece, I have some cavils about the Drury Lane production. The general level of audibility is not as high as it was in New York. One or two performances (especially that of Sweeney's daughter, Johanna) are not up to snuff. I even, heretically, find that Harold Prince's production is too busy in the opening scenes, so that attention is drawn to the sweeping movements of huge iron gantries and bridges and away from what is being sung.

That still, fortunately, leaves plenty to admire. Eugene Lee's set, for example, is masterly : a complete Victorian foundry with a glass-roof that reflects different colours, rusty iron beams, platforms with decaying handrails. It is both a marvellous environment for the show and a statement about industrial exploitation (and a fig for my old friend, John Mortimer, who wrote about it the other day as if it were simply decorative chic).

The central performances are also strong and resilient even if they cannot entirely expunge memories of Len Cariou and Angela Lansbury on Broadway. Denis Quilley's Sweeney, with ashen face topped by sadistic grey curls, has just the right quality of monomaniac obsession. His eyes gleam with passion when he sights his hungry blades; his body becomes active with joy at the prospect of revenge; and, when his task is accomplished, he lays his razors to rest with infinite care and awaits his own death with open-armed readiness. It is a lovely piece of acting as well as being strongly sung.

Sheila Hancock's Mrs Lovett also leaps across the footlights. For my taste, she is a little too robustly comic instead of being a woman who stumbles naively and thoughtlessly into mayhem. But with her tufts of orange hair sticking out of her head like bull's horns and with her fiercely rouged cheeks, she offers an almost Dickensian image of raddled elderly desire. I was also much impressed with Andrew C. Wadsworth as the young romantic lead who was several cuts above his Broadway counterpart.

In the end Prince's production also achieves a fine momentum and one comes out of the theatre feeling one has seen a musical like no other: one in which a fierce rage against society is offset by music that throbs with a suppressed tenderness.

For some stomachs, the show may be strong meat. But for those who long for a musical that explores exciting new territory, it will be a must. Attend, as they sing in the show, the tale of Sweeney Todd.

'The Fringe, The Fringe Is To Blame'

Debate at the ICA: 8 July 1980

About a hundred and fifty people, most of them theatre workers, gathered at the Institute of Contemporary Arts in London on Sunday afternoon for a debate promisingly billed as 'The Fringe, The Fringe Is To Blame'.

It was sparked off by a trenchant *Observer* piece by Michael Coveney in which he suggested that the classic tradition in English drama was in danger of withering away because young directors preferred 'the safe and subsidised studio ghetto' to the challenge of large stages. John Ashford, ICA theatre director, had retaliated on BBC World Service that the Fringe had acknowledged the classics but that its real business was with the issues that affect society now.

I went along hoping for a vigorous re-match and some pointers as to current Fringe thinking: what I got was about as exciting as a minor bout in some provincial baths on a wet Tuesday.

Admittedly Coveney came out of his corner jabbing fiercely in all directions: he landed some neat punches on the soft underbelly of *Time Out*-ish theatre criticism (the kind of thing that begins 'As a Marxist gay, I find little that is relevant in *Much Ado About Nothing*'); on Fringe classic productions (Shared Experience's Cymbeline is like a one-man band doing Beethoven's Ninth) and on the twilight world of regional studio theatres ('a couple of loyalists going in to see this week's Howard Barker play while the main audience is pouring into *Private Lives*').

Enough there, I would have thought, to goad the audience into a rash, fierce blaze of riot. Instead, we get a lot of rambling self-justification, ritual attacks on the critics (we even had some clown from the People Show inaccurately claiming that the *Guardian* had sent its Motoring correspondent to review their work at the Royal Court) and a few bursts of tired venom against such Aunt Sallies as the Arts Council, the National and the RSC.

But even if it was an unfocused discussion it did at least suggest that the Fringe (an admittedly amorphous term that covers everything from the Aba Daba Music Hall to Eugene O'Neill at the Warehouse) has to decide what its role is in the 1980s. It was born out of the political optimism and creative buoyancy of the late 1960s when a lot of people really did believe that an alternative theatre could contribute to, and even help to mould, an alternative society. Economic recession, political disillusion and a growing awareness that it will take more to change Britain than performing a clown-show in Willesden High Street have put paid to that particular dream.

This is not to deny that the Fringe movement has been intensely valuable. It has thrown up such writers as David Hare, Howard Brenton, Stephen Poliakoff, Barrie Keeffe. It has given us such consistently reliable theatres as the Bush, the Half Moon, the Richmond Orange Tree, the Theatre at New End. It has even, though not without a good deal of nervous soul-searching, dipped a toe into the West End with *Accidental Death Of An Anarchist*, and proved that it can attract a whole new audience without contaminating its idealism.

But this touches on the real problem the Fringe faces. Is it to be a hermetically-sealed institution that preaches only to the liberal converted? Or is it to be a greedily ambitious, outward-looking movement that seeks to take over the commanding heights of the British theatre? Someone said on Sunday that it began as a 'cultural sideswipe at what was happening in the society 12 years ago'. But while that was perfectly legitimate then, I don't think one can go on forever luxuriating in the purity of impotence. The point of an opposition party is that it has to be ready someday to take over the government: I only wish I saw more signs of mainstream theatre scooping up Fringe talent, and of people on the Fringe, vehemently battering at the doors of the citadel. The curse of British life, in fact, is that any form of power is assumed to be a sell-out. Hence the persistence of terms like Establishment and anti-Establishment.

I only wish our theatre had something of the guiltless mobility of New York: when a show like Elizabeth Swados's *Runaways* or Lanford Wilson's *Talley's Folly* makes if from Off-Broadway to on Broadway people don't sit around examining their conscience but delight in the chance to catch a wider audience. But then, we in Britain believe that the fewer people see a particular work of art, the better it has to be.

Which is why, despite his sweeping condemnations, I take Coveney's side in the Fringe debate. For too long it has been an article of religious faith that it is automatically better to work in a small studio than on a main stage, that it is somehow reactionary to put on a classic, and that to get involved with either of the major national ensembles is to flirt with the devil. There is blame on both sides; and I wonder if our big institutions do all the talent-scouting they might.

But if our theatre is not to become a middle-aged monopoly, then our best young Fringe talents have to start bidding for the regional playhouses, clamouring to work on the big national stages and sacrificing some of their sectarian elitism. There is certainly a place for small, studio theatres : but if they continue to absorb the best talents of the idealistic young then, sure as eggs, the larger playhouses will either wither away entirely or fall into the hands of bland mediocrities.

Macbeth

Old Vic: 5 September 1980

With one flying, scarcely credible leap the Old Vic *Macbeth* takes us back about a hundred years to the days of barnstorming, actor-manager Shakespeare. This three-hour-plus production is filled with prolonged, Irvingesque blackouts between scenes, a supporting cast many of whom would qualify as walking shadows and a roaring boy performance by Peter O'Toole that is about as subtle as a battering-ram.

Not that the director of this shaming venture, Bryan Forbes, has been entirely idle. We, presumably, have him to thank for the three sexy Witches who, far from being wild and withered in their attire, look as if they shop at Fortnum and Mason's. To him also, I guess, belongs the credit for licensing such ham that the audience sniggers when Macbeth goes berserk at his own banquet and Lady M. announces: 'Think of this good peers but as a thing of custom.'

And who else to laud but the director for slowing down the whole rhythm of the play (one that cries to be done without interval); for failing to create any sense of evil, and for prefacing each scene, while a stool is added or subtracted to the set, with little bursts of Shakespeare Muzak.

And what of Mr O'Toole? Gaunt, lean, good-looking, he obviously brings a romantic presence to the part of Macbeth; but that is not enough. He delivers every line with a monotonous tenor bark as if addressing an audience of deaf Eskimos who have never heard of Shakespeare. He makes no distinction between passages of reflective soliloquy and those of obvious rhetoric like the 'renown and grace is dead' speech after the discovery of Duncan's corpse. And he misses any hint of irony, humour, or real thought. It was P.G. Wodehouse, who memorably said that that 'tomorrow and tomorrow' speech has got a lot of spin on it but, as delivered by Mr O'Toole, it is hit for six like a full toss. Every line is delivered as if it were the climax; and so you never for a second feel this Macbeth is descending into a hell of his own making.

For the rest there is a pretty, nondescript Lady Macbeth from Frances Tomelty, a bluff, noisy Banquo from Brian Blessed, and varying degrees of inadequacy from a supporting cast that even Wolfit might have found wanting. Two shining exceptions are David Sumner as a well-spoken Ross and Marjorie Bland as a genuinely-alarmed Lady Macduff. But the whole venture reeks of old-fashioned fit-up Shakespeare in which everyone stands back to let the star do his number. The trouble is Mr O'Toole's Macbeth is simply a dashing athlete who never persuaded me that he wanted to be king in the first place.

The Romans In Britain

Olivier: 17 October 1980

Howard Brenton's *The Romans In Britain* is an epic play with only one idea in its head: that the invasion of Celtic Britain by Romans and Saxons bred in our ancestors inextinguishable dreams of empire manifested again today in Northern Ireland. But there is such a vast disproportion between the extravagance of the form and the banality of the thesis that one is reminded of the dotty Bavarian monarch who built a complex subterranean machine simply in order to have his dinner-table rise up through the floor.

I am sorry to write thus of Mr Brenton since I admire his talent: he is an imagistic thinker with a gift for muscular language. But this play, which moves between the Caesarean invasion of 54 BC, the Saxon raids of AD 515 and the British presence in Northern Ireland in 1980, displays those abilities fitfully. Mostly we are treated to sensational excess (lots of blood and buggery) combined with woolly thinking. What, for instance, does it prove about empire to have Julius Caesar and his soldiers disappear stage right and reappear a few minutes later stage left as camouflage-clad British soldiers on a night raid in Derry? Does Mr Brenton seriously believe that a simple theatrical trick like that does even a particle of justice to the whole complex history of the British involvement with Ireland?

I am equally suspicious of Mr Brenton's preoccupation with violence. An Irishman is strung up from a tree while his throat is cut; a Roman soldier carves up a druid's bum as a precursor to rape; blood spurts out repeatedly from stabbed and wounded bowels and thighs. You may argue that this is nothing compared with the recorded violence of history. But to display such an orgy of killing in the confines of one play is to suggest one is more interested in writing a neo-Senecan shocker than in analysing the many strands of the impulse to empire.

Just occasionally Mr Brenton's native talent shines through all the licensed mayhem. The portrayal of Julius Caesar (Michael Bryant being lethally ironic) as a brutal pragmatist dictating *aperçus* to his travelling historian is wittily credible.

But the overall impact of the play and of Michael Bogdanov's production is of a hollow prodigality. What does it, in fact, tell us? That 'a Roman spear, a Saxon axe and a British army machine-gun' are all comparable weapons of invasion celebrating the same dread impulse. But to take 57 characters and close on three hours of stage time to put across such a simple point strikes me as mountainously excessive.

And although good actors, like Stephen Moore as the manic intelligence officer, Yvonne Bryceland as a Celtic matriarch and John Normington as a nervy cook, make their impact, the final impression is of a blood-boltered agitprop pageant. I accept totally that Mr Brenton finds the hunger for empire anathema; but in order to savage such a crucial historical phenomenon I suggest you first have to understand it.

My Dinner With André

Theatre Upstairs: 6 November 1980

Something weird and wonderful is currently happening at the Theatre Upstairs. It is a two-hour play called *My Dinner With André*, directed by Louis Malle, in which two men discuss their own experiences and attitudes to life with absolutely enthralling candour. So many evenings in the theatre are spent listening to tired fictions that it is quite startling to come across something that deals, wittily and exactly, with recognisable life.

The two men are Wallace Shawn, a roly-poly writer and actor who turns up these days in a lot of American movies, and André Gregory, a highly-rated New York director who some time ago mysteriously disappeared from the scene. Meeting in a Manhattan restaurant after a long interval, these two old friends launch into a structured conversation that is part autobiography, part debate. For almost an hour Gregory describes a series of picaresque adventures (can they all be true?) that involved working with Grotowski in Poland, meditating in the Sahara, going back to New York with a Japanese Buddhist chum and joining a Scottish commune. Shawn then counters this mystical tourism with an account of his own happy life as a Manhattan writer and battle between the two men is fruitfully joined.

What emerges is a fundamental division of attitude. Gregory, whose opinions are a strange blend of Mailer's *American Dream* and Whitman's *Leaves Of Grass*, sees modern America as a cancerous society to which the only alternative is little monastic communities of like-minded friends: Shawn, a contented pragmatist, actively rejoices in work, companionship, a stable sexual relationship and more mundane things like waking up to coffee, the *New York Times* and another chapter of Charlton Heston's diaries. But what is enriching about the play is the way it expands beyond friendly argument into a deep conflict between a neo-Lawrentian life of feeling and modern scientific rationalism.

I found it a dense, funny, quirky, deeply articulate play that inevitably causes one to take sides. (I voted more or less the straight Shawn ticket.) Alas it only plays till Saturday after which Malle intends to film it. But I hope it has a longer theatrical life because it gives you the rare sensation of going to hear a play and coming out having met two talkative, intelligent men with something vitally important to say.

1981

You can prove anything you want from statistics. Also from a theatre year embracing 250 first-nights. You could argue this was a rather so-so year. Regional theatres, by and large, fell into the set-book syndrome. The West End offered its usual quota of transient comedies, farces and whodunnits. Even on the Fringe there were recurring plays about the agony of hitting 32 and the lost hopes of the 1969 generation.

But against that one would have to set Peter Hall's Oresteia *at the Olivier – brave and bold if not entirely successful – and new plays of the calibre of Friel's* Translations, *Bond's* Restoration, *Nichols's* Passion Play *and C.P. Taylor's* Good. *What began to disturb me, however, was the short life-expectation of so many good new plays. Friel's* Translations *and Mike Leigh's* Goose Pimples *(which, incidentally, offended the Union of Muslim Organisations by showing its Saudi hero boozing and whoring) at least made it from Hampstead to, respectively, the Lyttelton and the Garrick. But a work like* Restoration *got its statutory short run at the Court, was then ignored by the reps and had to wait almost a decade to be lovingly restored by the RSC. Why couldn't the Royal Court tour it round the country?*

Augury of the year was the success of Cats *at the New London. It was an innovatory show put together by people who obviously cared about the literary source rather than by rip-off merchants plunging their sticky fingers into bankable classics. What one didn't know at the time was that its popularity would set the tone for the decade: one in which the British theatre would become internationally famous less for the quality of its new writing that for its efficiency in producing hit musicals.*

There were other pointers to the future: Harriet Walter as Helena, David Suchet as Shylock, Antony Sher as an uncomprehending Arab in Mike Leigh's play all established themselves as front-rank players. And Adrian Noble's productions of The Duchess of Malfi, *which reached the Roundhouse from Manchester, Ostrovsky's* The Forest *and Ibsen's* A Doll's House *suggested that the classic tradition was in safe hands.*

Passion Play

Aldwych: 14 January 1981

The title of Peter Nichols's *Passion Play* at the Aldwych contains, as you might have guessed, a deliberate pun; for this is a play about sexual love and suffering and the fragile line between them. More specifically, it concerns marital infidelity; but, in its revelatory honesty, it is light years away from the standard West End adultery comedy and certainly sent this spectator out of the theatre shaken and more than a little stirred.

James (Benjamin Whitrow) and Eleanor (Billie Whitelaw) are a 25-year-married couple with grown-up children and a life of cosy routine: he restores pictures in his garden-studio whilst she sings in heavenly choirs. Their peace is shattered by the predatory Kate whose middle-aged lover has recently died and who fastens on James as the ideal replacement. So far, so familiar. But Nichols sharpens the format first of all by bringing on stage the alter egos (embodied by Anton Rodgers and Eileen Atkins) of the two main characters and then by showing us the domestic consequences of blithe adultery: the midnight rows, the visits to the shrink, the marital crack-up, the difficulty of parting even when passion is dead.

What I like about this rich, complex, wordy play is that it is both sensitive to the sadness at the heart of many modern marriages while at the same time conveying the absurd side of adultery. In typical Nichols touches, James and Kate time their lovemaking to broadcasts by his wife's choir ('This is the Agnus Dei – I'll have to be going soon') and a wife can tell when her husband is having a fling by the sound of the loose change for the phone jingling in the trousers of his jogging-suit.

But although the play is full of good, comic observation and uses the alter egos in a manner that's a cross between O'Neill's *Strange Interlude* and Coward's *Blithe Spirit*, the real core of it is a sense of bewilderment and desolation at the final insufficiency of illicit love. 'The Christians took over the language of sexual passion and used it for their own purposes', grumbles the atheistic James. And as we listen to the music of the Mozart Requiem and the St Matthew Passion, we see that Nichols is presenting, with total honesty, a familiar modern dilemma: that the fidelity proposed by moralists leads to imprisoning tedium while the infidelity of the liberationists produces pain and suffering.

Sometimes the technical virtuosity is a bit self-conscious. Sometimes the jokes ('We all need a stiff one', cries someone as an orgy looms) are a bit obvious. But I can think of few modern plays that have caught so well both the exhilaration and embitterment of love, and Mike Ockrent's production, played against a twin-levelled steel-and-glass set by Patrick Robertson, is deft without being slick. It is also punishingly well-acted. I can't put a pin for excellence between Whitrow and Rodgers as the two baffled, ruffled, child-like husbands and Whitelaw and Atkins as the stoically suffering wives. Louise Jameson as the catalyst in Reger lingerie also has just the right heartless sexuality. But the real test of the play's truth is that it leaves a large part of the audience, I surmise, feeling much like Claudius after seeing that touring version of *The Mousetrap*.

Cats

New London: 12 May 1981

Cats at the New London is an exhilarating piece of total theatre that demolishes several myths at one go: that the British can't get a musical together, that our dancers are below American standard, and that musicals with a literary source always dilute their origins. As anyone who recalls John Dankworth's *Sweeney Agonistes* will confirm, T.S. Eliot's verse often cries out for music.

But the particular triumph of *Cats* is that it never simply becomes a series of isolated feline spectaculars. For a start John Napier has designed a wonderful environmental rubbish-dump set made up of huge tyres, rusting cars, dustbin lids and old bicycles from which the cats playfully emerge. Even more crucially, director Trevor Nunn and composer Andrew Lloyd Webber have raided Eliot's *Collected Poems* and some unpublished work to give the show a strong framework: a midnight pussy-convention ('The Jellicle cats meet once a year on the night when we make the Jellicle choice') to choose one cat worthy of redemption. In this case it is the bedraggled glamour-puss, Grizabella, who is rescued from a life of solitary Bloomsbury prowling.

What is heartening is the way the poems are integrated into the occasion. Thus Gus the Theatre Cat (beautifully played by Stephen Tate) is seen as a wistful, white-haired Victorian relic dreaming of palmier days. He is then transmogrified (or transmoggified) into Growltiger, the cutlass-bearing Pirate cat who terrorises the Thames and who is unseated by Mongolian hordes. This becomes the excuse for much air-cleaving Oriental leaping reminiscent of the Peking Opera and for Siamese-cat hissing from behind giant, green fans. Our breath suitably taken away, Growltiger reverts once more to Gus laconically telling us 'These modern productions are all very well' and still reminiscing over 'Fireforefiddle, the Fiend of the Fell'.

But, although the show is all of a piece, Gillian Lynne as choreographer and associate director, has conceived some brilliant moments. Wayne Sleep's magical Mr Mistoffeles does some head-spinning turns, leaps and dives; the Macavity number develops from a bluesy duet into a big ensemble routine; and the Jellicle Ball, with its somersaults, spins and catapult-motion, has that quality of terpsichorean joy I last saw in Bob Fosse's *Dancin'*. The show is packed with dance but it never kills the language or overpowers the strong individual characterisation such as Paul Nicholas's sleek, black, fur-lined Rum Tum Tugger or Elaine Page's mournful, spangled Grizabella who evokes the Tottenham Court Road at three in the morning.

Many hands have made *Cats* work. But in the end one comes back to Lloyd Webber's remarkable ability to find tunes that fit each specific feline. And to Trevor Nunn's dazzling staging: he has cats' eyes glowing in the dark, he uses every inch of the auditorium space and he also keeps a balance between an Eliotesque preoccupation with time and memory and sheer outgoing exhilaration. The highest compliment

I can pay is that I don't think the poet himself would have felt that his material had been tarnished or betrayed.

What's Got Into Drama?

Modern British plays: 9 May 1981

I have been taken to task by a colleague for suggesting, in my review of Franz Xaver Kroetz's *The Nest* at the Orange Tree, Richmond, that it was the kind of play no British dramatist could write. What kind of encouragement to young writers, he wanted to know, was that? Probably none at all. But, ever anxious to be helpful, I do believe there are vital lessons to be learnt from the prolific Bavarian playwright.

Kroetz's play, let me remind you, is about a young married couple just starting a family and struggling to make ends meet. The husband, in an effort to earn some overtime, dumps what turns out to be poisonous industrial waste. As a result, his own child is severely harmed. But who finally is to blame? The hero blames his boss; the boss blames him and says that, if he kicks up a fuss about it, he will give him his cards and make sure he never works for anyone in the haulage business again. In the end the hero counters this intimidation by joining his union. 'In the union', he discovers, 'you are not alone.'

What makes Kroetz's play unusual is its respect for its characters and its positive, optimistic conclusion: qualities I find notably lacking in much recent British drama. Take, for instance, Elaine Morgan's *What's Got Into You?* which recently turned up at the Tricycle Theatre. This dealt with very similar territory to the Kroetz. Once again there was a young married couple, a long discussion about the economics of having a baby, a pervading sense of domestic pressure.

But whereas Kroetz even-handedly shows the complexity of domestic life (it's partly the wife's determination to have the best of everything, including mother-to-be cream against stretchmarks, that drives the husband into taking on extra work), Ms Morgan uses her play to make cliché feminist points about the blunt-witted husband. Kroetz is making damning observations about materialism, advertising, consumer expectation at large: Ms Morgan is setting up a male Aunt Sally for the pleasure of knocking him down.

But what really troubles me about so many new British plays is their lack of faith in human beings, political systems or the possibility of change. Hanif Kureishi's *Outskirts* at the Warehouse is a classic case.

Clearly it is the work of a promising, intelligent young writer. But its cynicism seems to know no bounds. Environment, upbringing, social factors turn one of its characters into a South London Fascist. But his friend who escapes, via education, talks of 'a paste of learning thinly spread over me – to make me tasty for genteel employers'. So in the end there seems little to choose between illiberal brutality and liberal education: a conclusion that I find impossible to swallow.

At which point someone is bound to say that drama has no obligation to find solutions or to give the spectator some kind of moral uplift. But then I think it has. All great, indeed all good, drama, throughout the centuries has given spectators, if not practical answers, at least the courage and determination to go on living.

When you come out of a performance of *Three Sisters* your soul may have been wrung to its very depths. But you don't feel like killing yourself, partly because you may have seen something of your own agony and frustration represented on stage and partly because the characters themselves believe there is some discoverable purpose to life. As Olga says, 'Maybe if we wait a little longer, we shall find out why we live, why we suffer. Oh, if only we knew, if only He knew. . .' Even Beckett's Winnie in *Happy Days*, buried up to her neck in sand, ends the play with a long, silent smile at Willie, who gazes back at her. All is not lost.

A basic function of drama is to provide us with moral sustenance and some assertion of spiritual valour. What is depressing is that any dramatist who now tries to cater to this need is regarded as an incurable sentimentalist.

One of the best plays ever done at the Warehouse was Ron Hutchinson's *The Irish Play*. It abounded in images of chaos, violence, and discord; but at the end a little girl who had been waiting all evening to do her number in a pageant at Coventry's Irish Club solemnly stepped forward and solemnly picked out a tune. Mr Hutchinson was not suggesting that the Irish problem can be resolved by little girls with violins. He was, I believe, simply suggesting there was some inner spirit that could never quite be crushed. And for this he was abused instead of being applauded.

This is not to argue for a drama of false Panglossian cheer or Pollyanna sentiment. It is simply to say that there is something about the public act of sitting at a play that gives you a hunger for the tiniest sliver of hope: it's the old Dr Johnson thing about art giving you the capacity to either enjoy life or endure it.

Which brings me back to Kroetz and *The Nest*. He shows that life encompasses the tragic (such as the near extinction of a child), that we are often weighed down by a petty materialism, that people are often victimised by those in power. But he also shows that people can learn and that authority can be answered. In short, he sends you out feeling more positive than when you went in. Of how many recent British plays can one say as much?

Letter To The Editor

Hanif Kureishi: 14 May 1981

Sir, – It is possible I have misunderstood my own play *Outskirts*. In his article 'What's got into drama' Michael Billington suggests that *Outskirts* is a cynical and despairing piece; and he sees a depressing trend in British drama exemplified in it.

As the play touches on the issues of fascism and racialism it is of course serious, and it is occasionally bleak. Yet Michael Billington is well aware that most of my plays have been concerned with the increasingly worrying attack on the liberal values he and I support. Not all my plays can be 'witty, hearty, and embattled' as he said of *The Mother Country*. But they have all been attempts to illuminate and discuss areas of freedom under pressure.

While I do not provide instant answers, I do show in *Outskirts* that fascism can be rejected, which it is by the two women in the play. And this is a crucial moment, almost the point of the play, the uplifting episode which Billington doesn't refer to in his article or in his review of the play.

I have always hoped that if theatre couldn't make people act, it could at least make them think. I wouldn't like to think Michael Billington left my play in despair. I'd like him to realise that I do believe in certain values; that is why my plays are about their suppression.

And I'd like him to realise that it isn't easy to maintain these values; that they have to be fought for every day, because they are being eroded every day. This isn't easy and it isn't simple. My plays are part of the process of resistance: they show what is happening.

And if plays about England today don't have him coming out of theatres snapping his fingers, they at least contain some truth; and that in itself is a liberating, heartening thing. It's a move in the game, not the end of it. The rest the audience can do for themselves

Yours sincerely,
Hanif Kureishi.

Restoration

Royal Court: 22 July 1981

In a thin year for new plays, Edward Bond's *Restoration* towers like a colossus. I do not say it is a masterpiece: merely that its stylistic wit, moral complexity and theatrical force (aided by Nick Bicât's dozen songs) are of the kind one associates with classic drama. At the very least, it is Bond's best play since *Bingo*.

What is fascinating is the way the past unlocks Bond's imagination. We are in eighteenth century England: a world of cruelty, injustice and iron privilege. Indeed the action hinges on Lord Are's casual murder over breakfast of his unwanted wife, a mine-owner's daughter who he has married for money. Having despatched his wife with foppish indolence, Lord Are then seeks to pin the deed on a guileless, illiterate footman, Bob Hedges. And the rest of the play consists of a battle between Bob's black, justice-hungry wife and the fortified privilege of aristocracy.

Simply stated, it sounds a conflict between good and evil, the exploited and the exploiter. But Bond is cleverer than that. For a start he makes Bob a stubbornly hypocritical peasant lad who willingly shops a fellow-footman caught stealing the silver. In one extraordinarily powerful scene we see Bob tying his colleague to a chair and bundling him into a chest. So, by a fine irony, Bob the victim of injustice is himself a boss's man. And to add to the complexity, Lord Are's mother (Irene Handl in sumptuous form as a fish-fattened aristo) throws her mountainous weight on the side of justice.

At the bottom of it all I suspect Bond is saying something straightforward: that justice is every man's right but a caste system's play-thing. But what is heartening is that he gets right away from the playing-card simplicities of agitprop and that he makes his points through laughter. Indeed, the scene in which Lord Are (Simon Callow, full of brutal languor) wanly rapiers his wife who, for various reasons, is dressed as a ghost, is one of the funniest things on the London stage. Lines like: 'I can't recall she mentioned a fancy-dress breakfast,' pour out of Mr Callow with Wildean profligacy: yet only gradually do we realise the full import of this depth-charge episode.

If there is a problem, it is that there is almost too much to digest at one sitting (but when could one last say that of a new play?). Nick Bicât's songs, played by a rock group atop the mobile bridge of a setting designed by Hayden Griffin and Gemma Jackson, act as an incisive comment on the action; but Mr Bond's lyrics and the variety of Mr

Bicât's tunes, ranging from the semi-hymnal to the ballad-like, take some absorbing alongside a plot of near-Congrevian intricacy. The music has the right dislocating effect, but it also makes the theatrical brew almost over-rich.

Irene Handl and Simon Callow play the Ares with high, lethal style. And, on the other side of the class system, Philip Davis as the truculent Bob, Debby Bishop as his black wife, and Nicholas Ball as the shopped colleague are, rightly, no plaster saints but complex victims of a loaded system.

This long, three-hour play has more layers still than I have indicated; but it is a very long time since I have come out of the Royal Court feeling that I have seen something not merely promising but also rich in achievement.

The Mayor Of Zalamea

Cottesloe: 13 August 1981

Those of us who have long nagged on about the need for a wider range of world drama in the British theatre will take heart from the triumph of *The Mayor Of Zalamea* at the Cottesloe. Written around 1644 by the prolific Spaniard, Calderón, it is a fast, exciting, incident-packed drama on the theme of justice. It tells a good story. But it also boasts plenty of moral complexity.

Calderón is really opposing two kinds of justice: the natural one of the peasant versus the narrow one of the military. We are in a small Spanish town where Philip II's troops are billeted en route for Portugal. An arrogant Captain falls obsessively in love with the daughter of Crespo, a rich peasant farmer. Having failed to win the girl openly, the Captain whisks her off to a forest and rapes her while his followers bind her father to a tree. But when Crespo becomes Mayor, the stage is then set for a conflict between his desire for instant justice and the tribal code of the Spanish army: a deadlock that is resolved only by the arrival of the king himself.

To reveal more of the plot would be to spoil the pleasure of future playgoers. But what Michael Bogdanov's on-rushing, bare-stage production brings out is not only Calderón's breakneck pace (as far as I can work out, the events all take place within about 36 hours) but also his moral subtlety. Crespo, the stubborn, honour-loving peasant, is obviously the wronged party; but Calderón also makes him a wily tactician prepared to gaol his son simply to advertise his own impartiality. At the same time, the army is seen as a rampageous gang that closes ranks in time of trouble, yet the senior general, Don Lope, is charmed and fascinated by Crespo's rock-like tenacity.

If there is a problem with the play today, it is making a modern British audience accept the premium the Spanish place on honour and virginity. But this production proves the theatrical law that if a character believes in something with sufficient intensity the spectator will accept it too. In this respect the supreme performance of the evening comes from Michael Bryant as Crespo. He makes him a wiry, nut-brown, white-bearded figure with triangular Spanish face and a rooted conviction that 'honour is the offspring of the soul of man'. To Mr Bryant these are not mere words. There is something about his pouchy eyes, his unflinching stance, his patriarchal authority (son and daughter always look nervously at him before making a decision) that tells you his beliefs spring from a life spent close to the earth.

But one also has to accept what Milton called 'the sage and serious doctrine of virginity'. And again modern cynicism is dispelled by the steadfast sobriety with which Leslee Udwin as Crespo's daughter describes the Captain's assault to her pinioned father. Bogdanov aids her by having the incident acted out in shadow even as she describes it; but Ms Udwin herself commands the stage by the stoicism with which she recounts her ravishment and the sense she gives of a life destroyed. And in a strong cast Basil Henson as a faintly Osbert Lancasterish General and Daniel Massey as the patrician Captain (full of dirty tricks) shine out.

Why The Show Must Go On

19 October 1981

Ten years ago (to the very month) when I became drama critic of this newspaper, the British theatre seemed a relatively secure and self-confident place. It had a definable structure. Arts Council grants crept up annually. Writers kept on writing. Indeed in London alone it was possible in September 1971 to see new plays by Nichols, Gray, Mortimer, Ayckbourn, Hampton, Bolt, Frayn and Bond while the Royal Shakespeare Company was knocking us out with a repertory consisting of Gorky, Joyce, Etherege, Pinter and Brook's shattering *Dream*. Happy days.

Many things have happened in the intervening decade, some good, some bad. But the most obvious is that we have seen the bottom dropping out of the commercial end of the market. Partly it's the result of economics: a night out for two in the West End now requires a capital investment only slightly smaller than putting down a deposit for a flat. Partly it's the result of the growth of an omnivorous subsidised theatre.

But partly it's the result of the contempt with which the commercial theatres, during the golden years, treated the paying customers: I believe the public is now getting its revenge for all those years of thick plays, thin programmes, overpriced drinks and clattering usherettes. Going to the West End has always felt like trespassing on someone else's property. Going to the National, a local rep or a fringe theatre is more like stepping into a place of your own.

But even if the West End is now the victim of the very market forces it has always pinned its faith on, good things have happened to the theatre over the past decade. Ten years ago Peter Hall (then about to take up a key post at Covent Garden) said the great problem was to prevent our institutions becoming "institutions". Miraculously, our two big national companies have retained their vitality. At the RSC, Trevor Nunn and Terry Hands have reached early middle-age without dwindling into a bored complacency: to take only two recent examples, their respective work on *Nicholas Nickleby* and *As You Like It* communicated a life-enhancing joy.

And at the National, in spite of the dire predictions when it opened, Peter Hall and his team have avoided the feeling of glass-case museum theatre: my feeling is that the further out on a limb they go, the better they are. Even Howard Brenton's *Romans In Britain*, for all its theatrical flaws, was the kind of work that only a living organism would undertake. And, by giving us a taste of Molière, Calderón, Schnitzler, Von Horvath, they have begun at last to dent our customary xenophobia.

However, far and away the most significant thing to have happened in the theatre over the last decade is the way the values of the one-time alternative theatre have begun to permeate the main-stream. I don't just mean in obvious ways such as the transformation of *Educating Rita*, *Duet For One* and *Accidental Death Of An Anarchist* into West End hits. Even more significant is the way in which fringe techniques have become part of popular theatre. The wall, for instance, that once separated stage and audience has now come crashing down. Go to *Barnum* at the Palladium, for instance, and you find the cast mingling with the audience before the show begins just as they do in John Caird's production of *The Twin Rivals* at Stratford's Other Place. And what was *Nicholas Nickleby* but a great assemblage of all the devices we have seen in fringe productions over the years: actors playing multiple roles, the incorporation of narrative into drama, bodies being used to form inanimate objects? Even the Meyerholdian notion of the actor as acrobat and athlete was an integral part of a hit play like *Jumpers*.

In short, two things are currently happening: the theatre as a profit-making venture is in trouble while the theatre as an expressive medium is more alive with possibilities than ever. And this leads me to wonder where we are heading over the next decade. What will the theatre be like in 1991? It may seem, of course, that it will be under greater threat than ever once the revolution in home entertainment takes place.

With the arrival of video cassettes, discs, cable and satellite television, it sounds as if there will be less and less reason to venture out of the house in search of entertainment. But my hunch is that the technological domestic revolution is going to have a pulverising effect on cinema while paradoxically stimulating the hunger for the live event, whether it be drama, opera, ballet or concerts.

My guess is that theatre (partly because of the long-term effect of Thatcherite economics) will shrink in size over the next decade but increase in intensity. In other words, the comfortable middle-brow play that gives one a passable evening out will be in trouble because people are going to hunger for a unique experience.

This may take many forms: the gargantuan project (look at the current appetite for epic ventures like *The Greeks* or *The Ring*); the big gaudy musical; the vaudevillian play; the microscopically exact studio classic; the bravura performance; the opulent extravaganza; the play that tackles subjects forbidden by an increasingly cautious television. Look around and you'll see it's happening already. What are the shows you can't get into? *Cats*, *Barnum*, *Amadeus*, the Stratford *Doll's House*, the Brighton Theatre's *Brothers Karamazov*, the Birmingham Rep *Candide* – all productions that belong uniquely to the theatre.

I also detect an important geographical shift in where theatre happens: one that Keith Dewhurst predicted in these pages a good six years ago. I see people venturing less and less into a dirty, decaying, pricey West End of London where it's virtually impossible to purchase a decent cup of coffee and a sandwich (why do we have nowhere quick and efficient and cheap like Manhattan's Stage Door Deli?).

Instead, I see theatre happening more and more in the suburbs where people actually live. In London this has already happened with the growth of neighbourhood theatres in arts-conscious boroughs like Camden and Hammersmith. But I see no reason why this movement shouldn't spread through London, Manchester, Leeds, Birmingham and indeed all the big cities.

Significantly, nearly all the big club theatres of the North are situated in the heart of the suburbs: that, I believe, is where the next generation of playhouses will also spring up. In Paris, anything remotely progressive always appears to be happening at the end of the Metro line: so too I predict exciting forays to Colliers Wood and Hendon Central.

In fact, if I had to lay my head on the block and outline the shape of theatre in 1991, I would predict the following.

The closure of anything from a third to a half of current West End theatres. A growth in popularity of big arts centres like the National and the forthcoming Barbican where you can eat and drink as well as go to a play or a concert. The subsidence of those repertory theatres that fail to find a policy, a style, an identity that is peculiar to them. An outcrop of neighbourhood playhouses, nearly all of them in converted buildings rather than purpose-built theatres. A concentration on those things which the theatre does better than any other medium: the spoken word, imaginative spectacle, politically dangerous content.

As for who will be running what, I predict the National will be in the hands of a triumvirate (Gill, Rudman, Bryden?), that Adrian Noble and John Caird will have succeeded Nunn and Hands at the RSC, and that Peter Lichtenfels of the Traverse will be in charge of the Royal Court. These are all hunches. But one thing I am sure of: a decade hence the theatre will still be here fulfilling its historic function of keeping the drama critics off the streets.

All's Well That Ends Well

Royal Shakespeare Theatre: 18 November 1981

Stratford's main house productions this year have been very patchy. But Trevor Nunn's production of *All's Well That Ends Well* strikes me, even in the breathless rush induced by a late curtain, as an incipient masterpiece. It takes a dark difficult play and turns it into that rarest of things: a realistic fairy tale.

Very like Guthrie in his ecstatic 1959 version (which I never thought to see bettered) Nunn distinguishes clearly between the play's separate worlds. The Countess of Rossillion (Peggy Ashcroft playing with a wealth of humorous silver-haired compassion) occupies a Chekhovian world of wicker chairs, towering ferns and chiming clocks. The fistula-stricken French King inhabits a Novello court packed with peacock captains who vault, fence, dance, and sport like Ruritanian princes. And when the action moves to the Florentine wars we are in a world of brass bands, smoke-filled estaminets and peachy nurses who might have stepped out of *Oh What A Lovely War!*

But although the action – framed by John Gunter's pillared Victorian conservatory set – floats anachronistically between several periods and worlds, it has in this production a binding emotional reality. Thus Harriet Walter's tender Helena is not a ruthless Shavian go-getter but a love-stricken medico's daughter, seemingly always on the verge of tears and bursting with undeniable passion.

At first there is a teasing playfulness about her selection of Bertram as a husband through the process of an elimination dance at court. But Nunn turns this to naked anguish when Mike Gwilym's ferocious Bertram spits out 'I can't love her' with Strindbergian intensity. You feel she can't help loving this utterly worthless man; and the end acquires a bitter irony as tentatively holding hands, they fade into dusk and the pain of an unequal relationship.

What is impressive, however, is the way Nunn throughout keeps the balance between comic hoopla and emotional pain. Stephen Moore's Parolles is, for example, a splendidly conceived braggart dandy decorated in white scarves like a walking Christmas tree. Yet the famous scene when he is literally hoodwinked and exposed is both funny and uneasy.

We laugh as a fork is scraped against a silver salver to produce the sound of torture instruments. Yet when he describes Bertram as 'a foolish, idle boy but very ruttish' we realise he speaks the blunt truth. And the realism of his interrogation, even down to the proffered cigarette and glass of water, has something of the cruelty of the gulling of Malvolio.

What Nunn has done is to reconcile the diverse elements of a 'mingled yarn' of a play. There is something wholly modern about Helena's reckless pursuit of a man who is an unredeemed monster. Yet when in the elegiac final scene the conservatory doors are flung wide open and she returns apparently from the dead to claim her man, we also seem to be in the realm of some twilit fairy tale. This is pure theatrical alchemy and it is achieved by putting real, suffering people into an unreal situation.

It is also the result of some very good acting to which I would add the names of John Franklyn Robbins as the tetchy monarch transformed from chairbound invalid to epauletted dancer, and of Robert Eddison, who surrounds Lord Lafeu with an aura of benign wisdom. By the end you have been taken into a world of magic; but one in which the lovers live painfully ever after.

The Oresteia

Olivier: 30 November 1981

Peter Hall's production of *The Oresteia* at the Olivier is certainly very daring. But does it work? For the first two plays of Aeschylus's great trilogy, I have to admit that the conventions chosen by Hall and his translator, Tony Harrison – masks, an all-male cast, rough alliterative Anglo-Saxon kind of verse – were like insurmountable barriers between me and the work. Only in the final, fantastically difficult play, *Eumenides*, do the conventions become a bonus with triumph being snatched belatedly from the jaws of Morpheus.

The first problem is that of the masks. You can rationalise till you're blue in the face (and some very strange arguments are used in the programme to justify the masks) but the blunt Emperor-has-no-clothes truth is that masks make language very difficult to hear and deny the actor one of his most basic weapons. Of course they were used in the Greek theatre. But that was partly because the occasion was a religious ritual, partly because one actor (as here) played more than one role and partly because in theatres seating up to 15,000, the facial features had to be exaggerated.

To employ them today (whatever the intellectual motive) seems to me as perverse as making a movie without sound or doing Shakespeare in a mock-Elizabethan playhouse. What was an accepted convention for the Greeks for us becomes an arty device.

Only in the third play, *Eumenides*, do the masks become something more than an obstacle. Agamemnon has been murdered by Clytemnestra. She, in turn, has been killed by her son Orestes. In the final play Apollo and the ancient Furies are locked in a terrific conflict over the morality of the murder. A hung jury cannot decide the issue and, as Athena finally resolves things, Aeschylus deliberately moves the action onto another plane and the masks at last come into their own.

The most chilling moment in the whole evening is the assembly, one by one, of the Furies, white-masked, gory-locked and to a sound like the murmur of innumerable bees. Their transformation into kindly beings (by a series of political bribes) and their final exit through a silent, standing, astonished Olivier audience is also a moving piece of theatre.

But in the earlier plays the masks so distance the spectator (this spectator anyway) as to leave him detached and unfeeling. Harrison argues that the mask and its language 'compel us to keep our eyes open in situations of extremity when we might otherwise flinch away in horror and stop looking'. This is absolute poppycock. I've seen *The Oresteia* at the Burgtheater in Vienna and in Peter Stein's magnificent Berlin Schaubühne version and can report that the audience, confronted by recognisable human beings, had rather less difficulty than here in keeping their eyes open.

Time and again the style adopted here alienates (in the Brechtian sense) the spectator and drastically limits the text's emotional variety. Take the return home of Agamemnon. He enters on a mobile trolley, spear-wreathed and adorned with skeletal horses' heads. In his mask he represents one attribute: bluff militaristic might. But given a human face (as he was by Peter Stein) it was possible for him to pause on the threshold and suggest an apprehensive foreknowledge of his death. Likewise Clytemnestra, in an unvaried rouge-streaked gold mask, cannot begin to convey the human subtlety (the guilt under the gilt, so to speak) of the murderous intent underlying her extravagant supplications.

What is extraordinary about this *Oresteia* is that it leaps effortlessly over the hurdle where other productions fall. Stein botched the *Eumenides* because, I suspect, he couldn't accept the divine intervention and the blatant endorsement of male supremacy. But Hall's version here really begins to work. The alienation-effect that has kept us lightly chilled in the first two plays pays off precisely because it enables us to see the contrived absurdity of the arguments. When Apollo, seeking to justify matricide, says, 'The mother of what's called her offspring's no parent but only the nurse to the seed that's implanted,' one is permitted to scoff.

The imagery of this third play is also infinitely more expressive : there is a fine moment when the body of Orestes sways and ripples under pressure from the Furies before making a slow motion escape like a marathon-runner trudging through mire. And the judgment on Orestes, with the jurors dropping their pebbles into one of two downstage urns, is as engrossing as it must have been in 458 BC.

The production also boasts one other unequivocal success: Harrison Birtwistle's music. Scored for six musicians on either side of the stage, it punctuates the action ceaselessly: jagged percussion for the Chorus's fragmented verse, screeching woodwind wails for Cassandra's cries, amplified harp when the trial reaches its most intense. Instead of being a detachable adornment, the music becomes an inseparable part of the event.

In the end the test of any production of *The Oresteia* is whether it sends you out feeling you've encountered drama's first masterpiece or endured an act of piety; and my feelings, as you may have gathered, were somewhat split.

For the first two plays I felt starved of blood, passion, excitement, emotion as I stared wanly at these hollow-eyed masks from which emerged this indigestible alliterative verse, beating like rain on a corrugated-iron roof. But with the trial of Orestes the language thins out, there is a deliberately ironic contrast between the beaten-gold masks and the tarnished arguments, and we feel a precarious order has been spun out of chaos. What starts as a dehumanised experiment at last achieves a perfervid ritual excitement.

1982

You could feel the recession beginning to bite. Early in the year a dozen West End theatres were dark. The RSC, having moved into its new home at the Barbican, muttered darkly about permanent closure. The Royal Court was shut for a month at Christmas. The Riverside Studios and the Roundhouse raged against the dying of the light. The bulk of the regional reps had long summer lay-offs. This was Thatcherism in action.

People also woke up to the fact that a lot of new writing was playing to very small audiences. The Theatre Writers Union, in fact, published a report called Playwrights: An Endangered Species? *which addressed the whole murky problem. It talked of 'the tendency for new work to be shunted into small spaces and, in fact, for new work to be deliberately written for small spaces and small audiences'. One didn't have to look much further than the Barbican – a handsome space greeted with unceasing vitriol by the more splenetic critics – where Shakespeare and* Peter Pan *prospered in the main theatre while an epic piece like Peter Flannery's* Our Friends In The North *was automatically consigned to the Pit. I welcomed the new building while questioning RSC policy.*

At least in Stratford the young Turks (supervised by the old Hands) made their mark: Adrian Noble with King Lear, *Ron Daniels with* The Tempest *and Barry Kyle with* The Shrew. *The National also enjoyed its best season to date on the South Bank. Richard Eyre left a gilt-edged calling-card with* Guys And Dolls, The Beggar's Opera *and* Schweyk In The Second World

War. *Gill's* Danton's Death, *Bogdanov's* Spanish Tragedy *and Hall's* The Importance *also confirmed the British theatre had not lost its talent for resurrecting the past.*

Where, however, were the big new plays? Stoppard's The Real Thing *had a rare element of personal pain and Frayn's* Noises Off *was a superb piece of technical wizardry. Terry Johnson's* Insignificance *and Doug Lucie's* Hard Feelings *put down markers for the future. But the noisily assertive public plays of the Seventies were conspicuous by their absence. Plenty of solid achievement in '82; but not much sign of wide-ranging adventure.*

Critic Versus Creator

Debate at the Warehouse: 2 February 1982

'We ought to do this more often,' said Peter Jenkins after chairing a Warehouse discussion on Friday about Theatre Criticism and the Future of New Writing. My own instinctive reaction was that we ought to do it less often. Nothing seems to me to be gained by pitting three theatre practitioners against three drama critics and then leaving them to thrash around a topic so vague as to be meaningless. All we got on Friday was the intellectual equivalent of cock fighting.

Admittedly the evening began with Mr Jenkins putting to the panel (David Edgar, Dusty Hughes, Max Stafford-Clark representing the creators, James Fenton, Michael Coveney and myself the critics) a perfectly reasonable question: what ought the critic to expect of a writer and the writer of a critic? Mr Fenton answered somewhat obliquely by attacking present outmoded critical practices: too little space, he argued, for the Sunday men, too little time for the harassed overnight reviewers. Mr Coveney vehemently demurred and I vehemently concurred and, having split our own defence, the goal mouth was left wide open.

What dismayed me, however, was not the constant bombardment from our own penalty area – those in the appraisal business must themselves expect to be judged – but the unrealistic view of criticism that came from various sources.

Dusty Hughes (who has been on the game himself and ought to know better) envisaged the critic as some kind of reporter on what passed between the play and the audience: the critic, however, is a partial witness rather than a mutual observer. Max Stafford-Clark thought the critic ought to get his hands dirtier and become much more informed about the theatrical process: all very well but the more a critic gets involved in the going-to-rehearsal syndrome, the less equipped he is to offer an uncorrupted reaction.

Michael Bogdanov (from the body of the hall) passionately argued that the critic should be helping shape the theatre of the future. That seems to me reasonable. The only problem is that, however many prescriptive articles a critic may write, the ultimate theatrical power rests in the hands of managers and directors. Advice is often given; very rarely taken.

But the real problem with this kind of discussion is that the critic is made the scapegoat for all the theatre's ills. David Edgar, in the course of a very sane and witty account of the way the late-Sixties explosion in new writing had failed to change either society or the theatre in the way hoped, rather marred his case by talking of 'the ambiguous critical response to Howard Barker, Edward Bond, Howard Brenton'.

If the response has been ambiguous, may it not be because these three very talented, varied writers have produced an uneven body of work? Because one admired Bond's *Saved, Bingo, The Bundle* and *Restoration*, does one also have to praise *The Worlds* and *Summer*? Because Brenton is a fine theatrical poet, does one have to treat *The Romans In Britain* as a masterpiece? Even a critic committed to the cause of new writing is in gross dereliction of duty if he does not point out a play's weaknesses.

The question we never got round to answering at the Warehouse, however, was what the critic expects of a writer. It is a dangerously loaded question because critics who go into theatres with too rigid a set of rules lack the capacity to be taken by surprise.

My own shorthand answer would be that I expect a play to link the private and the public worlds, since people are the product of both their psychology and their social environment. That I expect a play to offer a complicated, deeply felt response to life rather than a series of received ideas. That I hunger for a marriage of rich language and powerful images. That I want some instruction in how to live rather than a demonstration of spiritual negativism. Most good plays, from *Hamlet* to *Destiny*, fulfil those conditions.

The problem with new writing at present is that there is almost too much of it. Partly out of economic necessity, too many playwrights sprint to the typewriter with half-formed ideas. Also organic development as a writer becomes very difficult when promising, embryonic talents are snapped up to cater for the ever-expanding video industry. I can't blame young dramatists wanting to work in TV and films; I can however sometimes blame them for failing to recognise that writing for the theatre is a specialised and difficult craft that takes time to learn.

We never got round (and I share the collective guilt) to discussing these issues at the Warehouse. What we got was an understandable, pent up frustration from the writers and a ratty, beleaguered defensiveness from the critics. Before the next such event, I hope the organisers will pick a more specific topic, ask the participants to make a prepared opening address and acknowledge the existence of women in composing the panel. Then at least we might get less of a cock fight.

Noises Off

Lyric Hammersmith: 25 February 1982

Reviewing a Bamber Gascoigne play ten years ago, I dogmatically claimed you could never have a classic farce about actors. The essence of farce, I suggested, was the destruction of bourgeois propriety. Now Gascoigne's Cambridge contemporary, Michael Frayn, has shattered that rule with a pulverisingly funny play, *Noises Off*, at the Lyric Hammersmith, which shows the precarious illusion of theatre reduced to total chaos.

'One minute I'm stepping through the stage door. Next minute I'm stepping off the edge of the world.' So claims Paul Eddington's god-like director in the third act. And that is exactly what Frayn's play is about. It is not simply a machine for creating laughs. It is about the booby-trapped minefield of theatre itself in which one false move, one missed cue can destroy a carefully created fiction. In one sense, it panders to our sadistic delight in things that go wrong; in another, it is a very intelligent joke about the fragility of all forms of drama.

What is amazing, however, is the number of variations Frayn plays on this theme. In the first act, he shows us a horridly plausible sex farce full of sheikhs, adhesive sardine plates, de-frocked girls and de-trousered men being rehearsed in Weston-super-Mare. By the second act, we are backstage at a matinée in Goole where the company's internal sexual rivalries have reached boiling point: the frenzied whispers and frantic mime suggest *Othello* directed by Mack Sennett. In the third act we see an on-stage performance at Stockton-on-Tees where both play and company have disintegrated and where Ionesco's definition of farce ('a plunge into madness') is being lived out.

It is easily the funniest modern farce since Peter Shaffer's *Black Comedy*. And the reason is that Frayn has rooted it in a totally believable world. In the first, crucial act, he not only creates an authentic play-within-a-play (*Nothing On*) about a sex-mad estate agent taking over a country cottage for a bit of nookie. He also creates a libellously funny team of actors: the Stanislavskian one who has to have a psychological motive for exiting with a sardine plate, the furiously inarticulate one who can never complete a sentence, the benign old drunk never sure when to enter ('I thought I heard my voice'). And all are ruled over by a sardonically lecherous director who, when everyone is crawling round the stage looking for a lost contact-lens, wanly inquires: 'Is this going to happen during a performance?'

If I have any reservation, it is that the mimed backstage quarrels of the second act are so technically ingenious they almost kill one's laughter. But Frayn's ability to combine exact observation with the vertiginous lunacy of farce returns in the third act where Nicky Henson does a breath-taking fall down the stairs that matches Robert Hirsch in Feydeau and where the arrival of unscheduled characters explodes the play-within-a-play: to see three identical burglars enter illegally where only one is plotted is the kind of farce engineering it is hard to do justice to in print.

Michael Blakemore's production also combines mechanics and humanity and he has created, presumably in a short time, a genuine farce ensemble. I can only do brief justice to Paul Eddington's cardiganed deity of a director, Patricia Routledge's hysterical maid who wheels around the furniture as if it were subtly poisoned, Michael Aldridge's woozy old sot who has to be guarded like a sheepdog, Rowena Roberts's farce heroine, wandering around in a blue slip and a total daze, Nicky Henson's male lead, always on the verge of implosion.

All inhabit both the real world of farce and the unreal world of backstage life; and it is precisely the conjunction of those two that makes this both the thinking man's *No Sex Please We're British* and slapstick Pirandello.

Beyond The Footlights

Lyric Hammersmith: 6 April 1982

Like English cricket, weather and oratory, the Cambridge Footlights Revue is never what it once allegedly was. But *Beyond The Footlights* (the prize-winning 1981 sample), has found its way into the Lyric Hammersmith, and, even if it doesn't set the town ablaze, it introduces one to some highly talented performers and shows a particular gift for literary parody and for pricking the excesses of the privileged Cambridge life.

For me the best sketches nearly all involve attacks on cultural monuments. The Jane Austenish classic novel (or perhaps the genteel teatime telly version of it) gets a wonderful going over in a scene where a poke-bonneted female seeks a domestic position with a lordly master. 'You have your mother's eyes I think,' he remarks peering down his aquiline nose. 'Yes, in my reticule,' she calmly and ghoulishly replies. And equally devastating is a Shakespearean Masterclass in which a bow-tied directorial guru gets a willing actor to try and cram every single human emotion into his rendering of the one word 'Time': memories of the RSC's South Bank Show teach-in came flooding back unbidden.

But if a long and crowded show has any consistent point of view, it is one of even-handed apolitical restraint. It puts the boot, successfully and impartially, into American funding of the IRA, twitchy public-school-Trot folk singers, spy-obsessed dons who see themselves as part of the Apostolic succession and the halo of privilege surrounding Cambridge life in which clubs like Campaign for Real Cognac might plausibly flourish. Looking neither left nor right and favouring mild topicality over manic absurdism (we even get a song and sketch about the Falkland Islands), the show exudes a calm, unflustered wit and an air of faintly Olympian detachment.

In the end, however, it is the individual talents that matter. And I was especially taken by the work of Emma Thompson (very good on showbiz kitsch and the breathy clichés of award-winning actresses), Stephen Fry, who has the omniscient repose of a natural butler, and Hugh Laurie who, as a jaunty American folk singer, encapsulates the show's whole mood of benign scepticism when he sings 'everybody must have a cause – it's so much easier than thinking.'

Valmouth

Chichester: 20 May 1982

Sandy Wilson's musical, *Valmouth*, has now pitched camp at the Chichester Festival Theatre. Ever since its first appearance in 1958, it has had the chic mystique of a cult show. But, even if some of the claims made on its behalf are a touch extravagant, it emerges in this spectacular revival as a fascinating hot-house plant: a louche *Brigadoon* about a fantasy village rippling with myriad perversions.

I recall that Tynan's original objection to it was that Sandy Wilson had coupled the verbal wit of Firbank's novel with inappropriately lightweight melodies. But this seems to me the very point (or counterpoint) of the show: that Firbank's high Catholic camp is balanced by tunes full of sweetness and nostalgia. Valmouth itself is a decadent watering place where the cock emphatically crows and where sins are very much what they used to be. But, melodically, Wilson has the guile to portray it as a place of pastoral innocence.

It would be foolish to relate the story, except to say that passion unequivocally spins the plot. Lady Parvula, a visiting sophisticate, is smitten hip and thigh with a recalcitrant shepherd ('Oh,' cries Fenella Fielding, giving her best performance in years, 'I want to spank the white walls of his cottage.') Niri-Esther, a dusky Tahitian beauty, is equally enamoured of upstanding Captain Dick Thoroughfare, accompanied everywhere by a nautical chum ('We were pals together on the ocean'). And in this land of erotomania the wheels are oiled by an Oriental masseuse who could best be described as a black Pandarus.

What keeps the show afloat, however, is the blend of silky indecency with romantic tunes. The former is best embodied by Robert Helpmann as a dubious ecclesiast, Cardinal Pirelli, excommunicated for baptising a dog. And Sir Robert, with rubious lips and wide-spread eyes suggesting all the cardinal vices, gives a wonderful leer to some of the classic Firbankian lines such as the one about the uncontrollable lady granted a Papal audience: 'It seemed she kissed his toe and then went on to do much, much more.' And Mr Wilson's capacity to write blithely fetching tunes is seen in 'What Do I Want With Love', put across by Robert Meadmore's shepherd with affecting directness.

Admittedly there are times when the cloistered decadence cloys and at three hours' length the show could still do with some judicious trimming. But, among the drab foothills of the postwar British musical, it still represents a purple peak. And John Dexter's production and the designs by Andrew and Margaret Brownfoot give it a pleasantly dreamlike quality.

The costumes suggest a blend of Erté and the Chelsea Arts Ball: Judy Campbell's husky Mrs Hurstpierpoint is particularly resplendently clad in protuberant feathers and pearl chinstrap and at one point appears like a sequinned bat loosed from Hell.

The show is also cast up to the hilt with Miss Fielding positively oozing unsatisfied sexual hunger, with Bertice Reading hitting the back wall of the theatre with every syllable as the matchmaking masseuse, and with Femi Taylor radiating a supple, lithe sexuality as her amorous niece.

But what the show proves above all is that musicals, like plays, can be ahead of their time; and that now in the post-permissive age we have caught up with *Valmouth*, which sets the libido to music and finally suggests that Unhappy is the Land that has no Eros.

A Doll's House

The Pit: 19 June 1982

Some evenings in the theatre acquire an almost holy intensity. And Adrian Noble's magnificent production of *A Doll's House*, newly arrived at The Pit in the Barbican Centre, is one such. It is partly to do once again with the power of great plays in small, intimate spaces. But this is not merely Ibsen played in the round: it is Ibsen viewed in the round as well.

By that I mean that Mr Noble sees the play as infinitely more than a pioneering feminist tract about a doll-wife who finally achieves liberation. In this production it is about a whole group of people struggling to free themselves from either the burden of the past (the play could very well be called *Ghosts*) or their own natures. For Nora this is done through her historic domestic exit, and for her husband, Torvald, through being shocked into awareness of the cosseting, protective role he has long played. But the blackmailing Krogstad and the widowed Mrs Linde achieve a different kind of freedom through the pooling of their solitude in marriage.

Still the play is titled *A Doll's House*: and the central dynamic comes from Cheryl Campbell's extraordinary Nora. She takes huge risks, playing the whole first act on a high-pitched note of giggling, gurgling, coquettish, even petulant, near-frenzy: she is dangerously vivacious as if the strain of living a constant lie (playing the kitten-wife while having engineered her husband's recovery) were tearing her asunder. She catches brilliantly the riven complexity of Nora who is both in thrall to others (Krogstad) and who at the same time enjoys wielding sexual power over Dr Rank: never before have I seen the moment in which she allows him to caress and fondle her silk stockings, delicately running his fingers through them, played with such Pinterish finesse. But it is precisely because Ms Campbell's Nora is such a schizoid, suicidal near-hysteric that the final discovery of her real self becomes not merely moving but cleansing.

It is a powerful but in no way obliterating performance, since Stephen Moore offers us an almost definitive Torvald: no paternalist villain but someone trapped inside the role of the doll-husband. Mr Moore, with a feathery voice issuing from inside a strong frame, wonderfully suggests patronising kindliness. But his real strength comes when Nora presents him with the truth of their relationship: his hands flutter through the air in sawn-off, ineffectual gestures, his vowel-sounds turn harsh and ugly and, like Max Beerbohm's tailor, he is in the ungainly position of crawling on his knees while shaking his fist.

But the great virtue of this production is that every character is seen from his or her point of view. Bernard Lloyd's Krogstad is no satanic heavy but a reformed criminal quietly yearning for status and recognition. John Franklyn Robbins's Dr Rank is an astonishing study of a man approaching death with the formal suavity of one going to a wedding. And Marjorie Bland's Mrs Linde brings on with her the melancholy aura of provincial solitude and a passionate need for contact. Using Michael Meyer's translation, it is a production that gives you infinite new perspectives on a great classic without in any way advertising itself: I would class it amongst the best things the RSC has done in the whole of its 22 years.

Insignificance

Royal Court: 13 July 1982

A lot of modern plays run out of ideas. Terry Johnson's *Insignificance* at the Royal Court runs into almost too many . But if the action is over-stuffed with colliding notions and conceits, it is a fault in the right direction; and for me the play confirms the impression made by Mr Johnson's *Days Here So Dark* (which dealt with the primordial strangeness of the Outer Hebrides) that he is a young writer of peculiar promise.

Set in a New York hotel room in 1953, *Insignificance* brings together four American icons: though the characters are never named as such, they are clearly inspired by Albert Einstein, Marilyn Monroe, Joe Di Maggio and Senator McCarthy. The white-haired Germanic Prof is sitting in his room working on complex calculus when his space is invaded by a series of visitors. The Senator threatens to prosecute him and shred his calculus unless he supports the President's anti-Soviet atomic energy programme. The Actress offers her brain in exchange for his body and tries to stop him succumbing to government blackmail. And the Ball Player is trying to reclaim a wife who has become erotic public property.

I spent much of the play's length guessing at Mr Johnson's exact intentions. At times, he takes a Stoppardian delight in the juxtaposition of once-living legends. At other times, he suggests America is a society where knowledge is equated with power: the Senator learns a new word every day and the Actress delights (in one lovely sequence) in demonstrating the Theory of Relativity with the help of model trains and flashlights. At other times, in the exposure of the Ball Player as a jealous, gum-popping cuckold and the Actress as a haemorrhaging wreck, Mr Johnson seems hooked on the mortal fallibility of the famous.

He tosses all these balls in the air in a work that is very much an elegant, mathematical construct rather than a slice of life. But even if the ideas are sometimes self-cancelling (if knowledge without understanding is a curse, isn't it pushing one's luck to give us so many pop-science demonstrations?) and even if it is impossible to sum up the American malaise in four emblematic characters, Mr Johnson retains my theatrical interest because he is that rare creature: a moralist with wit. He writes with responsible gaiety. Yet his play is also a passionate statement about the significance of all human life and the danger of shifting the responsibility for our society into the hands of the famous few.

It is also right that, in a play about the penalties of star-worship, Les Waters's cool, air-conditioned production should be an ensemble affair. Obviously Judy Davis's Monroesque Actress, fresh from shooting the ventilation-shaft sequence in *Seven Year Itch*, takes the eye, but what Ms Davis does admirably is to combine a wide-eyed, child-like inquisitiveness with a messed-up adult despair; she is both breathy waif and helpless stray. But she is never allowed to swamp Ian McDiarmid's brilliant walking walrus of an Einstein who listens keenly to others with a saintly, omniscient tact; or Larry Lamb's towering, bat-swinging ball-player with a pathetic belief in fame as an insulation against hurt; or William Hootkins's rotund Senator oozing sweat and menace.

Mr Johnson sometimes chews off more than he can bite. And, in a democratic play about individual responsibility, it would be refreshing to meet a non-legendary character. But, at a time of slack dramaturgy, Mr Johnson's conceptual polish is quite a tonic; and it is good to meet a young writer for whom fame is a snare, rather than a spur and who urgently believes our destiny lies in ourselves rather than the stars.

Other Places

Cottesloe: 15 October 1982

Harold Pinter obviously believes in saving the best till last. The first two plays in his new triple-bill at the Cottesloe, *Other Places*, are strange, comic and fascinating but you would know they were by Pinter if you met them in your dreams. However the third play, *A Kind Of Alaska* (which strikes me on instant acquaintance as a masterpiece) moves one in a way no work of his has ever done before; and it gets from Judi Dench a performance that will brand itself on the memory of all those lucky enough to see it.

The play was inspired by Oliver Sacks' book, *Awakenings*; and it is about *encephalitis lethargica* (or sleeping sickness) which claimed some five million victims in the years from 1916 to 1926. What we see is a girl-woman, old in years but young in experience, coming to life again after a 29-year coma. She was struck still like marble in the act of putting down a vase at the age of 16. Now she wakes in a white bed in a high-windowed room unable to recognise either her sister or the man who has watched over her. She is sad, bemused, fretful, questioning, conscious of having been on a strange journey but unable to get her emotional bearings.

It is a perfect theatrical metaphor for Pinter's fascination (which runs through the whole triple-bill) with the no-man's land between life and death. Most people have at some stage had the feeling that family, friends, lovers are phantoms in some dream; and this play uses an uncommon instance to tap a common experience. But it is also particular, moving and direct. It harks back to a lost upper-class world. It shows the weird comedy in being warmly greeted by relations you don't recognise ('You've aged – substantially', the heroine abruptly says to her grey-haired sister). It also, crucially, says that with this disease the watchers suffer more than the watched.

Never before have I known a Pinter play to leave one so emotionally wrung through; and much of the credit, in Peter Hall's exact production, belongs to the incredible Judi Dench. Her great, sad eyes roam the strange room seeking comfort. She struggles to walk, arms extended like a condor's wings, as if motion were a human miracle. Yet through her performance comes a sense of recollected gaiety. Face glistening, she cries 'Of course I laughed, I have a laughing nature'; and Ms Dench, an actress to her fingertips, gives one a sense of a deep, buried happiness. To convey a feeling of being re-born is a rare achievement; and it is reinforced by the amazed, compassionate stillness of Paul Rogers and Anna Massey as the unrecognised relations.

But if this play deals emotionally with the theme of half-life, *Family Voices* (already heard on radio and done as a platform performance) handles it on Pinter's more familiar comic-metaphysic level. Two characters, a mother and son, sit on chairs framed against a vellum-background. She hungers for contact with her seeming-dead child. But Pinter treats the idea of the great chasm between kith and kin by highlighting the son's occupancy of some eccentric lodging-house complete with homosexual cop and landlady's lubricious daughter catching buns between her toes: it is a funny play (nicely acted by Nigel Havers and Anna Massey) about a tragic situation.

And a reminder that Pinter is also a born revue-sketch writer comes with *Victoria Station*, in which Paul Rogers plays a flat-capped, foul-mouthed controller of radio-cabs desperately trying to make contact with an aberrant driver hunched over the wheel of his Ford Cortina. You could see it as a study in power and panic; or you could take it as a return to Pinter's early surrealist sketches. Either way, it means you will never sit in a radio-car again without having an image of some god-like figure trying to control traffic from his glass booth. And it contributes to an extraordinary evening that shows Pinter's gift for pinning down the dream-like oddity of all waking existence.

The Real Thing

Strand: 12 November 1982

Tom Stoppard has always been an intellectual gymnast. Rarely, however, has one gone to his plays for their emotional truth. But in *The Real Thing* he combines some fly Pirandellian games with an unequivocal statement about the joyousness of shared passion. And the result is that rare thing in the West End (or anywhere else for that matter): an intelligent play about love.

At first, it seems as if we are in characteristic Stoppard country: clever people making clever remarks as an architect rumbles his wife's infidelity by revealing, as she vivaciously returns from a Swiss trip, that she had taken everything but her passport. But the rug is pulled from under our feet (always a pleasant theatrical sensation) as we realise that this is a scene from a play, *House Of Cards*; and that the playwright, Henry, is in the throes of an affaire with Annie, the wife of his leading actor. Henry and Annie abandon their respective partners and set up house; and what follows is an examination of whether their own passion is 'the real thing' or a shiny simulacrum.

Stoppard is, most ingeniously, doing two things simultaneously in this play: questioning whether one can ever write about love and at the same time pinning his faith on it. Henry is a cricket-loving, politically orthodox dramatist who seems to have imbibed the romantic values of the middle-of-the-road pop (Neil Sedaka, The Supremes, Brenda Lee) he so vehemently admires. But although this somewhat Stoppardian figure claims he can't write love, we see him experiencing its desperate pangs as Annie has a brief Glaswegian fling with the actor she is playing opposite in *'Tis Pity She's A Whore*. By the end pain has transmuted him, and the assumption is that he will be a better writer and a richer man.

None of this is revolutionary: what makes the play so fascinating is Stoppard's running intellectual commentary on the ideas he is presenting. Is Love unliterary? Do we inherit our notions of 'good writing' from what the good writers tell us? If you judge music by its emotional impact, is one man's Procul Harum another man's Verdi? Do concepts like justice, patriotism, politics have any existence outside our subjective perception? All these notions are profitably buzzing around inside a play that is also an endorsement of authentic private passion.

My one serious doubt about the play concerns the figure of Brodie, a convicted left-wing arsonist in whose rotten play Annie wants to appear: Stoppard sets up a too-easy conflict between Henry, the sophisticated wordsmith, and Brodie, the unlettered man who writes from the heart. What disturbs me is the unspoken assumption that impassioned political drama is irreconcilable with irony and finesse. But this is the one flaw in a play that itself constantly questions the nature of reality (in one superb scene Annie's forthcoming lover reveals his own passions through the mask of Jacobean rhetoric) while making a positive statement.

Much of course depends on the svelte smoothness of Peter Wood's production, with the seven mirrored panels of Carl Toms's set constantly rising to usher us into another bit of simulated reality. And there is a stunning performance by Roger Rees as Henry: all nervous impulse and growing panic as he grabs at a telephone, claws at a bookcase or simply follows Annie's departure from a room with hopeless resignation. Felicity Kendal's Annie also subtly combines impishness and passion, surrender to the moment and rock-fast affection. And Jeremy Clyde and Polly Adams play the other couple (at times it's like a hip *Private Lives*) with due conviction. There is even more to the play than I have adumbrated; but this piece proves conclusively that Stoppard can write from the heart while keeping the cerebrum still spinning like a top.

1983

Intriguingly, it was a year in which form made a comeback: there seemed to be a renewed interest in the play *aspect of play-making. In the seventies a lot of our younger dramatists were prone to slap raw, bleeding chunks of dialogue down on the stage, thereby creating some exciting but perishable drama. But in art you cannot afford to ignore the imperatives of rhythm, structure and shape.*

This didn't mean in '83 a return to the rigid format of the well-made West End play, so much as an experiment with the possibilities of narrative. Hare's A Map Of The World *set its dialectical arguments within the framework of a filmic recreation of a Bombay conference. Hampton's* Tales From Hollywood *gave its portrait of European exiles living in a Californian lotus-land the aqueous structure of a dream. Brian Thompson's* Turning Over *showed how the jumbled, crisis-ridden experience of shooting a documentary in India was turned into sixty minutes of smooth television. Mamet's* Glengarry Glen Ross *borrowed the structure of a whodunnit to give us both a withering indictment of capitalist incentive-schemes and a tribute to the desperate men who made a dubious system work. It was good to see all these writers paying attention to form as well as content.*

It was also a year in which the big public play made a brief comeback, not least with David Edgar's Maydays *on the main Barbican stage. What was cheering was the way Edgar's analysis of the collapse of the late Sixties revolutionary impetus reached out beyond the theatre and became a matter of editorial debate: here was theatre once again annexing the territory increasingly left to TV documentary.*

Peter Hall published his Diaries, *exposing both his own vulnerability and the complex workings of a big institution. Yuri Lyubimov took the Lyric Hammersmith by storm with his* Crime And Punishment *which rose above scissors-and-paste adaptation to bring out the tensions between nightmare-evil and Christian redemption. A number of women dramatists made their mark including Sarah Daniels with* Masterpieces, *Debbie Horsfield with a trilogy (*The Red Devils, True, Dare, Kiss *and* Command Or Promise*) for*

Liverpool Playhouse, and Marcella Evaristi with Commedia. *Theatres were still struggling for survival, but at least it was a year of marked individual achievement.*

Hard Feelings

Bush: 4 February 1983

They shop at Camden Lock, they eat at Routiers, they drink at Rumours. But Doug Lucie in *Hard Feelings*, which Oxford Playhouse have brought to the Bush, is doing something more than pin down the lifestyle of London's new swingers. He is suggesting in this pugnacious and funny play that there is a whole generation around that puts style before content, fashion before feeling, and show before basic human sympathy.

His setting is a house in Brixton in April 1981. Venetian blinds seal off this privileged barricade from the street riots outside and enable the inmates to get on with their middle-class games. Viv, who is looking after the property for her ex-pat parents, rules this particular roost with a lethal smile. And, as the action develops, we see her declaring silent war on Jane, a Jewish girl studying to be a solicitor, and on Jane's militant boyfriend. The other tenants and hangers on, including a rock musician and a glossy model, are forced to come out for Viv while Baz, a young entrepreneur who fixes frisbee-contests, squats uncomfortably on the fence.

One could carp at the easy irony that plants these domestic power battles in the midst of an erupting borough. But Mr Lucie writes with clear-eyed precision about a new generation of Oxford graduates who treat life as an endless party in which you come as the person you would most like to be. They watch *Casablanca* for the clothes. They hang up glamour prints of Hitler. And their only reaction to the Brixton riots is to complain about the damage to their car aerials. What lifts the play above a puritan diatribe, however, is partly Mr Lucie's sure sense of comic detail and his complex regret for a lost generation. In that sense, the best character is Baz: a sympathetic loner reared on Henry James and now devoting his life to footling entrepreneurial ventures. He proves that under Mr Lucie's fierce moralism there is a genuine dramatist alert to the poignancy of human waste.

Seeing Mike Bradwell's production a second time also reinforces my feeling that there are few better displays of group acting around. Frances Barber's brutally stylish Viv, Chris Jury's bewildered, owlish Baz, Jenifer Landor's cruelly persecuted Jane, and Ian Reddington's parasitic musician, veering between Humphrey Bogart and Gilbert's Pirate King, are all exemplary. But what the play does above all is combine accurate social reporting with a lament for the lost tribes of the new England. I commend it highly.

Theatre In Moscow

11 April 1983

Six o'clock on a chilly Tuesday evening in Moscow's Taganskaya Square. A crowd of around three hundred, youngish, fur-hatted and undeterred by the thin drizzle, is milling around behind the crush barriers that seal off a redbrick public building. They look on, with spaniel-eyed envy, as the lucky ones flash a paper document at the security guard and are admitted to the privileged warmth of the building.

This is not a meeting of some inner Soviet Council, simply a nightly ritual enacted outside Moscow's most exciting and celebrated theatre, the Taganka. Tonight sees a performance inside the Taganka's smaller, 600-seat house of Bulgakov's *The Master And Margarita* directed by the company's celebrated *auteur*, Yuri Lyubimov. Those outside have gathered an hour before curtain-time in the faint hope of securing a return-ticket for a production that has been in the repertory for over six years: those with a ticket are about to see a breathtaking Meyerholdian production that I would rank amongst the theatrical experiences of a lifetime.

But the experience outside the Taganka is not uncommon. Going to see a fashionable, newish, rather sexy rock-opera at the Lenin Komsomol, my Novosti guide and I are accosted several times in the street by eager ticket hunters. And this is the first, crucial point to make about Moscow theatre: it is phenomenally popular. In London, Paris and New York, the main problem these days is persuading people to go to the theatre. In Moscow there are not enough seats to satisfy demand. And this in a city where there are 28 permanent companies (covering drama, ballet, opera, music and children's theatre) each with an average of 20 productions in its repertoire. Given a nightly change of programme, this means that in any one week there are over 160 productions on offer. And still it's hard to get in.

Why, though, this inordinate appetite for theatre? Partly because tickets are cheap (the top price is three roubles and the official exchange rate is roughly one rouble to the pound sterling). Partly because alternative Moscow night life is not exactly seductive; a rash visit to a local bar involved sipping a lethally sweet cocktail in a Stygian crypt. But I suspect a British Embassy friend put his finger on it when he said that the theatre in Moscow offered the prospect of 'intellectual adventure'. The myth is that Moscow theatre is full of museum-classics and hortatory plays about productivity norms. The truth is that old plays are constantly re-evaluated (I saw a production of *The Cherry Orchard* at the Sovremennik that would have been damned in Britain for its radicalism) and that new, non-propagandist plays are being written. Theatre, as always, remains the most potentially dangerous of the arts.

It would be absurdly naive, of course, to pretend that, in Moscow theatre, anything goes: Lyubimov's latest venture, a non-musical *Boris Godunov*, has been put into cold storage after 42 objections were raised by the official scrutineers. But, within the parameters of political orthodoxy, you can still say quite a lot on the Moscow stage. The Moscow Art Theatre is currently staging a play, *Thus We Will Win* by Mikhail Shatrov, that deals with the struggle for succession just before Lenin's death and that raises some fairly uncomfortable historical matters such as the crushing by Lenin of trade union leaders who wanted a larger say in party affairs. You don't have to look too far to find modern parallels.

Soviet dramatists also seem to be fascinated by the question of whether the new consumerism means a loss of spiritual aspirations. The Mayakovsky Theatre is currently mounting a satirical comedy, *Look Who's Here* (featuring Andropov's actor son-in-law) that updates *The Cherry Orchard* by showing a nouveau riche hairdresser, surrounded by thuggish cronies, trying to buy up the property of an old impoverished family of writers. And a play I saw at the Moscow Art Theatre, *Old New Year* by Mikhail Roschin, again juxtaposed a working-class family grabbing up consumer durables with a group of ascetic trendies sitting around on cushions pouring scorn on materialism: both attitudes were found significantly wanting.

I gather that the current upsurge in new writing (the Soviet copyright agency handled about 300 new plays last year, though not all found a stage) dates from the early 1970s when it was realised people were hungry for plays about social issues rather than bogusly optimistic propaganda: symptomatically, I noticed a faint embarrassment when I asked someone about the heroic statues of Stakhanovite workers that decorate one of the famous Metro stations. But although Western nihilism hasn't exactly penetrated the Moscow stage (no Beckett on the grounds that 'we have our own Absurdists'), I was assured by one official that 'plays used to have to end happily: now our drama is closer to life.'

Yet although Moscow theatre has clearly moved on in the last decade, overall I was struck by the sense of familial continuity. Our Kleenex theatre is based on rapid turnover and instant disposability. In Moscow old actors are revered. Productions are very gradually replaced: there are 80 new shows a year. The past is there to be learned from. Valentin Pluchek (who runs the Satire Theatre and who has the beaming, Buddha-like features of his cousin, Peter Brook) made a sound point when he said that the Stanislavsky tradition of scientific naturalism is carried on by Efremov, director of the Moscow Art Theatre, and that the Meyerholdian legacy of revolutionary Expressionism has passed to the controversial Lyubimov. We bury our theatrical dead: in Moscow, they quote theirs.

This sense of continuity – of being part of an age-old family business – has its good and bad side. I glimpsed the good side when I went to a preview matinée for theatre folk of a new play at Mossovet's 150-seat Studio theatre in a converted cinema. The play itself, *A One-Wheeled Stove*, was an affectionate picture of village life in the style of the primitive painter, Lubok. Politically, it was interesting in that the only unsympathetic character on stage was the head of the local collective, a party hack, who kept bursting in on his motorbike and bullying everyone to increase their milk yield. But what fascinated me was the occasion as much as the play. When it was over, three of the leading actors got up and made speeches offering detailed criticism of the play we had just seen: praise was given here, advice there. One bull-necked veteran from the Maly Theatre went on to suggest that actor-directors like himself were far too respectable and established and that 'studio theatres like this offered the only hope for the future'. It was rather as if, at the end of a preview at the Bush, Donald Sinden were to get up and tell the cast how to tighten the second act and to suggest that the Fringe was where it was at.

The bad side of this familial continuity is that youth is often kept waiting in the wings. I heard everywhere about the outcrop of new writing; but one 'young' playwright I met was hovering around 40.

And when I asked Anatoly Danilov, deputy theatre chief at the Ministry of Culture, what the main problems were, he was fairly blunt. He said: 'You can count our leading directors on the fingers of one hand: Efremov, Lyubimov, Efros, Goncahrov, Zakharov. But who will head our theatrical art in the years to come? Where are the young directors who want to direct plays and administer our large companies?'

One week's intensive theatregoing, of course, gives one only fragments of the truth. But what is significant about Moscow theatre is that it crystallises some of the paradoxes within the Soviet system. Authority wants art to be constructive; yet it has to recognise that great drama is built out of conflict, dialectic and criticism. It wants art to be cheap and available to all; and so it is, yet there is no getting away from the faint air of privilege that surrounds a sold-out performance of a successful show.

I came away from Moscow, however, genuinely surprised by the stylistic variety of the fare available and by the overwhelming sense that theatre there matters. Moscow in the end is a theatre-mad city and drama seems as central to its everyday existence as the curlicued sugar-stick domes of St Basil's Cathedral which once led the English actor, Alec Clunes, to ask if they said St Basil's all the way through.

A Patriot For Me

Chichester: 13 May 1983

John Osborne's great, neglected play is the kind of work for which the Chichester Festival Theatre was built. It is a huge, complex, epic work, with 84 characters and 23 scenes spanning the Austro-Hungarian empire from 1890 to 1913. And its successful realisation in Ronald Eyre's production took me back to the halcyon early days of Chichester when you would expect to find a big new play by Arden or Shaffer each season.

Why does Osborne's play work so well? Partly because it fulfils one of the basic functions of drama. It combines the study of an individual with a portrait of a society. Osborne's hero, Alfred Redl, is a vain, brilliant, ambitious, reclusive career officer in the Austro-Hungarian army. And it is because that world is male, elitist and full of role playing that it provides the perfect cloak for Redl's closeted homosexuality. What we see in the play is Redl gradually coming to terms with his own nature; and, once he has recognised it, finding that he is trapped in a vicious web of spendthrift promiscuity that leads to his enlistment as a spy for the Russians and his ultimate ruination.

Osborne doesn't give you any obligatory nut of message. What he does is to encapsulate his ideas in concrete theatrical images; and nowhere more so than in the famous drag ball which once gave the Lord Chamberlain palpitations. It is a brilliant device: a group of elegantly gowned, silhouetted figures listening to an aria from *The Marriage Of Figaro* and slowly revealed to be men. The scene is ribald, coarse and funny with Nigel Stock as a square-chinned Queen Alexandra-like figure rebuking his acolytes – 'Mind your wimple' – and going into ecstasies at the thought that a real woman has been inserted into the clan. But the point of the scene is that these are all Austrian army officers; and that their disguise is a larger metaphor for Redl's own self-deception.

More than in the original production, this version brings out Osborne's own intensely ambivalent attitude towards homosexuality. In one perfectly balanced scene Redl, discovering his lover is going to marry a countess, claims a detailed, proprietorial knowledge of the man's body; to which the countess replies with a withering attack on the physical consequences of gayness. It is a first rate scene because it springs out of Osborne's own tensions: a seeming regard for any hunted minority combined with a tangible Swiftian horror at bodily decrepitude.

Admittedly Ronald Eyre's production misses one or two tricks: an early scene with Redl and a whore overlooks the sub-textual taunting at his impotence. But although the production needs a bit of playing in, it occupies the Chichester stage admirably; and Carl Toms has set it shrewdly against a background of neutral grey screens on to which are projected images of a leisurely Austrian café society and a harsher world of bleak military gymnasiums and Russian spy-holes.

Alan Bates as Redl also captures very precisely the transition from a stiff, ramrod-backed junior officer, sitting on the edge of a chair in case it creases his uniform, to a hedonistic, indulgent colonel: he is particularly fine in the scene of his blackmail, which he greets with the stone-faced impassivity of the officer class. And George Murcell as the Russian colonel, Sheila Gish as a creamy bosomed countess, David King as Redl's admiring superior lend weight to the supporting roles.

But the chief delight of the evening is that it confirms Osborne's stature as our finest creator of isolated, self-discovering heroes and that it once more puts the Chichester stage to epic use.

Prejudices

10 June 1983

A drama critic has, by definition, to be a quick-change artist. He, or she, should be capable of responding in a given week to a wide variety of entertainments: a Shakespeare revival, a new Howard Barker, a rare Racine, *The Two Ronnies*. One doesn't have to like everything; but one should be capable of reacting with the same forthrightness and vigour to a classic revival at the National, an anti-nuclear play on the Fringe, an American musical in the West End, and Ken Dodd playing in some 'magnificent shed' in the sticks.

But, as Joe E. Brown said in *Some Like It Hot*, nobody's perfect; and it might be as well to confess that there are some forms of entertainment (not all confined to the theatre) to which one is personally immune. John Gielgud once said that it must be agony for critics having to review time and again some performer whom they dislike. A far greater agony is slumping in one's stall and being confronted by some brand of entertainment that produces an aesthetic allergy.

Top of my own particular hate-list is anything to do with puppets or marionettes. Like most adult failings, this can be traced back to childhood experience. I can never forget being taken, with a school- party, at the age of ten, to the old Birmingham Rep Theatre in Station Street (where I later had many exhilarating evenings) to see the Salzburg Marionettes performing a miniature Mozart opera. All I can say is that if you have never sat at the top of a very steep theatre watching a lot of prancing mannikins on wires murdering Mozart in a manner Salieri would have envied, then you have never known what Hell is like.

I have, of course, since come to realise that puppets come in all shapes and sizes: that there are glove-puppets, rod-puppets, wire-puppets, life-size puppets and a whole aesthetic of puppetry ranging from Punch and Judy to the Japanese Bunraku Theatre. Yet confront me with these squawking, parody simulcra of humanity and I become like Ben Jonson's Zeal-of-the-Land Busy who rushes into the puppet-show at the end of *Bartholomew Fair* crying 'Down with Dagon, down with Dagon, 'tis I will no longer endure your profanations.'

I am sure it is indefensible. But it is rooted in the same thing that makes me howl with boredom at the prospect of an animated cartoon in the cinema: a dislike of anything that reduces the infinite excitement of human beings to jerky, squeaking, one-dimensional limited representations. When I go out to the theatre I crave flesh; preferably spiced with a little blood.

Next to puppets comes mime: one of the nastiest four-letter words in the theatrical language. I exempt mime which is part of a larger theatrical structure. Where would *Hamlet* be, for instance, without the dumb-show played before Claudius at the court, though I've always thought Ophelia had a point when she asked 'Will 'a tell us what this show meant'? I also, paradoxically, exempt ballet, which I love for its colour, its beauty, its exquisitely choreographed patterns.

What I can't really take is the solo mime artist who spends so much time walking into the wind (something people actually do with their heads down) with many a corkscrew turn of the body and with tiny, shuffling movements, pressing his hands against imaginary plate-glass windows, or compressing the history of the world into three minutes. I accept that mime is a highly disciplined skill and that someone like Marcel Marceau has raised it to the level of genius. But the prospect of a whole evening watching someone use the elaborate machinery of mime to convey something that speech could often convey in a sentence is to me the quintessence of boredom. Mime is a weapon in the theatrical armoury. When it becomes the whole armoury itself, I make an excuse and don't go.

I concede that these are blind-spots: temperamental flaws hard rationally to justify. But there are other forms of theatre where my dislike is much more explicable. Plays, for instance, where the first act is set in the year 2007 and the second 'half-an-hour-later'; musicals where newsboys run across the stage shouting 'Extra, extra' (it happens in *Bugsy Malone*); allegorical works where the characters are labelled The Man, The Woman, The Child, The Lavatory-Attendant; evenings where an artist's complex viewpoint is reduced to resounding banality – which reminds me of the classic story of a *Henry V* in battle-dress at the Mermaid which began with a character coming out on stage and telling the audience 'This is a play about war' to which Mr Peter Dews responded with a stentorian cry of 'Wrong'.

I also dislike the growing tendency to sectionalise and compartmentalise the theatre. I realise that there are many members of the community who have causes they wish to propagate and unique experiences they wish to convey. But if I confront a company calling itself, say, Single-Parent Masons in Milton Keynes, I tend to feel that I am being excluded or that the territory covered will be, shall we say, a little narrow.

One goes to the theatre to enlarge one's understanding and to escape from the confines of what John McGrath always dubs one's white, male, middle-class Oxbridge background. But a theatre that appeals exclusively to a single group (the young, OAPs, Seventh-Day

Adventists or whatever) is one that loses sight of the medium's ability to cut across the social barriers of age, class, sex and race.

I could easily add to the list things I dislike in other media: TV sitcoms that reduce life to 28-minute temporary crises; those eternal telly documentaries about battleships; movies that combine high-tech sophistication with a junky, strip-cartoon vision of life; self-referential films about the agony of making films with directors philosophising in echoing, luxury hotels in Upper Dalmatia, while outside it rains.

But these are simply my personal lists of pimples on the surface of the arts. On the whole, I believe critics write best out of enthusiasm; and I certainly set out for the theatre with a desire to be uplifted, instructed and entertained. I can, I hope, take just about anything; unless, perhaps, it be a futuristic, allegorical play by a Serbo-Croatian puppet-company in which, during the interval, a figure in black cap and silken pantaloons mimes the ending of the world. At that, even I might jib.

Great And Small

Vaudeville: 26 August 1983

Forget the intimations of disaster and stories of provincial walk-outs: *Waiting For Godot* got precisely the same treatment. Far from being a no-no, Botho Strauss's *Great And Small* is the most striking, original and entertaining new play in London; and, though its theme is loneliness and alienation, it handles it with a jaunty, nerve-tingling freshness.

It could be called *Lotte's Odyssey*; for its heroine, a graphic artist separated from her husband, goes through life enthusiastically seeking human contact but meets only a solitude and isolation greater than her own. We first see her on a Moroccan package-holiday where she finds (as on most such trips) greed, hate, jealousy, envy. Back home, she peers through neighbours' windows and vainly tries to strike up a friendship. She rents space in an apartment-block where she is chillingly told, 'In principle each room is its own responsibility.' Old friends rebuff her, family-life turns out to be a sham, bosses reject her advances. She ends up talking to God and to total strangers in doctors' surgeries; but she goes on her way doggedly believing that love still exists.

Obviously Strauss is not the first dramatist to see modern society as a series of isolated cells never making contact. but what makes his play unusual is its springy humour and its total lack of self-pity. Lotte, far from bemoaning her fate, is like a tail-wagging puppy, always waiting to be stroked and never able to understand why she gets a kick instead. Strauss is clever enough to make you see why people flinch from Lotte's bright-eyed, wet-nurse eagerness; yet at the same time he gives you a sharp, vivid, surreal portrait (one 17-year-old is reduced to living in a tent where meals are passed under the flap) of a society where solitude has become endemic.

Admittedly one scene involving a street-fracas between a Turkish gastarbeiter and his wife doesn't mean much in an English context; and I was puzzled by the director's omission of one crucial image in which a massive book Lotte is looking at starts to bleed. Otherwise I have nothing but praise for Keith Hack's ebullient production set by Voytek in a towering perspex cage and backed by music from Ben Mason which has echoes of twenties German jazz and Ibert-like eccentricity. The production's very lightness ironically counterpoints Strauss's vision of a society where each man has become a marooned island.

Glenda Jackson also gives an astonishing performance as Lotte: crop-haired, long-necked, deliciously nosy, she has the blithe fixity of purpose of a comic character yet at other times the frightening ability of a Beckett heroine to stare into the abyss. She doesn't tell us what to think; she presents the woman as she is which is one of the hardest things to do in acting. And, in a talented cast, Barry Stanton is very funny as her journalist-husband and petrified boss and Brian Deacon has a good scene as a chess-playing computer-expert terrified of Lotte's accosting technique. Those who regard *The Second Mrs Tanqueray* as avant-garde may hate the play: all true modernists will love it.

Tales From Hollywood

Olivier: 2 September 1983

I admired Christopher Hampton's *Tales From Hollywood* enormously when I saw it in Los Angeles last year. There seemed a wicked chutzpah about offering that city a play about the culture-clash between Californian values and the emigré European writers who landed up in Tinseltown in the 1940s. But a second viewing of the play, in Peter Gill's diamond-sharp production at the Olivier, makes it look a much richer and more moving work built around a series of multiplying antitheses, personal, geographical and historical.

In shape, the play has the quality of a dream. It posits the idea that Ödön von Horváth, the Hungarian writer who was actually killed in a freak Paris accident in 1938, arrives in the slightly surreal world of wartime Hollywood where Johnny Weissmuller knows Thomas Mann and Schoenberg plays tennis with Harpo Marx. Horváth thus becomes the narrator guiding us through this topsy-turvy community in which hucksters thrive, in which Hitler's quest for *Lebensraum* is judged by its effect on European grosses and in which a great writer, Heinrich Mann, is a contract hack living out the *Blue Angel* story in his private life. But Horváth also becomes the epitome of the politically passive, acclimatising writer, with an American-Jewish girlfriend, in stark contrast to the abrasive Marxist Brecht who remains as anachronistic as a sausage in a greenhouse.

Obviously Hampton's play has a documentary fascination. But what is impressive is not merely the scalpel-like wit of the dialogue but also the number of conflicts Hampton manages to embrace. A figure like Heinrich Mann (beautifully played by Philip Locke as a silvery, displaced ghost) embodies the pathos of exile and Joyce's remark that 'history is a nightmare from which I am trying to escape.' Yet we are constantly reminded that he and the other sun-kissed emigrés were at least surviving while Europe itself was burning.

And the play is built around a series of interlocking tensions between the tragic innocence of America and the guilty awareness of the Europeans, between the need some writers feel to observe society and the compulsion others have to change it, between personal discomfiture and cosmic upheaval. It is a play that can make you laugh at the crassness of Hollywood producers appalled to discover that Edward II was a faggot and that can, at the same time, move one at the tragic cuckolding of Heinrich Mann by his voluptuous, hard-drinking wife, Nelly.

What is equally impressive is Hampton's ability to combine easy, graceful writing with pure theatrical surprise. 'Eden paid for out of other men's dreams' is a lovely description of a Hollywood tycoon's paradisal pad. And yet any tendency to luxuriate in the supple dialogue is jolted by such moments as Brecht's arrival down the centre-aisle with house-lights full on and his ability to dictate terms by bringing on his own lawn and signpost for a scene in his garden. In a sense, the conflict between Brecht, the anarchic Utopian, and Horváth, the guileful humanist, lies at the very heart of this deep-revolving play. And it is typical of Hampton's maturity that just when he makes you think Horváth has won the argument, he brings out of the cupboard his guilty complicity with the Nazis in 1934. It is a play that throws numerous ideas out to the audience and allows them the privilege of making up their own minds.

Peter Gill's production also gives you the feeling of hard-edged vignettes within the framework of an undulating dream: Alison Chitty's designs (her best at the National) consist of mobile trucks outlined against the space of the Olivier and a huge beige poster of old Hollywood movies. Michael Gambon's Horváth, a bulky, white-suited figure, padding around the stage like a caged animal, also captures precisely the feeling of an outsider gradually warming to his environment. And there is fine work from Billie Whitelaw as Nelly Mann, a figure of good-hearted coarseness unable to withstand the pressures of exile, from Ian McDiarmid as Brecht, stubby, unshaven, impish and sly, and from Guy Rolfe as Thomas Mann, forever viewing life as if someone has sent it him to review. Far more than in Los Angeles, I felt as if I was seeing a play that took a fascinating slice of cultural history and transmuted it into the complexity of art.

Glengarry Glen Ross

Cottesloe: 22 September 1983

You won't hear much better dialogue on the London stage than you get in David Mamet's *Glengarry Glen Ross* at the Cottesloe. The play is filled with the spiralling obscenity and comic bluster of real-estate salesmen caught off-guard; yet underneath that there is fear and desperation. Mamet says that he admires his characters' pragmatic individualism, but to me the piece comes across as a chillingly funny indictment of a world in which you are what you sell.

It takes time to plug into the patois. The first act, consisting of three duologues that take place in the scarlet-sinister booths of a Chicago Chinese restaurant, echoes with talk of 'leads' and 'boards' and 'closers'. It transpires that the characters are mainly salesmen whose very survival in their company depends on their ability to fix up juicy appointments (leads) that will enable them to firm up Floridian land-deals (closers) and so enable them to get a winning position on the office sales graph (the board). One is an ex-sales virtuoso desperate to regain lost status; another is a middle-aged man subtly blackmailing a colleague into carrying out a midnight robbery to get the best leads; another is a sharp hustler button-holing a total stranger almost as if he were executing a homosexual pick-up.

I would not be so cruel as to reveal what happens in the second act, which takes place in the paper-strewn real-estate office the morning after the internal robbery. What really counts is Mamet's brilliant use of language to depict character and attitudes. 'Anyone lives in this office lives on their wits', says Richard Roma, the brashest of the batch. And you see the sharp contrast between the wheedling, ingratiating, fake-matey tone adopted towards a welching client and the big-mouth, four-letter abusiveness with which they bombard the head desk-wallah who never has to go out on the streets. Mamet (as in *American Buffalo*) conjures up a world in which violent words are used to mask fear, shield panic, hide feelings, and deflect attention from the fact that the top two salesmen get prizes while the bottom two face the sack.

I wouldn't class the play with *Death Of A Salesman*, which poignantly shows how the American dream of individual initiative has been soiled by the corrupt ethos of the sales-pitch. But what Mamet does is show how the fight for survival bends personal morality: in this world you implicate a colleague in crime for the sake of a puny reward and you proclaim fellow-feeling while grabbing someone else's territory. Mamet stops short of attacking the system; but he paints a vivid, cruel, often hilarious portrait of a hermetic and tacky order in which people camouflage fear under a wealth of blue-streaked street-talk.

Bill Bryden's production, with the help of two very good sets by Hayden Griffin, exactly catches this feeling of a nervous, closed society. And there are riveting performances from Jack Shepherd as the white-suited hustler backing away from people as he gets more vocally aggressive; from Derek Newark as a flannel-suited blusterer bullying the very man from whom he most needs help, and from Karl Johnson as the sweaty-palmed office-manager surveying his desperate charges with the quiet guilt of one who never has to venture out into the jungle of the hard sell.

Freshwater

Riverside Studios: 28 November 1983

'The English stage has rarely seen so bizarre a performance as this,' said Nigel Nicolson, introducing Virginia Woolf's *Freshwater* at the Riverside Studios. He had a point; for here was a satire on eminent Victorians first performed at a private Bloomsbury party in 1935 now being played in 1983 by a group of French writers and intellectuals with

Ionesco as Tennyson, Alain Robbe-Grillet as Charles Hay-Cameron, drama critic Guy Dumur as G.F. Watts and Nathalie Sarraute, a dapper, silvery octogenarian, as James the Butler.

The short evening, under Simone Benmussa's direction, certainly had the playful, indulgent air of a private charade: when Ionesco's tiny wife, as Mary Magdalen the maid, fumbled her lines when announcing that the coffins had arrived to accompany Julia Margaret Cameron and her husband to India, the audience gave her a round.

But the play itself, depicting a proto-Bloomsbury group on the Isle of Wight in 1870, also emerged as a fascinating curiosity. Nigel Nicolson suggested it was a Woolfian allegory about the falsity of Victorian values and the intolerable presumption of men. To me, it shows Virginia Woolf writing in the tradition of English nonsense-humour of Gilbert, Edward Lear and Lewis Carroll, and even ironically echoing Shaw's *Heartbreak House* which had itself capitalised on Bloomsbury.

Thus we see Ellen Terry posing as Modesty for G.F. Watts before escaping to flirt with a young naval lieutenant on the Needles. As they spoon, a huge porpoise (played by Snoo Wilson in a black bowler with an immaculate sense of porpoise) swims by and gulps down Ellen Terry's wedding ring. Tennyson tears up *Maud* on discovering that Ellen, presumed dead, is alive after all. And Queen Victoria (embodied by a blue-chinned, implacably masculine historian, Jean-Paul Aron) finally arrives to bestow a peerage on Tennyson and the Order of Beauty on Watts.

Admittedly the play undergoes something of a sea-change in Elisabeth Janvier's French translation. In the original the philosopher Cameron, gazing wistfully at a marmoset, pronounces 'Life is a dream.' To which Tennyson wittily replies, 'Rather a wet one, Charles'. When that becomes 'La vie est un rève' – 'Plutôt pollué Charles', a very English double-barrelled pun goes out of the window. But Simone Benmussa's stylish production – in which the sea is evoked by two black-clad figures solemnly carrying a painting of 'un bateau' across the stage – transforms a piece of nonsense humour into something with the dreamy madness of the Theatre of the Absurd.

That impression is heightened by the presence of Ionesco, owlish and bearded like seventeen pards, as Tennyson reciting 'Viens dans mon jardin, Maud.' Even more bizarre was seeing Nathalie Sarraute, progenitor of the new novel, as a white-gloved butler proclaiming her vision of the future. But the most accomplished performances came from Joyce Mansour as a cigar-puffing Julia Cameron, Florence Delay (Bresson's Jeanne d'Arc) as an ethereally beautiful Ellen Terry, and Guy

Dumur (proving that critics are born actors) as the arrogantly cuckolded Watts. The evening, which ended with a huge birthday cake being wheeled on for Ionesco, certainly proved that whoever is afraid of Virgina Woolf it isn't French intellectuals.

Jean Seberg

Olivier: 3 December 1983

For the past few weeks it has been impossible to take a stroll round the block without someone rushing up a telling you what they thought of *Jean Seberg*. Now, at last, I can reveal that it is neither the biggest disaster since the bombing of Pearl Harbour, nor a particularly stirring theatrical event. It is simply a rather dogged, trite bio-musical (better than *Marilyn* but not as good as *Evita*) that is well-staged and boasts a couple of decent numbers, but leaves the heart and mind serenely untouched.

The story it tells is certainly a sad and pathetic one: of the small-town Iowa girl who gets snapped up by Preminger at 17 to play Saint Joan, gets savaged by the critics, becomes a symbol of the French New Wave in *Breathless*, marries Romain Gary, supports the Black Panthers, is systematically discredited by the FBI, and takes her own life in Paris in 1979.

In Julian Barry's book and Christopher Adler's lyrics, Jean Seberg emerges as a naive and hapless victim of the American success-ethic, of a Hoover smear-campaign and of her own involvement with revolutionary politics. But in attempting to elevate this unhappy woman into a symbolic American martyr, the musical is impaled on its own pretensions. It does, in fact, unequivocally, identify poor Jean with Saint Joan. Initially, it shows Preminger shooting the Shavian trial scene in a Parisian square supervised by a black-cowled Inquisitor who turns out to be J. Edgar Hoover ('Maybe you're here to shoot *Saint Joan* but I'm here to try Jean Seberg'). And the climax of the musical is the public burning of the Jean/Joan heroine after she has rounded on her tormentors and accusers.

Clearly the show's creators think they are breaking new ground by writing a musical tragedy (Verdi beat them at that game). In fact, they have come up with a politicised version of an old-fashioned Hollywood biopic. But there are hints in the show that if only they had pursued their gift for irony, they might have produced something far more exciting. Late on in the evening (two hours sans interval) there is a moment when a group of grey-masked, white-coated doctors do a gentle, soft-shoe number around the figure of the stricken heroine: the contrast between the glitzy style and the astringent content does give one a jab and hints at what might have been.

Mostly, however, it is a rather savourless musical staged with merciful speed and dash by Peter Hall (Jean's transformation from hick French immigrant to red-dressed epitome of chic is very deft) and acted unexceptionally. Kelly Hunter is perfectly presentable as the young, innocent, puppy-faced Jean, watched over by Elizabeth Counsell as her haggard, close-cropped older self. Joss Ackland in the impossible role of Romain Gary (musicals can never handle writers) does a very interesting Alan Brien impersonation, but Michael Bryant, gamely taking over as J. Edgar Hoover, can do nothing except look menacing atop a mobile podium. John Bury's set, a dissected Paris apartment block with a screen in the middle, at least clears the space for the action: but the energy gradually drains out of a musical that aims for Shavian resonance without a smidgen of Shaw's buccaneering wit or bully-boy gusto.

1984

Orwell's nightmare predictions for 1984 may not have been fulfilled but, in the theatre, the whole subsidised structure looked perilously fragile. Grant increases were well below inflation level. The National's scheme to launch five separate companies, under different directors, was in peril even before it started. The axe was poised over the Royal Court. In the regions, prolonged summer closures became commonplace. The contrast with France was instructive. There the Socialists, who came to power in 1981, more than doubled the theatre budget from 271 million to 664.6 million francs. The Thatcher government seemed more concerned to sustain Fortress Falklands than to support the arts.

There were some good new plays around: Frayn's Benefactors, *Hutchinson's* Rat In The Skull, *Hastings's* Tom And Viv, *Pownall's* Master Class, *Page's* Golden Girls. *But even the best plays were on a relatively small, televisual scale and many of them (including Poliakoff's* Breaking The Silence *and Nicholas Wright's* The Desert Air*) looked back to the past rather than engaged with the present.*

One refreshing sign was the emergence of a number of counterweights to the two big national companies. Ray Cooney created the Theatre of Comedy and enlivened the West End with Loot *and* Two Into One. *United British Artists weighed in with Albert Finney in* The Biko Inquest. *Honest Ed Mirvish poured his Canadian millions into the Old Vic which brought us Philip Prowse's version of* Phaedra. *And the Orange Tree, Richmond gave us one of the year's best revivals in Tolstoy's* The Power Of Darkness.

As always, there was also plenty of good acting about: Glenda Jackson in O'Neill and Racine, Judi Dench as Mother Courage, Sheila Gish as Blanche Dubois, Brian Cox in Rat In The Skull, *Ian McKellen in* Wild Honey, *Gerard Murphy in* The Devil And The Good Lord. *But, against that, there was an increasing reliance on showbiz glitz, an ever-greater dependence on tourists and a feeling that the British theatre was like some wickerwork edifice built on stilts: one push and the whole thing could go toppling over.*

Tom And Viv

Royal Court: 10 February 1984

I had expected Michael Hastings's *Tom And Viv* at the Royal Court to be a scurrilous attack on T.S. Eliot for his treatment of his first wife, Vivienne Haigh Wood. In fact, it comes across as a tender, probing, quietly moving study of a haunted marriage: one that begins in haste and ends in Viv being institutionalised. It shows her as a grievously wronged woman; but it also suggests her love for Eliot remained constant and that she is threaded through every line of poetry he wrote in his richest years.

The surprise is that Eliot emerges as just as much a tragic figure as his wife. Hastings (spanning the period from 1915–47 in seven crisp scenes) depicts him as a riven figure who discards America, marries into English upper middle-class respectability and discovers he has a sick wife to whom he can offer neither sexual passion nor spiritual comfort. I was reminded of Edmund Wilson's essay in which he says that Eliot went to England and 'evolved for himself an aristocratic myth out of English literature and history'. Out of marriage too, it seems; for what we see is an awkward Jamesian expatriate who grasps eagerly at the status and security provided by association with the upper crust and then finds only the silence, pain and torture of a profound misalliance. 'Poor Tom's a cold' seems to be the verdict.

In Tom Wilkinson's marvellous performance – tall, stooping,

emotionally throttled and even in youth looking like the 'aged eagle' of *Ash Wednesday* – we get an image of a man who confronts domestic crisis with dry precision.

Of course Hastings's purpose is also to rescue Vivienne from obscurity and to show that she was unwarrantably certified insane in 1935. And here he is partially successful. He presents us with a woman who is by turns larky, unstable, ailing, mercurial. But, on the evidence here she seems as much the victim of upper-class reticence as of Eliot's incapacity: she has a chillingly comic first scene with her whaleboned mother in which her menstrual problems are discussed in a series of archly circuitous metaphors. No wonder, you feel, she turned into an odd-ball prankster.

But the heart of the play lies in its portrait of a sterile marriage. Here (though no outsider can ever know the truth) Hastings is very good at conjuring up a world of brutal heartache. He pins down moments of fitful togetherness such as Tom and Viv amiably fighting over a box of chocolates and bashing out fictive readers' letters to *The Criterion*. But the basic image is of two singular, lonely people separated by a metaphorical pane of glass, a literal one even when Viv stands behind a window reading one of her poems while the solitary Eliot kneels downstage taking the Catholic baptismal vows.

Hastings, a strangely unclassifiable writer, has in fact come up with that relatively rare thing – a plausible play about literary people. It can be argued that he has blurred the line between fact and fiction and apparently invented incidents like that in which Viv pours a tureen of melted chocolate through the Faber's letterbox, thereby damaging a manuscript of Roy Campbell's poems and a translation of the Bhagavadgita. But even if it isn't true, it is in character; and it offers a potent image of Viv's wildly signalling desperation and of Eliot's literal unreachableness.

The real test of the play is how it makes you feel about the characters. I can only say that it made me feel sorry for Viv, doomed, ostracised and living out her last years in incarcerated gentility. But (though it rather irrelevantly raises the old hare of the poet's thirties fascist sympathies) it never made me dislike Eliot: indeed it made me want to go back to the poetry to seek out the vein of personal angst behind the impersonal mask.

As a piece of theatre, it is quietly absorbing. I wasn't bowled over by the set by Antony McDonald and Jock Scott with its mix of realism and symbolism: a painted backwall of manicured lawns and country-house elegance and sliding, semi-institutional glass panels in the foreground.

But Max Stafford-Clark's production is extremely well-acted. Julie

Covington's Viv has exactly the right strained, tense, blanched look of a woman caught between implacable good breeding and a desperate need for the solace of love. Nicholas Selby and Margaret Tyzack etch in the Haigh Wood parents, trapped inside the mores of their class. And there is a choice performance from David Haig as Viv's brother, Maurice, sailing through life in a cloud of amiable density.

Mr Hastings may well have been prompted by outrage at the cruel injustice of the treatment meted out to Viv but I feel something of Eliot's lonely gravitas has infected the spirit of his play. It is written in a cool, expository prose; but the poetry, as so often, is in the pity.

Starlight Express

Apollo Victoria: 28 March 1984

Starlight Express, Andrew Lloyd Webber's new musical, is a hymn to the age of the steam train. But the ultimate irony is that it takes a £1.4 million John Napier set, a multiple-level roller-skating track, and a Spielbergian flow of special effects to celebrate a pre-electric heaven. Not, in fact, since Lionel Bart's *Blitz* has London seen a musical where the technology so totally dwarfed the minuscule content.

The show seems to have started out as a simple Cinderella story about a humble steam engine, Rusty, that gets involved in a race with diesel and electric trains and finally triumphs. But somewhere along the line this tenuous fable was turned into a giant Concept. Put the actors on roller-skates to simulate trains. Transform the theatre into an environmental playground half way between a rollerdrome and a motorised disco. Bring in a huge swivelling crane and have a back-wall that dissolves to introduce the magical force of the title. The result is a computerised fairy story, a theatrical *Star Wars*, in which the human element is constantly struggling to get out.

I don't deny that it is all done with mechanical ingenuity. When one first enters the Apollo Victoria, John Napier's set takes one's breath away. The front stalls are completely surrounded by a skating arena. More switch-back track curves and swoops around the auditorium. Miniaturised trains glide round the theatre, lights gleaming like the eyes in *Cats*. And when it comes to the races that punctuate the action, retractable handrails suddenly appear and video screens unfold to chart the progress of the racers when they disappear from view. But it is a comment on the fallibility of technology that interference from an outside broadcast van on the first night damaged the sound of the climactic number. Even though a hand mike quickly retrieved things, it proved that those who live by the machine can also perish by it.

The blunt fact is that Lloyd Webber's music and Richard Stilgoe's lyrics might be more enjoyable if they were not surrounded by such a vast carapace. The first number to really grab me was 'He Whistled At Me', which worked because Stephanie Lawrence as a pink-suited steam buff was allowed to stand centre stage and communicate a recognisable human emotion: unfulfilled longing. And there was a nice wit about 'Uncoupled', in which Frances Ruffelle's unattached Dinah literally spelt out the pathos of being a carriage without a marriage, a van without a man. But too many of the numbers, sharply-rhymed though they are, seem to me swamped by Trevor Nunn's busy production and by pounding disco orchestration.

In *Cats*, the balance between spectacle and emotion was well-nigh perfect and the final ascent to the skies lifted the spirits. But here when the cast finally hymn the 'Light at the End of the Tunnel', I was reminded of Raymond Briggs's classic remark that what that often signified was simply an oncoming train.

Death Of A Salesman

New York: 6 April 1984

The salesman is a mythic figure in American drama. He represents optimism and illusion on one side, the bitter taste of failure on the other. And, by a strange quirk of fate, two of the greatest American plays about the drummer-as-hero have opened on Broadway within the space of a few days. One is David Mamet's *Glengarry Glen Ross*. The other is Arthur Miller's *Death Of A Salesman* which brings Dustin Hoffman back to the New York stage in triumph after a gap of 16 years.

At first, Hoffman may seem an unlikely choice for Miller's 63-year-old Willy Loman. Isn't he too young and slight to play this exhausted dreamer? But Miller has been quick to point out that Lee J. Cobb, who created the role, was only 37 when he first played it; and that in the original script Willy was a 'shrimp' which was altered, for Cobb's benefit, to 'a walrus'. But Hoffman presents us with a short, sharp-featured little shrimp of a man constantly dwarfed by his two sons and having to stretch even to kiss the woman in the Boston hotel-room. Hoffman's Willy (in Michael Rudman's beautifully-cast production) is a little man; but he dreams big.

What is remarkable about Hoffman's performance is that it captures all of Willy's devouring insecurity. 'I still feel kind of temporary about myself,' says Willy at one point; and Hoffman presents us with a man who in his sad sixties still doesn't quite know who he is. He flashes thin, nervous little smiles at newcomers. He drops into little bursts of vaudevillian hoofing at moments of happiness. He playfully butts his wife with his rump or puts his hand on her breast to prove to himself she is his support. Yet he implodes with anger when she interrupts him and at times reverts to the impotent rage of childhood. In the crucial, cruel scene in Howard's office when he is fired, Hoffman goes berserk, almost ripping the phone from its socket and making fierce inhalations through his cavernous nostrils.

Hoffman may not yet have the baggy, crumpled pathos of Warren Mitchell's fine Willy Loman. What he offers us is a consummate, detailed piece of *acting* that shows us Willy as the victim of a phoney dream. Originally, the American Dream implied fulfilment of self through work and achievement. But Miller shows how, in Willy's world, the Dream has dwindled into success through charm, jokes, personality, riding on a smile and a shoeshine. Hoffman's Willy is an exciting performance precisely because it depicts a childish elder who is destroyed by his easy acceptance of society's values. Hoffman, in fact, is a doomed kidder.

But *Death Of A Salesman* is not a one-man show; and Rudman's production at The Broadhurst excited me more than its National Theatre counterpart because every role is perfectly cast. Willy's wife, Linda, is not that great a part since she is given little life outside the kitchen and bedroom; but Kate Reid gives a memorable portrayal of a seamed, tired woman grown used to being dominated by Willy yet still filled with the compassion that comes from sharing a long life with someone.

John Malkovich (a highly regarded member of Chicago's Steppenwolf Theatre company) also gives a stunning performance as Biff that evokes the young Brando. Tall, muscular, with a tight mop of clenched hair and a Marciano-jawline, Mr Malkovich adopts a staccato delivery that suggests Biff has to fight his way through the thickets of language and relates to people physically in a manner that indicates he does not belong in urban America. One test of Mr Malkovich's potential is that you can easily imagine him in a whole line of parts: Stanley Kowalski, Hotspur, the younger brother in *Long Day's Journey* and even, in years to come, Willy Loman.

Death Of A Salesman is an important evening in many ways. One is that it proves Hoffman's technique has not been impaired by years in the movies. It also demonstrates that it is possible to combine a study of an individual, an examination of familial ties and a critique of society: Miller, quite simply, puts an amazing amount of America on to the stage. And it is important to be reminded of that at a time when everyone seems to be writing mother-son, mother-daughter, father-and-children plays of minimal social resonance. I sat through one such, Harvey Fierstein's *Spookhouse*, in a state of numbed boredom and disbelief.

If America is to produce great plays again, it has to raise its eyes from analyst's-couch drama about the predatory nature of family life and address itself to social and political concerns. Sam Shepard does that obliquely in *Fool For Love*. David Mamet in *Glengarry Glen Ross* presents a tragi-comic vision of capitalism in action. And Miller in *Death Of A Salesman* shows us an individual and a family crucified by acceptance of the false values of success and salesmanship in which personality becomes a commodity. Miller's play deserves more than a long run: it should be a model for all those young dramatists who cannot see beyond their own fragile egos.

Strange Interlude

Duke of York's: 9 April 1984

'Pardon me while I have a strange interlude,' says Groucho in *Animal Crackers* before lapsing into an interior monologue. And that is a sign of how much Eugene O'Neill's inordinate, nine-act, four-hour-plus drama – the big hit of the 1927 Theatre Guild season in New York – had entered the public consciousness through its characters' revelation of their private feelings in a series of prolonged asides.

But seeing *Strange Interlude* revived today at the Duke of York's (an act of lunatic daring which no serious theatregoer can afford to miss), I am struck less by O'Neill's use of inner monologue than by his ability to combine social comedy with poundingly obsessive themes in the story of a woman's life over 30 years. The play has already been compared to soap-opera. In fact, it is more like Wagner opera in which motifs and ideas are introduced and brought together in voluptuous fusion. It may not be a masterpiece; but it seizes you warmly by the throat and rarely relaxes its grip.

It is the story of one woman, Nina Leeds, and her possession of three men: Nina leads and others follow. The daughter of a university professor who has lost her athlete lover in the First World War, she marries a shallow advertising man whose child she aborts when she discovers a record of family insanity. She fulfils her hunger for motherhood by being impregnated by a neurologist, Edmund Darrell, in a spirit of would-be clinical detachment: in fact, she and Darrell become lovers but never allow themselves to reveal their son's true parentage. Finally, after her husband's death, she falls gratefully into the arms of an old-maidish Jamesian novelist, Charles Marsden, who has platonically adored her since childhood.

It sounds like melodrama; and indeed there are times when you have to swallow large doses of the improbable. I can't believe that in 1921 a woman would have instantly had an abortion because of a belief in inherited lunacy (this is Ibsen's *Ghosts* gone mad).

But what binds this extraordinary play together are O'Neill's psychological leitmotivs: there is a woman's simultaneous need for security, sex, platonic love and children; the notion of the present as a strange interlude between past and future; the idea of happiness as the closest we ever get to understanding good; above all, there is the belief that you cannot meddle scientifically in human emotion. And if you want proof of O'Neill's remorseless eye for truth, you simply have to contrast the years of agony that follow the experiment of begetting Nina's child with the glib coupling that accompanies a similar operation in the movie, *The Big Chill*.

I wouldn't claim that O'Neill was an original thinker. He shopped around in Schopenhauer for his notion of immutable human character. Even the idea of dramatising the sub-text had been used by Alice Gerstenberg in a play called *Overtones*. What finally makes *Strange Interlude* memorable is O'Neill's ability both to understand profound human needs and to see their comic consequences.

And the monologues serve the dual function of showing what goes on behind the smokescreen of social intercourse (as in a famous scene in *Manhattan*) while offering devastating comments on character. There's a wonderful moment when Nina's newly-dynamic husband rushes hectically in only for the novelist Marsden to observe crushingly: 'What a fount of meaningless energy he has tapped.' O'Neill, as I've long maintained, was a very funny writer.

Keith Hack's production, staged inside a functionally beautiful white clapboard box designed by Voytek, gets the comedy across with the aid of a superbly silky, prissy performance by Edward Petherbridge, who looks like a tightly furled umbrella, as the neutered novelist.

But it is Glenda Jackson as Nina who gives the production its core of mystery: she captures all the contradictions of Nina's delight in and disgust with the men she possesses and her restless, questing hands constantly caress her body and the air around her as an index of her inner turbulence. Brian Cox also plays her doctor-lover on the right note of anguished self-debate, and James Hazeldine lends the adman husband a sporty lightness.

In New York, it was once said that one doesn't attend *Strange Interlude*: one enlists for it. But although the last hour declines in quality it is worth rushing to the colours if only because the play proves that O'Neill was that rare writer: one who detects mankind's absurdity without forfeiting his compassion.

Simon Callow

26 April 1984

Do theatre directors have too much power? Are our actors and writers being squeezed out of the decision-making processes and reduced to nothing more than hired hands? Peter Nichols, to judge by his interview (*Arts Guardian*, April 16), bruisedly thinks so. So, even more passionately, does Simon Callow, who has just written a pugnaciously candid book called *Being An Actor*. It ends with a ringing manifesto seeking the creative union of the actor and the writer 'without the self-elected intervention of the director, claiming a unique position interpreting the one to the other'.

I think this view is tragically myopic and historically unsound. But before taking on Mr Callow, let me say that I welcome his fascinating book partly because it gives a graphic account of the actor's life and partly because it helps to rend the veils of secrecy which normally surround the British theatre. For years our theatre has been run with a closeness that makes the Mafia look positively self-advertising (try finding out the box-office takings from a commercial management). Then last autumn came the invaluable Peter Hall Diaries which lifted the lid off the artistic, political and industrial crises which threatened to cripple the National Theatre. Now comes Mr Callow's book which reveals what goes on in the rehearsal-room.

Mr Callow has set down naught in malice. What he has done is to record the frustrations and glories of being a modern actor, disclose the working methods of directors like Gaskill, Dexter and Hall, pinpoint the internal contradictions of a collective like Joint Stock and offer sharp insights into admired individuals ('Shaffer's is a theatre of gesture'; 'The price of David Hare is eternal vigilance'). But although his book is a unique account of an actor's life in mid-career, I cannot buy the thesis that underpins it and the manifesto to which it leads.

Broadly, this argues that the modern theatre directors have acquired an almost dictatorial power, that the imposition of a director's or company's style threatens the dramatist's individuality and that our theatre will only be restored to health when self-governing companies start to hire directors according to their needs. As an actor, Mr Callow is an exciting over-reacher; but here he has chewed off more than he can bite.

For a start, he writes as if the tragedy of twentieth century British theatre is that it has been colonised by directors: I would say that its tragedy is that, until recently, it hasn't. While Russia had its Stanislavsky and Meyerhold, Germany its Reinhardt and Brecht, France its Copeau and Dullin, we had Basil Dean. Throughout Europe the idea of the creative director working with a permanent company has long been accepted: our theatre, predominantly commercial until a quarter of a century ago, has traditionally regarded the director as a superfluous functionary. For proof, look at a document produced by the Society of West End Theatre Managers in the 1950s which defined directors, astoundingly, as 'liaison officers between the workers and the management'.

Our theatre lagged behind the rest of Europe for the first half of this century precisely because the director was, in Tynan's words, 'a tolerated stranger engaged ad hoc and invited only for a strictly limited period'. That situation began to change only with the establishment of institutions like the Royal Court, the RSC and the National and the arrival of a new breed of intelligent interpreters like Hall, Gaskill, Dexter, Richardson and Nunn.

Even then our attitude to truly innovative directors remained punitive and suspicious. Joan Littlewood spent most of her time at Theatre Workshop in under-subsidised penury and only survived through commercial transfers which finally undid her company. Peter Brook, wanting to set up a theatrical laboratory free from the assembly-line pressures of the major companies, could get no funds in London and so set up camp in Paris. The East Germans gave Brecht the Theater am Schiffbauerdam and the West Germans gave Peter Stein the Schaubühne: we seem to rejoice in giving our pioneers the boot.

My problem is that I simply do not recognise the theatre Mr Callow describes. He sees one vitiated by a power-hungry directocracy: I see one that has gained in strength and stature through the belated recognition of the director. Nor do I recognise the process Mr Callow describes whereby great works are flattened out in the interests of directorial ego or company style. Musically, he argues, we accept that Telemann is not played like Tchaikovsky. 'But Shakespeare', he writes, 'is played like Chekhov or Feydeau, Büchner is played like Brecht and so on.'

This strikes me as so much tosh. Was Trevor Nunn's spare, no-tricks-up-the-sleeve *Macbeth* really played like his detailed, naturalistic *Three Sisters*? Was Peter Gill's invigoratingly ascetic *Danton's Death* remotely like John Dexter's colourful, processional *Galileo*? Every good director has his signature; but only a bad one bends every play to suit his style.

Mr Callow seems to see strong directors as the actor's enemy: I would claim they are often their best friends. A supposed martinet like Dexter not only had the imagination to cast Michael Gambon as Galileo but revealed in him a new toughness and obduracy. Actors like McKellen and Jacobi did fine work with the Actors Company and Prospect but it was only when they joined the allegedly director-dominated RSC that their full potential was realised. And, to take an obvious current example, Peter Gill's new production of *Venice Preserv'd* taps a heroic style of acting from Pennington, McKellen and Lapotaire entirely in keeping with Otway's play. First-rate directors do not treat actors like Über-marionettes: what they may do is unlock qualities that have previously been dammed up.

But what of the future Mr Callow envisions? I accept his point that actors should increasingly be part of the decision-making process. 'How can you be passionate about anything in which you have no involvement?' asks Mr Callow reasonably. And, given that we have a new breed of politically aware, intellectually-trained actor, it seems absurd that they should be isolated from the power-bases of companies big and small. The work of Joint Stock (and a project like *Nicholas Nickleby*) also confirms the tangible sense of commitment that comes from actors being in at the beginning.

A more democratic theatre is one thing. But to argue from that that 'the rise of the director is a recent phenomenon which on balance has by no means proved its value' is absurd. I could list a hundred productions (including Joan Littlewood's *Oh What A Lovely War!*, Brook's *Dream*, Hall's *War Of The Roses*, Gill's Lawrentian trilogy, Barton's version of *The Greeks*, Havergal's *Men Should Weep*) which owed much to beneficent directorial influence. What really worries me is Mr Callow's vision of a theatre in which actor and writer commune with each other without benefit of an interpreter. That was precisely what happened with Irving at the Lyceum and Beerbohm Tree at Her Majesty's and the result was, with the exception of Shaw's *Pygmalion*, one of the blankest periods in British dramaturgy on record.

Mr Callow has opened up an important subject. But since it has taken the director several centuries to acquire more than a precarious toehold in the British theatre, I suggest it is somewhat premature to start thrusting him (or her) into the street. Directors obviously need actors. But actors may require directors every bit as much. And that is true even of the provocative Mr Callow.

Richard III

Royal Shakespeare Theatre: 21 June 1984

Antony Sher has long been limbering up (if that is quite the word) to play Richard III. Even his Tartuffe had a whiff of Crookback about it. And now he makes a vigorous, compelling, totally deformed and yet astonishingly mobile Richard in Bill Alexander's fundamentalist new production at Stratford that sees the play squarely in terms of sin and redemption, good and evil.

Mr Sher certainly presents an astonishing image. On his first entry through the back doors of William Dudley's chancel-like set, he seems small, dark and jovial. But, as he tells us he is not shaped for sportive tricks, he levers himself forward in giant leaps on two crutches that descend from his arms. These crutches not only make him the fastest mover in the kingdom, they become a staff to beat Lady Anne's attendants, a phallic symbol to probe under her skirt, incisors to grip Hastings's threatened head, a sword to frighten recalcitrant children with, and a cross to betoken Richard's seeming saintliness.

The result is twofold. Mr Sher's spindly legs, protuberant knees, bent frame, make him a symbol of pitiable deformity. At the same time he is a figure of active, energetic evil who can bound across a room in one leap to fix an enemy with a basilisk stare. It is a performance filled with that most exciting of all theatrical qualities: danger. You see that in the scene with the adolescent Duke of York whom Mr Sher passes back and forth to Hastings as if he were a parcel he were about to tear to pieces. But Mr Sher also makes Richard a Satanic joker crying, with weary impatience, 'men shall deal unadvisedly sometimes' after having murdered half his relatives.

For my money Mr Sher keeps up his sardonic mask almost too long so that the final scenes lose tragic weight. But it is still a superb Richard, both fleet and demonic that reminded me of W.C. Fields's remark about Chaplin: 'The guy's a goddam ballet dancer.'

For the rest Mr Alexander's production is pageant-like, religious and morally straightforward. It is typified by the way it puts Richard, at the last, in black armour on a black horse and Richmond in gold plate on a gold palfrey. And even in the Bosworth scenes the set retains its perpendicular side-walls and religious effigies, with Richard finally stabbed with a crucifix-shaped sword.

It is a viable interpretation but it underplays the element of calculating power politics and makes the work more a mad medieval morality than a study of deviousness and brutal pragmatism. But then, ever since the *Wars Of The Roses*, I have always thought this play only makes total sense if you have seen the political backstabbing that produces a Richard Crookback.

For all Mr Alexander's protestations, it is very much a star centred evening. But Malcolm Storry contributes a dry, witty Buckingham, Roger Allam's Clarence goes melodiously to his death before being popped into the malmsy butt and Patricia Routledge's Queen Margaret is a plausibly embittered hag wrapped in a flag. I just wish Brian Blessed could curb his instinct to play Hastings as if he were the Laughing Cavalier.

But, in fairness, Mr Alexander handles the stage with confidence (there is a fine phantasmagoric coronation with Richard and his Queen barebacked under red robes) and gives us a persuasive, if conventional, reading. The evening, however, belongs to Mr Sher, who vigorously enshrines Blake's precept that energy is eternal delight.

If I Were Peter Hall . . .

17 September 1984

What would I do if I were sitting in Peter Hall's chair at the National Theatre? That is the question. And it immediately reminds me of Kenneth Tynan's remark, inverting Oscar Wilde, that a critic is someone who knows the value of everything and the price of nothing.

Power without accountancy is the prerogative of the journalist down the ages; and it is easy to construct a Platonic ideal of what a theatre ought to be when one doesn't have to administer budgets and check production costs.

I also start from the premise that the National Theatre we have is more or less on course; any organisation that can come up with productions as good as the current Chekhov, Feydeau, Otway, Sophocles and Mamet has to be doing something right. I was strongly critical (as the Hall Diaries confirm) of the present regime during its early years. But recently, if you ignore an aberration like *Jean Seberg*, it has achieved a consistent level of quality and, most refreshingly, kept faith with such living dramatists as David Hare, Christopher Hampton and Howard Brenton.

But good can always be better. And the first thing I would do (on the king-for-a-day principle) is to re-establish the idea of a World Theatre season. It is, of course, possible to romanticise Peter Daubeny's famous Aldwych festival and forget that it could sometimes involve watching a minor Turkish musical in a half-filled theatre with a small-scale parking meter stuck in one's ear. However, those Daubeny seasons from 1964 on also brought us untold riches (who can ever forget Krejca's production of *Three Sisters*, Koun's *The Birds*, Wadja's *The Possessed*, Bergman's *Dream Play*?). What is more those seasons had a perceptible influence on British theatre. I doubt, for instance, if we would ever have got round to the plays of Eduardo de Filippo if it had not been for the importation of works like *Napoli Milionaria*.

I should like to see the Lyttelton given over, for one month each year, to the best of foreign theatre. It seems to me a shame and a scandal that something as brilliant as Strehler's *La Tempesta* (which I saw in Paris) or Stein's *Three Sisters* (which I have heard about from Berlin) never gets to London. Raise the question of foreign imports at the NT and the response is much the same as Alfred Doolittle's to morals . . . 'Can't afford 'em, guv.' But I believe, if one wants something badly enough, there is always a way.

With the help of commercial sponsorship and the temporary transfer of the Lyttelton repertoire to a regional theatre (yes, I know about the problems of cross-casting), it would surely be possible to bring us the work of Mnouchkine and Chéreau, Stein and Strehler, Bergman and Besson. Without regular exposure to alien styles, our theatre is endangered by a suffocating smugness and a rooted belief that naturalism is the only style.

My second National reform would be to institute a more cohesive repertoire. It is of course an easy parlour game to sit down and list the 20 plays the National ought to do regardless of cost, popularity, actor and director availability. But my point is that the National repertory for the last 21 years seems to have been built on the principle of a-bit-of-everything-and-not-much-of-anything. Occasionally one gets interesting juxtapositions like *Wild Honey* (Chekhov heading in the direction of down-right farce) and *A Little Hotel On The Side* (epic French farce with real people). One also gets sudden bouts of Americana with Mamet, Shepard, Odets, Loesser, Kaufman and Hart all jostling for a place in the repertory. But I often get the impression (the same is true of the RSC) of piecemeal planning in which productions are isolated events rather than part of a determination to work a particular theatrical seam.

So what would I do?. One thing, for sure, is to attack some of the still unconquered peaks of world drama. French classical tragedy is a glaring example. Christopher Fettes has shown the way with his astonishing productions of Racine at the Lyric Studio and Glenda Jackson is to give us her Phèdre at the Old Vic. Yet (with the exception of an evasive British Raj *Phaedra Britannica* which was neither flesh nor fowl) the National has consistently ignored Racine and Corneille for the whole of its history. Likewise, the Sturm and Drang drama of Goethe and Schiller remains a closed book at the National, though for years I have heard mutterings about a version of *Die Räuber* knocking about. Maybe the plays are not stageable any more (though I recall a stirring version of Schiller's *Wallenstein* done by an Oxford theatre company years ago). Still, unless we give them an airing we shall never actually know.

I should also like to see mini-seasons in which one play was related to another. Do a one-off revival of a rare classic and it doesn't have much meaning: if it fails, it can also kill off that writer for good. But it would be fascinating, for instance, to see Euripides's *Iphigenia In Aulis* played in conjunction with Racine's *Iphigenie* and Goethe's *Iphigenie Auf Tauris*. Equally I would go a long way (well, as far as the South Bank) to see what happened if you put together a season of Ibsen's early verse plays (*The Vikings At Helgeland*, *Love's Comedy*, *The Pretenders*) or indeed of his late symbolic dramas (*The Master Builder*, *John Gabriel Borkman*, *When We Dead Awaken*).

The stock response to such suggestions is that critics might go but no one else would. Can we be sure? If I have noticed one thing about popular taste over the past five years, it is that there is a growing hunger for the inordinate. Put on something average and people may or may not come. Put on something epic and exhausting (*The Greeks*, *The Oresteia*, *Nicholas Nickleby*, *The Ring*) and you have to dust down the crush-barriers.

In case this sounds academic or high-minded, let me add that there are plenty of other things I should like to see the National Theatre tackle. How about a season of post-war British plays, comprising *The Cocktail Party*, *The Living Room*, *The Entertainer*, *Roots*, *The Workhouse*

Donkey, *Black Comedy*, *Old Times*, *Knuckle*, *Absurd Person Singular*? There is a whole batch of modern plays more honoured in the study than the performance. And, although the RSC caught something of a cold with *The Happiest Days Of Your Life*, I wouldn't mind seeing the National dip a further toe into the spring of popular comedy and farce, and checking out whether there is still more to be discovered about Ben Travers or Philip King. All I seek is a more visible sense of purpose.

My third change at the National (it's going to be a busy day) would be structural. I should endeavour to sign actors up on long-term contracts (18 months seems to me a reasonable minimum). I should also try to achieve a sense of identifiable companies working within the same building. The one director who has famously managed to achieve this is Bill Bryden. He has built up a particular troupe of tough, hairy, proletarian actors: Jack Shepherd, Derek Newark, Trevor Ray, James Grant have appeared in virtually all his recent productions and have shown that a company style is simply the product of continuity and long-range commitment. If Bryden can do it, I see no reason why other directors such as Peter Gill and Michael Bogdanov should not create their own commando units dependent on group loyalty.

In an ideal world there are other changes I should make (many dependent, I fear, on union negotiations). I would open the three theatres on Sundays (when London is awash with people) and close them on Mondays. I would have free public dress rehearsals when anyone could come in. I would have a permanent mobile company (as opposed to a temporary one) that could tour any time to schools, factories, theatreless communities.

I would also make manifest (as the Royal Court does) attendance figures for the productions so that the public could see for themselves what was popular and what was not. I would have a suggestion box in the lobbies so that audiences could register complaints or nominate work they would like to see – all in the democratic spirit of that Tom Phillips poster, The National Theatre Is Yours.

The logic of that poster is that everyone (critics included) thinks he has a right to determine National Theatre policy. I don't envy Peter Hall his job for that reason and also because, as his Diaries make clear, he has to turn an intricate industrial complex into an artistic organisation. By and large he has pulled it off. But the National, as it prepares to celebrate the 21st anniversary of the company, is still susceptible of radical improvement. If it were not, it would be a dead duck rather than a living organism.

Letter To The Editor

Peter Hall: 27 September 1984

Sir, – Michael Billington writes that the National Theatre, by and large, is successfully on course. And I am grateful to him for saying kind things about me personally. But I still find irresistible the chance to answer some of his points.

For instance, two of his main dreams for the NT – were he to find himself its director – are central but, alas, unfulfilled parts of the policy I agreed with my board some eleven years ago: annual world theatre seasons, and Sunday openings. 'If one wants something badly enough, there is always a way,' Michael Billington claims. But he's wrong. There isn't. Not if there simply isn't the money around.

We have tried and failed for years to get funding for world theatre seasons, either from the state or from a commercial sponsor. The British theatre *is* too parochial, *is* too cut off. And Peter Daubeny's seasons – which I was proud to be associated with during my time at the RSC – did have an enormous influence on the future of British drama. But it seems they can't happen in the eighties – certainly not in anything like the form in which we gave them at the Aldwych in the Sixties. It is not just that the genius of Peter Daubeny is, sadly, no longer with us. The economics of life have changed.

And as for our country footing the bill, we have a curious situation where the Arts Council is responsible for funding art produced in Britain, and the British Council for funding British art abroad. But no official body is responsible for bringing foreign art to Britain. I'm not therefore surprised that Michael Billington saw the Milan production of *La Tempesta* in Paris. The French government spends vast sums in its attempts to make Paris the capital of artistic Europe once more. London is slipping behind because we have had a series of governments which don't care so much about these matters.

Of course we should be open on Sundays. The South Bank is full of visitors then. The Festival and Queen Elizabeth Halls give concerts; the Hayward Gallery shows exhibitions; the National Film Theatre screens movies. All are jammed with people. We alone are shut on the best day of the week for people to enjoy theatre in comfort, without rush. Why? Because we cannot afford the swingeing overtime costs. Musicians don't claim overtime for Sunday working.

Among the other things Michael Billington would want as director are 'a more cohesive repertory' and 'a more visible sense of purpose'. Well, we have a demonstrable purpose: put simply, it is diversity of repertoire. I try to stage, to the very highest standards, a mixture of plays – classic, new, and neglected – about which I, and those who are directing them, feel passionately. That seems to be what audiences respond to as well.

The problem of a more cohesive repertory – that is, seasons of linked plays (post-war drama, Sturm und Drang, or Revenge plays) – is that it can work only if the people putting it on have a real obsession to do it. Once you persuade an unwilling director to do a questionable play merely because it fits a season, you're dead. On the whole, I think it is critics and scholars who are drawn to seasons with a theme; I'm not sure they interest the public too much. Michael Billington wonders what would happen if I presented together Ibsen's early verse plays: *The Vikings At Helgeland*, *Love's Comedy*, and *The Pretenders*. I suspect that not many people would be there to see them, unless I found – which would be very difficult – directors who burned to put them on.

Michael Billington has, though, perceptively noticed a growing hunger for the inordinate. There he is absolutely right. Unexceptional revivals of classics no longer draw the crowds. Unique events, or discoveries of old works newly translated, or new plays, do in fact far better. Of the 149 productions that have been staged since we opened on the South Bank, 67 were new plays or new translations of unknown plays. Nearly all played to excellent business.

There are some suggestions on which I won't, for the time being, comment in Michael Billington's vision of what he would do if he were in my chair. These either make me think that he is prescient, or that he had his ear extremely close to the ground. But if I were sitting in *his* chair, I would start a vigorous campaign with my fellows to protest against the performing arts being diminished by the desperate financial pressures put upon them over the years by successive governments of both parties.

The arts have not really been supported creatively since the sixties. It is time we woke up to that fact. We could all then do so much more to entertain and to thrill our public.

(Sir) Peter Hall.
National Theatre,
London SE1.

Leonard Rossiter

8 October 1984

I find it sad that the weekend TV and radio-news bulletins harped so much on Leonard Rossiter's fame as the accident-prone smoothie in the Cinzano commercials with Joan Collins. For Rossiter – who died on Friday night at the age of 57 during a performance of *Loot* at the Lyric Theatre – was a great comic stage and television actor who always left behind an indelible outline: the accosting profile, the lizard-like tongue, the manic gleam in the eyes always suggested a man in the grip of an *idée fixe*.

I first saw him at the Belgrade, Coventry in 1963, in one of his finest roles: Fred Midway in David Turner's *Semi-Detached*. The character is a Jonsonian insurance-agent ready to sacrifice his entire family to his dream of status, power and wealth. Rossiter, who started life as an insurance-clerk, seemed to understand him completely. He ran his hands lightly over his encyclopaedias like Rubinstein caressing a concert grand, unloosed viperish sneers at an indiscreet daughter and shot out his long, stiff-jointed legs like pistons on one of his prized railway engines. Rossiter painted an unforgettable portrait of a lunatic, Machiavellian schemer and seized on the line 'We'll have nothing spontaneous here' as the key to the character. Olivier played the role in London with misplaced naturalism: Rossiter offered us a stylised monster.

The perfect fusion of actor and role, however, came with Brecht's *The Resistible Rise Of Arturo Ui* which played in Glasgow, Edinburgh and Nottingham before finally conquering London in July, 1969. I would place this high on the list of the greatest comic performances I have ever seen. Rossiter told me years later that he didn't particularly like or admire Brecht; but he completely fulfilled (with the help of Michael Blakemore's direction) the Brechtian principle that 'the actor must make himself observed standing *between* the spectator and the text.' The play translates Hitler into a daemonic Al Capone gangster; but Rossiter constantly showed the fear and absurdity behind the mask of brutality. On his first entrance he burst like a clown through a paper-screen, spoiling the effect by the fact that he left a mass of brown paper clinging obstinately to his teeth: immediately we saw that Ui was man who could never live up to his mental image of himself. Like Chaplin in *The Great Dictator*, Rossiter made evil funny. His superb performance also, for the first time in Britain, made Brecht popular at the box office.

Arturo Ui was a hard act to follow. And for some time Rossiter seemed to be casting around for a vehicle to contain his outsize talents. He did, however, essay *Richard III* at Nottingham in 1971 and a year later was a brilliant Davies in *The Caretaker* at the Mermaid, offering a radical alternative to Pleasence's original creation. Rossiter gave us a cawing, predatory scarecrow-figure aspiring to class; his voice was pseudo-genteel and when a dirty, dust-covered counterpane was thrust into his mitts he handled it with the visible distaste of a Pinero dowager.

Rossiter wasn't simply a superbly inventive comic actor. He was also very good at playing social upstarts. His portrayal of Rooksby in Eric Chappell's *The Banana Box* at Hampstead in 1973 (with Frances de la Tour) gave birth to the TV series, *Rising Damp*. I also remember him at the Old Vic in 1976 in Feydeau's *The Purging* as a toiletware manufacturer with delusions of grandeur ('Today France – tomorrow the world') dreaming wistfully of models decorated with the Cross of Lorraine. And in the same year at Greenwich he turned Molière's Tartuffe into a dandified arriviste running a carefully-crooked little finger along the lacy fringes of Elmire's bosom as if looking for faults in the workmanship.

In recent years, *Rising Damp* and *The Rise And Fall Of Reginald Perrin* turned Rossiter into a household name. But TV stardom in no way blunted his great comic capacity for playing men who were prey to some ungovernable obsession. In Michael Frayn's *Make And Break* in 1980 he played a workaholic executive who couldn't even take off a girl's shoe in the course of seduction without squinting at the brand-name; yet there was also a hint of tragedy about his determination to discover what it was his colleagues found in Buddhism or Beethoven that eluded him. And Rossiter died at his peak playing Joe Orton's Inspector Truscott as a slightly dim suburban sleuth.

Rossiter was an instinctive freelance who eschewed the security of the big national companies which is sad since there were many classic roles one would have loved to see him play. But he leaves behind a wealth of film and TV work (*Tripper's Day* is currently going out on ITV, his BBC *King John* is still to come).

Above all, he leaves us with the ineradicable memory of an actor who could show the monstrosity lurking inside ordinary men and who could conjure up suburban daemons. Great comic acting is often about single-mindedness; and Leonard Rossiter conveyed better than anyone I know the tunnel-vision of the truly possessed.

Two Into One

Shaftesbury: 20 October 1984

It may be a rash thing to say but Ray Cooney's *Two Into One* at the Shaftesbury strikes me as a classic farce. It made me laugh as much as the National's recent Feydeau and the Lyric Hammersmith's *Charley's Aunt*; and the reason is that, like all first-rate farce, it starts with a plausible premise and builds to a fever-pitch of delirium in which the world seems to be spinning into madness.

Like G.F. Newman's *An Honourable Trade* at the Court, it deals with the sexual peccadilloes of politicians but is less concerned with social comment than pulverising the audience. It starts with Donald Sinden as a Home Office Minister, staying at a Westminster hotel with his wife, asking Michael Williams's pin-striped civil servant to book him a room at the same venue for an afternoon's romp with one of the P.M.'s secretaries.

Unfortunately, the adulterous suite turns out to be adjacent to the marital chambers; and while the Minister's wife, unexpectedly ducking out of a matinée of *Evita*, is trying to lure the civil servant into her bed, next door her husband is hoping to achieve consummation with one of Mrs T's trusties. But sex, of course, becomes an ever more remote prospect as a Chinese waiter, an irate manager and a vice-sniffing lady MP invade the premises, and as the civil servant shuttles back and forth trying to fulfil the dual roles of ardent lover and ministerial helpmeet.

As in all farce, the wages of lust is frustration. But what keeps the plot boiling is Mr Cooney's uncanny ability to pile one mad invention on another so that the civil-servant (much the juiciest role) is gradually forced to assume the identity of a Norwich GP making a BMA-sponsored movie, *A Bit Of The Other*, with a gay friend. And Michael Williams gives a superb display of baffled respectability as the Whitehall-wallah blinking through his tortoise-shell specs as randy wives scatter deodorant down his Y-fronts, hotel staff mistake him for an uncontrollable sex fiend and his minister bounces him back and forth like a rubber ball. Jonathan Lynn, who should know, once defined farce as the worst day of your life; and Mr Williams beautifully suggests a man living through a nightmare.

Donald Sinden is no less funny as the rantipole, benzedrine-filled Minister making good use of his slow, dismayed turn of the head with eyes wideningly aghast: at one point he even manages to kangaroo-hop round a hotel-room with a woman's wig (don't ask me why) stuck between his cheeks. Lionel Jefferies as the empurpled manager ('There's far too much sex in this hotel and I'm not having any of it'), Derek Royle as an Oriental waiter and Barbara Murray as the voracious wife also display the jet-propelled egoism of true farce, and, under Mr Cooney's agile direction, Terry Parsons's sets slide sleekly back and forth.

Edward Bond

23 November 1984

'Basically I'm a comic dramatist. I'm not a tragic writer.' So says Edward Bond. And there are those who might think it was a fairly robust definition of comedy that could embrace such incidents as the baby-stoning of *Saved*, the cannibalism of *Early Morning* or the punctured ear-drums and blinding of *Lear*.

But I think Bond has a point. Some of his plays (above all *The Sea* and *Restoration*) are very funny. He may confront human degradation but he also has the optimism and detachment of the comic writer. And in person he somewhat belies one's preconceived notion of him as a stony puritan. He sends me up, in the course of a long conversation, for asking if *The Pope's Wedding* and *Saved* (two Sixties plays about to be revived by the Royal Court) were written from a sense of outrage. He also sends himself up saying at one point, 'I don't know how to write plays – this will come as no surprise to you – and every time I sit down to write I say I don't know how to do this play.'

Any conversation with Bond is bound, sooner or later, to bring up the question of violence. I brought it up sooner by asking if he had ever witnessed the kind of violence he depicts in *Saved*. 'I haven't seen particular incidents like the ones in the play. The nearest I've been to real violence is being caught in air raids in wartime with bombs coming down that you think will kill you. But the expression of physical violence is merely the full-stop at the end of the sentence. The ingredients are there all the time. What strikes me when you see physical violence break out on the streets is that it tends to be amazingly ordinary. Extraordinarily ordinary. People handle knives as if they were cups and saucers. But you seem to be obsessed with violence,' he says.

Not obsessed. Just curious at the seeming change in Bond's attitude from his moral detestation of violence in *Saved* to his implied acceptance of armed insurrection in a play like *The Bundle*. What is he exactly? Pacifist? Democrat? Revolutionary?

'I'm not a pacifist. I love peace too much. Pacifism for me is summed up by Gandhi, who said that what you should do if you were a Jew in Nazi Germany is kill yourself. And my question is: do you kill your children? I believe we are not innately aggressive but that violence is a cultural problem.

'But do I want a revolution tomorrow? Oh God, we should be on *The World At One*. I would like society to be changed tomorrow; but you can't change societies mechanically. You don't change society by changing the people in power. You've got to change human consciousness, which is a man-made thing. If we tried to shoot the ruling class tomorrow, the ruling class would probably shoot us first. It's interesting to consider whether, if there were a serious social disturbance in Europe, tactical nuclear weapons would be used by governments against the people they now claim to be defending. That would be a real possibility.'

Bond utters such extreme statements with a mixture of disarming candour and impish provocativeness. He reminds me of Marshall McLuhan in that he comes out with spiky aphorisms that then get extended into spiralling generalisations. Thus: 'In a way we always have a culture that's a generation behind a technological culture: I think, for instance television is the twentieth century's greatest gift to the nineteenth century'. What he means by that is that TV is used to reinforce a pre-existing culture, that it's run by the same kind of people who run our law courts or our prisons, and that working people only get on TV as clowns or people with social problems.

But what, I protest, about the work of people like Trevor Griffiths, Tony Garnett, Ken Loach, David Leland? 'Of course, there are people whose work I admire very much. But they're not in charge of the stations. They're given slots. I would say the ruling class is very sophisticated in the way it licenses elements of opposition.

Bond disclaims any blue-print for Utopia ('You end up with William Morris'). But, given that he wants to change human consciousness, does he think the theatre has a role to play? 'Yes, because the need to act or perform is one way communities have of creating the ideas they live by. In a sense, the theatre is poetry. I'm a Marxist but I believe very much in poetry. Because all around me I hear people speaking poetry. If you go into a supermarket, you hear people speaking it. In a supermarket, they ask practical things like, 'I want that tin. I want that packet'. It's not Arts Council poetry, which has no practicality. When they say it, they smile or they gesture and sing to each other and provide rhythms to each other. The girl at the cash desk will provide a rhythm which someone else will answer. That seems to me what poetic language is really about'.

A lot of Bond plays are about the poetry of the everyday. But he extends the idea, saying that theatre should take the broadest concepts, 'all the ideas that the dead gods left hanging around when they went away', and relate those to people's actual lives. What is more he doesn't want to work in little theatres but in opera houses, big theatres, television even. But is there, I ask, any room for escapism in the theatre?

'No'.

'Why not?'

'I don't believe in narcotics. Unless somebody is in desperate pain. Unless it's a terminal case.'

'But if more people want to see *42nd Street* than a difficult new play, is that bad?'

'Yes'.

'Why? Because it's turning their minds off?'

'Yes. I don't believe in just switching off, especially in a public medium. Why don't people go along and play some records on their own and have a dance? I wouldn't stand up with my placard and say The Day Of Wrath Is At Hand. That would be extremely impolite. But there is a special function to the theatre. It's a community function. And therefore one doesn't go to the theatre to be consoled with what should not be consolable. I mean, I'm a comic writer. I believe the stage should always be entertaining. But it should be the laughter which comes from knowledge, from identifying the fraudulent and the fake. If the laughter is simply sneering at people or the oddity of the world, then I don't see any point in it.'

But if Bond wants theatre to change human consciousness, why does he set so many of his plays in the past? He answers reasonably, 'I dislike that socialist theatre which says junk the art of the past. It's like saying, forget the wheel.' He adds that he wants to cheer when they have that vote at the end of *The Oresteia*. 'Even though it's a lot of old gangsters rigging things, it's still a victory for human understanding. One thinks, that's my species and we can do that'.

He denies, however, that the bulk of his plays are historically based. 'Is *Early Morning* set in the past? There are airports and cinema queues in it. Is *Lear* set in the past when it's really an anti-Stalinist play? Only about half my works are set in the past. A play like *The Worlds* is set in a modern, terrorist society and has had about seven performances. If I have set plays in the past, it's not because the past interests me but because I want to know how we got here. We can only find out where we are by looking at where we've been. I've also looked at the past to point out the inadequacy of past answers. Shakespeare can enunciate human needs supremely but he cannot say how you fulfil those needs in our society.'

For the moment Bond is keenly awaiting the revival of his Royal Court plays ('Watching them in rehearsal, I didn't know what was going to happen next'), has a play with the National Theatre called *Human Cannon* set in the Thirties and Forties, and is engaged on a trilogy of nuclear war plays for the Royal Shakespeare Company to be spread over two evenings. 'It's no use just saying nuclear war is horrible. You have to find ways of explaining why these wars occurred; and what would happen afterwards. Once people come out of their command bunkers, they'd either have to shoot the survivors or the survivors would shoot them. You'd then have to have a gangster society or a socialist society.'

It is an idea that intrigues Bond ('I would dearly love all the war dead to come back to the Cenotaph service – they'd butcher the lot of them'). But although Bond says provocative things, it is hard to convey in cold print the fact that he often accompanies them with a wry smile: it's not that he doesn't believe them but that he also enjoys pushing an idea to its limits.

He also brings to the drama a moral anger at injustice, a missionary zeal to change things and a private vision of one day creating his own writers' theatre that would extend the catchment area for playwrights and change the rules of the game: 'I have no answers. I have all the questions. I know we're not asking the ones people want us to ask. What we have to do is go back to the questions of the ruled and not of the rulers.'

1985

By the mid-Eighties the British theatre was in decidedly rocky shape. In 1985 the average grant increase to subsidised companies was 2%: well below inflation level. The West End was being kept precariously alive by foreign tourists: in the first nine months of the year overseas visitors made up 44% of the audience. Once a vital centre of world theatre, London now yielded the title to Paris where one went to see the latest productions by Strehler, Bergman, Mnouchkine or Chéreau.

Even the language in which we discussed the arts was gradually being debased. We now talked of 'investment' rather than subsidy. We no longer justified theatre on the grounds of spiritual nourishment or intellectual stimulus: we talked of 'an important strand in our export drive'. Most sinister of all was the admission by the Government that the vocal opposition of people like Sir Peter Hall to their funding policies prejudiced the chances of an all-round increase in subsidy: a denial of the long-established British principle that subvention came with no strings attached.

Of course, individual institutions still did lively work. The National gave us Bill Bryden's production of The Mysteries *and Mike Alfreds's ensemble vision of* The Cherry Orchard. *The RSC more contentiously went into partnership with Cameron Mackintosh on* Les Misérables, *but bravely put Peter Barnes's* Red Noses *onto the main Barbican stage though Edward Bond, Howard Barker and Granville Barker were carefully confined to the Pit. The Royal Court, though dependent on a $50,000 boost from Joe Papp and presenting an increasingly Americanised repertoire, at least kept the flag flying with Timberlake Wertenbaker's* The Grace Of Mary Traverse. *The Bush brought us Kroetz's* Through The Leaves *from the Edinburgh Traverse, the Half Moon jauntily revived* Sweeney Todd *and the Edinburgh Festival imported a stunning Japanese* Macbeth.

But the regions generally played safe, new writers were increasingly swallowed up by television and – in the case of Hanif Kureishi – cinema and, particular excellences aside, the broad picture was of a theatre struggling to keep its head above water.

The Mysteries

Cottesloe: 21 January 1985

Saturday in the Cottesloe began with the fall of Lucifer and the creation of Adam and Eve. It ended, almost twelve hours later, with Judgment Day. Bill Bryden's production of *The Mysteries* achieved completion with *The Nativity* and *The Passion* being joined by *Doomsday*; and the result, for all present, was an unforgettable piece of communal theatre. But the interesting question is why, in an age of scepticism, an audience should be so stirred by a piece of medieval religious drama.

Theatre is a great persuader: if a writer believes something strongly enough, that passion will transmit itself to an audience. And because the men who put together the York, Wakefield, Towneley and Coventry cycles sincerely believed that human beings had betrayed the freedom given them by God, we too accept that premise.

What is more the plays are always human, earthy and concrete. Thus when the God of *Doomsday* appears before us to lament the prevalence of sin and his disappointment in his creation, he tells us: 'To sadden me man straightway sought, Therefore me rues that I the world began.' He speaks like a grieving father rather than a pompous divine.

Tony Harrison's version of all three plays grasps this fundamental point: that although the works embrace a variety of styles, including farce, irony, spectacle and sermon, they are written in a sharp, bright language that makes the cosmic colloquial. Sometimes Mr Harrison's drumming alliteration bounces off the brain. But he has a wonderful grasp of the down-to-earth ('When I am dead' says Cain 'bury me in Wakefield by quarryhead'). And he often clarifies the source without distorting it. Thus Christ's original final lines on Judgement Day ('And thei that mendid thame whils thei moght, Schall belde and bide in my blessing') here movingly become: 'But they that mended all their miss Shall abide with me in endless bliss.'

But the other reason why the plays work on a modern audience is that Bill Bryden's production combines democratic celebration with theatrical sophistication. You can either promenade at floor level (where the gain in immediacy is offset by the occasional loss of view – I missed Mary's delivery of Jesus) or you can sit upstairs (where you see the plan of action better).

The emphasis throughout is on the plays' roots in ordinary life: thus Brian Glover's God strips off his hempen cloak to become a man in cloth-cap and braces, and Karl Johnson's Risen Christ appears among his followers in shabby fawn overcoat and reveals a hearty appetite for bread and fish.

But although Bryden and his designer William Dudley highlight the everyday (even the overhanging, guttering lights are shrouded in domestic objects from dustbins to colanders), they combine the simple with the spectacular; and breathtakingly so in the climactic *Doomsday*. Adam and Eve emerge from 4,600 years in limbo in a black drum-shaped cage. Satan and Beelzebub escape from the sewers for the Harrowing of Hell and later dispatch the unsaved souls into the giant maw of a waste disposal unit. Christ is resurrected from inside a padlocked magician's cabinet.

The most astonishing effect of all is the vision of writhing souls in torment, for which the black drapes behind God's throne part to reveal a gigantic Ferris-wheel shaped like a globe: and inside this revolving sphere the damned swing from the struts in perpetual agony. This is the most Wagnerian of Dudley's effects and it stuns the senses. But the success of *Doomsday* lies in its constant oscillation between images of nightmare retribution and festive release. Christ is borne off to Heaven on a fork-lift truck decked in billowing white cloth. And the funeral of Mary, mother of God, becomes a moving working-class ritual with a town band snaking through the audience playing 'O sad farewell' until the coffin bursts open and Mary is carried off on bowers of roses towards reunion with her son.

Bryden swathes *Doomsday* in an orgy of theatricality. In the process the excitement of the play comes through, but the fire-and-brimstone theology gets slightly buried. It must be difficult to make damnation real to a modern audience. But when those sitting on the left hand of God are singled out for punishment, the mood is one of faint jokiness; and when a few members of the audience are pitchforked into the waste-disposal hell, it is all a bit of a lark. I believe this should be played with unabashed severity. Without that the whole postulate of the Medieval Mysteries is shaken and the idea of divine redemption diminished.

Bryden makes us believe totally in good: he has less success with evil. But he has master-minded an extraordinary ensemble achievement and, from his team of regulars, I would invidiously single out Karl Johnson's heart-piercing Christ, Robert Stephens's Pontius Pilate, suggesting some Gogolian provincial mayor, Jack Shepherd's self-abasing guilt-ridden Judas and Dinah Stabb's Mary, full of inner illumination.

The music, performed by The Home Service and directed by John Tams, also captures a variety of styles from folk-rock to Sally Ally tunefulness. But what is most extraordinary about *The Mysteries* is that, through the sheer imaginative power of the production, it penetrates and sometimes even shatters the agnostic detachment of a modern audience.

Me And My Girl

Adelphi: 13 February 1985

The revival of *Me And My Girl* at the Adelphi sets the British musical back 50 years: 48 to be precise, since it was in 1937 that this condescending romp first wowed the British public. Now, despite the addition of extra songs from the Noel Gay canon, a revised book by Stephen Fry and a lively comic performance by Robert Lindsay, the show is chiefly remarkable for its patronising and sentimental view of British working-class life.

Is this to take it too seriously? I don't think so, since musicals, as much as plays, express certain values. What this show, the story of a Lambeth Cockney who turns out to be the long-lost Earl of Hareford, says quite clearly is that there is an unbridgeable gulf between the social classes; and that while the aristocracy may be decadent and effete, the proles are ignorant louts redeemed only by their capacity for true love.

Bill Snibson, the upwardly mobile hero, may stay faithful to his Lambeth sweetheart. But the whole musical rests on an extended coals-in-the-bath joke about the inappropriateness of a barrer-boy let loose among the county set, where he gropes the women, sucks sherry through a straw, and eats peas off his knife.

Of course, the book, by L. Arthur Rose and Douglas Furber, is on the side of Bill and his girl Sally who finally undergoes an Eliza Doolittle-like transformation. And the show's most famous number, 'The Lambeth Walk' (which spills out into the Adelphi stalls like a Cockney Bacchanal), is meant to be a sign of working-class, pearly-king vitality. But 'God bless 'em' is no better an attitude than 'How quaint they are'; and the show's strident sentimentality is in stark contrast to the spare realism of Maugham's *Liza Of Lambeth*.

Even on the pure entertainment level the show suffers from a threadbare plot (as in *Waiting For Godot*, nothing happens twice). What keeps the evening tenuously afloat are the amiable Noel Gay songs (though I don't care for the transformation of 'Leaning On A Lamp Post' into a slow tempo romantic number) and the comic inventiveness of Mr Lindsay, who manages to take some of the offensiveness out of the prole-gaucherie gags.

He plays Bill, in fact, as a hunched-shouldered, brown-bowlered Cockney anarch with a great capacity for lungeing at girls and furniture and missing, and for coming up with snappy retorts. 'Do you know my daughter May?' inquires a beaming duchess. 'No,' he replies, 'but thanks for the tip.'

Emma Thompson sings soulfully as his naive Cockney mate, but must have to grit her teeth to deliver lines 'Everybody knows Joan of Arc was married to Noah.' Susannah Fellows reveals a nifty pair of pins as a predatory aristo (who, incidentally, is tamed by having her face slapped), and Roy Macready makes his mark as a solicitor who looks as if he has done a lot of soliciting. But Mike Ockrent's cutesy production (complete with tap-dancing family portraits) cannot disguise the fact that the show is snobbish codswallop. It is also based on a thundering lie: that life in Lambeth is inherently preferable to that in a comfortable country estate.

Pravda

Olivier: 3 May 1985

Fleet Street offers a broad target; and *Pravda*, the new comedy by Howard Brenton and David Hare at the Olivier, scores a few bullseyes as well as several outers. It is neither a work-play like Wesker's *The Journalists* nor a debate on press freedoms like Stoppard's *Night and Day*. Instead it is a boisterous, swingeing, sometimes crude satire on the degradation of newspapers by overweening tycoons and the mayhem of mercantile capitalism; and it harks back to the same authors' *Brassneck* and even further to Jonsonian comedy of humours.

Its main theme is the rapacious absorption of chunks of the British press by a tough South African entrepreneur, Lambert Le Roux. Starting with a Leicester daily, he eats his way into Fleet Street via a tit-and-bum tabloid (*The Tide*) before devouring the ailing, upmarket *Daily Victory* and installing a bright young protégé as editor.

At first he is more omnivorous businessman than power-mad Citizen Kane. But when his appointee threatens to run a piece on plutonium leaks hushed up by the Ministry of Defence, Le Roux savagely exercises his proprietorial rights and sacks his award-winning editor. From then he degenerates into a beleaguered fanatic, practising the Japanese art of Toyinka in his Weybridge home, but always one step ahead of his enemies and a living embodiment of bare-toothed capitalism.

The play, as broad as it's long, is described in the Methuen edition as a 'comedy of excess'; and that seems, if anything, an understatement. But Brenton and Hare, with a good deal of bilious wit, pick off a number of targets. The willing surrender of newspaper trustees to rogue elephants like le Roux. The treatment of newspapers as a mere commodity alongside sports-centres, hotels and restaurants (they might have added cable television). The topsy-turvy world of the Lobby system whereby 'the only way you can have the confidence of Ministers is to have the confidence never to repeat what Ministers say.' The glib hucksterism of the bingo-parlour end of Fleet Street. They even touch on the failure of papers to respect confidential sources.

Brenton and Hare write with abundant comic zest; and they make numerous telling points, such as the hypocrisy of newspapers which celebrate the free-market economy complaining when they fall victim to it. But although many scenes have an exuberant cartoon-like quality (not least that in which Le Roux descends on the *Victory* office like a Springbok Caligula and fires at random effete hacks with names like Cliveden Whicker-Baskett), the play as it progresses runs into a central problem.

Le Roux himself is, on the one hand, a monster unleashed by Thatcherite capitalism. But he is also a man of iron certainty striding like a Colossus through what he calls 'the great melancholy of business'. He enlists a dangerous sympathy purely because he is the only character on stage possessed of a vision; and one feels that Brenton and Hare, having unleashed this spider from the bottle, cannot entirely control him. Like Richard III, he takes over the play; and one finds oneself waiting impatiently for his every entrance.

This is partly because he is superbly embodied by Anthony Hopkins. He utters every sentence with precise Afrikaans over-articulation as if the rest of the world are idiots. He thrusts his big bull-like head forward as though constantly braced to charge. He smiles with malign satisfaction at the reduction of newspapers to global formulae. And, in the very funny scene in his Oriental Surrey bath-house, he pads delicately round the stage like a disciple of Noh. Mr Hopkins presents us with a man who is almost certifiably mad; but who also has the chilling single-mindedness of those with tunnel-vision.

David Hare's production, staged on a wide V-shaped Hayden Griffin set that achieves swift transitions from Frankfurt sports-hall to Fleet Street office, offers a number of other performances that have the sharp outline of lightning sketches. Basil Henson as a Latin-quoting elitist editor, Peter Blythe as a biddable Tory smoothie, Ron Pember as a suicide-prone survivor of the great Beaverbrook massacre of 1952 are very funny; and it is no fault of Tim McInnerny as Le Roux's protégé and Kate Buffery as his left-wing wife that they emerge as slightly impotent wimps.

Unlike vintage satire, the play doesn't really possess a moral positive: it is hard to deduce from the evidence what kind of Fleet Street the authors ideally envisage. But it is a highly entertaining and scabrously funny play that rightly uses the Olivier stage to expose some of our current sickness.

'Theatre Writing: Why And How?'

Debate at the Royal Court: 11 June 1985

The Royal Court, home of many a theatrical revolution, nearly witnessed another one on Sunday afternoon. A packed house had assembled for a Playwright's Forum on the topic of 'Theatre Writing: Why And How?' It was intended as the highspot of a weekend-long celebration of the fact that, with the publication of *Pravda*, Methuen now have 500 plays in print: itself an extraordinary feat and a reminder that, whatever the problems afflicting new drama, a hunger for plays still exists.

Under the low-key chairmanship of Michael Attenborough, six empanelled playwrights were invited to kick off by talking about the pleasures and problems of writing for the theatre. Louise Page spoke of the hazards of writing for large casts. Stephen Lowe of the dramatist's familiar uncertainty as to whom he was addressing. Then up spake Margaretta D'Arcy who had hitherto been gazing at her colleagues as if they were rare tropical fish.

Misunderstanding Attenborough's jokey reference to the selected speakers as 'condemned people', she launched into an intemperate attack on the theatre as a premature killer and source of mental illness. Theatre, she sagely proclaimed, was dead, was a drug, 'makes us into passive spectators unable to control what is taking place'.

How many of us, she challengingly enquired, had been to the theatre in the past month? A majority raised their hands. How many, in the same period, had been on a demonstration? A tiny few. She seized on this as triumphant vindication of her point, as if the mere act of theatregoing turned one into a lobotomised zombie and as if demonstrating automatically toppled governments.

Uproar ensued as Ms D'Arcy barracked successive speakers, Hanif Kureishi and Mustapha Matura, though not her husband John Arden, who made some disturbing points about the alienation of playwrights from the current theatrical set-up. 'The structure of theatre,' he intriguingly remarked, 'has not advanced as fast as the imagination of playwrights.' That idea was left hanging tantalisingly in the air as Ms D'Arcy advocated the dissolution of the forum and the opportunity for everyone to have his say (who had ever denied it?). Finally she left, with a small band of followers, to conduct a seminar in the circle bar. Her departure was greeted by the majority with fortitude.

I report these spoiling tactics if only because they nearly capsized an afternoon devoted to the genuine crisis facing British playwriting and because they demonstrated, all too vividly, how those who most loudly trumpet total freedom of speech often monopolise that right.

What followed, after the procedural chaos, was a lively and well-tempered discussion but one that confirmed my own instinctive feeling that the British theatre right now is on the brink of losing everything achieved in 30 years. We have fine actors, directors, designers, writers. We have the necessary institutions. We even have, precariously, our international reputation as a centre of world theatre. What we don't have, thanks to candle-end Government economies, is a theatre that is working to anything remotely like its full potential. Cut-back on investment in the arts is not a saving: it is a waste. And it is this fact which is inducing a palpable despair amongst theatre practitioners.

The point was most forcefully put on Sunday by Philip Hedley, artistic director of the Theatre Royal, Stratford East. 'There is,' he said, 'a tragedy haunting this conference.' And the tragedy to which he referred is that young writers are hamstrung and constrained by the present stringent theatrical economies.

He gave a precise example of a new play he had received, full of excellent dialogue, set in a GLC evening-class. The characters were confined to two students, a caretaker and a teacher. In real life, he said, any such class would be shut down because of insufficient numbers; but the dramatist had not written in more for fear of limiting the play's chance of production.

Hedley's most potent argument is that fourteen productions have in the past thirty years moved from Stratford East into the West End but that, on current budgets, only two of those shows could now be staged. Shelagh Delaney's *A Taste Of Honey* may have had a cast of five; but, as Hedley pointed out, Joan Littlewood's production had a jazz-band in the box which would today be 'unimaginable luxury'. Right now he wanted to commission Barrie Keeffe to do an updated version of *The Alchemist* but how could you ask a dramatist to undertake such a project with six characters? 'The money,' said Hedley with a ring of passion in his voice, 'has got to be invested in the playwright.'

He is right. British drama at the moment is bedevilled by a prevailing littleness: small casts, small plays, small ambitions. Partly it is a result of the prevailing economics. But it is also a result of what Louise Page accurately called 'the rise of the studio play and the little black box'. We have over the past fifteen years constantly seen new drama shunted into those conscience-saving adjuncts to big theatres and the consequence has been the growth of a new generation of dramatists with neither the opportunity, gift nor temperament for handling large spaces. We need to get new plays out of the ghetto and back on to main stages.

What emerged from Sunday's talk-in is that dramatists currently feel like an endangered species: excluded from the interlocking relationships of the big companies, under-commissioned and thinly rewarded for their work, untutored in the use of sizeable casts. What is also clear is that the crisis is not next year, it is now. The year is half-way over and I can count on the fingers of one hand the really stimulating new plays I have so far seen: Brenton and Hare's *Pravda*, Stephen Wakelam's *Deadlines*, Nigel Williams's *My Brother's Keeper*, Alan Ayckbourn's *Woman In Mind*, Robert Holman's *Today*.

But what can be done to stimulate new drama? The Arts Council, for a start, could ensure that the allocated £200,000 was actually spent by theatres on new plays and not on roof-repairs. Artistic directors could formulate long-term new play policies (as happened at Liverpool Playhouse); the public (all those people who buy Methuen plays) could be more adventurous.

But dramatists themselves have a responsibility (as Mustapha Matura insisted on Sunday) to tell good stories and also to remember that the word playwright, like shipwright or wheelwright, carries with it implications of a highly specialised craft.

The Mahabharata

Avignon: 16 July 1985

We assembled around seven o'clock on Saturday evening in an amphitheatrical stone-quarry fourteen kilometres outside Avignon after a boat-trip up the broad-banked Rhône. As the sun edged down behind the cliff-face of the quarry, Peter Brook's production of the great Sanskrit epic, *Le Mahabharata*, began. Eleven hours later, with the birds singing in the Provençal dawn, the show finished with a vision of Paradise with sitars playing and candles bobbing gently in the onstage river.

We were the first audience at this year's Avignon Festival to have seen *Le Mahabharata* as it should ideally be experienced: not as three separate evenings but, as in Jean-Claude Carrière's adaptation, a dusk-to-dawn epic dealing with the birth of heroes and legends, a world-shaking family quarrel and a final exhausted calm.

It was, in every sense, an unforgettable experience comparable to the kind of day-long ritual audiences must have undergone in Athens in the 5th century BC. One put up with the mild discomfort of the tip-up seats and the occasional bout of tiredness; for what one was seeing was the cycle of human affairs presented in a single night.

What is also worth stressing is that *Le Mahabharata* is a triumphant vindication (if one were needed) of the work Brook has been doing in Paris over the past eleven years. There are still those who wonder why Brook has chosen to work abroad with his own international company rather than churning out product for our classical theatre.

But this production shows him forging a fabulous narrative theatre that combines the lyrical magic of *The Conference Of The Birds*, the austerity of *Les Iks*, the knockabout farce of *Ubu*. Holy and Rough theatre (to use Brook's own terms) combine in a work that is like Shakespeare's Histories in its vision of dynastic conflict and universal disorder.

Each of the three plays that make up the epic also has its own distinct tone. The first, *La Partie De Des* (The Dice-Game), is rich in myth and magic. It begins with Vyasa dictating 'le grande poème du monde' to a scribe and shows the origins of the two clans – the Pandava brothers and their cousins the Kauravas – whose conflict leads to global disaster. Karna, the child of the sun, is born in a billow of torch-smoke, wreathed as a boy in garlands while a bow and arrow is placed in his hand.

But although the first play shows the growing quarrel between the rival cousins and leads to the fatal dice-game in which the Pandava leader (Mathias Habich) gambles away his inheritance, it is full of piercing images of tenderness. At one point the five Pandava brothers all harmoniously share the same bride and lie down in front of her with their mother, Kunti, at their head.

And in the second play, *L'Exile Dans La Fôret*, we get a sense almost of pastoral idyll as the brothers go into retreat and eventually become part of a court where an entertainer plays out a puppet-show behind a crimson curtain. But the inevitable conflict approaches and in the third part, *La Guerre*, we are plunged into a world of darkness, torchlight, smoke, bloodshed, the death of successive heroes and the destruction of kingdoms before the arrival of the dawn and a sense of healing harmony.

What does it all mean? On a narrative level, it is a basic decline-and-fall story of rival family factions destroying the very universe that is their inheritance. But what makes it enigmatic for a Western audience, unversed in Indian epics, is that moral blame is never apportioned, words like sin and evil are never used and that the great god Krishna foresees and laments the coming holocaust but seems powerless to prevent it.

If a general principle emerges, it is that human beings must find order within themselves to create an ordered universe; and to me there is one crucial exchange in which the Pandava leader is asked the miracle of life and says that 'Each day death beats at our door yet we live as if we were immortal.'

The ultimate meaning of *Le Mahabharata* is for each individual to discover. But Brook gives it a direct link with our century in a monumental explosion of blinding intensity that bursts out of the quarry and fills the stage with sulphurous smoke: I met an Indian professor who said it was out of keeping with the original but to me it was a brilliant reminder of the looming destruction under which we all live.

For the most part, however, Brook evokes chaos and disorder

through the simplest means: a shower of white arrows criss-crossing in the night, Karna propelling a single chariot-wheel across the sand-caked stage, warriors splashing heedlessly through the river that was once the source of creation. It is like an elliptical *Wars Of The Roses*. But it also ends with an intense Shakespearean feeling that, after the dark night of the soul, comes the overpowering human need for renewal.

Brook's international company also helps gives the work a universal quality. There is no attempt at a spurious Indian ethnicity; and there is a whole range of remarkable performances from Maurice Benichou as Krishna regarding mankind's self-destructiveness with immeasurable sorrow, from Mamadou Dioume as a volatile, giant-like Pandava warrior, from Matthias Habich as the clan's blond, whipcord-muscled leader, from Mireille Maalouf as the eye-bandaged queen, from Bruce Myers as the war-forged Karna.

It is very much a story of mothers and sons, fathers and children and it is this that gives it a poignant human dimension as well as a sense of cosmic upheaval. Without question this production is the masterwork of Brook's later period and a tribute to the perservance of himself and Jean-Claude Carrière in making an enthralling dramatic entertainment out of a work five times as long as the Bible.

I only pray we one day see it in Britain. It is an extraordinary philosophical epic that acknowledges death, destruction and decay while enhancing the mystery of life itself.

Les Liaisons Dangereuses

The Other Place: 27 September 1985

I am wary of novel adaptations. But for the second time this year (Shared Experience's *Pamela* was the other) an epistolary novel turns up trumps with Christopher Hampton's brilliant version of Laclos's *Les Liaisons Dangereuses* at Stratford's Other Place. Mr Hampton has used one work of art to create another in which sexual power games are dissected and exposed with Firbankian verbal wit.

As in Laclos's famous literary bombshell (published in Paris in 1782), we see two calculating predators using sex as a weapon of revenge. Working like a campaign strategist (and it is no accident that Laclos himself was a military tactician), the Marquise de Merteuil spurs on her former lover, the Vicomte de Valmont, to attack the citadel of the 15-year-old, convent-reared Cecile Volanges's virginity. But the complicating factor is that the Vicomte is himself obsessed by conquering the prudent, God-fearing wife of a provincial magistrate. So we see the cynical seducer himself becoming a slave of passion; and the result is both the destruction of virtue and the wholesale exposure of vice.

Hampton's achievement is to have preserved the satanic magnetism of the twin conspirators while going all-out for social comedy. But this is comedy of the highest theatrical kind: edged with danger, replete with pain and forever reminding us that lives are being ruined with the flick of a well-turned phrase. Seizing, for instance, on a tiny episode in the book, Hampton shows the Vicomte using a bare-backed courtesan as a writing-desk to pen a letter to his would-be mistress; but no sooner has the Vicomte sprayed us with double-entendres than we see the object of his passion almost choking to death with sexual guilt.

As in the book, the main characters are monsters; but they are compelling monsters. And Hampton skilfully brings out Laclos's implicit feminism in the scene where the Marquise justifies her role as 'a virtuoso of deceit' by explaining she is the product of a double-standard society where sexual conquest can ruin a woman while enhancing a man's prestige.

Both erotic and painful, comic and tragic, the evening keeps one in a constant state of conflicting emotion. And where Hampton takes liberties with the original, such as ending with the sound of the guillotine that awaits these silk-swathed egotists, they are justified by history. But what is heartening is that moralising is kept to a minimum. Bob Crowley's set, with its latticed screens and rumpled beds, delicately suggests a sun-lit salon full of imprisoned butterflies, and Howard Davies's production leaves it to us to deduce that we are watching the last gasp of a doomed class.

The casting is also exemplary. Alan Rickman seems born to play the Vicomte, whom he endows with a drawling, handsome languor and a genuine sense of spiritual shock at discovering he may be in thrall to love. Lindsay Duncan matches him perfectly as the avenging Marquise who is like a porcelain beauty gifted with the calculating brain of a chess-master: she is spared the character's final facial disfigurement but her panicky, hunted look as she settles down to cards, registers just as powerfully. Juliet Stevenson, as the Vicomte's prey, though unflatteringly coiffured, strikes a note of authentic feeling in this hot-house world.

Giraudoux described the book as 'the one French novel that gives us an impression of danger'. What Mr Hampton has done is turn it into an elegant comedy with the menace of a stiletto.

Torch Song Trilogy

Albery: 3 October 1985

Harvey Fierstein's *Torch Song Trilogy* at the Albery is rather like Neil Simon re-written by Barbara Cartland. It is stuffed to the gills with gags (some good, some pure push-button laugh-raisers). At the same time, its vigorous defence of the family pieties is the kind of thing that Victorian ladies stitched on their samplers. For all its touted Broadway success, it strikes me as a corny, sentimental rag-bag of an evening redeemed by a virtuoso performance from Antony Sher.

Sher plays a stilettoed, slim-hipped New York drag-queen (though nothing like the 'Amazon woman' lazily referred to in the text); and in the first play, *The International Stud*, we follow the agonies of his on-off relationship with Ed, a bisexual Brooklyn teacher. What hits one, however, is Mr Fierstein's willingness to go for instant effect rather than consistent characterisation. His hero, Arnold, yearns for romantic love, tragic torch-singer status, and at the same time makes with the one-liners like a gay Henny Youngman.

Mr Fierstein knows how to pace a scene; and there is one good one (the best in the whole evening) when Arnold pleads desperately with his lover by phone for an explanation as to why he has been deserted. Sher catches brilliantly Arnold's mixture of swivel-eyed panic, grovelling self-abasement and sharp-tongued acerbity: it is a scene straight or gay can easily identify with. But even here Mr Fierstein's penchant for pokerwork moralising shines through with lines like Arnold's 'How can you show any respect for anyone if you won't be yourself?'. Mr Fierstein is like a tub-thumper with jokes; and a scene where Arnold is mimetically ravished in a gay bar is like an Awful Warning on the horrors of loveless sex.

This ambivalence runs right through the evening. In the second, least interesting play, *Fugue In A Nursery*, Arnold and his new male-model lover, Alan, are invited for an improbable weekend in the country by Ed and his spouse. As the two couples exchange partners, wisecracks and reminiscences on a king-sized bed, this becomes a cross between *Private Lives* and *I Love My Wife*.

But it is in the final play, *Widows And Children First*, that Fierstein's determination to be both finger-wagger and gag-man reaches its apogee. The time is five years later; and the situation is dramatically interesting. Arnold's lover is dead and he himself is desperately keen to become adoptive parent to a 15-year-old ex-delinquent living with him for a probationary period. I find this moving and fraught with possibilities.

But what we get is *La Cage Aux Folles* farce with Arnold trying to conceal the situation from his Mrs Portnoyish mother; and jokes come before truth so that when the young boy asks Arnold's panic-stricken mum how he could possibly be the rapist she takes him for since he's wearing a three-piece suit, she cries: 'I don't know – maybe you got a wedding after.' Lines like this are a dead giveaway.

What this leaves out of account, however, is Sher's magnetism as Arnold. Mr Sher is nothing like the big, plump, cumbersome figure the text implies. But what he gets across superbly is Arnold's chameleon nature: he is gossipy-camp with his phone-friend, Murray; fussy mother-hen with his would-be son; sober best-chum with Ed's distracted wife. Not even Mr Sher can reconcile one to the play's glaring inconsistencies (Arnold's casually-regarded lover is translated, once dead, into the romance of a lifetime in order to shore up campaign speeches about the homosexual capacity to feel). But his lightning transitions from raw emotion to waspish wit paper over the cracks in Mr Fierstein's text.

There is also good work in Robert Allan Ackerman's production from Rupert Frazer as the lantern-jawed, bi-sexual Ed, from Miriam Karlin, who works hard to keep the Jewish mum this side of caricature, from Barbara Rosenblat, as a smokey-lung'd torch-singer and especially from Ian Sears as Arnold's level-headed son. But the blunt fact is that this four-hour show is constantly torn between having its hand on its heart and its tongue in its cheek. Reluctantly, I came to the conclusion that Mr Fierstein is interested in the zinger not the song.

The Castle

The Pit: 18 October 1985

Writers change. I complained a week ago of the lack of internal dynamic in Howard Barker's work. But *The Castle*, his most recent play and the second in the Barker season at The Pit, suggests he has matured massively as a dramatist in the last few years. It combines narrative thrust with scorching language and poetic power to make it, along with *Pravda*, the most exciting new play in London.

The news that it is set in medieval England after the Crusades may not make the heart soar; but Barker uses this setting to stage a complex battle between the male and female principle. We see Stucley, a feudal lord, returning to his domain after a seven-year absence to find it has been turned into a secular commonwealth and that his wife has taken a witch as her lover. He quickly sets about restoring male values: he commissions a captive Arab mathematician he has brought back from the Crusades to build him a massively fortified castle and gets his bishop to rewrite the Gospels to assert the powerful virility of Christ. What follows is a fascinating spiritual tussle in which competitive masculine destructiveness does battle with compassionate female creativity.

At one point one of the village women, speaking of children, says to a soldier, 'We birth 'em and you kill them.' But the play is far more than a simplistic championing of matriarchal values. Obviously it has strong parallels with Greenham Common and could be taken as a metaphorical Bomb-play; what makes it a stirring theatrical fable, however, is that the issues are never clear-cut.

Stucley's circular-towered fortress is, in its perverse way, a visionary idea; and, conversely, in a scene of stomach-churning power, women sacrifice themselves and their children in the ultimate protest against a brutish patriarchy. Barker, through historical parable, is raising a vital moral question: how far could, and should, women go in order to change the values of society?

But what gives this play such force is Barker's language which is tart, comic, rich-textured and hard-consonanted. Some may baulk at its insistent use of anatomical four-letter words but they're always nouns, never expletives. And what is encouraging is that idiom is matched to character. When Stucley, able to build a castle but unable to father a child, cries to his wife 'I spent enough juice in you to father forty regiments,' the language is a direct embodiment of an authoritarian swagger. Throughout I was reminded of Cocteau's definition of theatrical poetry as something that should not be light and flimsy but 'thick like the rigging of a ship and visible at a distance'.

Mr Barker's apocalyptic second act may not have the theatrical tension of his first. But this is, by any yardstick, a major play and both Nick Hamm's production and Stewart Laing's design economically suggest epic deeds in a studio space: witness the forest of black ladders used to evoke the building of the castle.

Ian McDiarmid also colours Stucley's baronial bullishness with a brilliant waspish irony; and there is admirable work from Harriet Walter as a lesbian magician gradually transformed into a worshipped icon; from Penny Downie as Stucley's instinctively fertile (though not with him) wife for whom child-bearing is natural fulfilment; and Tony Mathews as a pliable cleric ready to rewrite the New Testament and to wear a toolbag in place of a mitre.

Fatal Attraction

Haymarket: 28 November 1985

Bernard Slade's *Fatal Attraction* at the Haymarket is one of those plays that defies a critical act. So below I offer the random questions that came to me in the course of this preposterous thriller.

1. Why must murder mysteries always be set in cut-off country houses or, as here, the remote Nantucket beach house of a fading film star? Judging from the theatre, you would think murder was a rural pursuit exclusively indulged in by the relatively affluent.

2. When the film star's ex-husband is stabbed at the end of the first scene, do we care? As George Jean Nathan wrote: 'If a character comes on and is popped off before we get to know him, it is dollars to free passes we don't give much of a hang if he is murdered, who murders him, or why he is murdered.'

3. At what point did it become fashionable for characters seemingly departed (in this case a lurid photographer) to make Gothic re-entries? I traced this back myself to Clouzot's film, *Les Diaboliques*. The results ever since have been suitably diabolical.

4. When did it become popular to spice stage thrillers with bisexual chic? The turning point, I suspect, was Ira Levin's *Deathtrap*. Gore Vidal said the advantage of bisexuality was that it doubled your chances of a date on Saturday night. But isn't there something a bit creepy about the idea of it as an incentive to murder?

5. Isn't it fatally selfconscious to make your detective (here Denis Quilley doing an impersonation of William Bendix) a cultural connoisseur? When, catching a bar or two of the Bartok Concerto for Orchestra, he enquires, 'Isn't that the von Karajan recording?'

6. How can the memorably fetching Susannah York be expected to get away with a line like, 'No one has ever accused me of being sexy'?

7. If in the course of a single day, a film star's husband was murdered and then she herself was raped by and stabbed his assailant, wouldn't she be invited to pop down to the station-house for a little questioning?

8. Why must stage thrillers always be so trivial when a TV series like *Edge Of Darkness*, a film like *Defence Of The Realm* and a novel like *Hawksmoor* has shown they can deal with serious issues?

9. Isn't the form itself a one-way ticket to oblivion? On Broadway in the Thirties there were 58 mysteries in eight seasons. Not one has survived.

10. When the star's agent (Kate Harper) breezes in saying. 'I was on my way here with a script,' why didn't the cast take the hint and offer to play that one instead.

1986

A feverish year. The Sunday Times *launched a nasty campaign against Sir Peter Hall and Trevor Nunn suggesting, none too subtly, that the former had exploited National Theatre hits like* Amadeus *for his own gain and that the latter had absented himself unduly from the RSC to launch a thriving commercial career: both charges were stoutly rebutted by the individuals concerned but inevitably some of the mud stuck. What was dismaying was that this campaign of vilification – quickly seized on by the rest of the right-wing press – distracted attention from the British theatre's real problem: Government indifference and a pathetic Arts Council drama budget of £26 million incapable of sustaining a network of national, regional, touring, Fringe and community theatres.*

I spent much of the year sitting in committee and talking to theatre-workers as a member of the Cork Enquiry into Professional Theatre in England: a stimulating and eye-opening experience. What struck all of us was that the two big national companies, through no fault of their own, were inexorably absorbing about 50% of the Arts Council's drama budget: we calculated that it would cost £16.2 million to restore the balance between the national companies and the rest which obtained in 1970. We proposed the enhancement of specific regional companies, determined both by geography and artistic quality, to give them national status: though many of the Report's recommendations were put into practice this one, alas, still awaits implementation.

Two other features stood out this year. One was Frank Dunlop's success in turning the Edinburgh Festival into a Daubeny-type World Theatre Season: we had Ninagawa's Medea, *Wajda's* Crime And Punishment, *Bergman's* Miss Julie *and* John Gabriel Borkman, *Gomez's* Blood Wedding, *the American Wooster Group. What with Nuria Espert directing* Bernarda Alba *in Hammersmith and the London International Festival of Theatre going strong, it was a good year for internationalists. The other keynote of the year was the way playwrights used the past to comment obliquely on the present: Frank McGuinness's* Observe The Sons Of Ulster, *Pam Gems's* The Danton Affair, *Howard Barker's* Women Beware Women. *Good work resulted; but one still wished for more direct comment on the particular spirit of our times.*

Theatre In Japan

3 March 1986

Japan is a culture of violent contrasts: one in which the ancient art of haiku rubs shoulders with high-tech and in which your snapshot of a Shinto shrine is likely to be backed by a dreaming sky-scraper. And nowhere is this contrast more evident than in the theatre, where you can move easily from the arcane rites of Noh business to the wilder excesses of show-business. After a week sampling Tokyo theatre, my eyes were dazzled by an amazing parade of images: I was also disturbed by the almost total dependence on commerce.

Tokyo theatre resembles our own in one major respect: sheer quantity. On any one night, the city offers some 40 shows: in the country at large, there are some 500 groups. All else is bewilderingly different. For a start, state subsidy is so small as to be barely visible: 'tears in the eye of a sparrow' as one director poetically put it. Many productions are mounted by two giant entertainment-complexes, Shochiku and Toho (who last year brought Ninagawa's *Macbeth* to Edinburgh). Others are sustained by a mix of commercial sponsorship, box office and low wages. Mrs Thatcher would love it.

The most surprising sponsors are Tokyo's huge department stores, many of which house their own theatres. I took a lift to the ninth floor of the chic, chromium-black Parco One to see a play directed by Ninagawa, about the failure of Sixties revolutionary dreams: it was like going to Harvey Nichols to see the latest David Hare.

Sometimes the contrasts make one rub one's eyes in disbelief. I talked to the director of the new Ginza Theatre which will seat 774 people, cost almost as much as our own National, and play host to the international avant-garde: it will open in March 1987 with Brook's *Carmen*. Ironically, Brook's first request was that this spanking new department store playhouse be made to look as ruined as possible.

I do not mock this department store drama (where would Tokyo be without it?), but there is a glaring contrast between the cheque book culture of the big stores and the struggle to make ends meet of many resident companies. A director of one of the most famous, Haiyuza Gekijo, whose repertoire ranges from Shakespeare to Brecht to modern Japanese drama, told me that their actors hand back 25 per cent of their earnings in films and TV to the company (a common practice).

A director of a smaller group (staging a competent version of *Twelve Angry Men*) told me that his actors were paid only expenses. In Japan there are neither actors' trade unions nor agents. And while the big stars earn a fat living, most actors subsidise the theatre by outside work. It happens here too; but in Japan the sweatshop and the playhouse sometimes seem uncomfortably close neighbours.

What also separates Japan from Europe is that they favour neither the consecutive long-run nor the revolving repertoire. Big productions often play for a month: if popular, they go on tour and are brought back at regular intervals. In Tokyo this leads to a constant turnover of productions: as many as a thousand a year. It also leads to some strange paradoxes. This week sees the return to Tokyo, for close on the 500th performance, of a popular actress as Blanche Dubois in *A Streetcar Named Desire*. The fact that she is 80 doesn't seem to worry anyone.

But this passion for antiquity has its benefits. And the most obvious is that you can still see, amid the frantic urban hubbub of modern Tokyo, such traditional dramatic arts as Noh Theatre (which dates back to the 14th century), Kabuki (which started in the 17th century) and the Bunraku Puppet Theatre (which began in 1871). I focused on Kabuki, partly because I had seen Noh and Bunraku in London; partly because I was intrigued by Beatrice Lillie's remark, in creating a number called Kabuki Lil, that 'These Kabuki plays go on for six months with only one intermission.' A pardonable exaggeration; but one that does scant justice to a stunningly beautiful and moving art-form that takes the pejorative sting out of the phrase 'museum-theatre'.

Kabuki (deriving from a verb meaning 'to wear a strange costume') is a highly colourful mixture of acting, song and dance. It originated in a religious dance of ecstasy performed at Kyoto in 1603 by a woman named O-kuni. It evolved into a popular art, produced its own repertoire and today there are some eighteen oft-revived Kabuki plays fitting into different genres. All Kabuki productions, however, have certain features in common. One is the hanamichi: a two-metre wide catwalk running from the stage to the back of the stalls. Another is the presence of onnagata: men who play women's roles, dating back to an edict of 1629 when female prostitution was rampant. A third is the interaction of music and drama with the actors taking their cue from the singers' lines.

I saw one of the most famous of all Kabuki plays, *Kanahedon Chushingura*, dating from 1748 and based on a famous incident in which forty-seven retainers exacted revenge for the death of their master. It started at 11 am, finished around 9 pm and (with the help of an excellent earphone translation) I found myself gradually ensnared in its web. At first, I felt like an alien spectator at some religious ritual: the audience (mostly women) applauded familiar business, cheered on their favourite actors and clearly delighted in the exaggerated portrayal of the villain with dilated nostrils and popping eyes.

But I came to see that there is more to Kabuki than brocaded costumes, falsetto singing, melodramatic gesture: behind it lies a severe and haunting restraint. In one scene Enya, a lord guilty of drawing his sword in the Shogun's palace, commits ritual suicide. In Western theatre this would be an excuse for a display of blood and guts: in Kabuki it becomes a prolonged ritual.

Enya emerges dressed in the pale garments of death. Straw mats are solemnly laid out by his grieving servants. Sprigs of sacred trees are placed at the corners of the mats. Enya slowly withdraws his sword, wraps it in paper leaving the tip exposed and then meticulously draws it across and up his belly, watched by his wife and her handmaidens in white kimonos. The scene, played out in dumb-show to plangent music, tears at the heart through its quiet understatement; and there is an astonishing moment of realism when a servant massages his master's death-cold fingers to prise the sword from his grasp.

Kabuki offers something we have lost sight of in the West: the expressive power of ritual. It also, in this instance, provides acting of true artistry from the star onnagata, Tamasaburo, Japan's most popular actor. Watching him play a fugitive lady-in-waiting in love with one of Enya's followers, I was reminded of something Chekhov wrote: 'When a man spends the least possible number of movements over some definite action, that is grace.' Tamasaburo does not caricature femininity: he embodies it. At one point, he uses his long kimono-sleeves to echo the distant outline of Mount Fuji: at another, he sketches in his future, wifely duties with tiny, needle-threading movements. You may baulk at the sentiments and at the denial of women any place in Kabuki: you cannot deny you are in the presence of a spell-binder who transforms female impersonation into art.

Authentic Kabuki is pure theatre: Tokyo also shows how it can dwindle into showmanship. At another theatre there is a show billed as 'Super Kabuki' starring a popular actor-manager, Ennosuke, and written by a modern Japanese Professor. It bears the same relation to the real thing as a John Player knock-out game to a five-day test. It is called *Yamato Takeru*, is set in the twelfth century and sends its eponymous hero on a series of Herculean quests.

As old-fashioned Lyceum spectacle, it is incredible: the hero conquers hordes of barbarians like a Japanese Errol Flynn, wipes out a prairie-fire, rides out a sea-storm and, after his death, rises from his mausoleum transmogrified into a swan and flies out over the heads of the audience suspended on wires. Ennosuke makes Donald Wolfit look like a shrinking violet. But although the play is a tribute to the unification of Japan, I felt it was even more a celebration of the canonisation of its star: as he flew past me, Ennosuke bathed graciously in our applause. A clear case of swanupmanship.

But Japanese theatre is not exclusively concerned with the past. Shingeki (or 'New Theatre') dates back to 1909 and has taken many forms: Western imports, new plays, performance art. In Tokyo there have recently been plays on political corruption, school violence, the identity crisis of the young. I caught Kunio Shimizu's *Tango At The Winter's End*, directed by Ninagawa and starring his Macbeth, Mikijiro Hira, as a radical actor of the Sixties who returns to his childhood home, is driven into madness by his alienation and, unable to distinguish between reality and illusion, finally strangles his mistress. Without a knowledge of Japanese, it is impossible to judge the play's literary skill. But what struck me, as so often in Tokyo, was the play's visual and visceral power, proving that Ninagawa's *Macbeth* was no flash in the pan.

Ninagawa's production thrillingly embodied Shimizu's lament for a lost generation; and afterwards he told me that this year (as well as bringing his all-male *Medea* to Edinburgh) he will be directing *Oedipus*, a rock *Odyssey* and *Blood Wedding*. An enticing prospect.

But Japan's imagistic passion can also lead to the kind of overblown scenic extravagance I recently deplored in our own theatre. I went finally to a musical called *Dreaming* based on Maeterlinck's *The Bluebird* and directed by Keita Asari, who last year produced *Madam Butterfly* at La Scala. The music itself was tinny and tuneless: what we were treated to was a demonstration of hydraulics in which stages ceaselessly rose, fell, heaved on huge chunks of arboreal scenery and did everything but solicit our applause. I could have been in any theatre in the West End or Broadway. And it left me concluding that Japanese theatre can be stunning when it draws on its own country's rich past and present and equally decadent when it relies on the worst excesses of occidental showbiz.

The Threepenny Opera

Olivier: 15 March 1986

I was fascinated to read in the National's programme for *The Threepenny Opera* that the *Red Flag* condemned the 1928 Berlin production as 'culinary theatre, totally lacking in concrete social awareness'. Whatever claim to revolutionary status the work has stems from its ironic, low-life inversion of the operatic form; and that point goes crucially missing from Peter Wood's bland, smooth, pretty new production at the Olivier where the only irony is that the show is sponsored by Citicorp and Citibank.

Irony is the key. Brecht himself in a conversation with Giorgio Strehler in 1955 (recorded in the Methuen edition) explained the show's underlying idea. 'Beggars are poor people. They want to make a grand opera but lack money and have to make do as best they can.' What Brecht underlined was that the actors' effort to achieve something grandiose ended each time as a fiasco. And the one production I have seen that got anywhere near that was Philip Prowse's recent Opera North version which showed a group of Buñuel-type tramps invading a plush Belgravia mansion, tying its occupant to a chair and presenting her with a travesty-opera before cutting her throat.

Mr Wood's production has no such savagery and no such framing device: it is basically a pleasant bourgeois spectacle with some indestructible Kurt Weill tunes. You get the general idea from the opening 'Mack The Knife' ballad when a jokey, black-plumed funeral cortège slow-steps across the stage, after which designer Timothy O'Brien evokes London through the descent of Georgian churches and monuments from the flies. It is clever and amusing but it distracts you from the actual lyrics which portray Macheath as an arsonist, rapist and child-murderer. It also begs the fundamental question of who is putting the show on: clearly not a group of beggars parodying a bourgeois form, but a well-drilled National Theatre company.

Without that central irony (what I wonder, does Mr Wood think the title means?) what you get is a show; but, even on that level, mordancy and bite are often undercut by fiddly distractions. Thus, while the Peachums are reacting with horror to the news of Polly's marriage to Macheath, we are watching a bed flying out and a church flying in; and, while Eve Adam as Jenny Diver is singing (very well) the haunting 'Song of Solomon', the purity of the moment is undermined by the wheeling on of a bed-bound Macheath swathed in whores.

The real passions in this production seem to be decorative, from the swivelling round of the Turnbridge whorehouse set for a smoke-filled rooftop chase of Macheath to the sporting of canine masks by the Victorian rozzers. The result is that the genuine ferocity of a number like 'What Keeps A Man Alive' ('Begin by bringing food, not education') springs out of no consistent context and the spectacle of beggars brandishing their crutches at the audience leaves our withers unwrung.

There is, however, always the music; and the success of the evening lies in Dominic Muldowney's basic respect for Kurt Weill's orchestrations and the fact that the eleven-strong band is never allowed to drown the singers (who, incidentally, are miked).

There is also, appropriately, a peach of a Polly from Sally Dexter who builds on the excellent impression she made in *Love For Love*. She sings with full-throated directness, convinces you she might well have taken over Macheath's gang and in the Barbara Song beautifully expresses sexual fulfilment by spreadeagling her arms and sliding slowly down the bed-rail.

I was less persuaded by Tim Curry's dapper, kid-gloved camel-coated Macheath; like most of the cast, he sings well but I miss any hint of sexual or personal menace. I don't think Macheath should be cuddly. But amongst the gang, one actor shows what can be done with a small role and that, predictably, is Michael Bryant whose Crookfingered Jake is a real character with curly-brimmed bowler, elephantine lugs, drastically curtailed trousers and a determined bustle that doesn't prevent him always missing the vital action.

But in the end, for all the exactness of Robert David MacDonald's translation, this is prettified Brecht. It ducks the central question ('criminals are bourgeois: are bourgeois criminals?'). But more crucially, it never lets you see that the work is meant as a rough travesty of grand art put on by a poor company. It finally lacks both irony and steel.

Romeo And Juliet

Royal Shakespeare Theatre: 10 April 1986

As we enter the Stratford theatre, a rock group is playing mood-indigo music, a black guy is cruising round the marble-smooth stage on roller-skates and there is a pervasive whiff of black leather. We are instantly closer to the world of *Starlight Express* than star-cross'd lovers. And, as Benvolio arrives on a motor-bike and Tybalt turns up in the Veronese square in a low-slung red sportscar, it becomes impossible not to dub this the Alfa Romeo and Juliet.

Michael Bogdanov, in short, has set the play unequivocally in Verona 1986. The result is hip, cool, clever and witty; a painless revitalisation of a play that, for my money, never lives up to its advance publicity as a great love-tragedy and that depends too much on the faulty postal service between Verona and Mantua. But though this is the first *Romeo And Juliet* in years I have truly enjoyed, I have a nagging worry that the RSC is starting to decorate Shakespeare rather than explore him and that the Leavisite purism of the Sixties is being replaced by the pure Take-it-or-Leavism of the Eighties.

To be fair, Bogdanov's flair for Guthriesque invention works spectacularly well in the first half, where he creates a complete society in which everyone has a defined place. Montagues and Capulets are rival families living under a Mafia prince with Capulet himself an urban predator working from a green-marble desk and staggeringly indifferent to his daughter's welfare and his wife's affair with cousin Tybalt. Capulet also throws some spectacular thrashes: at the big one, Tybalt essays Memory on the saxophone (thus becoming the Prince of 'Cats') and Mercutio, the original Gucci loafer, jives headlong into the pool with his partner.

This is a world of rich kids, fixed marriages and tough deals where, when two people meet, it's business at first sight; and for once Bogdanov creates a real sense that, by falling in love, Romeo and Juliet are defying the local customs. He also thinks the concept through so that Friar Laurence here becomes a jovial Fernandel-figure on a bicycle meticulously removing a pressed flower from inside his wallet. And the big fight in the main square acquires a mixture of jocularity and venom with Michael Kitchen's laid-back Mercutio taunting Hugh Quarshie's chain-brandishing Tybalt by spreadeagling himself across the bonnet of his priceless motor.

But all this Bogdanovian invention builds to a point which is that young love is as vulnerable as it ever was to parental exploitation and cruelty: more so since Richard Moore's crude tycoon of a Capulet is ready to slap his daughter around to get his way. And after the two lovers are safely dead (Romeo, incidentally, expires by shooting up after a peculiarly creepy encounter with a Mantuan fixer), they are instantly transformed into gold statues before which the survivors smilingly pose for the paparazzi. Renaissance tragedy is thus transformed into social critique.

My one doubt about all this is that the production skims over the verse like a speedboat over water instead of working through it. Time and again the language is accompanied by soft rock: thus when Romeo, after the balcony encounter with Juliet, cries 'The grey-eyed morn smiles on the frowning night, Chequering the eastern clouds with streaks of light' an electric guitar slides sinuously in adding its own comment. This reduces Shakespeare to the status of a librettist; and I am reminded that Bogdanov has already staged *Romeo And Juliet* in Tokyo with music by the self-same Hiroshi Sato. In Japanese theatre, as I recently discovered, image and music often take precedence over the word: what troubles me is that Stratford is beginning to head the same way.

I also feel here a quicksilver production is masking some so-so acting. Niamh Cusack's Juliet has possibilities (I can imagine her in the tomb madly playing with her forefather's joints) but her voice lacks texture and colour: the same goes for Sean Bean's likeable but raw Romeo. Much the best work comes from Robert Demeger (the Kick Theatre's Lear) as the exuberant friar lighting up a fag with relief after despatching the lovers; from Richard Moore and the stylishly fetching Anna Nygh as the quarrelling Capulets; and from Mr Kitchen as an insolently nonchalant Mercutio, even if his death could chill us more.

Bogdanov and his designer Chris Dyer (using blown-up computerised images as a backdrop) have come up with a swift, sharp *Romeo* for the Eighties: I simply temper my enthusiasm with a caution that one goes to Shakespeare at Stratford for text and acting as well as an audacious directorial concept.

Andrew Lloyd Webber

12 May 1986

'Whatever Lola wants, Lola gets,' runs a song from *Damn Yankees*: and I sense that, in musical terms, the same may be true of Andrew Lloyd Webber. He certainly started young. He wrote his first musical, a version of *The Importance Of Being Earnest* at the age of nine and some of the tunes were published in a magazine called *Music Teacher* (a collector's item if anyone still has a copy). He wrote a fan-letter to his idol, Richard Rodgers, when he was twelve and was summoned to meet the great man. And, as a boy, he was befriended by director Vida Hope who showed him how musicals were staged. While his schoolmates collected pop records, he bought cast-albums: 'Everyone thought I was mental because you had to be a Beatle: not me.'

Lloyd Webber's subsequent career is proof that dedication pays off. News that he had bought the Palace led me to surmise that the Royal Family were about to be displaced: in fact, it was the Palace Theatre where he now works from a handsome office-cum-boardroom at the top of the building. It's a rather different existence from the hero of his next project (*The Phantom Of The Opera*, opening at Her Majesty's in October) who lurks in the dripping cellars of the Paris Opera and who lures the young singer he loves into his bedroom in the sewers and vivaciously shows her his coffin-bed. At least, he did in the movie.

The significant thing about Lloyd Webber is that (in tandem with collaborators such as Tim Rice, Richard Stilgoe and Trevor Nunn) he has always managed to anticipate popular taste. By any logical standards, musicals about Jesus Christ, Eva Peron, cats and railway-trains sound doomed to instant closure; Lloyd Webber and his varying teams have made them work. Now, at a time when the musical is rapidly becoming a branch of industrial technology, he is going back to an old French centime-dreadful. What does he know that we don't?

'A lot of people have had the idea of using the story as the basis for a musical but any previous versions I'd seen were joky, campy, penny-dreadful melodramas. Then I found a copy of the old Gaston Leroux book which has been out of print for many a long year. I read it and found it was not simply the story of a man who'd had printer's acid thrown over his face but about a girl and a man who was born very ugly and was desperately keen to communicate somehow. It was a big operatic plot. I played the first version of the score to an old theatrical friend who said: "You've taken one big step backwards towards the world of Rodgers and Hammerstein." I was delighted because I've always wanted to write for a conventional orchestra and write real love songs and do my own 'Some Enchanted Evening'. I hope it's going to be about slightly old-fashioned theatrical values because it's absolutely imperative the musical now goes back to the direction it was taking during the years of Rodgers and Hammerstein and the best of the Americans.'

Why imperative exactly? 'What has happened in the last two or three years is a little alarming because money and technology have taken over from real theatre values. Ah-hah, I hear you cry, what about *Starlight Express*? But I never thought of that piece in theatrical terms. It started out as a Cinderella-story about a diesel, electric and steam train and followed the Cinderella-myth in detail down to the heroine losing a piston and the Prince going to put it back on. It was intended to be done for 400 children but Trevor thought that was a lousy idea, felt it would be much better in a larger form and hit, very brilliantly, on the idea of the roller-skating. He has turned it into an event. But it was only intended as a bit of froth and, if I'd been planning my career with a map, its the last piece in the world I would have chosen to follow *Cats* with. The one thing one can say for it is that, as pop theatre, it works and that the show, in the form it finally took, needs that set.'

Mr Lloyd Webber claims he has never been in the business of creating sense-blitzing mega-spectacles that appeal to the laser-minded. Seeing

Evita again in Manchester last week he was reminded that Hal Prince's production deploys little more by way of a set than a screen, a bridge and trucks. Even *Cats* (which this weekend will have run for five years solid at the New London) is, he claims, a much simpler show than most people remember, and he is appalled at the way some subsequent versions, like the one in Hamburg, are so full of razzle-dazzle lighting and movement that you can't even hear the overture. And he confesses to being no lover of hi-tech product like *Time* where, he says, 'for all the tremendous technical expertise, the understanding of the musical is simply not there.'

So it's back to the future with Lloyd Webber. But the most heartening news of all is that he wants to do something about the curse of the modern musical: the wall of amplified sound that destroys any sense of human reality or spatial relationships on stage. 'I don't think we want to know about anything more computerised. And one thing I want to see in *Phantom* is how far you can push an audience by keeping amplification to an absolute minimum. The problem is audiences have lost the art of listening; they've also, because of recording and the quality that CD can produce, become used to an unreal perfection. I went the other day to hear the Elgar Cello Concerto in the concert hall – not played by my brother, I should add – and my friends complained they couldn't hear the cello all the time. What they meant was that they were used to hearing it on the Jacqueline Du Pré recording which has an artificial balance. Somehow we have to get people in the theatre to listen to real sound.

That may be possible in *The Phantom* because Lloyd Webber has conceived it in operatic terms. 'The phantom himself is a composer which leaves me with the challenge of writing his own version of *Don Juan Triumphant*. But the basic score is operatic and for the first time in a musical I'm writing for a soprano voice. All the other female leads have been chest-roles and much more akin to the pop-voice. The highest you can get if you're a chest-singer is the D above middle C and the lowest is the A below so you've really only got nine or ten notes to play with. We hope to have Rosie Ashe (who was in the Miller *Cosi* on television) playing the other opera-singer, Carlotta and – though she doesn't know it yet – she starts with a run that goes up to the top D. We're not messing around in this one.'

But in discussing what makes a good musical, Lloyd Webber comes back time and again to the word 'structure'. There are already fourteen drafts of *The Phantom* in the room bearing witness to his quest for the ideal structure. But what exactly does he mean by that word? 'Is the libretto right? Is the music right for that particular bit of the story? Are echoes of the music to be heard in other parts of the score? How exactly do they interweave? Nobody, I hope, notices that the beginning of *Cats* is a fugue and that the middle of the Jellicle Ball is fugue and that the resolution comes in a later theme. But for me it's the crucial thing on which the score depends, just as the whole of *Evita* is based on a tri-tone and goes round in a complete circle.'

For the future, Lloyd Webber would like to work on a small-scale project (he has been looking at Dickens's *The Signalman*) and is keen to do a project with Tim Rice again. For the present, he is spending his days and nights orchestrating *The Phantom Of The Opera* (which Hal Prince will direct probably with multiple casts) with occasional time out to attend meetings of the South Bank Board. He has about him the look of perennial youthfulness that often attends success. It'll be fascinating to see whether he can in *Phantom* create a Luddite musical that will explode the new technology and restore the musical to the exploration of a human dilemma in song.

Subsidised Theatre

5 July 1986

The theatre can be a hysterical place. So too can Fleet Street. Ever since the shock-horror story about Peter Hall and Trevor Nunn appeared in the *Sunday Times* (was it really more important than the prospect of Commonwealth sanctions against Britain?), the right-wing press has been baying for blood. Resignations have been called for in the *Telegraph* and the *Mail*. Not content with having driven Ian Botham out of cricket for two months, Fleet Street now wants to topple two of our best directors from their perch. We truly do hate success in this country.

Of course, there is a crisis in the theatre (when wasn't there?) but it has nothing to do with the earnings of Hall and Nunn. There is a deep crisis in the commercial theatre: partly because ticket-prices have reached a level few people can easily afford, even more because of the dearth of American visitors. One West End manager told me that he doubts if there will be any serious plays left in the commercial theatre in five or six years time, and it is true that every day we are edging a little closer to Broadway's neon sickness.

In the subsidised theatre, there is a longer-term, equally debilitating crisis. Persistent subsidy-cuts over the past few years have led to caution, conservatism, smaller casts, fewer new plays, the virtual disappearance of permanent companies, the loss of a whole generation of radical experimenters, a spreading blandness.

Of course, there are pockets of resistance (the twin nationals, the Court, the Glasgow Citz, the Edinburgh Traverse, the Royal Exchange, the Bolton Octagon). But subsidy, which was initially meant to encourage initiative, adventure and access, has now become a tenuous life-support system enabling most companies to stagger from one crisis to the next. Our subsidised theatres have not actually closed, but, as Benedict Nightingale wisely said, theatres can go artistically as well as literally dark.

Peter Hall has spoken out against this: Trevor Nunn has been less vocal. But now they are being treated as if they were the source of our malaise rather than the architects of the two companies that have done more than anything to offset it. The shrill and violent tone of the attacks on them personally also disguises the fact that there are important principles involved concerning the relation of subsidised to commercial theatre and the nature of directors' contracts.

Long before the present Fleet Street fandango, the current Enquiry into English Theatre (set up by the Arts Council but independent of it) was looking at both these issues among myriad others. I happen to be part of the Enquiry team, chaired by Sir Kenneth Cork, and we shall be issuing our Report in mid-September. I cannot pre-empt its findings. But, speaking as a critic, it's fair to say that for many years there has been concern about the hazy, ill-defined relationship between subsidised and commercial theatre. Back in the 1960s some of us asked questions about the way major regional theatres (such as Bristol Old Vic) went into partnership with commercial managements to try out new plays. Today the situation is even more complicated. Precisely because subsidy has, in real terms, declined national and regional theatres are forced to become even more entrepreneurial. What we lack are any clear, firm guidelines ensuring that the bulk of the profits go back into the originating company's coffers while directors, designers, actors get their proper reward. This goes way beyond the Hall-Nunn issue: I know of one occasion where a freelance director earned six times as much from a West End transfer as the regional company that initiated the project.

The other issue of principle concerns directors' contracts: what we need is a balance between commitment to a company and freedom to do outside work. As long as directors have to accept a cut in salary by working in the subsidised sector, they are going to want to do freelance productions. They are also going to want to spread their wings.

But the triumphant triumvirate at the Glasgow Citizens – Giles Havergal, Philip Prowse, Robert David MacDonald – show that it is possible to have a high profile in the outside world while also running a first-rate company. What we need, though, are clearer, sharper guidelines.

Clamouring for the instant resignation of Hall and Nunn solves nothing: all it does, in practice, is foster a philistine distrust of subsidised theatre. But just supposing they were to collect their cards tomorrow morning, what would happen? The National would be left without an obvious successor since few directors relish the prospect of running large institutions. It's also worth noting that the best-equipped candidate for Hall's job, Richard Eyre, is a man with extensive film and television interests which would have to be accommodated. And supposing Nunn were to cut his ties with the RSC? They would simply be left without the services of arguably the best director in the country. In both cases, the gain would be zilch.

I would not argue the National and RSC are perfect. The National's current programme lacks flair: the RSC's acting strength sometimes looks wobbly in the middle-ranks. Neither company does enough to explore world drama. But the good news is that next year the National is to import visiting foreign companies and the opening of the RSC's Swan has unlocked the neglected English classic repertory. Judged over a long time-span, the two companies under Hall, Nunn and Hands have managed to stay amazingly fresh. The real problem that we face is how to sustain our two national companies while building up our regional and experimental theatre through fresh injections of cash and enterprise.

In due time, I think there should be new blood at the head of both national organisations (David Aukin moves into the NT this year as Executive Director). But I don't think the agenda should be set by anonymous Insight teams who can't even get quotes from the critics right. What really worries me, however, about the present witch-hunt atmosphere is not that Hall and Nunn will become sacrificial victims (I suspect the present attacks will only encourage their resolve to stay) but that the idea of subsidised theatre itself will be tarnished by right-wing philistinism.

Observe The Sons Of Ulster Marching Towards The Somme

Hampstead: 26 July 1986

Irish plays generally do badly in England. But I hope that Frank McGuinness's fiery, funny, eloquent and moving *Observe The Sons Of Ulster Marching Towards The Somme* will have audiences flocking to Hampstead Theatre. Written by a Catholic, the play fuses criticism with compassion and Michael Attenborough's production wants little by comparison with Patrick Mason's original which I saw in Belfast last autumn.

What is extraordinary about the play is that it is both a lament for the brave men of the 36th (Ulster) Division who died at the Somme in July 1916 and an evocation of the death-wish inherent in their culture and history. Seen through the memory of an old survivor from the Protestant Ascendancy, the play charts the course of eight Ulster volunteers from barrack-room initiation to almost certain extinction. Pyper, the central figure, is a guilt-ridden, death-seeking artist sexually drawn to a young Enniskillen boy. The other pairs are a Coleraine baker and miller, a couple of Belfast boyos noisily beating the lambeg drum and a lapsed preacher forced into blaspheming humiliation by a half-Fenian boy.

McGuinness's central point is that the courageous Ulstermen took with them into the trenches their prejudices and antique instincts and that they were more obsessed with the Fenian than the Hun: before going into combat they even replay the Battle of the Boyne with men astride each other's shoulders imitating King Billy and King James. 'In the end,' says the older Pyper looking back in anger, 'we were not led, we led ourselves. . . . We wished ourselves to die and in doing so we let others die to satisfy our blood lust.' What happened in the Ulster Division was, in short, both the product of Protestant history and something that left its mark upon the future.

The miracle of the play is that McGuinness throughout retains his double perspective: sorrow for the men and fear of their history. In the very funny barrackroom scene (McGuinness, incidentally, is a great admirer of Ayckbourn) he shows the wide-eyed Coleraine baker swallowing the wildest stories about the three-legged Fenian women. But when the men pair off during their home-leave in Ulster he shows them individually becoming aware of the shadow of the death. And in the powerfully moving climax in the trenches he reserves his pity not for the privileged Pyper, reneging on his Carson-ridden background, but for these trusting, foolhardy, unquestioningly brave men singing 'Heaven is my home' and exchanging their Orange sashes before going to the slaughter. Less sentimental and class-ridden than *Journey's End*, this is one of the best plays about war since *The Silver Tassie*.

Michael Attenborough's production lacks the blood-red hand of the Ulster flag that dominated the original version. But, with two survivors from the first cast, it is finely acted and there is especially powerful work from John Bowe as the guilt-drenched renegade from the big house, from John Rogan as his angry, red-eyed older self crying 'Ulster has grown lonely', from Ciaran Hinds as a bombastic Belfast bully and Reece Dinsdale as an awakened innocent. Dermot Hayes's landscape opens up onto vistas of hell and Ilona Sekacz has come up with a stunning score that evokes both the beating of a Lisburn drum and the insistent sound of gunfire. A second viewing confirms that this is a major play by a writer who understands the poetry of theatre.

Dead Wood

Kew Gardens: 2 August 1986

Criticism used to be a sedentary occupation. These days, with shows like *The Dillen* and now Lumière and Son's *Dead Wood*, you have to walk to work. This extraordinary agitational spectacle, devised and directed by Hilary Westlake, takes one on a promenade through the Royal Botanic Gardens, Kew, in gathering darkness both to evoke the sights and sounds of the world's rain forests and to lament their tragic destruction. The result is something rare; a show that manages to be popular, political and avant-garde all at the same time.

The evening starts with the audience (over a thousand of them on the first night) squatting on the lawn just inside the Victoria Gate picnicking, drinking and listening to a Bolivian folk-band: as someone remarked, the atmosphere was a bit like a Sixties Hyde Park pop festival.

As darkness falls, we move in a lengthy crocodile through the Gardens and are assailed by strange images: two toucans in the branch of a tree, chimps cavorting in a clearing like something from *Greystoke*, armies of insects in black leather marching up and down a slope like totalitarian guardsmen. The accompanying commentary is often whimsically dire but the sights have a kaleidoscopic splendour.

We then arrive in front of the Palm House where a group of white-suited Victorians are posing, prancing and sipping tea to a minimalist Jeremy Peyton Jones score that suggests these characters live in Glass houses: they even tango with exotic animals in Prince Monolulu head-dresses before retreating into the illuminated pavilion.

Retracing our steps we find the night-forest populated by black-garbed bats, cawing birds, mobile fungi before arriving in front of a neo-classical temple from which a modern tycoon ironically justifies the plundering of the earth's rainforests: the profits are vast, the benefits enormous and at least there will be folk-memories of parrots, monkeys, mandrills and marmosets to remind us such creatures once existed. As he speaks, a moving mosaic of forest species assembles in front of him only to disappear once more into the night.

People say propagandist theatre is dull: this alfresco extravaganza (a co-production between Lumière and Son, the Watermans Art Centre and Earthlife) proves otherwise. It makes the point that, at current rates, the world's rain forests will be extinct within 40 years but it does so through taking one on a magical mystery tour. 'I'd rather spend the evening sheep-dipping,' a Sloaney voice muttered behind me as we trekked through Kew Gardens. Though David Gale's text is woolly, Ms Westlake's ambitious concept exposes the futility of such urban myopia. One more performance tonight: worth the detour.

Medea and Blood Wedding

Edinburgh Festival: 25 August 1986

Accustomed to dining off scraps, theatregoers in Edinburgh this year are confronted by a feast. In two days we have seen two masterly productions of great tragedies: Japan's Toho Company in Euripides's *Medea* and Spain's Compania Jose Luis Gomez in Lorca's *Blood Wedding*. The former vividly demonstrates the theatrical power of ritual, the latter that of heightened poetic realism.

Last year the Toho Company astonished us with *Macbeth*. This year they have the added bonus of playing in the courtyard of the Old College at Edinburgh University: the setting is like a miniature version of the Palais des Papes in Avignon and it is extraordinary to watch the story of Medea's savage infanticide being enacted against a background of mellow brick and neo-classical columns. It reinforces the point that this is a play about uncontainable violence erupting in a world of Corinthian order.

But this all-male, Kabuki-style production by Yukio Ninagawa also raises profound questions about the mystery of acting. In the last 18 months I have seen three actresses play Medea with valiant realism; yet none has moved me so much, or so convinced me of Medea's paradoxical love for her slaughtered children, as Mikijiro Hira does here. It is hard to explain how a man playing a woman can come closer to maternal passion than most actresses.

The answer lies partly in the ritualistic power of Ninagawa's production. Medea's two sons are established early on as tender, white-faced victims who execute a stately dance to plangent music: their curled, fleecy wigs even suggest lambs awaiting slaughter. But Hira himself also evokes a woman torn between revenge and love. At first his Medea is like some ornate, barbaric princess with silvery, cushioned headgear, raven dark hair, a tasselled veil hanging from his cheeks, bare artificial breasts, a technicolour Kabuki costume. As he gets closer to the murder, he strips down to a maroon, priest-like gown that emphasises the sinuous contortions of his body.

Seeing his sons for the last time, he rolls with them on the ground in a final, earthly embrace. And, once the murder is accomplished, he is last seen – in a sensational coup de théâtre – rising in a dragon-winged chariot in the night sky high above the rim of the college buildings.

I have always questioned the Peter Hall argument that Greek tragedy needs to be stylised; but Ninagawa's production proved that the Kabuki mixture of drama, dance and song offers a key to Attic drama. The passion becomes more intense precisely because it is choreographed. Thus the Chorus of Corinthian women here become a non-individualised group in black beehive-like headpieces who register their grief by plucking shamisen (balalaika-like instruments), who wheel and career around Medea like attendant bats and who are implicated in every stage of her tragedy: as she plucks a knife from the ground and advances thunderously upstage to the murder, the Chorus fling aside their black cloaks to reveal a blood-red lining underneath. Ninagawa also uses music to heighten emotion: the chords of a Bach suite endlessly resound as the poison crown is borne to Creon and as the murder is achieved.

But what is finally impressive about this production is that, as in Kabuki itself, there is emotional realism within the ritual grandeur. Medea, in the original, asks why she should hurt her children to make their father suffer. Here you sense the cost to Medea of her crime by the way in which Hira's fringed veil sweeps the ground as he crawls along it or by the final, despairing wave to his departing children. This is theatre of stylised gesture and choreographed image; but it transcends the language barrier because at its heart lies a core of emotional truth about a mother's love for her offspring.

Grieving motherhood and a Greek sense of fate are also at the centre of Lorca's masterpiece *Blood Wedding*; and Jose Luis Gomez's spare, lean, highly musical and deeply moving Madrid-based production at the Royal Lyceum captures a sense of tragic inevitability.

Lorca based the play on a newspaper story about a bride from Almeria who on her wedding day ran off with her former lover: the jilted bridegroom followed them and the two men killed each other. What is uncanny about Lorca's play is its ability to move from realism to surrealism as he literally brings on stage the Moon and Death in the shape of a beggar woman.

Gomez's production flawlessly conveys the play's shift of mood and sense of disaster hanging over the characters. There is something disturbingly Oedipal about the bridegroom's relationship with his mother, whom he hugs, teases, slaps playfully on the rump. The Bride and her former lover Leonardo (a dark Lawrentian figure in a felt hat) circle round each other before the wedding with predatory fear and sexuality. And the wedding ceremony itself is implicit with doom: the bride wears black, the festal table is strewn with rose petals, the revellers pour blood-red wine down their throats and the groom's mother (the magnificent Gemma Cuervo) talks sensuously of once licking hands tainted with her son's blood.

Gomez makes you feel the tragedy springs both out of landscape and character: he offers a constant visual reminder of the bare, scrubbed Andalusian hills and an aural one of pounding horses' hooves symbolising the instinctive forces that drive Leonardo and the Bride onwards.

He also copes effortlessly with the intervention of super-human agencies: as the woodcutters move to the forest with scythes, the moon is embodied by a pale, bald, naked woman, and a cowled, hunched beggar becomes the symbol of death. His production is the precise realisation of Lorca's text evoking both the punitive cruelty of Spanish soil and the power of elemental passion. It is like Greek tragedy with the crucial difference that life goes mundanely on. When, at the last, the mother says 'we have terrible days ahead' you sense the continuous human struggle to survive after life has touched the very extremity of feeling.

Woman In Mind

Vaudeville: 5 September 1986

Any lingering suspicion that Alan Ayckbourn is a boulevard light-weight should be ruthlessly dispelled by *Woman In Mind* at the Vaudeville. It is about female frustration, despair and madness and shows its heroine torn between reality and fantasy, God and the Devil. Yet, without trivialising its subject, it also manages to be very funny. Much improved since its Scarborough premiere last year, it goes even further than *Just Between Ourselves* in pushing Ayckbourn's Comedy of Pain to its extremist limits.

Julia McKenzie plays (superbly) Susan, a middle-aged woman concussed by a blow on the head from a garden-rake. In the real world, she is tormented by the insufferable smugness of her vicar-husband, the lousy cooking and paranormal enthusiasms of her sister-in-law and the unbroken silence of her son who is part of a Trappist order in Hemel Hempstead.

After her concussion, she is prey to visitations from a fantasy-family for whom she is the perfect wife, mother and sister, Britain's leading historical novelist and a cherished figure to be fêted with Dom Perignon 1978 in mid-morning. What makes the play technically adventurous and spiritually unnerving is that Ayckbourn allows the two worlds to collide as Susan finally spirals into total madness.

As our leading feminist dramatist, Ayckbourn is obviously writing about what happens to women when they are made to feel redundant as wives and mothers. 'Sex,' Susan says to her husband, 'was once something we did together, like gardening – now I have to do that on my own as well.'

Much of the play's comedy springs from the vivid hideousness of Susan's surroundings: the unspeakable husband who has neglected her for the sake of a 60-page history of the parish since 1386 and the appalling sister-in-law who sprinkles Earl Grey tea on the omelettes and who puts a visiting doctor to flight at the prospect of her dessert.

Ayckbourn is clearly writing about what drives women to distraction. But just as *Way Upstream* was a fable about evil, so this play, I believe, is really about the failings of modern religion. Susan's husband has turned the church into a specialised antiquarian interest. Her sister-in-law is the victim of psychic self-delusion and believes her dead husband is inscribing messages on her ceiling. And Susan's son represents a cranky, narcissistic sectarianism. Failed by God's representatives and Christian love, Susan literally flees into the arms of the

Devil; and although Ayckbourn is no Teilhard de Chardin, his play is quite astonishing in even airing spiritual issues on the degraded West End stage.

It is a much deeper play than it looks. It also works far better on a proscenium-stage than in-the-round because it is easier to establish the sheer otherness of Susan's alternative world: Roger Glossop's set and David Hersey's lighting create a sinister, seductive, J. M. Barrie-ish ambience full of receding poplars, marble statuary, Byzantine mazes. Ayckbourn's favourite set, a garden, turns from secret paradise into living nightmare.

Julia McKenzie also brings to Susan an extraordinary mixture of shrewdness, longing, hope, despair. Her face offers a total map of the emotions: one sees the light dim in her eyes as her son cruelly tells her she would have ruined any daughter as well. It is the performance of her career; and she is admirably abetted by Martin Jarvis as the cardiganed vicar who talks in italics as if he has a portable pulpit and by Peter Blythe as the secretly admiring doctor who hides his emotions behind a guilty, nervous bray.

Maybe Ayckbourn (who directs with utter assurance) hasn't quite cracked the problem of the surreal climax. What is remarkable is that our most popular playwright has written a savage tragi-comedy about the light that failed.

Kafka's Dick

Royal Court: 25 September 1986

'This is persecution.'
'No it's not. It's biography.'

That laconic exchange from Alan Bennett's *Kafka's Dick* at the Royal Court gets close to the heart of this witty, elegant theatrical phantasmagoria. For Bennett's theme is the way we pick at the details of dead artists' lives with necrophiliac glee as a substitute for understanding their work. We live in a culture, he suggests, where the nature of E. M. Forster's relationship with an Egyptian tramdriver or the size of Kafka's penis is more important than the mystery of their art: and, in the end, the play is a plea for the dignity of privacy and for engagement with the work rather than the man.

The form in which Bennett casts his ideas is certainly unusual. The play begins with Kafka's famous request to Max Brod to burn his stories, novels and letters, though Bennett is shrewd enough to suggest that the desire for obliteration is accompanied by an artist's vanity. Bennett then shifts into a middle-class modern world where Sydney, an insurance agent is beavering away at an article on Kafka for *Small Print: The Journal of Insurance Studies* to the despair of his uncomprehending wife.

Max Brod then bursts in through the French windows, having urinated on the family tortoise, which transmogrifies into Franz Kafka. So we are confronted by the comic spectacle of a Kafka student coming face to face with his literary hero, by frantic attempts to conceal from the resurrected writer the extent of his world-fame and ultimately by the arrival of Kafka's brutish father in a belated attempt to vindicate himself to posterity.

It is a bold and original conceit even if there are times when the spray of verbal jokes is not sustained by the necessary internal dynamic. But what Bennett is writing about is fascinating and important: the creation of a scholarly industry around dead writers (there are, apparently, 15,000 Kafka studies in print), the decline of criticism into a quest for arbitrary connections and, above all, our craving for the myth of the artist who is despised and rejected in his own lifetime.

Bennett rams the point home by showing how hardly anyone can actually stand the revenant Kafka: Sydney, in particular, looks on in impotent fury as his despised wife becomes the one person to form a rapport with this gangling literary ghost who has (in a good phrase) 'that kind of social ineptitude people mistake for sincerity'.

In the end Bennett spells out his intentions almost too literally: Kafka is put on trial behind a walking-frame belonging to Sydney's over-looked, geriatric father (another theme is the way academic investi-gation often conceals a cruelty to the living) and Sydney has a spotlit speech containing the nut of message about the consoling myth of the artist's wretched life.

We could have deduced that from the surrounding action. But Bennett writes with real mordancy about Kafka's father who decides that the only secure toehold on posterity is to be judged a monster since normality is thought to be uninteresting. And Bennett actually gets across a crucial critical point about Kafka, in a speech where he microscopically studies the movements of Sydney's wife, which is that his nightmarish visions were always based on a detailed realism.

It is a play in which formal perfection is often sacrificed to exuberant theatricality and in which there are almost too many ideas; but it is held together by Bennett's overriding, humane belief that our joy and delight in artistic creation has been replaced by nit-picking analysis and prurient fact-gathering.

The play is also bound together by Richard Eyre's expressive production and William Dudley's ingenious design which translates us from Kafka's enclosed domain to grey suburbia to a campy Heaven. And there are two unforgettable performances from Roger Lloyd Pack as a hunched, stooping, ashen Kafka and from Jim Broadbent as his bullet-headed, self-vindicating father as well as good ones from Geoffrey Palmer and Alison Steadman as the encased suburbanites. It is a far-from-perfect play: but at least it puts a timely and eloquent case for the primacy of art over parasitic biographical intrusion.

The Cork Report

27 September 1986

I was sent to Coventry with Diana Rigg. I went to a school just outside Darlaston to see Theatre Foundry playing *The Good Person Of Setzuan*. I bumped into Ken Dodd, who has strong views on subsidy, at the Key Theatre, Peterborough, and spent an engrossing Saturday night at the Bolton Octagon watching *No Orchids For Miss Blandish*.

I also – along with fellow-members of the Inquiry into Professional Theatre in England – went to a weekend retreat in Sussex for the business of hammering out the recommendations. Being part of the team was, for me, exhausting, educative and informative. Having no experience of official reports, I was also fascinated by the process: I sometimes feel that, like the lady in Webster's play, I was 'drawn arsie-varsie into the business'.

It all began with a phone-call last December from Dickon Reed, then Drama Director of the Arts Council, asking if I would go and talk to Sir Kenneth Cork, the Chairman of the Theatre Inquiry, about the kind of questions it should be addressing. By the end of an hour with the wily, shrewd Sir Kenneth, I realised I was irrevocably committed. 'It should be a lot of fun,' he promised. It was.

There was vague talk, at the start, of monthly meetings. What followed was infinitely more hectic than that. We were being asked to make a report – the first in 16 years – into English theatre, looking at its overpowering needs and determining funding priorities. We had our first meeting in January and were asked to offer our findings by September.

We spent most of March on the road visiting theatres up and down the land and taking written evidence. In April and May we took oral evidence from individuals and institutions. In June we split up into small working parties to come up with specific proposals. The rest of the summer was spent in the hard process of hammering the report – with its 95 recommendations – into shape.

When I say it was educative, I mean that. Critics, on the whole, concern themselves with judging the end-product. As a member of the inquiry team, I was forced to see how that was achieved. I was struck by the resilience of all the theatre people I met. I was also struck by the fact that much of English theatre – outside a handful of privileged companies – is like a sweatshop: a creative one but still a sweatshop.

People often work from dingy, overcrowded offices and the pay-structure is quite appalling. I soon learned that, for actors, Equity minima have become the norm and that most are on £120–£140 a week; that designers, to make a living, often have to take on five commissions at once; and that directors of prestigious theatres are often on salaries that people in, say, television or journalism would laugh at. As the report indicates, the English theatre (and I suspect this goes for the whole UK) is subsidised by the people who work in it. Our communal researches also confirmed my suspicion that too much of the available talent is tending to cluster round London.

Substantial proof comes in fascinating tables assembled for the report by Ian Brown, the Inquiry Secretary, and his assistant, Rob Brannen. One analyses the repertoire at Arts Council-funded building-based companies from 1971 to 1985. Over a 14-year period, musicals have gone up from 4 per cent to 9 per cent, Ayckbourn (whom I much admire) has shot up from 0.5 per cent to 5 per cent, new work is down from 15 per cent to 11 per cent and classics (i.e. any play written before 1945) are down from 18 per cent to 8 per cent. The decline in the last, related to small casts and prevailing caution, is appalling: what it means is that the whole classic repertoire – outside Shakespeare – is in danger of disappearing unless something is done fast.

So what can be done? The report makes a number of practical recommendations: the establishment of national companies in the regions, the nomination of national new writing theatres, a financial boost for touring theatre, black theatre, theatre for Young People and Community Theatre. We have costed the proposals: the total is £13.4 million.

We have also looked at ways of raising the money. It is clear, from the inquiry press conference, that the most controversial is the proposed levy of 1 per cent on the BBC licence fee and ITV profits (tax-allowable in their case). Asked how the broadcasting authorities would react, Sir Kenneth Cork replied 'The turkey doesn't like Christmas'; but it still is a practicable, sensible way of the media repaying the debt they owe to live theatre. 'What debt?' they may say. But a glance through the *Radio* and *TV Times* quickly reveals the extent to which they depend on talent nurtured and trained by the live theatre. Consider the two most prestigious drama series launched in the autumn schedules.

On BBC, it is *The Monocled Mutineer* written by Alan Bleasdale who learned much of his craft writing for regional theatres in the north-west. On ITV it is *Paradise Postponed* written by John Mortimer, a theatre-dramatist of long standing, and boasting a cast virtually all of whom have stage-based careers: Michael Hordern, Colin Blakely, Paul Shelley, David Threlfall, Zoë Wanamaker, Eleanor David.

If our theatre withered away through neglect, television (and cinema too) would be infinitely the poorer. And while some TV companies, such as Granada and Thames, already recognise their debt through encouragement of writers and directors, the majority don't. If theatre is to be treated as nursery, someone has to pay.

I also believe our report makes an impeccably logical, iron-clad case for increased public funding of theatre: specifically, to restore the differentials between the national companies and the rest. The figures alone make the point. In 1970–71 the two national companies received 30 per cent of the Arts Council drama budget. By 1977–78, they received 39 per cent of the total. In 1985–86 they got 47 per cent.

The Government, rightly, recognises the need for a National and an RSC. It also recognises the need to fund them at an adequate level: hence the Priestley and Rayner Reports. But while the national companies have been brought up to a proper level of funding, everyone else has fallen behind.

As the report points out, to restore the differentials of 1970 would require an additional £16.2 million. Even to restore the differentials of 1977 would need an extra £7 million. If the nationals are now funded more or less properly, then it follows – as the night the day – that everyone else needs to be given a comparable boost.

After the press conference this week, I was asked several times 'Will the Report be implemented?' I believe it will. This report will not go away. Nor will Sir Kenneth Cork. He is prepared to fight tooth and nail for it at the highest level. He also made a very significant comment on *Channel 4 News* on Wednesday night. Pressed on possible government reaction to the report, he said unequivocally that an expansive, properly-funded theatre would, with an election looming, be 'the best possible vote-catcher'.

It is true: there are votes in the arts. And to hear it said so loudly by Sir Kenneth Cork, a sharp-brained accountant who hates what he calls 'pie-in-the-sky', made nine months communal slog worthwhile.

1987

The bad news was that the Conservatives were re-elected for a third term. This meant that commercial success became the prime criterion of artistic value. Arts Minister Richard Luce put it succinctly in a post-election speech when he announced that 'the only test of our ability to succeed is whether or not we can attract enough customers.' By that criterion, Pinter would have been finished after The Birthday Party, *Arden after* Serjeant Musgrave's Dance *and* The Mousetrap *is the greatest play of the century.*

Not only was the right to fail banished: one also had a sense of expectations constantly being lowered. In his first two seasons at the Royal Court in the mid-1950s, George Devine managed to stage eight and twelve productions respectively. In the late 1980s, Max Stafford-Clark could only afford to stage four main-house productions a year. When Peter Hall founded the Royal Shakespeare Company in 1960 the idea was to form a crack classical troupe equally capable of tackling Shakespeare and new work. Even as the director of Jean Seberg, *he would, I think, have been astonished to find the company in the late Eighties staging no fewer than four musicals:* Les Misérables, Kiss Me Kate, The Wizard Of Oz *and* Carrie. *What was depressing was how few people seemed to find the situation intolerable. Thatcherism had re-set the agenda.*

It couldn't, however, entirely squash the curiously resilient spirit of the British theatre. The West End, aside from Follies *and the eruption of shining stars like Maggie Smith and Barry Humphries, was its usual lacklustre self. After a false start with* Julius Caesar, *the RSC had a lively season at Stratford including Deborah Warner's* Titus Andronicus *and Nicholas Hytner's* Measure For Measure. *The Gate in Notting Hill, though receiving not a penny from the Arts Council, gave us two startling evenings in Marivaux's* The Triumph Of Love *and an erotic version of a Twenties Japanese novel,* Naomi. *And no year that included visits from Ninagawa, Stein, Bergman and Vasiliev (with Viktor Slavkin's* Cerceau*) could be easily written off. It was the old story; some glowing, individual nights but a prevailing sense of unease.*

A View From The Bridge

Cottesloe: 14 February 1987

In any critic's life there are certain red-letter nights. The new production of *A View From The Bridge* at the Cottesloe is emphatically one of them. In the first place it shows Michael Gambon unequivocally shaking hands with greatness. But Alan Ayckbourn's immaculately detailed production also banished any doubts about Arthur Miller's play and vindicates its claim to be a modern tragedy.

In the past I have always thought of the play as a powerful social drama bidding for tragic status through the imposition of a choric commentator. But Eddie Carbone, the Brooklyn longshoreman whose love for his niece leads to an act of betrayal, now emerges as a tragic hero. His passion, blind, self-destructive and unstoppable, is his fatal flaw. And even if it doesn't, like the passions of Oedipus or Phèdre, shake the foundations of the state, it leads to a violation of the Sicilian-American tribal laws and brings about the hero's death. Eddie lacks the self-awareness that the rules say tragic heroes should possess; but maybe it's time we changed the rules.

The problem with the play has always been Alfieri, the Italian lawyer who acts as Eddie's counsellor and a moral spokesman. Do we really need him to tell us what to think? But as played by James Hayes, he emerges less as a fount of wisdom than as a beneficent observer who may not have all the answers. He tells Eddie that 'the law is nature' and that he must let his niece go. But the whole point of Miller's play is that there is a natural justice that exists beyond the law. Strictly speaking, Eddie observes the law by informing on the illegal immigrants in his house: Marco, the older immigrant, breaks it by getting his revenge. In the end, Miller suggests, human actions have their consequences in a way that transcends legal propriety.

But what gives this production its tragic weight is Michael Gambon's towering performance as Eddie. In the first place, he actually looks like a longshoreman: big, barrel-chested, muscular-forearmed, he has the physique of a man who could work the docks and heave coffee-bales. But what makes Gambon exciting to watch is that he charts Eddie's emotional life through physical actions. He stabs a tablecloth angrily with a fork when his niece gets a job, he turns with electric vehemence when he hears the immigrant Rodolpho call her 'beautiful', his eyes roam restlessly over a paper as the young lovers court, his knees sag and buckle as he learns, after his fatal phone-call to the authorities, that two other illegal immigrants are in the house.

Alfieri famously says of Eddie that 'he allowed himself to be wholly known': so much is true of Gambon. But the extra dimension to his performance lies in his tenderness and melancholy. At moments, he and Suzan Sylvester's Catherine sit quietly touching in unspoken love. And when Eddie confesses to his wife 'It's breaking my heart', it is in the uncomprehending tones of a man whose impact on the world has always been physical. Like Brando, Gambon has the capacity to suggest a buried sensitivity lurking inside a truck-driver frame; and what I shall remember from this magnificent performance is its blend of power and sadness.

But Gambon is aided by a superb production by Alan Ayckbourn which combines minute detail with a sense of large issues at stake. When Eddie, for instance, plonks a whisky-bottle down in the Christmas crib it is a potent reminder that he is violating the household-gods. Even the way Ayckbourn brings up the roar of the Brooklyn traffic as the immigration-officers arrive adds to the sense of momentousness. But what I like most is Ayckbourn's willingness to let us see there are two sides to this story: when Adrian Rawlins's excellent Rodolpho prances vivaciously round the sitting-room singing 'Paper Doll' you see exactly what it is that goads and infuriates Eddie.

All the performances are in key from Elizabeth Bell as Eddie's aggrieved wife to Michael Simkins as the immigrant Marco for whom family is the law of life; and Alan Tagg's set, with its looming vista of Brooklyn Bridge, implies the wider community beyond this microcosmic home. Tragic heroes, we used to be told, have to fall from a great height. What this production proves is that it's the intensity of the despair rather than the depth of the descent that makes for true drama.

Serious Money

Royal Court: 30 March 1987

Caryl Churchill's *Serious Money* at the Royal Court is a play for fresh businessmen. It assumes the audience either knows or will quickly deduce the roles of a fan club, a concert party, a white knight or an arbitrageur and is up to date in dirty take-over tactics. But even if your knowledge of the City is pretty shaky, it is hard to resist the show's satirical exuberance and ensemble attack.

There are many reasons why the show works. The most basic is that you feel Ms Churchill, the director, Max Stafford-Clark and the cast are as fascinated by the City's frenzied energy as they are appalled by its moral unscrupulousness.

The story they tell is a complicated one; but it is about the intersection between a Sloaney futures-dealer's investigation of her brother's death and a ruthless take-over bid by Billy Corman, a corporate raider, for a plodding old firm symbolically named Albion. En route it involves New York bankers, a Peruvian businesswoman, a Ghanaian importer and a Tory Cabinet minister. But its main thrust is that the new, post-Big Bang City is merely the old writ crude and that the Square Mile is a place where no bad deed goes wholly unrewarded.

What Ms Churchill captures superbly is the restless dynamic of the modern City. 'I work on the floor of LIFFE,' proclaims Lesley Manville's supercharged Sloane referring, of course, to the London International Financial Futures Exchange, where the basic commodity is money. But the rancid joke at the heart of the play is that, for a whole new generation of dealers and traders, making money breed has become life itself.

It is clearly a world where class is subordinate to acumen and where a Cockney with a CSE in metalwork can get ahead as fast as a girl from the shires. Sex, Ms Churchill suggests, is also an after-thought: one very funny scene shows an American banker and a Peruvian tycoon comparing Filofaxes as they unavailingly try to make a simple date.

The form of the play is also the key to its energy since Ms Churchill has cast much of it in a rhyming verse that suggests a weird mix of Hilaire Belloc, Cyril Fletcher and provincial panto. Sometimes it is just doggerel: at others it trimly encapsulates a point. 'If it was just insider-dealing,' a City apologist points out, 'It's not a proper crime like stealing.'

Though there is a sudden drop in momentum early in the second half, the cast of eight do an astonishing job in steering us through the complex narrative. Gary Oldman, with gingery locks and a creepy tache, is a whirlwind of mono-maniacal energy as the take-over bandit, and equally good as a gilts dealer hauling himself up from the gutter.

Lesley Manville, as the upper-crust heroine, shows that a cut-glass accent can conceal a heart of stone, and there is impressive work from Alfred Molina as an American banker playing Buckingham to the take-over king's Richard III, from Linda Bassett as a stockbroker distancing herself from the foul deeds under her nose, and Allan Corduner, in five roles, including a Cabinet minister, uttering dire threats to the City-slicker in the interval of *King Lear* at the National.

The heartening thing about Max Stafford-Clark's production is that it attacks the City's greed and fear with zest rather than self-righteousness; and Brecht himself would not have been ashamed of the irony of the final song by Ian Dury and Chaz Jankel, which makes the Court's roof reverberate with the City's impassioned hymn to 'Five More Glorious Years'.

Julius Caesar

Royal Shakespeare Theatre: 10 April 1987

Dear Terry Hands,

I have just seen your new production of *Julius Caesar* which opens the season at the Royal Shakespeare Theatre in Stratford. It has its points (such as being played straight through without interval) and is mounted with your customary visual flair. But I was frankly shocked by the rawness – with two shining exceptions – of the company and left pondering what I perceive as a growing crisis in Shakespearean acting in Britain today.

On the visual side, I was puzzled by one thing: the permanent surround Farrah has designed for the 1987 season. It looks like three sides of a redbrick courtyard in one of the new universities erected in the 1960s. As the evening proceeds, one perceives it takes lighting well: I liked the blood-streaked rays along the back wall and the projected imprint of Caesar's body after his death. But, as a basic image, it is not exactly cheering. It also emphasises the vastness of the Stratford stage and, in these days of reduced cast-sizes, makes Rome seem a savagely depopulated city.

When it came to the play, I wondered if there was a governing directorial concept. The only one I detected was the inevitability of assassination in a brutal autocracy. David Waller plays Caesar, very well, as a bull-necked tyrant greeted by kow-towing slaves, forcing Cassius into an act of humiliating public submission and literally kicking Metellus Cimber aside like a dog in the Senate. This Caesar, smug and brutish, is clearly a nasty piece of work. But if he is so nakedly Fascist, doesn't this rather detract from Brutus's moral qualms about his murder? Would he have worried about carving him as a dish fit for the gods? Wouldn't all Rome, in fact, have risen up against such a vulgar totalitarian?

But this brings me to the acting: traditionally one of the prime motives for going to Stratford. Aside from Mr Waller, there is one performance which justifies the trip: Roger Allam's Brutus. Mr Allam has a voice, dignity and that vital Shakespearean ability to weight a phrase so as to give us an insight into character.

When he says, after the assassination, he will go into the pulpit and 'show the *reason* of our Caesar's death', his emphasis on the noun exposes the flawed liberal assumption that you can persuade people into acceptance. I was also moved, for the first time, by Brutus's acknowledgment of Portia's death: as Mr Allam revealed she 'swallowed fire', he burned the letter bearing the news and poignantly watched it fade to ashes.

Mr Allam is first-rate. But why is the rest of the production so undercast? We know Sean Baker, having seen *Principia Scriptoriae*, to be a promising actor. But why do you encourage him to play Cassius – from Caesar's point of view rather than his own – as an envious hysteric so busy shouting his complaints to the world at large that he would obviously have been arrested on sight?

And while Nicholas Farrell is very adept at conveying a quintessential English decency, is he really your idea of a manipulative playboy like Mark Antony? Why also ask him to do the impossible which is, in the Forum, to control and steer a crowd who here only exist as voices on tape? Surely the scene is meaningless unless we can see him exercise his demagogic skill on actual people as they cry 'Let's stay and hear the will.'

When I talk of the crisis in Shakespearean acting, what I mean is this: because of the impoverishment of the arts in this country, there is much less Shakespeare now being done in regional theatres. As a result, actors are being thrust into major roles on the Stratford stage while still relatively unversed in Shakespeare. It is a cruelly exposed place in which to serve one's apprenticeship.

I also suspect, because of the general decline of verbal culture, actors are losing the ability to relish Shakespeare's irony, ambiguity and play of imagery which was a cardinal feature of Peter Hall's policy in creating the RSC.

I realise it is early in the Stratford season and that, as the year progresses, the company will obviously mature. But on the evidence of *Julius Caesar* – and many of last year's productions – I am worried that actors are losing the ability to handle Shakespeare's language with a witty, confident intelligence that used to be an RSC hallmark. It worries me. I hope, in your new role as the RSC's sole Artistic Director, it also worries you.

Yours sincerely,
Michael Billington.

Antony And Cleopatra

Olivier: 11 April 1987

I asked yesterday if we are facing a Shakespearean-acting crisis owing to dearth of opportunity and growing disregard for language. Time alone will tell. But I can say, with ringing certainty, that there is no hint of crisis in Peter Hall's new production of *Antony And Cleopatra* at the Olivier. It is not only the most intelligently spoken Shakespeare I have heard in years but it also contains two performances from Judi Dench and Anthony Hopkins that, in their comprehensive humanity, rank with Ashcroft and Redgrave at Stratford many moons ago.

Like all great Shakespearean productions, Peter Hall uncovers meanings in the text that may seem obvious but that have never hit one so penetratingly before. For me this production is rooted in prophesy and dream. From the Soothsayer's first predictions to Enobarbus's tart comment that the new-found amity between Antony and Octavius cannot hold, everything that happens is foreseeable and foreseen. It is all there in Shakespeare. But I have never before been so aware that this is not a tragedy (like *Hamlet*) of constant narrative surprise but one in which a pattern is fulfilled.

But Peter Hall also deliberately heightens the extent to which the characters exist in a state of intoxicated fantasy. When Michael Bryant's admirable Enobarbus begins his famous speech about Cleopatra's barge, it is in the casual tone of an old sweat reporting what he has seen: as he continues, he gets carried into an imaginative trance from which he has to be roused.

Similarly when Judi Dench's Cleopatra describes her Antony ('His legs bestrid the ocean'), she does so with the intensity of someone recounting a dream. 'Nature,' she says, 'wants stuff to vie strange forms with fancy.' I was reminded, strangely, of *A Midsummer Night's Dream* in which Shakespeare also deals with the transubstantiating power of love.

What this means in practice is that the production – played in Jacobean costume against Alison Chitty's circular, blood-red surround with broken columns and fragmented porticoes – is about two chunkily real people living out some epic fantasy.

And no one could be more real than Judi Dench's breathtaking Cleopatra. She is capricious, volatile, the mistress of all moods who in the course of a single scene can switch easily from breathy languor ('O happy horse to bear the weight of Antony') to cutting humour ('How much unlike art thou Mark Antony' to an effeminate messenger) to a pensive melancholy ('My salad days when I was green in judgement') at the frank acknowledgment of the passing years.

Ms Dench ensures that Cleopatra's sexual magnetism lies not in any Centrefold posturing but in emotional extremism: she can be highly funny, as when she rushes for the door in affronted dignity at being told Octavia is thirty, and highly dangerous as when she fells a messenger with a right hook. Ms Dench even gets over the notorious hurdle of the last Act (how often has one waited impatiently for Cleopatra to die?) by looking for the precise meaning of each speech and by achieving a kind of fulfilment on 'Now the fleeting moon no planet is of mine.' After the boggling inconstancy of her life, Ms Dench goes to her death with single-minded certainty.

She is no way, however, o'ertops Anthony Hopkins's magnificent Antony: a real old campaigner (you can believe that he ate 'strange flesh' in the Alps) for whom Alexandria represents escape and fantasy. Mr Hopkins, who like many heavyweights, is extraordinarily light on his feet, externalises the conflict in Antony between the soldier and the lover: when recalled to Rome he prowls the stage hungrily like a lion waiting to get back in the arena.

But what I shall remember most is Mr Hopkins's false gaiety – and overpowering inward grief – in the short scene where he bids farewell to his servants. From that point on, the knowledge of death sits on Antony; and when Mr Hopkins says he will contend even with his pestilent scythe, it is with a swashbuckling bravura that moves one to tears.

But the strength of this production lies in the way every role has been reconsidered. Tim Pigott-Smith does not play Octavius as the usual cold prig but as a man who combines calculation with passion: it is a superb study of a power-lover who delights in spotting and playing on other men's flaws.

Michael Bryant's Enobarbus is also played, fascinatingly, not as a contrast to Antony but as someone who delights in aping his master's drinking and womanising and who even, as I have indicated, shares in the erotic dream to which he has fallen prey.

I have always, to be honest, had my doubts about this play, feeling that the later stages camouflage in poetic glory what they lack in emotional dynamism. But Hall's production, cinematically dissolving one scene into another and then playing it with due deliberation, banishes my qualms. It is about two middle-aged people – carnal, deceitful, often sad – seeking in love a reality greater than themselves.

Follies

Shaftesbury: 23 July 1987

Follies at the Shaftesbury is a musical for grown-ups. It deals with adult themes – the disappointments of middle-age, the delusions of memory

– in a musical style that is witty, allusive, yearning and melodic. Instead of simply assaulting the senses, it also uses the unique properties of the theatre in a deeply poetic way. If the title hadn't been booked already, it could have been called *Ghosts*.

What we see on the stage of the Shaftesbury is very different from the 1971 Broadway original. Stephen Sondheim and James Goldman say in the programme that 'what started out as a quiet sea-change has resulted in a brighter and more optimistic show with four new songs and an entirely new book.'

The basic framework, however, remains as before. We are still on the stage of New York's Weismann Theatre (about to be pulled down) for a reunion of old *Follies* girls and for a revelation of marital discontent: we get to see the cracks in the facades of two particular married couples, Ben and Phyllis Stone are rich, busy, (he's in Wall Street, she's on more committees than a Rockefeller), childless and unhappy. Buddy and Sally Plummer are also rich and busy on their Arizona ranch but he is unfaithful and she has never conquered her romantic love of Ben. What gives the situation poignancy is that we see the two couples as they are now and as they were when young.

It is this that lends the musical its overwhelming emotional richness; and the device is extended far beyond the two main couples. The first image we see is of silvery, spectral chorines emerging through a swirl of mist; and throughout, the tough, feisty old *Follies* girls are watched by their lissome younger selves.

Time present is merged with time past; and the infinite theatrical possibilities of this become apparent in a number like 'In Buddy's Eyes'. We see the mature Sally singing a number of pure romantic self-deception, to the man she truly loves, about how she is still prized by her husband. At the same time we witness the young couples, about to take the wrong turning that was to damage their lives, gazing in wonderment at the 1939 World Fair. Pure theatre.

I also find it hard to think of a precise theatrical parallel for Sondheim and Goldman's poetic mingling of past and present. Barrie in *Dear Brutus* shows how, even in changed circumstances, we would still be what we are. Peter Nichols in *Passion Play* (like this, directed by Mike Ockrent) showed the single self split into two halves. Sondheim himself in *Merrily We Roll Along* went on to reverse theatrical time so that the show starts with middle-aged despair and ends with youthful optimism. But I cannot think of a play or musical in history that has earned so much pathos from the constant, aching contrast between what we were and what we become.

My only cavil is at the compulsion to make the show 'more

optimistic'. The original *Follies* ended with Ben launching into a jaunty, top-hat number that climaxed in mental breakdown and orchestral cacophony: even in the concert version, it emerged as a brilliant theatrical device. Now Ben goes into a witty, Astaire-like routine, 'Make The Most Of Your Music', that suggests the divided self can be put together again ('What you do is construct yourself by the way you conduct yourself').

Sondheim and Goldman are entitled to say that their attitudes have changed. But the final reconciliations have a patched-up quality which runs counter to the logic of a story that suggests we nearly always marry the wrong person.

Sondheim's other new songs are superb. 'Country House' is a vintage comic number – crackling dialogue in song – in which Daniel Massey and Diana Rigg as Ben and Phyllis run through a shopping-list of things, from foreign travel to child-bearing, to divert them from their boredom. Ms Rigg, who throughout plays with a cool, sexy, acidic wit, also has a wonderful, second-act, ironic striptease that is both full of clever internal rhymes ('If his idea of ecstasy is to see what he expects to see') and a comment on a character who is fundamentally still a Follies girl in Schiapirelli's clothing.

Indeed it is in the second half that the show's theatrical mastery becomes truly apparent for Sondheim launches into a gigantic, full scale pastiche of the Follies while still retaining his preoccupation with time, memory and marriage. 'Buddy's Blues', robustly delivered by David Healey, is a burlesque number evoking Weber and Fields but actually dealing with wracking infidelity. And Julia McKenzie sings, with crystalline purity under a crescent moon, 'Losing My Mind' which is both an old Helen Morgan-type number and a revelation of her character's inner turmoil. Sondheim is using pastiche to develop character.

Maria Bjornson's designs are also a vital part of the evening's abundant theatricality. They are spectacular without simply being displays of light engineering and in the second act achieve astonishing parodic verve. Skull-capped chorines wearing their hearts on their abdomen descend Busby Berkeley-type staircases. Young lovers climb into elevators in tilted skyscrapers reminiscent of Lucio Fanti's sets for *The Hairy Ape*. Dancers emerge from piano strings as if plucked out by magic.

But the secret of Mike Ockrent's beautifully-marshalled production is that the voluptuous style is never allowed to dominate the emotional context. And, in addition to the excellent central quartet, there are show-stopping contributions from Dolores Gray who sings 'I'm Still

Here' in a voice both creamy and clear and from Lynda Baron who kicks off the dance-number, 'Who's That Woman', with buxom élan. The whole point of the routine is that a gang of ageing tappers and hoofers are shadowed by their silvery, wraith-like younger selves; and it is through that kind of mirror-image that *Follies* makes its eloquent statement about humanity being both at the mercy of time and capable of triumphing over it.

Miranda

Chichester: 31 July 1987

John Gale, director of the Chichester Festival, says in the current programme that you can never please everyone. Some people find the plays too avant-garde: others not avant-garde enough. It took me a while for the implications of this to sink in: that there are people around West Sussex today who think a season comprising *Robert And Elizabeth, An Ideal Husband, A Man For All Seasons* and now *Miranda*, is dangerously avant-garde. Perhaps Mr Gale next season should give them a real radical shocker. *East Lynne*, perhaps?

But what, I hear you ask, is *Miranda*? To my generation, it conjures up an image of Glynis Johns as a mermaid in a Gainsborough movie. On this occasion, it represents a comedy by Beverley Cross 'after Carlo Goldoni' and set in a Chichester-like cathedral city 30 years ago.

The heroine is the owner of a ramshackle period inn whom the local worthies want out so they can develop the site to build a luxury hotel. But since she is unbudgeable, three of the city's male élite (an aristocrat, an archdeacon and a captain) all decide to compete for her hand. She interviews the applicants and makes a choice that will surprise no one who has seen Goldoni's *La Lacondiera* or even managed to stay awake for the previous two hours.

I am interested in Mr Cross's observation that our cathedral cities are full of dirty capitalist tricksters eager to destroy our heritage; but my interest stops there. What this fatally misconceived show proves is that you cannot take the conventions of a past dramatic era and apply them willy-nilly to the present.

In Goldoni's Venice, for instance, where masks were current, it would have made sense for the heroine to adopt a series of disguises as she interviewed her suitors. But in Fifties Britain it seems preposterous when Mr Cross's heroine, allegedly an ex-opera star and actress, dons the roles of Millamant, Carmen (thus making her Carmen-Miranda) and Coward's Amanda to test her wooers.

Nothing in the evening makes any logical sense, least of all the notion that ancient statutes would be dug up to debar an unmarried woman from running a Fifties pub; and the air of unreality is compounded by Wendy Toye's production and Penelope Keith's central performance.

Ms Keith, we are asked to believe, is a working pub proprietress. At one point she even goes into the kitchen to whip up a little concoction. Yet throughout the evening she sports a series of glittering rhinestone gowns that suggest she is on her way to a royal wedding. This is not theatre: it is a fashion parade. By playing Miranda as an eccentric, actressy toff, Miss Keith also knocks on the head one of Goldoni's original points which is that practical middle class wisdom is inherently superior to aristocratic pretence.

It is pointless, however, to belabour one duff show that is neither the best of Cross nor good as Goldòni. What disturbs me are the wider implications. Chichester is the very model of a Thatcherite theatre in that it proudly announces it receives neither state nor local subsidy and survives through the box office, self-generated income and sponsorship. But season by season its choices get ever blander and much of its artistic energy is siphoned off into the studio where this year they are playing Marivaux, Frisch and Shakespeare.

A major theatre that once took a few risks (even as recently as 1983 with the superb revival of Osborne's *A Patriot For Me* that stirred up local hostility) is now a symbol of safety and caution. Chichester is fully entitled to have the theatre it wants. What worries me is that in five years' time we may end up, if the art of the drama is increasingly made to depend on box office and business sponsorship, with a whole nation of Chichesters.

Perdition

Royal Lyceum Studio, Edinburgh: 19 August 1987

On Monday night a condensed version of Jim Allen's *Perdition* was given a public reading at the Royal Lyceum Studio in Edinburgh. Outside the theatre there was a peaceful demonstration, though at least one banner accused Jim Allen of 'Dancing on the Graves' of Nazi victims. Inside the theatre the mood was one of restless curiosity. My own immediate impressions were as follows:

Firstly, that the reading of the play demystified it and robbed it of the spurious excitement attaching to a work theatrically outlawed. It strikes me as nonsensical that one should be able to walk into any bookshop and buy a copy of the text but that the play should be considered too 'offensive' to put on a public stage.

Secondly, that *Perdition* is vehemently anti-Zionist without being anti-Semitic. It specifically impugns the Zionist leaders who allegedly co-operated with the Nazis, even after five million Jews had been exterminated, without showing anything but the gravest compassion for the victims of the camps.

Thirdly, that it failed as drama because it is an indictment masquerading as an impartial courtroom debate. One of the oldest rules of dialectical drama (applied by writers from Shaw to Trevor Griffiths) is that you give the strongest arguments to the side with which you least sympathise. In this play Dr Yaron, a fictional Hungarian gynaecologist accused of collaborating with the Nazis in 1944, puts up a tame defence of his actions and at the last emerges as a self-flagellating figure craving judgement. There is interest but little tension because Mr Allen's mind seems made up from the start.

Initially it appears as if there is the prospect of genuine moral debate. Dr Yaron is, in fact, suing his former assistant, Ruth Kaplan, for libel in publishing a pamphlet accusing him of collaboration (as is well known, this is based on the real case of Rudolf Kasztner and Malkiel Grunwald: in 1955 an Israeli judge endorsed the charge against Kasztner of complicity with the Nazis but three years later the verdict was overturned on appeal).

The essence of Yaron's argument is that for the members of the Jewish Council in Hungary in 1944 the only alternative to some form of co-operation with a vulture like Eichmann was execution, and that by secret bargaining it was possible to save 18,000 Jews from deportation to Auschwitz. At this point Mr Allen touches on a crucial moral dilemma. Given Nazi extermination policies, was it better to engage in a heroic but possibly futile resistance or to negotiate with the devil and save as many lives as possible? Properly examined, that subject alone could make a fascinating play.

But Mr Allen broadens his attack to suggest that the roots of Yaron's collaboration lay in pre-war efforts by Zionist leaders to reach an accommodation with the Nazis: that, in principle, they accepted the idea of racial separateness and that, in practice, they put the ideal of creating a permanent homeland above the preservation of their own people.

It is a breathtaking charge but, in dramatic terms, it doesn't stick because Mr Allen never permits it to be seriously refuted. Through the mouth of Miss Kaplan Mr Allen alleges, for instance, that in 1933 the Zionist Federation sent a memorandum to the Nazi Party offering to co-operate, and criticising Jews abroad for boycotting the regime. Egged on by her counsel, she even goes on to suggest that the Zionists were 'Hitler's favourite Jews'.

But when she herself is cross-examined, it is about her own mental stability and about the actions of Dr Yaron rather than about the historical veracity of her claims. Under the guise of a pseudo-forensic debate Mr Allen throws out provocative accusations, many of which go unchallenged.

On the basis of this edited, 90-minute version I would say that *Perdition* raises massive historical issues without fully exploring them. It offers anti-Zionist certitudes rather than the tang of argument, leaves serious charges suspended in mid-air and judges the actions of the past from the comforting stance of the present.

But I also believe that the play should be given a full scale production (Ken Loach's Edinburgh reading is capably performed by a cast of six including David Calder, Ian Flintoff and Caroline Gruber) for one very basic reason: as Jimmy Reid said last week in a debate on Soviet literature, the essence of democracy is that no one has the right to decree what is unacceptable. With all respect for Jewish sensitivities, I believe *Perdition* should be seen first and judged later.

Macbeth

Lyttelton: 19 September 1987

In my whole theatregoing lifetime I have never seen a production as achingly beautiful as Yukio Ninagawa's *Macbeth*, now at the Lyttleton. In his hands the play seems less an anatomy of evil than a lament for the waste and destructiveness of vaulting ambition; and through it all runs what Virgil called 'the sense of tears in mortal things'.

Ninagawa's production has the quality of a legendary story being retold. Two withered crones (a device also used by Suzuki in his production of *The Trojan Women*) part a walled curtain and then squat at the side of the stage with their thermoses watching events unfold: sometimes they peer round to get a better view and when Macbeth sinks into mindless barbarism they unashamedly weep. They act as a silent chorus commenting on the vanity of human greed.

What makes the production so startlingly different from our own approach to Shakespearean tragedy, however, is its sheer lyricism. The action is set in 16th century Japan; the wars between rival chieftains have reached exhaustion point and the samurai sit at Duncan's feet demonstrating a new-found cohesiveness.

But we glimpse much of what passes through a transparent, latticed screen: behind that the dominant images are of a blood-red sun, a throne made out of embossed golden armour and the famous falling cherry-blossom which symbolises mortality as well as beauty. On top of this, Ninagawa makes use of a throbbing, plangent score in which I detected the Fauré Requiem, the Samuel Barber Adagio for Strings and a Purcell Chaconne.

We are used to seeing *Macbeth* presented in Stygian gloom: here it is surrounded by colour and light. But Ninagawa is not simply presenting us with great pictures. He has a vision of the play based on the transience of earthly power: the armoured throne sits on stage throughout, as part of a Buddhist altar, mocking those who vainly seek to occupy it.

Macbeth himself (with Masane Tsukayama replacing Mikijiro Hira whom we saw two years ago in Edinburgh) is also presented as the ideal hero plummeting from a great height. We first see him astride a battle-weary white palfrey: the perfect image of the warrior-knight. Even at the last he is still capable of despatching a dozen opponents with sublime ease. He seems less the usual frenzied psychopath than a great man corrupted by the will to power.

But if any one performance leaps over the language barrier, it is that of Komaki Kurihara as Lady Macbeth. Young, beautiful, raven-haired, she unequivocally caresses the hilt of her husband's sword: sex and dominance are for her indistinguishable.

But she is at her most moving in decline. In the short scene with Macbeth before Banquo's murder, she sits gazing wanly at herself in an oval mirror: a poignant image that suggests both the need to don a false face and the eyes as windows of the soul. And in the sleepwalking scene, her pale, lilywhite hands are constantly seen reaching heavenwards into the light as if trying to expunge the blood by invocation rather than by cleansing.

What makes this a great production, however, is that it combines regret at human madness and folly with awareness of earthly beauty. As Lady Macbeth gathers up the knives to kill the grooms, the dawnbirds start to sing. Birnam Wood comes to Dunsinane in the shape of a mobile forest of cherry-blossom. As Macbeth reaches the pit of despair, the fiery orb of the sun changes instantly to the colour of ash.

Instead of simple moral condemnation, the production offers a poetic meditation on the way all human striving is subject to the passage of time; and as the old women close the curtain on Malcolm before the end of his final speech, we realise that even his beneficent reign is no more than a beam in the eye of eternity.

And Then There Were None

Duke of York's: 9 October 1987

The West End is in desperate crisis. Coming cold on the heels of Mr Archer's droopy little piece, we now have a ritual exhumation at the Duke of York's of Agatha Christie's *And Then There Were None* (né *Ten Little Niggers*) which has the unmistakeable aura of seaside weekly rep in the late Forties and which is so preposterously bad it has acquired the dubious status of camp.

Scan the West End lists, in fact, and one's heart sinks. Fifteen out of 32 current shows are musicals; the rest are equally divided between farces, thrillers, revivals and new plays. Two of the musicals (*Follies* and *Phantom Of The Opera*) are excellent. Two of the plays (*Serious Money* and *Les Liaisons Dangereuses*) are first-rate imports from the subsidised sector. The rest range from middling-good to galvanised tat. We are promised new plays from Peter Shaffer and Ronald Harwood; but we are getting perilously close to Broadway when the whole artistic credibility of a West End season hinges on two new works with star names.

But if the commercial theatre is artistically wan, the subsidised sector is financially beleaguered. Intramural reports suggest the National (which is doing fine work) faces new problems because the Arts Council cannot deliver monies already vouchsafed; the RSC has had to be bailed out at the Mermaid; the Lyric Hammersmith is threatened with closure.

Out in the regions, enterprising work is obviously being done in Manchester, Glasgow, Leicester and Derby. But it is a sign of the times that this new Christie production stems from Nottingham Playhouse: a theatre which, under John Neville in the 1960s, presented Calderón and work from the Shakespeare Apocrypha (*Sir Thomas More*) to large audiences. If Mrs Christie is the New Realism, you can keep it.

Meanwhile back at the Duke of York's some good actors are doing their best to prove there is life after artistic death. The action takes place in a country house on a Devonshire island cut off from any contact with the mainland or reality. In Kenneth Alan Taylor's wooden production, the characters enter one by one through the upstage french windows and then pause at the top of the steps to announce their credentials before doing a pantomime walk-down into the living room.

Once there, they proceed to deliver Mrs Christie's perishable dialogue ('Is Lady Constance Cumlington here?') with all the vivacity they can muster. A disembodied voice then warns them they are all guilty of someone's death; and, with that deductive facility for which the English are famous, they realise they have all been invited to this remote spot by 'U. N. Owen – or, by a slight stretch of fancy, Unknown'.

You have to say one thing: Mrs Christie got away with murder. As the characters are bumped off one by one, she twists the original nursery-rhyme into the most outlandish shapes. Remember 'A bumble bee stung one'? The height of risibility is reached when Miriam Karlin (who has given a lively study of a moral watchdog in pebble specs) slumps forward in her chair from, I had assumed, listening to the dialogue. But a colleague, suspecting something rummy, crosses to her side, delves into her garments and fishes something out, triumphantly announcing 'A hypodermic syringe – the modern equivalent of a bee-sting.'

After this, a mood of revelry ran through the house. Thus when John Fraser's Judge turned towards Glynis Barber's nubile secretary and solemnly intoned 'Vera Claythorne' a voice behind me murmured 'This Is Your Life.' Handkerchiefs also had to be stuffed in mouths when Ms Barber drew attention to the fact that, with all those corpses in the next room, there they were eating tinned tongue. As Jimmy Durante used to say, there are times when food is secondary.

Stepping gingerly over the bodies rolling in the aisles on my way out, it suddenly struck me the whole show had been mounted as an ironic metaphor for the state of the British theatre. The punitive, disembodied voice belonging to a figure no one has actually seen clearly stands for the Arts Minister, Richard Luce. The cornered, guilt-ridden figures tremulously awaiting the chop symbolise artistic directors who have failed to gather sufficient commercial sponsorship. And, at the end, the architect of elimination is left surrounded by nothing more than a Pyrrhic victory and a pile of corpses. Under the foul play lies a tract for our times.

Christopher Fry

19 December 1987

Tucked away in the ITV Christmas schedules (December 27 at 10.30 pm) is a new production of *The Lady's Not For Burning* starring Kenneth Branagh and Cherie Lunghi. It is being broadcast not because it gave a phrase, slightly modified, to Mrs Thatcher, but as a tribute to Christopher Fry who was eighty yesterday. The sharp-eared will also be able to detect the voice of Fry in the BBC showing of *Ben Hur* for which he (uncredited) wrote most of the script.

Fry, once in the vanguard of the poetic revival in theatre, was a major victim of the theatrical revolution in 1956. Talking to him in his elegant Sussex home, he doesn't sound much like a sacrificial victim. Mr Fry is spry, wry, resilient and anecdotal, reminding me that Kenneth Tynan, who attacked all he stood for, once wrote that no one was closer to the Aristotelian ideal of magnanimity. He only withdraws a little when you raise the whole subject of verse-drama, referring you courteously to an article he wrote seven years ago called *Looking For A Language*.

What is startling about Mr Fry is that the great apostle of theatrical poetry turned in the Thirties from schoolmastering to showbusiness. He wrote lyrics and songs (including 'I'll Snatch The Man From The Moon') for a 1935 revue, *She Shall Have Music*, and directed a tour of Ivor Novello's *Howdo, Princess* that brought him in touch with the raffish end of the market: one of the ASMs was thrown into prison for bigamy, the producer spent much of the investment money on playing strip-poker with the chorus girls and the tour collapsed in ignominy halfway through.

Raising his sights a little, Mr Fry turned to writing as a result of clerical commissions. A vicar asked him for something on the worthies of Sussex which led to *The Boy With A Cart* about Cuthman, who pushed his mother from Cornwall in a handcart. Next came *The Tower* for Tewksbury Abbey in 1939 which was seen by T. S. Eliot with whom Fry's name was for ever linked.

'I suppose he had some influence on me,' says Mr Fry, 'but to me the names of Eliot and Fry always suggested a pair of famous photographers who were around at the time.

'I first met Eliot in '39 and I remember asking him what I could do in wartime that didn't mean shooting people. He suggested the Fire Service but I told him that I had no head for heights. Eliot told me "You must specialise in basements." '

After the war, Fry found himself directing for Alec Clunes at the Arts and accepting £450 as staff dramatist with the understanding he would write something. Fry was paralysed by the commission and only began to write a play, ironically *The Lady's Not For Burning*, in the freezing winter of '46–47.

'I wrote the first act,' he says, 'with frozen hands and I remember one had to trudge off to Notting Hill Gate simply in order to get water. I had written in verse before but I suppose one of my main ideas was to take man out of his familiar domestic context. I felt that mankind was shut away from the rest of creation in a confined space between four walls rather than being seen as part of a single, unified world.'

The play is the story of the burgeoning love between a life-hating ex-soldier who desperately wants to be hanged and a suspected witch who does not want to be burned. But although the play takes place in '1400 more or less exactly', Fry himself is anxious that it be seen not simply as some colourful medieval romp. He remarks that Gielgud, who directed the hugely successful West End 1949 production, with himself, Claire Bloom and Richard Burton, had a yen to do it in modern dress. Fry himself directed a revival that turned the cynical ex-soldier just back from Flanders into the kind of khaki greatcoated drop-out often to be seen on the streets of post-war England.

On the subject of verse-drama, Fry refers me to his view, published in the magazine *Adam*, that 'in prose we convey the eccentricity of things, in poetry their concentricity, the sense of relationship between them: a belief that all things express the same identity and are all contained in one discipline of revelation.'

My own view is that a dramatist is entitled to write in whatever form he chooses and that there are signs, largely in the person of Tony Harrison, of dialect-poetry edging its way back into the theatre. But I cannot see that poetry has an exclusive monopoly on the unity of creation. Don't Chekhov's plays give us just that feeling while being written in the most basic naturalistic prose?

But what is important to remember now is that Fry's plays brought a neo-Elizabethan linguistic exuberance to a rather drab, post-war English theatre. They were also, in the Forties and Fifties, huge commercial hits. In 1950 Fry found himself simultaneously translating Anouilh's *Ring Round The Moon* for Peter Brook and writing *Venus Observed* for Olivier's new management at the St James.

'I was writing sixteen hours a day,' he recalls, 'trying to finish the play for Olivier who was very patient and good. But I got rather behind on the last act and I remember one day opening a parcel from Larry containing a typewriter ribbon and brush to clean the keys of my old

1917 machine. There was also a little note from Larry saying "I hope I'm not making you nervous." '

The comparison between Fry and Eliot is revealing. Where Eliot's plays domesticate poetry making it look like prose, Fry's plays expand into romantic rhetoric and lyric soliloquy. What both writers shared was commercial theatrical success and the ability to attract stars.

Edith Evans played the lead in the third of Fry's seasonal verse-plays, *The Dark Is Light Enough*, in 1954 and brought to the casting her own eccentric humour. 'I remember,' says Fry, 'the question came up of whether we should have Wilfred Lawson in it. Edith said "I can't remember whether I like him very much or not at all but I do remember he named his bicycle after me." '

After the Royal Court revolution Fry, who had been the darling of the old regime, became the outcast of the new. He turned increasingly to film-writing and found William Wyler and Sam Zimbalist inviting him to Rome for six weeks to rewrite *Ben Hur* from the Crucifixion to the end.

'In fact,' says Fry, 'I stayed a year and two months and virtually re-wrote the whole movie. I liked having a committee life and going down on the set to write in a couple of lines for Charlton Heston on the spur of the moment. From that I went on to *Barabbas* for Dino De Laurentis. I remember at one meeting about the order of the scenes he got onto a table and launched into a torrent of Italian waving his arms around and sounding like Mussolini. After this great histrionic display he turned to us and said "Of course you needn't pay any attention – it's only a suggestion." ' In recent years Fry has concentrated on writing for television, including a four-part life of the Brontës for YTV, and supervising occasional revivals of his work.

What he has discovered – a harsh fact which many of his successors are only just coming to terms with – is that the theatre goes in cycles and that many dramatists often enjoy a rich creative span of about a decade. But Christopher Fry views the past with content, praises the work of moderns like Pinter and Stoppard and at eighty, exudes a zest for life that seems vastly more important than being fashion's darling.

1988

In David Lodge's elegant fiction, Nice Work, *his heroine lectured on 'Condition of England' novels in the 19th century. This year saw the return of 'Condition of England' (even of Britain) plays. Confronted by the entrenched vulgarity of Thatcherism, the theatre began to fight back.*

Hare's The Secret Rapture *dealt brilliantly with the listlessness of virtue and the blinkered energy of the new politics. Ayckbourn's* Henceforward *was a dystopian comedy about our new technological nightmare. Doug Lucie's* Fashion, *imported from Stratford, outlined a world in which the ad-agency fixers and image-handlers had won effective political control. Pinter's* Mountain Language *offered pungent images of a society in which dissent was no longer tolerated and communication was strictly controlled. It was interesting to note that TV at the same time was questioning the state of the nation.* A Very British Coup *prophetically suggested that a combination of secret service dirty-tricks and tabloid mud-slinging would make a future Labour Government improbable. And* Blind Justice *– written by Peter Flannery – ended with the moral that 'In England we've forgotten the meaning of liberty – that is why we don't care about justice.'*

In the theatre, a number of institutions rightly challenged the classic supremacy of the twin national companies. Jonathan Miller launched a daring season at the Old Vic that included Racine, Ostrovsky and Chapman. David Thacker offered us excellent revivals of Ibsen and O'Neill at the Young Vic. Cheek By Jowl took to the road with Ostrovsky's A Family Affair *and the Sophocles* Philoctetes. *The Branagh-Parfitt Renaissance Theatre Company also struck gold with three Shakespeares that sold out both at the Phoenix and on tour.*

For all that, it was still difficult to get new, unsubsidised ventures off the ground. And the theatre still seemed to be living off the subsidy-explosion and expanded horizons of twenty years past. But at least in 1988 it took on an adversarial role and tackled head-on the ethos of the existing government.

Tom Stoppard

18 March 1988

Tom Stoppard recalls that during the run of *Rosencrantz And*

Guildenstern Are Dead on Broadway a woman rushed up to him outside the theatre and asked if he was the author of the play. With becoming modesty, he said Yes. 'Well,' she said, 'I want you to know that it's the worst play I ever saw in my life.'

Nothing like that has happened to Stoppard outside the Aldwych since the opening of *Hapgood*. All the same Stoppard, 36 hours after the first night, seems ruefully pensive. He envies the breezy élan of Cole Porter who, just before his own Broadway premieres, used to set off on a world cruise. In contrast, Stoppard is still fine-tuning the text of *Hapgood* and seems less than gruntled at the tone of some of the reviews.

'The play,' he says, 'has been written about as though it were incomprehensibly baffling. It doesn't seem to me to be borne out by experience. After all these years, one thing you learn is what's going on in an audience and by God you know when you're losing them. It's like getting a temperature: you can't miss it. My impression is that your ordinary punter has less trouble with it than some of our critics.

'But critical response is like a branch of natural history. It's a cycle as inevitable as that of the sea anemone. It's nice to be discovered as a bright young man but then the playwright gets older and the critic becomes the bright young man who's not going to be taken in. It's nothing to complain about. But the truth is you get over-praised when you're young and sandbagged a bit when you're older.'

Hapgood, on reflection, strikes me as taxing but penetrable: an engrossing theatrical equivalent of David Mamet's *House Of Games*. The problem is we are so used to up-front, single-issue plays we tend to get thrown out by a multi-layered, hydra-headed animal like *Hapgood*. I counted half a dozen issues whirling through it. Was it finally saying that if the laws of quantum physics are not susceptible of proof, then everything else is treacherously uncertain?

'No,' says Stoppard. 'That's too sweeping. If there's a central idea it is the proposition that in each of our characters – yours and mine are doubtless exceptions – the person who gets up in the morning and puts on the clothes is the working majority of a dual personality, part of which is always there in a submerged state. That doesn't seem to me a profound or original idea but I still find it interesting.

'The play is specifically about a woman – Hapgood – who is one person in the morning but who finds that, under certain pressures, there is a little anarchist upsetting the apple-cart. The central idea is that inside Hapgood One there is a Hapgood Two sharing the same body; and that goes for most of us.'

In that case who is Stoppard Two? Who is the sleeper lurking inside the genial, ironic, surprisingly boyish 51-year-old playwright, expensively accoutred in a brown suede overcoat and, give or take the overnight reviews, pretty much at ease with the world?

A pause.

'I haven't considered revealing my other side to more than one person at a time. But I suspect the genial interviewee is a sort of cover. I do have periods when I'm extremely cross with life and I try to behave well. My metabolism is much higher than it ought to be for a professional playwright and, as I get close to a first night, I try to do eighteen things an hour: if you go on like that you blow the circuits. I am a very emotional person. People wish to perceive me as someone who works out ideas in a cool, dispassionate way but I don't think that's my personality at all.'

Stoppard's double identity, even as a playwright, is territory that has been too little explored. His plays, from *Rosencrantz And Guildenstern* to *Hapgood*, have been analysed as if they were intellectual conceits: I suspect they only work because of their emotional ground-base.

That first play is anchored in what John Wood once called the 'bravery' of those two attendant lords whistling in the Elsinore dark. In *Jumpers* – more in the Aldwych revival than the original Old Vic production – you felt the pain of a marriage audibly splintering. In *The Real Thing* – more in the New York than the London version – you were aware of the torturing self-abasement that stems from the knowledge of infidelity. Stoppard reveals that his regular director, Peter Wood, is always on at him to up the emotional ante.

'Imagine,' says Stoppard, 'I write a play about astronomy because I've got all these fascinating things to say about Neptune and Ursa Major and that I also feature a married couple. Peter will say, these people are married and can we take their relationship out of the fridge? He always bullies me and says I am stingy about this side of things.

'For instance, there's a scene in *Jumpers* where George recalls the first day Dotty walked into his class and, because her hair was wet, he called her "the hyacinth girl". These lines give the play emotional leverage and make it a play about marriage rather than moral philosophy. Peter tries to get me to put a hyacinth girl into every play including *Hapgood*. I always think I've done it and he says I haven't. Peter is an advocate for the audience and tries to make the plays work for an imaginary spectator called Rupert who he believes was the bear of little brain. It's no good my telling him that was actually Pooh.'

Stoppard, I would claim, has a dual political as well as emotional identity. On the one hand there is the Stoppard who regretfully says, 'We live in an age where the leper is the don't-know.' On the other hand, there is the Stoppard of *Professional Foul* and *Every Good Boy*

Deserves Favour who has taken a clear stand on the question of human rights in the Eastern bloc. But even now Stoppard is wary of being dubbed a committed playwright.

'With Eastern Europe I don't feel I am carrying some kind of torch for the causes that might crop up in this or that play. Because what I do – which is write plays – is something whose problems are empirical. With *Professional Foul*, I didn't sit down to sound off about human rights. It happened to be Prisoner of Conscience Year in 1977 and Amnesty asked if I could write a play to mark the event. Well I obviously couldn't do a play about a couple who go Come Dancing in Prague. What happens is you sit down in a practical, level-headed way and you end up with *Professional Foul*.

'If you're writing plays or painting pictures, whatever your public postures, what you're trying to do is write a good play or paint a good picture. I still believe that if your aim is to change the world journalism is a more immediate, short-term weapon. But art is important in the long-term in that it lays down some kind of matrix of moral responsibility. It's on that one pins one's hopes of the thing lasting. I mean can you think of a play that has helped to change anything?'

I suggested that *The Normal Heart* did an effective job of raising consciousness about Aids.

'Fair enough. But will it last as long as *Ghosts* which hardly even mentions directly the subject of a transmitted sexual disease? My point is that plays work through metaphor. In the end the best play about Vietnam will probably turn out to have been written by Sophocles.'

If there is a moral touchstone in Stoppard's work it is probably to be found in children: the boy Sacha in *Professional Foul*, the son in *Hapgood*, and now the 11-year-old hero of the film, *Empire Of The Sun*, directed by Steven Spielberg, which Stoppard has adapted from the J. G. Ballard novel about a boy surviving the 1941 Japanese invasion of Shanghai. Why this enduring faith in children?

'It's to do with their innocence which isn't something they acquire but which is something they haven't lost. I do have an idea which crops up all the time, which is that children are very wise because they don't know how to be taken in. You can fool people if they are very clever but it's quite hard to fool a child. I think children start off with a sense of natural justice which is obscured through a process of corrupting sophistication.'

Stoppard actually seems to enjoy the nuts-and-bolts side of writing as much as the high-flying ideas. This week, for instance, he has inserted four speeches running to about eight lines into *Hapgood* because he knew something was missing: the precise point at which the heroine moves from entrapment to warning and realises that the technical traitor is also the person most anxious to help her son. Stoppard the brain-box is also the practical mechanic.

But that is just another symptom of Stoppard's double identity. He is the intellectual fire-cracker who writes about emotional havoc. The apostle of non-commitment whose stand on human rights is unequivocal. The thriving playwright (and ex-hack) still gnawed by thoughts of the public prints. The wordsmith who admires Ayckbourn because 'I have a predilection for plays that don't depend on lines you can quote.'

If he were not Tom Stoppard, who would he like to be? 'Someone who sings or plays a musical instrument well. It causes me intense grief that I can't do it or even tell good from bad. I'm not talking about being Placido Domingo. I'd just be happy to be someone who plays piano in a pub.'

As we finish talking we make our way down Carnaby Street with its extraordinary hungover Sixties aroma. 'I feel it should be in the V and A rather than out here,' says Stoppard. As he sets off in a taxi to do a television interview, his parting shot is that he can't wait to get the Sunday reviews over and done with, as if he were a tyro-playwright undergoing ordeal by criticism. I feel as if I've had a sudden, touching glimpse of Stoppard Two: the anxious self-doubting Thomas that still lurks under the poised, equable figure of the success-wreathed, acclaimed public playwright.

Faust

Lyric Hammersmith: 13 April 1988

You either surrender to Goethe's *Faust* or you don't. My own reaction, after watching the full seven hours of Parts One and Two at the Lyric Hammersmith, is one of astonishment: astonishment both at encountering this great mythic poem on the English stage and at the success of David Freeman and his 12-strong company in encompassing so much of it. Peter James says this production is crucial to the Lyric's future: it will, if there is any justice, guarantee it.

But how good a play is Goethe's *Faust*? George Steiner calls it 'sublime melodrama'. He argues that Goethe, unlike Marlowe, evades the tragic implications of the story in that his hero is saved and ends up with an act of Rousseauesque benevolence – draining the marshes to build a new society – before being borne away amidst falling rose-petals and an angelic choir. Following Thomas Mann, Steiner even argues that there was in Goethe a decisive *Burgerlichkeit*: a word implying middle-class solidity and confidence in the way of the world.

He may be right. But that is not how it comes across in performance, where the play emerges as something larger than a pseudo-medieval tragedy about a man who sacrifices his immortal soul to earthly pleasure. Goethe replaces the religious battle between good and evil with the opposition of activity and passivity. As Faust says in Robert David MacDonald's version, 'Life and Liberty are theirs alone who fight for them each day.' His discovery is that doing is superior to being; and, while this may undercut the sense of tragedy, it places Goethe at the forefront of modern thought.

In fact what is startling about Part Two is the way Goethe, even as he sends his character hurtling through time and history, anticipates modern ideas. Faust arrives at the bankrupt court of the Holy Roman Emperor. So what does he do? Invents paper money and thereby causes rampant inflation. Even more prophetic is the scene where Faust's old pupil, Wagner, creates artificial life in the shape of Homunculus: an alchemical hermaphrodite imprisoned in a glass bubble. In Mr Freeman's production the image of Linda Kerr Scott's test-tube baby propelling herself round the stage is impressive: a pity her words rarely penetrate the sealed bubble.

But this is a rare lapse in a production that keeps the balance between ideas and images. Mr Freeman saves his big Flo Ziegfeld effect for the Rocky Inlets of the Aegean Sea where Homunculus enjoys a mystical union with the sea-nymph Galetea. The stage suddenly explodes with cascading fountains and three downstage tanks, filled with splashing nymphs and naked philosophers, foam to the brim. Far more exciting than the hi-tech effects of big musicals, it unites Busby Berkeley and Bishop Berkeley and manages to create the effect of an aqueous paradise.

The key to David Roger's design, in fact, is the incorporation of earth, air, fire and water: we even get Icarus flying near a sun comprising a blazing, light-bulbed disc. But the success of the production lies in the fact that the images always reinforce meaning. The land-reclamation of the final scenes is evoked through something as simple as the rhythmic movement of stocking-masked figures lugging sandbags onto the stage to the tolling of a melancholy bell. Far from seeming like some Greenpeace Utopia, it suggests the immeasurable impossibility of Faust's task, but it is the pursuit rather than the goal that matters which, in the end, seems to me the whole point of Goethe's play.

The theatricality of the production is matched by Mr MacDonald's translation which accommodates Goethe's shifting styles and achieves a Byronic gaiety (appropriate for a play in which Byron is celebrated in the figure of Euphorion). Thus Mephistopheles, thrust into an alien world of classical sirens, announces, 'Though I know how to manage Northern witches, I'm none too happy with these foreign bitches.' And when asked to conjure up Paris and Helen he replies, 'You think one pulls such things out of the blue, A case of whistle and she'll come to you' in which the Bacall-like anachronism seems entirely fitting.

Simon Callow's Faust also embodies Goethe's point that continual striving is the very point of human existence. He shifts in this version from tormented medievalist to modern man to, at the end, a bearded Tolstoyan patriarch sharing something of the great writer's passion for communal welfare. But although the play may not, technically, be a tragedy, Mr Callow endows Faust with what I can only call a tragic aura in his discovery of the spiritual emptiness of mere enjoyment.

Peter Lindford's Mephistopheles is sleek and witty and even brings a resonant sadness to his climactic lust for the angels who spirit away the body of Faust. And Caroline Bliss is not only memorably fetching as Helen but also gives dignity and weight to her stoic acceptance of 'earthly destiny' after the fall of Troy.

I would be a liar to deny there is the odd moment when you tune out of this epic play. (Great art risks boredom: only second-rate art is permanently entertaining). But not since John Barton's *The Greeks* have I seen such a stirring piece of reclamation and one that proves Goethe's *Faust* is not some theatrical dinosaur but a practicable, stageable possibility and a moving salute to the humanist idea of individual growth.

Uncle Vanya

Vaudeville: 26 May 1988

Michael Blakemore's production of *Uncle Vanya* at the Vaudeville shines like a good deed in a naughty world: it is a gem amidst the fake jewellery of the West End. For me it misses total perfection because of details of interpretation but, as should happen with *Vanya*, I found myself watching the end through a mist of tears.

Oddly enough, one of my doubts centres on Michael Gambon's Vanya. He is, of course, mesmerising to watch. A bulky figure in a crumpled linen suit, he presents us with a 47-year-old emotional adolescent. One of his first actions is to plant himself on a garden swing and, whenever Yelena weaves into view, he gazes at her with adoring eyes set in a lolling head.

Gambon has inherited Ralph Richardson's ability to exist in two dimensions at once. Half the time he seems to be living in a private dream: there is a magnificent moment when he is accused of being drunk and cries 'Possibly, possibly' in a voice so alien and remote it might be coming from a man under hypnosis.

Gambon offers a brilliant monument to ineffectuality: a man crippled by unrequited love and professional futility. But I am reminded of something Eric Bentley once wrote: that Chekhov's elegiac note is moving 'because the sense of death is accompanied with so rich a sense of life'. It is the element of might-have-been in Chekhov's characters that makes their waste so tragic. Gambon's Vanya for me just misses greatness because he is directed to play defeat from the start: all hope and dignity have been shredded. But Astrov points out that he and Vanya are the only two people of culture in the district; and although Gambon, brushing his hands across his thinning hair and erupting into childish fury, is wonderful to watch, he needs more of that Chekhovian thwarted rage for life.

There is, however, the sense of a real, tangible relationship between him and Jonathan Pryce's Astrov: it is summed up in the superb moment when Astrov essays a drunken dance and crashes into Vanya landing them in a tangled, jocular heap on the floor. But Pryce's magnificent Astrov also has that crucial sense of life's worth which is what makes its unfulfilment so moving.

He presents us with a damaged idealist who is quirky, eccentric, sensual and used to burying his pain in vodka: there is an unforgettable moment when he complies with Sonya's request not to drink and then, suddenly remembering the patient who died under chloroform, his eye steals longingly towards an unclaimed glass. Pryce gives us the might-have-been; and there is an exact psychological truth about the way he fondles Sonya with the thoughtless familiarity one exhibits to those one does not love.

At its best, Blakemore's production grasps the essential point that Chekhov's characters are painfully alive: there is intensity in their lassitude. That is why Imelda Staunton is the best Sonya since Plowright: she is a woman who is quite desperately in love, parroting Astrov's opinions as if they were her own and giggling over their midnight feast in sheer pleasure at getting him to herself. And the brave, falsely heroic smile she puts on at the doctor's departure is one of the most moving examples of a breaking heart I have ever seen.

It is also a sign of the production's merit that it rediscovers an almost forgotten character in Telegin, the impoverished landowner who lives on the estate. Jonathan Cecil plays him as a bright, buoyant man in middle-age, permanently affronted by the fact that people cannot remember his name. He gives you the man's whole history; and when he rushs from the room in terror at Vanya's explosive anger, you sense exactly the nervy vulnerability that led his wife to desert him.

But two performances need more Chekhovian intensity. Benjamin Whitrow's Serebryakov has a tetchy *amour-propre* but little of that sense – communicated by Lebedev in the Leningrad production at Edinburgh last year – of an arrogant peacock who treats the universe as if it were created for his convenience. And although Greta Scacchi is radiantly beautiful as Yelena, she doesn't use her body to the full: the character should have an offensively swaggering indolence which Astrov (in Michael Frayn's needle-sharp translation) actually describes as 'inadmissible'.

These are cavils, however, at a production which is strongly cast, excellently designed (Tanya McCallin's set has the right feeling of people thrown together in a cramped house outside which the landscape stretches to infinity) and which subsumes the comedy into the tragedy. At the end, with Vanya and Sonya together at the work-table and with her cradling his great baby's head in her arms, you feel the poignancy of starting life again on the flat when, as Desmond MacCarthy said, 'a few hours before it has run shrieking up the scale of pain.' I know of no more moving climax in world drama.

The Secret Rapture

Lyttelton: 5 October 1988

David Hare's great gift as a dramatist is for relating private despair to the public world. But his astonishing new play at the Lyttelton, *The Secret Rapture*, touches profounder chords than anything he has written before. It is partly about the corrosive effect of the Thatcherite ethos on human relationships; but at a deeper, quasi-religious level (and the title refers to a nun's union with Christ) it is about pain, martyrdom and the idea of fulfilment through death.

The framework is clear even if the final meaning is tantalisingly elusive. Two sisters are brought together by the death of their father, a

Gloucestershire bookseller (who seems, incidentally, to have lived in an incredibly baronial mansion). Marion is a junior Tory Minister, cool, managerial, intelligent, but lacking any gift for empathy. Isobel is part of a small-scale design firm: she seems to have inherited her father's humanist tolerance and unimpeachable pre-Eighties integrity.

Two events trigger the dramatic crisis. One is the sisters' attempt to solve the problem of what to do with their stepmother, Katherine: a young alcoholic wrecker whom their father had married late in life. Isobel is persuaded to give her a job in her firm with foreseeably disastrous consequences.

The other key event is the takeover of the firm by Marion's husband, the President of Christians in Business, which leads to rapid expansion and the ultimate ruination of a mildly thriving cottage-industry. But the thing that is really destroyed, by a combination of the anarchic stepmother and bruising capitalism, is Isobel's love for her partner, Irwin.

On one level the play is perfectly clear. Hare is saying (as he has done in every play and film he has written) that you cannot separate political and human values: that if you live in a society that sanctifies greed, worships money and excuses mendacity, it is bound to affect personal relationships.

But although Hare is a moralist, he is clever enough to see that few people are immune to the blandishments of capitalism. Irwin, a mildly talented designer and a nice guy, acquiesces in his firm's takeover when his salary is doubled. Hare doesn't condemn him; but the pay-off is that business expansion and incorporation kills off something that works.

As a portrait of our times, the play is lethal, accurate and witty. I know of no work that pins down so well the two-dimensionality of Thatcherism: the combination of sharp intelligence with limited vision. But I find it slightly harder to follow Hare's thinking when it comes to the subject of human pain. Through Tory Marion and her proselytising husband, he shows the impossibility of immunising yourself against agony and keeping family for weekends; and through Irwin, Hare depicts, with aching realism, the sense of emptiness that accompanies a broken love affair.

The problem for me is the character of Isobel. Hare says in the programme he is trying to buck a trend by creating a heroine rather than another maligned villain. But I was never really clear what she represented. Does she embody a supine English tolerance that allows itself to be exploited? Is she a shining example of integrity? Or is she a born martyr half in love with easeful death? She may be all of those things but I find her fuzzy rather than complex. Under Hare the sharp satirist I suspect there lurks a romantic who sees suffering and pain as proof of the validity of existence and who wants us to celebrate the idea of Isobel as a secular bride of Christ.

Jill Baker plays her very well as one of those women who measures everyone against the high standards of integrity they demand of themselves. But there is a dead giveaway when she says that you wouldn't think, to look at her, that she ever had a sense of fun: the truth is you wouldn't and that is because Hare has omitted to show that virtue can bring joy.

The other actors have an easier row to hoe. Penelope Wilton is superb as Marion whom she endows with a crisp, laundered sexiness and smug smiles of self-satisfaction at having made mincemeat of a delegation of Greens. Paul Shelley as her Christian husband, given to baptismal immersions in his swimming pool, is all scrubbed certainty. There is also excellent work from Mick Ford as the emotionally devastated Irwin, Clare Higgins as the alkie stepmother embodying what Schopenhauer called 'the tyranny of the weak' and from Arkie Whiteley as a silky young predator.

Howard Davies, after his work on Williams and Boucicault, caps a magnificent year at the National with a production that combines irony and heart even if John Gunter's designs, with their panelled walls and vast gardens, romanticise Gloucestershire bookselling. But, greatly as I admire Hare's ruthless analysis of the amorality of modern Britain, I question his transcendental assumption that goodness can only triumph through death.

Henceforward

Vaudeville: 22 November 1988

Alan Ayckbourn gets more daring with each new play. *Henceforward*, which had its Scarborough premiere last year and is now at the Vaudeville, offers an ultimately bleak vision of men, machines and society. But the exhilarating Ayckbournian paradox is that the darker it gets the funnier it becomes.

Three leitmotivs weave their way through this brilliant play. Ayckbourn is writing about the extent to which we are not only enslaved by, but also enamoured of, the technology we have created; about the artist's subordination of people to the restless quest for perfection; and about a nightmarish Dystopia (reminiscent of Anthony

Burgess's 1985) in which responsibility for law and order has passed into the hands of thuggish vigilantes.

The setting is the non-too-distant future. Jerome, the composer-hero, is holed up in a North London studio full of domestic squalor and sophisticated gadgetry with only a robotic child-minder, NAN300F, for company. But he is a man haunted by two obsessions. One is to express the sensation of love in abstract musical form. The other is to reclaim his 13-year-old-daughter whom his separated wife has not allowed him to see for four years. So he hires a young actress, Zoe, to pose as the ideal companion and impress both his wife and a welfare officer with his domestic bliss. But when Zoe realises he is recording every sound made in his studio, even down to their love-making, she flees from his reversal of normal values.

The first act takes its time: the second is biliously funny. But what is astonishing is the balance Ayckbourn achieves between comedy and horror. Behind the play lurks a terrifying vision of the artist who parasitically sucks the blood of those around him and who prefers the consoling perfection of technology to the messy contradictoriness of humanity; and there is a chilling moment when Jerome, asked to explain to his daughter why people are superior to machines, is reduced to tongue-tied silence. I was strongly reminded of Ibsen's *When We Dead Awaken* where the sculptor-hero ultimately confronts the futility of sacrificing love to the ideal of artistic perfection.

But Ayckbourn is also a comic writer and his play is a living demonstration of Bergson's theory of humour, which is that we laugh whenever the essential spontaneity of life is reduced to a series of automatic movements. In the first half, the child-minding android is like a cross between Mary Poppins and Daphne Du Maurier's Mrs Danvers. In the second half, suitably re-programmed, she greets everyone with the mechanical bonhomie of a TV chat-show host. Ayckbourn's great gift is that he doesn't bang home ideas didactically but expresses them visually; and the robot is both a constantly funny sight-gag and the ultimate symbol of sterility.

Ayckbourn's production and Roger Glossop's design, all synclaviers and screens, capture superbly the sense of a computerised fortress. This version also dents the myth that Ayckbourn's plays automatically suffer when given the West End star-treatment. Ian McKellen, normally a physically expansive actor, makes Jerome a walking embodiment of emotional repression. But the key to McKellen's truly perceptive performance is that he seems gauche, awkward and nervous when confronted by people and only truly alive when playing with his digital audio system or talking to his android.

Jane Asher makes the transition from the antiseptically brisk robot to Jerome's insecure wife with great comic panache. And, going in the reverse direction, Serena Evans as Zoe starts out full of tinkling-laughtered nervousness and winds up all robotic brightness. Michael Simkins as the welfare officer also hilariously makes the point that humans are now ever more encased in technology. It is a deep, black, disturbing comedy; but I suspect its haunting power derives from the fact that Ayckbourn is exorcising his own, and every writer's private fears. No art is created without sacrifice. The daunting question this play asks is whether the reward is worth it.

Single Spies

Lyttelton: 3 December 1988

I suppose Alan Bennett's *Single Spies* at the Lyttelton will go down in history as the first play to present the Queen as a major dramatic character. But the real fascination of this double-bill lies in the way it questions our accepted notions of treachery and, in different ways, makes a sympathetic case both for Guy Burgess and Anthony Blunt.

A Question Of Attribution is much the weightier and more richly-textured of the two plays. It deals with Blunt in his triple role as Surveyor of the Queen's pictures, international art historian and Communist spy. But Bennett subtly links Blunt's profession and his political beliefs by suggesting that, just as attribution in no way explains the mysterious enigma of art, so the tag of 'traitor' does nothing to solve the Blunt riddle. But Bennett goes further and demonstrates that, just as the restoration of painting reveals hidden depths, so the process of uncovering the ultimate spymaster is futile and never-ending.

These, however, are only the main themes of a play that is as multi-layered as the Titian canvases that are its focus. It begins with cat-and-mouse games at the Courtauld between Chubb, an MI5 officer who is steeping himself in art history, and an evasive Blunt. While Chubb sees all art as a progress towards realism, Blunt explains that 'art evolves but doesn't progress' and that a painter can only be understood in the context of his time: an ironic reflection of the fact that Blunt himself has to be seen in relation to the instinctive anti-Fascist leftism of the Thirties.

But the links between art and politics (Bennett's principal theme) become even clearer when Blunt seeks to interpret two Titian paintings. Bennett suggests that a picture cannot be 'solved' as if it were a visual riddle, just as Blunt cannot be cracked as if he were a code.

The play, however, takes off comically in the Buck House scene where Blunt comes face to face with the Queen. Lest anyone think this smacks of *lèse majesté* on the part of the Royal National, one should add that HM actually comes across as a canny operator who gives Blunt a much stickier time than the man from MI5. With serpentine skill, the Queen steers Blunt into a discussion of the palpably forged Vermeers. As Bennett's Blunt dabs his sweating palms with a handkerchief, you realise that he knows that the Palace knows that he himself is a walking deception who has been mistakenly attributed.

What is extraordinary is that in 75 minutes Bennett manages to raise, with wit and guile, a whole series of questions about art, aesthetics and treachery. His own performance as Blunt is still a shade tentative but Prunella Scales scores a small triumph as the Queen, radiating sharp-witted benevolence and possessive pride as she potters about the gallery muttering, 'This rosebowl was a wedding-present from Jersey.' Simon Callow, who directs, also gives a shrewd performance as the MI5 officer.

Mr Callow appears as Guy Burgess in Bennett's own production of *An Englishman Abroad*, a revised version of his early Eighties TV play. It is still a touching, funny account of the pathos of exile, showing Coral Browne sitting in Burgess's scruffy pad listening to old Jack Buchanan records. According to *Spycatcher*, Blunt once observed to Peter Wright that Burgess was a great patriot; and he here emerges as the epitome of the displaced person pining for London literary gossip and a new suit.

Bennett's humane sympathy for Burgess comes through but, like all work transferred from television, it seems a trifle thin-textured. You miss the location-work and, most especially, John Schlesinger's unforgettable final image of an umbrella-toting Burgess jauntily crossing a Muscovite bridge to the strains of *HMS Pinafore*: on stage, you get the moment but not the physical context.

Simon Callow makes Burgess both comic and sad and Prunella Scales captures the be-furred stylishness of Coral Browne. But while this play now seems anecdotal, *A Question Of Attribution* raises profound questions about the teasing unfathomability of both art and espionage and emerges as a minor masterpiece.

Electra

The Pit: 22 December 1988

Is Greek tragedy possible on the modern stage? Can one pierce through the dead conventions to get to the core of suffering? The answer is emphatically Yes. After Dexter's *Creon* and Donnellan's *Philoctetes* we now have Deborah Warner's production of Sophocles's *Electra* in the Pit; and the result is an evening of fierce lucidity and driving passion that never for a second makes you doubt you are in the presence of great drama.

What strikes one first is Sophocles's astonishing moral ambiguity. He makes it clear that Orestes is compelled by Apollo to avenge Agamemnon's death by killing his mother, Clytemnestra, and her lover, Aegisthus. Yet Sophocles's chief interest is in the character of Orestes's sister, Electra, who is motivated less by divine justice than her own obsessive hatred.

She is a female Hamlet (a point re-inforced by Kenneth McLeish's translation where she says, 'I am like Niobe, all tears') torn apart by the idea of her mother and Aegisthus making love in her father's bed. And when Clytemnestra points out that she sought a just revenge on Agamemnon, Electra screams back at her, 'Blood for blood, is that your law?' seemingly oblivious to the fact that is exactly the basis for her own actions. Is matricide justified? Sophocles leaves the answer up to us.

But, as in *Philoctetes*, one observes that he is both a master story-teller and a superb ironist. By delaying as long as possible the recognition of brother and sister, he focuses on Electra's unswerving resolution: nowhere more so than in the scene where she is confronted by her brother's supposed funeral-urn.

But Sophocles reserves the grisliest irony for the end when Aegisthus is poised over a shrouded corpse he assumes to be Orestes. 'Ask the queen to come,' he says. 'There's no need to fetch her, she's here,' is the reply: a moment as subtly savage as that in *Titus Andronicus* where Tamora feeds off her own sons.

As in *Titus*, Ms Warner pulverises the emotions not through an imposed concept but through a rigorous concentration on text and acting. There is also nothing in Hildegard Bechtler's stark, barewalled set that is not later used to powerful effect. If there is a gully inset into the flagstoned floor, it will eventually become an incarnadined canal. And if the palace of Mycenae is protected by a sliding, aluminium door, it will later reverberate to the awesome sound of the cornered Clytemnestra pounding it in vain.

The classic problem in Greek tragedy is, of course, the Chorus: over-individualised, they become distracting, acting in total unison they seem like Attic Tiller Girls. Here Ms Warner solves the problem brilliantly by giving us only five women of Argos similarly clad in russet mantles, reacting with apparent spontaneity to Electra's plight but drawn into a cohesive body by the weight of suffering. Only after Electra has been spurned by her collaborator-sister do they beat the ground collectively with the palms of their hands and only when the violence is unstoppable do they draw black veils over their faces in a gesture of unified grief.

The evening, however, depends on Electra and Fiona Shaw impressively rejects the minor league of pathos for the major division of tragedy. What is striking about her performance is its total unsentimentality. Crop-haired and clad only in a tattered black robe, Ms Shaw is less like the nightingale to whom Electra constantly compares herself than a scavenging bird of prey. Moreover there is nothing noble or beautiful about her passion: when she says 'I tear my own flesh raw in this palace of pain,' you realise you are in the presence of naked emotional violence. Ms Shaw chillingly presents us with a woman in extremis: her joy at Orestes's return is as excessive as her wall-clawing horror at his reported death.

Piers Ibbotson's Orestes seems less passion-driven, but Natasha Parry rightly plays Clytemnestra from her own point of view as a woman historically wronged, Sylvester Morand as Orestes's servant makes the reported death of his master in a chariot-race seem as exciting as the Grand National and Gordon Case as Aegisthus is like a proud lion aware that the cage-door is shutting behind him.

But the great thing about this production is that it allows one's sympathies to swing back and forth like a pendulum and leaves the Sophoclean moral conundrums finally unanswered.

1989

The decade ended with the deaths of Laurence Olivier, Samuel Beckett and Anthony Quayle; with Terry Hands announcing his resignation from the financially beleaguered RSC; and with the British theatre alternating, as usual, between bursts of glory and inspissated gloom. But that was no cause to despair

of a medium that in another country, Czechoslovakia, acted as the cradle to a revolution by providing the Civic Forum party both with a headquarters in the Magic Lantern Theatre and a leader in Vaclav Havel.

In fact, many of the best evenings I had in 1989 were spent on foreign soil: watching a vast audience crowd into Berlin's Deutschlandhalle for Chéreau's Hamlet, *marvelling at the poetic beauty of Stein's* Cherry Orchard *at Berlin's Schaubühne; or being erotically dazzled by Maddalena Crippa's sinuous Tamora in Stein's Roman production of* Titus Andronicus.

At home it wasn't such a bad year either. The two most exciting directors of the post-Nunn generation both came up with first-rate work. Adrian Noble's RSC version of The Master Builder *re-defined Ibsen for our age in a way that Howard Davies's overblown, MGM-melodrama production of* Hedda Gabler *at the National never did. And Nicholas Hytner not only gave us a moving, inspirational account of Joshua Sobol's* Ghetto *but also showed his versatility by directing the year's best musical,* Miss Saigon, *with piercing emotion and a restrained use of spectacle.*

New plays didn't exactly come thick and fast but a few registered strongly. I warmed to Peter Flannery's panoramic Singer, *which both gave a vivid picture of post-war Britain and explored the paradox by which a victim of the Nazi death camps himself turned rabid exploiter. Richard Nelson's* Some Americans Abroad *was also a deadly accurate account both of the sentimental Anglophilia of visiting culture-vultures and of the ferocity of academic in-fighting. Peter O'Toole's magnetic presence also made Keith Waterhouse's* Jeffrey Bernard Is Unwell *rather like a one-man* Godot. *But, against that, the Royal Court was compelled to close the Theatre Upstairs and the unacceptable face of sponsorship became visible at the First Night of the NT* Hamlet *where half-canned City types staggered in during Polonius's advice to Laertes. At least that kind of thing never happened when Arts Council mandarins were the ultimate dispensers of revenue . . .*

Directing Marivaux

27 January 1989

'I see,' Stephen Fry murmured to me one evening at the theatre, 'that you're putting your little botty on the line.' He was referring to a backstage announcement at the Barbican asking actors if they would like to enlist in something called The Michael Billington Project.

The reaction from friends and colleagues to the news that I was going to direct a play was generally 'You're very brave,' uttered in tones of farewell solicitude. The assumption was that I was raving mad to sacrifice my comfortable role as a hired gun for a position in front of the firing-squad. But why must theatre be a permanent war between critics and artists? There were will always be what Peter Hall called 'a creative tension'. But in America there is a long and honourable tradition of the critic-director symbolised by Harold Clurman, Robert Brustein, Charles Marowitz.

Andrew Porter of the *New Yorker* has directed operas as well as translating them. It seems to me a peculiarly British notion that commentators and artists should be forced to stare at each other from behind barbed wire with not even the occasional Christmas Day soccer-match in No-Man's Land.

In truth, the idea of directing came almost by chance. In December 1987, I gave a talk to the Stratford company about the role of the critic. I felt at first like Daniel going into the lion's den. In the event, I was courteously treated. I was also asked the inevitable question about whether critics should attend rehearsals. I said it was impractical and useless: all you did was sit around for a day nursing an impotence-complex. Far better, I said, if a critic got his hands on a play by directing it.

Over lunch, Greg Doran (then an RSC actor, now an assistant director) asked me if I was serious. Last August he repeated the offer, saying he foresaw a million problems but that a group of RSC actors would be free during the run of *The Wizard Of Oz*.

I got my first introduction to theatrical reality when he asked me to come up with a list of plays with small casts and running no more than an hour. So much for any mad scheme of doing Ibsen's *The Pretenders* or Schiller's *Wallenstein*. He also hinted that the Barbican Conservatory might be available as an unusual venue. Since I bang on endlessly about world drama, I came up with three little-known foreign plays.

One, Strindberg's *The Pelican*, was a devastating assault on devouring motherhood. Marivaux's *Slave Island* was a philosophical comedy about role-swapping. Another Marivaux, *The Will*, was about the conflict between desire and greed and the agonised contortions people go through in the name of love.

A group of actors gave up a Saturday morning last November to read all three plays. *The Pelican* was full of practical problems and handicapped by an odd translation ('I can't stand this smell of carbolic acid and fir twigs'). *Slave Island* was fascinating but a touch schematic. *The Will* emerged, in Michael Sadler's translation, as brisk, playable and funny.

But how does one start directing a play? I suspect my approach was made up of memory, observation and pellets of wisdom culled from interviewing practitioners. Two remarks stuck in my mind. One was Peter Hall's observation that it is foolish to start with a rigid concept: that you do the work on the floor in order to find the concept. The other came from a recent encounter with Peter Stein in Berlin: that actors must feel a sense of responsibility for what they are doing and that, as a director, he never put anything on stage that an actor didn't touch.

The role of the director is, of course, a subject of red-hot debate. My own hunch is that style is dictated by temperament. There are creative directors, like Peter Brook or Joan Littlewood, who are virtual auteurs capable of inventing new forms of theatre. There are many more, like Stein and Hall, who are superb interpreters of classic texts. There are others, like Jonathan Miller or David Pountney, who often come armed with a strong intellectual or social vision. In reality, I suspect their working-methods would be found to overlap.

The only thing I deplore is the sentimental, anti-director bias that is suddenly fashionable. It is perfectly articulated by Paul Daneman in the current issue of *Drama* magazine where he says: 'The cult of the director has almost strangled the life out of live theatre.' Oh, really. Has he seen *Fuente Ovejuna, The Secret Rapture* or *The Plantagenets*, which all prove that fine direction is in no way incompatible with first-rate acting?

As a diffident tyro, my only belief is that democracy works better than dictatorship. I was blessed with a highly gifted and intelligent cast – Jane Leonard, Ian Barritt, Paul Spence, Emma Hitching, Gordon Warnecke and Helen Sheals – and my first observation was that we had to agree on a way of doing Marivaux before we even started work.

The big decision was: should it be done in 18th-century period or modern dress? In the end, a consensus emerged for setting the action in the 1930s, both to avoid a feeling of stylised prettiness and in order to invest Marivaux's complex emotional chess-game with a hint of modern naturalism.

What have I learned from the rehearsal process? Many things: most of them, I suspect, obvious to professional directors. One is that directing is a process of constant adjustment. You plan moves for actors at home and then find everything looks different once you are confronted by real people. Also that directing is a matter of discovering the route rather than imposing the destination. It is no use telling an actor you want anger or disdain. Even in a play as devoid of sub-text or realistic detail as the Marivaux, the actor has to discover the biographical origins of an emotion in order to display its end-product.

I have also discovered that many of the problems are pragmatic. The actors (all doing the show for free in their spare time) suddenly get called for RSC understudy or line-rehearsals. The terrace of the Barbican Conservatory, where we are mounting the play, is a fascinating space but also unknown territory. Costumes have to be sorted out in people's meal-breaks. Moves that looked OK in the Clapham rehearsal room suddenly seem odd when people have to negotiate round a Conservatory tree.

But if there are countless headaches, there are also endless compensations. The fun of rehearsal (no one ever talks about that). The moment of breakthrough when, as happened last week, an actor unlocks a character by discovering a new accent. The sudden illuminating suggestion – made by Greg Doran at a run-through – about the need to acknowledge the audience. Every day the project changes like a living organism.

Will it work? For once, I leave others to judge. But at least I shall resume my aisle-squatting a bit more aware of the collaborative process of theatre: aware that things we, as critics, so confidently ascribe to the director, are often the result of the spontaneous combustion of rehearsal.

Mike Nichols, when asked what directing was about, said: 'Mostly it's about showing up. After that, everybody else does it.' I may not be a good director. But at least I can say I showed up.

Hands On Billington

Terry Hands: 2 February 1989

Some say the lark and loathed toad change eyes
O, now I would they had chang'd voices too . . .

Romeo And Juliet III sc V

Well actors do it – playwrights do it – I've even known producers do it. Let's all do it. Let's direct a play. The latest recruit to a much abused and more misunderstood profession is a critic, Michael Billington. It is an odd choice. Critics are soloists – directors, teamsters. I should have expected a desire to act, like Jack Tinker, or to write, like Irving Wardle. But no, Mr Billington, perceiving directors as auteurs or interpreters, has plumped for power.

His disarming apologia in Friday's *Guardian* before the first night (would we all could) shows how much he now qualifies that perception. In fact a director is much more teacher than tyrant. He coordinates.

The play is *The Will* by Pierre Marivaux, to be performed by the RSC on the Conservatory Terrace at the Barbican until February 13. In my adopted role of critic, for the first time at an RSC first night I feel unapprehensive.

The Terrace is an appropriate setting for the play – a greenhouse jungle ideal for Marivaux's predators. In *The Will* – a technically brilliant one-act – the Marquis and the Countess love each other but he has been bequeathed 600,000 francs provided he marries Hortense. If he doesn't, he loses 200,000 francs. Nobody wants him to marry Hortense – not even Hortense – and the play is the conspiracy of all the other characters to persuade him that the path of true love is worth 200,000 francs. In fact, by the end he has both Countess and cash – but then it *is* a comedy.

The play has all the difficulties of our own Restoration period. Nobody does anything – they simply talk, and activity of any kind has to be invented. Mr Billington's production is at its best in the confrontations between the Marquis and the Countess when he trusts the language and Jane Leonard expertly relates her growing exasperation to increasing assaults upon her garden. Here, word and action cohere to tell several stories. But he fails to relate the servants to the main theme – their cunning and bloodymindedness reflecting and underpinning their more mannered masters and mistresses.

It is partly focus – which in a French play means control of every word, every gesture (and does not include two musicians centre stage who don't play); it's partly stage mechanics. The movement of a Marivaux is as precise as a Swiss chronometer. Mr Billington gives us a sundial in an English summer.

It is not really his fault. He has simply responded to the translation, though that too is a director's responsibility. Michael Sadler has freely adapted the original into a text at once speakable and funny, but it has none of Marivaux's glitter and danger. Thirties costumes add to the Anglicisation, together with English diffidence, archness and self-consciousness.

These are assertive, greedy people. At one point a bird trilled in the Conservatory – it should have been an alligator. The characters talk of war, aggression, anger – we are given Parisian hanky-panky. The company achieve a surface of sorts but not a meaning. And there is no sex. From Marivaux's high style we descend to what is at best suburban Labiche.

I accept that directors should not go to rehearsals with all the answers. On the other hand, they should go with the right questions. And the first of these must be what is the difference between a French play and an English.

But the performance is fun. The actors flourish in the comfortable security of Billington's vision and if that reduces a sinister jungle to a genteel garden – at least it is a party to which we are all invited. It was full house on Friday night.

I hope it will not be Mr Billington's last outing as a director. He brought the best out of his actors, held his audience, and successfully assaulted a traditional theatre barrier. For me, it will be the last time. It is hard to criticise. I'd rather appreciate. It requires enormous experience to surrender to a performance and yet retain a pencil in hand or head.

At the end of the performance I went over to congratulate Michael Billington. 'No, no,' he said hurriedly. 'You can't talk to me. You're a critic.'

Iranian Nights

Royal Court: 20 April 1989

It was quite like the old days. The theatre was packed. The pavement outside was thronged. And the stage itself was being used to comment on a burningly topical issue. But the good thing about *Iranian Nights* by Tariq Ali and Howard Brenton at the Royal Court is that it transcends the immediate issue of *Satanic Verses* to explore the nature of tyranny, Britain's own responsibility for creating religious intolerance and the schisms within the Muslim community.

Shrewdly and ironically, the authors use the kaleidoscopic form of the *Arabian Nights* to further their basic purpose: to make a vital distinction between Islamic culture and its current Iranian interpreters. Thus we see Omar Khayam and Scheherezade seeking to divert a Caliph who turns into an intransigent modern Holy Man arguing that Islamic executions are bountiful. But the poet's retaliatory argument is that the strength of a religion lies in its ability to withstand heresy and that 'power, terror, Realpolitik' often masquerade as spiritual indignation.

Ali and Brenton approach their subject not with a self-righteous piety or po-faced dogmatism but with a rational sanity and cheeky wit: Britain is seen as a beleaguered isle where two Queens sit on a single throne and Islam is rocked by a blasphemous book that no one has read. But the authors' crucial point is that Islamic culture is rich, fable-oriented and, at source, far removed from the harshness of the modern mullahs. The single most effective moment in this hour-long show comes with a set of quotations from the prophet Mohammed: 'Whoever has no kindness has no faith,' 'Women are the twin halves of men,' 'Speaking the truth to the unjust is the best of holy wars.'

But as well as distinguishing between the prophet and his mouth-pieces, Ali and Brenton also make the point that Britain's Muslim community is divided and that our racial arrogance has fostered local fundamentalism. We see an educated Bradford son turning into an Islamic hardliner as a retort to racial abuse, while his semi-literate father argues against the absurdity of burning books and of the belief that Britain can become Islamic.

In a way the play is an apt pre-cursor to Caryl Churchill's *Icecream* which follows it on the Court stage, in that it, too, is about mutual cultural misconceptions. Only at the end does it turn into an outright gesture of solidarity with Salman Rushdie when his name climaxes a list of writers who have been banned and persecuted throughout history; but by then the show has earned the right to a political statement.

What is heartening, however, is that Ali and Brenton have cast their ideas in a highly theatrical, fabulist mould. Penny Cherns's production also gets three highly effective performances from Nabil Shaban as the authoritarian Caliph, Fiona Victory as a Scheherezade who finally breaks free from her enslavement, and Paul Bhattacharjee as the bemused poet. The strength of the piece, however, is that it is a humane plea for freedom of thought and the kind of thing that gives propaganda a good name.

Ghetto

Olivier: 29 April 1989

Joshua Sobol wryly admits in the National Theatre programme that the genocide of European Jews is a subject he tried to resist. But he tackles it head on in *Ghetto*, written in Hebrew and given in an English version by David Lan at the Olivier; and not the least remarkable feature of this astonishing play is that it debates moral issues in a form that has the headlong exuberance one associates with Yiddish theatre. But such paradoxes are partly what the play is about.

On one level, the play concerns the tactics of survival. The setting is the Vilna ghetto between January 1942 and September 1943. Jacob Gens, the leading figure on the Jewish Council, adopts a policy of pragmatic accommodation with the Germans and sanctions the formation of a Vilna theatre troupe. Hermann Kruk, the ghetto librarian, is a fierce proponent of underground resistance and produces a poster saying 'No theatre in a graveyard.' Meanwhile Kittel, a young, music-loving SS officer, rules over the city with a saxophone in one hand and a gun in the other.

Sobol is not the first dramatist to debate the ethics of accommodation. Arthur Miller's moving TV film, *Playing For Time*, dealt with the women's orchestra forced to play in Auschwitz. Jim Allen's *Perdition* used a pseudo-forensic approach to discuss the complicity of Hungarian Zionists in extermination policies.

But Sobol's achievement is that (like Miller) he does not use hindsight to adopt a comfortable moral stance but recreates the dilemma faced by people like Gens at the time. In one agonising scene, Gens is ordered by Kittel (in the midst of an orgiastic party) to murder half of the 4,000 Jews in a neighbouring ghetto. Gens bargains with Kittel until he gets the number down to 410. Rather than judge Gens, Sobol empathises with him and makes us comprehend his motives.

In the end, Sobol shows that whether you negotiate with tyranny or adopt a policy of armed resistance, you cannot counter its arbitrary cruelty: for all Gens's accommodation, the Vilna ghetto was liquidated in 1943. But Sobol's real point is that there is a life of the spirit – here embodied by members of the Vilna Troupe – that is less easily crushed. Sobol has seized on and intelligently used the historical fact that the troupe put on plays and revues even as Jews were deported to the camp at Ponar five miles up the road.

Auden, pointing to the practical impotence of art, famously wrote that no line of poetry ever saved a Jew from the gas chamber. But Sobol's point is that art, and specifically theatre, can simultaneously provide spiritual comfort, symbolic defiance and communal solidarity. Theatre is the abiding metaphor of the play; and Sobol makes brilliant use of it, from a satirical sketch about a Nazi rally to the inclusion of eight songs written by members of the ghetto and varying from plangent lyricism to a celebratory hymn to survival.

But Sobol's fascinating play also touches on something deeply mysterious: the relationship between oppressors and oppressed. As part of his damage-limitation exercise, Gens practises a Germanic efficiency. Conversely, Kittel is hypnotised not only by the troupe's lead singer but by the vivacity and energy of Jewish culture. It is as if he is seduced by what he is bound to destroy; and in one memorably queasy sequence initiates a lively group rendering of Gershwin's 'Swanee'.

Sobol has, in fact, found a fluid form, blending dialectic, drama, dance and cabaret, that precisely embodies what his play is about: the consolation and tenacity of art. And Nicholas Hytner has matched it with a richly expressive production that combines moral seriousness with theatrical exuberance. Bob Crowley's design, based on converging, multi-windowed ghetto walls, likewise has a pointed inventiveness; the librarian Kruk, for instance, is framed against a huge tower of books which says everything about the importance of written culture in the ghetto. And Jeremy Sams's arrangement of the ghetto music moves easily from lyrical fervour to Weill-like irony.

In a communal achievement, there are some strong individual performances. John Woodvine rightly plays Gens not as an obliging trimmer but as a man who brings an impassioned commitment to his belief that 'jobs mean lives'. Alex Jennings as Kittel also avoids all the usual war-movie clichés by playing the German officer as a smooth-faced figure who is parasitically dependent on the ghetto for spiritual sustenance. Maria Friedman as the ghetto's singer delivers her numbers with stunning directness and not a whisper of false pathos. And Paul Jesson makes the socialist librarian a figure of plausible rectitude.

Given the subject matter, you expect a punishing evening. The triumph of *Ghetto* (as both play and production) is that it takes an historical event and turns it into a testament to spiritual defiance, the durability of memory and the saving power of art.

The Cherry Orchard

Berlin: 20 June 1989

It is time, I think, to burn a few boats. Over the past quarter century I have seen Chekhov's plays done in a variety of styles. But Peter Stein's version of *The Cherry Orchard*, which has just had its premiere at the Schaubühne in Berlin, is, quite simply, the best Chekhov production I have ever encountered – even more remarkable, in its emotional abundance, than Stein's own legendary *Three Sisters*.

The Cherry Orchard, as Michael Frayn has pointed out, is the most elusive and difficult of all Chekhov's plays. It merges naturalism and symbolism. It depends more on mood than event. And it is haunted by

Chekhov's own observations in his letters that 'What has emerged in my play is not a drama but a comedy, in places even a farce,' and that 'the last act will be cheerful – in fact, the whole play will be cheerful and frivolous.'

Yet how do we square that with the emotion we undoubtedly feel at the destruction of the cherry orchard and the ruination of a family through their own heedlessness?

Stein's answer is to take all the play's ingredients (in the Berlin programme it is described, Polonius-like, as 'Tragedy. Comedy. Pastoral. Farce.'), and push them to their limits. In this version the realism is more realistic, the symbolism more symbolic and the farce funnier than in any of the dozen other productions I have seen. Stein's genius is for realising every moment on stage with maximum intensity: what emerges is a sense of life lived at fever pitch, touching the wildest extremities of absurdity and pain.

Realism today has become a drab word implying something photographic and low-key: Stein uses music, light, sound, design (by the brilliant Christophe Schubiger) and ensemble acting to restore to it poetic richness. Thus the famous first act, here beginning in shuttered darkness, is replete with a sense of *Heimat*, the joy of returning to one's ancestral roots. Jutta Lampe's Ranevskaya belies her grande dame appearance by leaping from chair to chair and kissing the nursery furniture with holy devotion while Karoline Eichhorn's Anya jumps in the air at the rediscovery of 'Mein Zimmer, mein Fenster'.

But the great moment comes when the shutters are flung open, light floods the nursery and we see a profusion of white cherry-blossom: for the first time I truly understood why the Gayev family couldn't bear to part with their estate.

But Stein's achievement is to show that realism at its height acquires a symbolic power. You see this most clearly in the breathtakingly beautiful second act. Schubiger's design consists of a long sloping escarpment, pocked with old tombstones and bathed initially in the fierce orange glow of the setting sun. But Stein also puts on stage a huge stack of hay into which Jutta Lampe hurls herself even as she is being warned that the estate must be sold: it provides the perfect metaphor for her own wilful, irresponsible childishness. This heightened realism merges perfectly with the symbolism which Stein also pushes, provocatively, to the extreme. Thus when we hear the famous sound of the breaking string, the backcloth is suddenly illuminated with a distant prospect of industrial chimneys and Kremlin domes implying the Revolution to come.

Any production of *The Cherry Orchard* raises the questions of where

Chekhov himself stands. Is he writing a poignant paean to the passing of the old Russia or hymning the inevitability of change? My own feeling is that he is recording an historical process with scrupulous objectivity; but Stein subtly adds another dimension which is our own late 20th-century awareness that the world of change embodied by Lopakhin and Trofimov will hardly lead to a social Utopia.

Stein shows the Gayev family as palpably absurd. Their beloved house is peeling and flaking; and their third-act party is a comic provincial hop straight out of Gogol, with very short men dancing with dowdy, needlessly tall women. But when Michael König's Lopakhin returns from the purchase of the estate he is on a manic high that contains an element of vindictive class triumph: there is a touch of incipient tyranny, which I have never sensed before, about the way he bursts into the revels and orders everyone to dance to his tune.

But Stein does not take sides. He does not imprison the play within a bourgeois or Marxist concept. He simply presents what is there to the full so that no crevice of the play is left unexplored. The relationship between Varya and Lopakhin, for instance, is exquisitely realised. Throughout the evening Dorte Lyssweski's Varya shoots shy, secret smiles at him while he mercilessly teases her. When, at last, they are left alone he almost buries his head in her hair, almost seizes her in his arms but is always checked by some fatal emotional inarticulacy. It is a perfect heart-breaking embodiment of the tragedy of love unspoken.

But every character is here conceived in the round. Werner Rehm is the definitive Pischik: an earth-larding provincial Falstaff lapsing into instant snores as he butts his head against the bookcase. Roland Schäfer's Yasha is the epitome of cocksure arrogance as he kisses the chambermaid while his mouth is still full of cigarette-smoke. And Gerd Rameling is a wildly funny Yepikhodov, even managing to interrupt Jutta Lampe's moving farewell to her house with another squeak of his boots: a superb example of Stein's ability to show that tragedy and comedy in Chekhov endlessly interweave.

This triumphant Gesamtkunstwerk is a landmark in modern theatre: a production in which Stein's visual richness goes hand in hand with his psychological understanding. It is also faithful to the spirit of Chekhov, if not to the exact letter. One of Chekhov's original images for the play was 'a branch of cherry blossom sticking out of the garden straight into the room through an open window'. That clearly stuck in Stein's mind because, as Firs sits dying in the abandoned house, suddenly and terrifyingly a lopped branch crashes through the shuttered window, shattering the glass to smithereens. It is a supremely eloquent image of the break-up of the old order which lies at the heart of this play's mystery.

A Flea In Her Ear

Old Vic: 10 August 1989

Our theatre at the moment is falling flat on its farce. After a soft-boiled Labiche at Greenwich (to which, in retrospect, I feel more indulgent) we now have a grotesque, stylised, nightmarish version of Feydeau's *A Flea In Her Ear* directed by Richard Jones at the Old Vic. A technique that worked well in Ostrovsky's *Too Clever By Half* proves fatally heavy-handed in Feydeau.

Before analysing the production, one should perhaps recall what Feydeau's masterpiece is actually about. It hinges on the impotence of Chandebise, the metaphorically upright head of an insurance company. Convinced that her husband's flaccidity is a token of infidelity, his wife sends him an anonymous love-letter making an assignation at a seedy hotel.

Unfortunately the letter is penned by her best friend and falls into the hands of the lady's husband, a splenetically jealous Latin American. Eventually all the characters (including butler, chambermaid and Chandebise's cleft-palated nephew) converge on the hotel whose drunken porter, Poche, turns out to be Chandebise's double.

This is only the main-spring of a plot which drives the characters, especially the hapless Chandebise, who is battered and humiliated when mistaken for the hotel porter, to the very brink of madness. But a fundamental rule of farce (equally applicable to Feydeau and Ray Cooney) is that the descent into delirium is only funny if it starts from a base of realistic credibility.

Jacques Charon, who directed the legendary National Theatre production of this play in 1966, put it definitively when he said: 'The aim is to be natural within the style; not to turn the style itself into a joke. Like Feydeau we have first to discover the reality of the characters; *des personnages vraies*.'

Mr Jones wantonly ignored that advice. For a start he presents the play not as an objective farce but as a subjective impotence-nightmare inspired by Chandebise's visit to a comedy at the Palais-Royal: a framing device that is more a symptom of ebbing craft than of Kraft-Ebbing.

Mr Jones and his designers, The Brothers Quay, also seize on Chandebise's insurance connections to plunge us into a world that is pure Kafka: mountainous filing cabinets stuffed with paper soar to the ceiling and Chandebise's nephew scuttles up and down a central ladder exactly like the giant insect in *Metamorphosis*.

But where the production comes seriously unstuck is in the second act when the characters repair to a hotel that, in John Mortimer's deft translation, is described as 'carved out of nougat'. That exactly sums up a style of kitsch rococo. What we have here is a smoky, slate-grey Dickensian hell-hole with a sinister staircase and dank rooms giving off an aroma of joyless lust. But Feydeau's whole point is that Chandebise's nightmare takes place in a world of sexual fantasy ('Coming into here looks like going into an enchanted forest,' someone observes.) If the set loudly proclaims that we are already in a living hell, then there is no place for the action to go.

One sees Mr Jones's point: that Feydeau creates a world of madness, hallucination and frenzy in which the ultimate nightmare is that one will be confronted by one's *doppelgänger*. But all that is in the text anyway, superbly embodied by the moment when an appalled Chandebise catches a glimpse of the off-stage Poche and announces, 'I'm asleep in my bed.' What Mr Jones forgets is that Feydeau's genius was for projecting real people into burlesque situations and that laughter (in somewhat short supply here) has its own cathartic power.

The best one can say is that a misconceived approach is followed through with rigorous consistency and that Jim Broadbent emerges with honour in the dual central roles: I particularly liked the way his mooncalf-featured Poche advanced to the footlights and gesturing at the bourgeois group behind him, announced: 'Nice family. Bit simple.'

But many of the other performances are strenuous without being funny. Why is Linda Marlowe as Madame Chandebise forced to deliver every line as if in a Joan Crawford melodrama? Why is Matthew Scurfield as the sadistic hotel manager given leanings towards the ballet? Why is Kevin Williams as the Latin husband (fiercely protective of Rose English as his towering Spanish spouse) so over the top that he has few comic resources left when he drinks a glass of boracic acid? A host of good actors is cast adrift in a production that clubs you over the head with its insights and that substitutes surreal distortion for Feydeau's portrait of a world gone mad in which every detail is mathematically precise.

The Master Builder

Barbican: 28 September 1989

Adrian Noble's production of *The Master Builder* at the Barbican is the theatrical event of the year.

We have a great, neglected, soul-searching Ibsen masterpiece; stunningly perceptive direction and fine design that strips the play of naturalistic clutter; and two performances by John Wood and Joanne Pearce that leave one emotionally drained.

Like many Ibsen plays, this one builds an upper-storey of symbolism on a ground-floor of realism. On one level it is the story of Halvard Solness, an ageing architect who is fearful of his younger rivals and exploits everyone for his work. Into his dry, cold, barren life steps Hilde Wangel: an ardent 23-year-old idealist whom Solness met ten years previously, when he kissed her 'many, many times' and promised eventually to buy her a kingdom. She has now come to claim her due – encouraging the vertigo-afflicted Solness giddily to ascend the spire of his own new house.

Ibsen is partly composing a self-portrait. The play famously derives from his infatuation with an 18-year-old girl, Emile Bardach, whom he met in the Tyrol in 1889. But the play is infinitely more than a record of a sexual obsession. Harold Clurman once suggested it might be subtitled *Sorrows of the Artist* and quite clearly Solness's, sacrifice of private happiness to public work, his panicky insecurity about younger rivals and his fear that his career adds up to nothing are a reflection of Ibsen's own darkest torments.

But while watching Mr Noble's remorselessly investigative production, another theme hit me. Surely this is a play about the eternal conflict between duty and desire. Solness's wife, Aline, is a slave to duty; Solness, paralysed by guilt over the burning down of their house and the death of their children, is chained to a living corpse, and even Hilde finally lacks the courage to wrench the master-builder away from his wife. But against the fetters of convention, Ibsen poses a world of joy and unshackled freedom that we aspire to but rarely achieve.

But the greatness of this production is that it probes the play's mystery without imposing a single meaning and it is helped by two effortlessly interlocking central performances. John Wood is such a forceful actor that he can sometimes unintentionally take over a play but here he gives a performance that is both generous and blindingly revelatory.

What Wood discovers in Solness is a man both irradiated by Hilde's presence and terrified of his own inner demons. In their opening encounter, he digs away at the truth of his first meeting with Hilde with a child-molester guilt complex, and Mr Wood's aquiline features are constantly wracked by the fear that his own success derives from some evil force. He gives us all of Solness's guilt, hunger for retribution and private despair – his final cry that his career adds up to 'nothing,

nothing, nothing' has a hammer blow Lear-like finality. Yet Mr Wood also conveys the sense of renewal that comes from Hilde's presence like a man startled by a sunrise. He does not so much play Solness as unravel him in a performance that wants nothing by comparison with Olivier's.

But Ms Pearce matches him in intelligence and intensity. Above all, she suggests that inside Hilde, the young idealist, lurks a sexual tease in a sailor-suit: she is constantly offering her mouth and body to Solness and then staging a tactical withdrawal. The moment of revelation comes when Ms Pearce says how exciting it would be 'to be taken' by a plundering Viking. Realising she has just issued an invitation to rape, she checks herself in appalled horror and the whole burden of Ms Pearce's performance is that Hilde is simultaneously a source of light and rejuvenation and ultimately as cowardly as Solness.

The other roles are well taken. Mrs Solness, whom Agate described as 'the dankest tank among all Ibsen's woeful cisterns', is played by Marjorie Yates as another guilt-ridden figure who cares more about the destruction of her nine dolls than her two children. Geraldine Alexander as Solness's book-keeper is a female fly helplessly caught in his web. And Duncan Bell as Solness's young rival has a sharpness that suggests he may have inherited his master's ego.

Richard Hudson's sets, all inclined walls and minimal furniture, also show that it is possible to divest Ibsen of realistic detail without lapsing into ostentatious Expressionism.

But everything about this engrossing evening is harmoniously exact and Mr Noble's specific triumph is to show that in exploring his own psyche, Ibsen states permanent truths about our own conflict between confining guilt and sky-reaching aspiration.

Hamlets

12 November 1989

Last year brought us a storm of *Tempests*. This year produced (what is the right collective noun?) a brood of *Hamlets*. I have so far seen four productions: Richard Eyre's at the National, Patrice Chéreau's from Nanterre, Ron Daniels's for the RSC and Yuri Lyubimov's for the Leicester Haymarket. And with these last two transferring to London this week and Chéreau's production re-opening in Paris on 1st December, it is a good time to ask what we have learned from the year of the moody Dane.

The single most striking fact is that we no longer see *Hamlet* purely as an anatomy of melancholy or a hoop through which a star-actor must jump. Read Agate's *Brief Chronicles* with its reviews of inter-war years *Hamlets* (Barrymore, Olivier, Gielgud, Tearle, Ainley) and you find that four-fifths of the space is given over to a discussion of how each actor measured up to the title-role: a reflection not only of Agate's temperamental bias but of an age dominated by heroic acting. Read almost any modern review and you will find that the main role is seen in the context of the directorial-visual concept and of the interpretation of key roles such as Claudius, Polonius and Ophelia. You can't have *Hamlet* without the Prince; but we have come to realise that he is no longer the sole focus of the play.

How has this come about? Partly, it is a simple matter of restoring the text. Pre-war, a full-text, four-hour *Hamlet* seems to have been an event: now it is commonplace. And the less you edit the play, the more you realise that Hamlet's debate on the revenge-ethic is only one of several issues with which it deals.

Take a simple example: if you cut the vital passage at the beginning of Act 2 Scene 1 where Polonius sets Reynaldo to spy on Laertes, you rush straight from Hamlet's 'O, cursed spite' to the distraught Ophelia's description of Hamlet's eruption into her closet. Perfectly possible; but it falsifies the play by making it seem as if Shakespeare's only concern was with the state of Hamlet's mind.

But along with a restoration of the text (though not, I have to say, in the case of Lyubimov) lies a growing awareness that *Hamlet* is a profoundly political play: one that deals not just with a tortured, individual soul but with the whole question of the governance of society.

You see this, for example, in the way Shakespeare pointedly contrasts Denmark and Norway. Voltemand has a crucial speech in which he describes how in Norway old Fortinbras has checked a mutiny by his nephew (who 'makes vow before his uncle never more To give th'assay of arms against your majesty') and re-integrates him into the society: in Denmark, Claudius tries to do precisely the same thing with Hamlet and fails. Shakespeare, as always, is fascinated by the mechanics of political power.

An extension of that is the way Elsinore itself, rather than the character of Hamlet, has now come to seem the play's determining factor: a point made in each of this year's productions. John Gunter's set at the Olivier is dominated by a towering, unequivocally martial statue of old Hamlet and by a court filled with Ucello-like images of battle. Antony McDonald's RSC Elsinore is an imprisoning institution full of crazily angled walls and Magritte windows giving on to swirling spindrift: the place, like the time, is out of joint. Lyubimov's designer, David Borowsky, goes even further by creating a vast, mobile hempen curtain that acquires a sinister volition of its own. And Richard Peduzzi's startling design for Chéreau is a raked wooden floor that, as the play proceeds, fissures and disintegrates into a honeycomb of traps, graves and sunken corridors.

But, as Professor Terence Hawkes has pointed out, *Hamlet* is a pluralistic play that, surprisingly, bears only the Prince's name. The reclamation of Claudius (Hamlet's 'mighty opposite') is a process that has been going on ever since Alec Clunes played him as a conscience-scarred figure in Peter Brook's 1955 production.

But I have been struck this year by the way other characters have come into renewed focus. I shall remember Richard Eyre's production (not having seen Ian Charleson's takeover) for Michael Bryant's staggering Polonius. Here was no doddering old fool but an aphasia-afflicted sad Machiavel who brilliantly distinguished between his parental concern for Laertes and his casual indifference towards Ophelia. And Nadia Strancar's Gertrude in Chéreau's production charted, more clearly than I have ever seen, every stage of the character's moral awakening, culminating in a profound death-wish.

So where does this leave Hamlet himself? Obviously part of the play's labyrinthine fascination lies in his character (unless, like Charles Marowitz, you dismiss him as 'a slob'); and Mark Rylance at Stratford, drifting through the court in striped pyjamas and white bedsocks, left behind one of this year's most indelible images.

But my contention is that in the Eighties our perception of the play has radically changed: that we no longer see Hamlet as Everyman or a romantically introspective figure but as a puzzling neurasthenic who, because he cannot govern himself (his treatment of Ophelia has been getting progressively more violent) is ill equipped to govern Denmark.

The ideal production, of course, is one in which a multi-faceted performance is matched by a total vision of the play; and, in recent years, I can think of only two examples. One was Kozintsev's Russian film in which Smoktunovsky's smouldering Prince was seen in the context of a bustling Elsinore reminding us, as Kenneth Tynan said, that a royal castle is like a vast hotel which somebody has to run.

The other was a strangely undervalued RSC production by John Barton in which Michael Pennington (against the bias of the times) gave us a Prince who was both sharp-brained and sweet-souled, living in a Pirandellian Elsinore obsessed with theatricality and role-playing.

The eternal challenge of the play, in fact, lies in the effortless meshing of character and society so that Hamlet's personal dilemma springs out of a vividly-realised public context. It rarely happens. Meanwhile we go on watching and waiting.

Coriolanus

Royal Shakespeare Theatre: 7 December 1989

It is twelve years since the last Stratford *Coriolanus*: an absurd neglect of Shakespeare's best political play. But the new production at the Royal Shakespeare Theatre, directed by Terry Hands and John Barton, has a lot going for it. Pace. Clarity. The best Volumnia in years from Barbara Jefford. But, in an ideal world, one would look for more dangerous animalism than one gets from Charles Dance's Coriolanus in order to sharpen the edge of political debate.

What makes this such a great play is Shakespeare's analytical power: as John Barton once pointed out, Shakespeare is neither right-wing nor left-wing but wing-less. Coriolanus is seen as a magnificent warrior, a psychologically damaged mother-worshipper and a potential threat to an evolving republic. The people, on the other hand, are suffering from famine at a time when the patricians are hoarding the grain-harvest, but are themselves easily manipulated by the Tribunes. Shakespeare does not so much take sides as show how the state is threatened by the tragic collision of opposing forces: for antique Rome read Jacobean England.

What is good about the current production is that it does not seek to tilt the play either way: it allows us to decide where we stand. It also implies, rather than re-creates, the past: Christopher Morley's set consists of three mobile siege-towers with the Romans, in costume terms, veering to black leather, the Volscians to scarlet greatcoats. And along the way the production makes a number of intelligent points.

The Tribunes are strongly contrasted, with Geoffrey Freshwater's bullish rabble-rouser of a Sicinius Velutus off-set by the ineffectual moderation of Joe Melia's Junius Brutus. The continuity of martial values is also brilliantly suggested at the end when Coriolanus's son ritually receives his father's sword from Volumnia while his mother looks grievingly on.

What I miss, however, in Charles Dance's Coriolanus is a sense of implacable danger. Mr Dance gives us many of the man's essential qualities: his psychological dependence on his mother, his solitariness (he is constantly placed down front gazing over the audience's heads), his antique, tribal valour. But there is a dragonish aspect to Coriolanus which Mr Dance has yet to catch. He also throws away too many key phrases: 'This Triton of the minnows' is a magnificent epithet for Sicinius but it here gets lost, and although in the great banishment-speech Mr Dance's body-language is good (as he hurls his coat to the ground in fine disdain) it is significant that the directors resort to an echo-chamber effect on 'There is a world elsewhere.' Olivier, one wanly recalls, had his own built-in reverberations.

Without a dictatorial Coriolanus, Shakespeare's point about the implied threat to the republic is stated rather than felt. But there is rich compensation in Barbara Jefford's magnificent Volumnia: why has this superb actress been given only two roles by the RSC in 30 years? She is, essentially, a voluptuous Volumnia whose hold over her son is dangerously sexual. Greeting him on his return from battle, she hands him over to his wife with palpable reluctance; seeking to calm him before his confrontation with the people, she shackles him in an iron grip; and, in the great plea with him not to sack Rome, she pinpoints the lines about him treading on his mother's womb 'that brought thee to this world'. Volumnia can easily be played as a sexless harridan: Ms Jefford interprets her as a passionate woman who dominates her son physically as well as spiritually, even to the extent of giving his face a resounding slap when he is recalcitrant.

But the other key roles are also strongly cast. Malcolm Storry's bullet-headed Aufidius is not simply a rude barbarian but an acute analyst of Coriolanus's character: Mr Storry has the priceless gift of making the language tangible so that when he says 'I think he'll be to Rome as is the osprey to the fish' the image comes resonantly alive. Joseph O'Conor also makes Menenius infinitely more than a wily patrician: he seems the only one capable of communicating sanely with the several, warring factions.

In what is normally seen as a male-dominated play, it is also worth noting that Hands and Barton give the women unusual prominence. Amanda Harris's Virgilia is no simpering wet but a loyal wife who vehemently thumps the tribunes for their banishment of her husband. And Jane Maud's Valeria is characterised in the programme as 'priestess of Diana' and, in the final peace-mission, is given unusual symbolic weight.

That is a sign of how the play has been intelligently rethought. The production also takes on board the point Anne Barton makes in the programme that Shakespeare, following Livy, sees Coriolanus as a threat to the balance of the state. But for the idea to be made manifest one needs a Coriolanus who is not only a truculent fighter but also a thrillingly horrific force of nature.

1990

The main drama of the year was at the Palace of Westminster. How well I recall those heady nights in late November as one delayed going to the theatre as long as possible in order to catch the Six O'Clock News *and dashed home as quickly as possible in order to see* Newsnight. *Delight in the PM's downfall was not just proof of an anti-Thatcher fixation (though I am ready to confess to that) but also evidence of a conviction that her hostility to public subsidy had damaged Britain's artistic life. The theatre in the Eighties achieved many things; but Thatcherism also bred a siege-mentality, excessive prudence and the sanctification of the box-office as the ultimate arbiter.*

The best news, artistically, in 1990 was that political theatre was still alive and kicking. I recall an hilarious edition of The Late Show *in which a number of practitioners were invited to speculate on its demise only to reveal that it was quietly flourishing. It was particularly hard not to be struck by the speed with which the British theatre reacted to the turbulent events in Eastern Europe.* Moscow Gold *by Brenton and Ali was nobody's favourite play, but it was a far-from-dishonourable attempt to pin down the process of change in the Soviet Union. David Edgar's* The Shape Of The Table *was also a mature, well-researched play warning that the leaders of Eastern Europe's new democracies would soon discover the insulating effects of power. Caryl Churchill's* Mad Forest, *initiated by the Central School of Speech and Drama, not only evoked the mood of fear and rancour in Romania but implied the country had witnessed not a revolution but a triumphal coup by Iliescu.*

Religion also returned to the theatrical agenda in David Hare's Racing Demon*: the vibrant first part of a projected state-of-Britain trilogy.*

One could hardly cheer about a year that forced the RSC to quit the Barbican for five months. But the Theatre Royal Stratford East had a vintage spell (with Wild Justice *and* Five Guys Named Moe*), the McDiarmid-Kent regime at the Almeida gave us high-grade actors' theatre and the Abbey Theatre, Dublin conquered London with* Dancing At Lughnasa. *All told it was, as the dethroned Tory leader might have said, a funny old year.*

RSC In Crisis

13 February 1990

Given the hysteria that has greeted the RSC's latest cash crisis, it is worthwhile trying to offer a few calming facts and pointers to the future.

(1) The RSC's financial problems date back to the early Sixties when an initial grant of £47,000 was wrung from a reluctant Arts Council. Almost from its inception the RSC was treated, financially, as less important than the National Theatre. That ludicrous imbalance has persisted up to the present day.

(2) The immediate crisis stems from two things. One is the Government's failure to honour the recommendations of its own Priestley Report, which examined the financing of the RSC and concluded in 1984 that it was seriously underfunded. Because it was not properly implemented, the RSC has lost nearly £6 million in subsidy over the last six years. The other key fact is the slippage of attendance figures to 75 per cent of capacity at Stratford and the Barbican over the past year. But the two facts are intimately related. An under-funded company cannot pay competitive wages and finds it hard to attract top stars. Audiences, already hit by mortgage-rises and high interest-rates, start to count the escalating cost of a night out at the theatre. But where, in all the coverage of the projected Barbican closure, is the attack on Government policies that have induced it?

(3) Artistic standards. These are hard to measure objectively but, judging from some of the rubbish written over the past few days, you would think Terry Hands was presiding over a company in the business of vandalising Shakespeare. There have been some duff productions (there always were). But in the last 18 months I have sat through Trevor Nunn's *Othello*, Nicholas Hytner's *The Tempest*, Adrian Noble's *The Plantagenets*, Ron Daniels's *Hamlet*, Terry Hands's *Romeo And Juliet* and Cicely Berry's *King Lear* without feeling that standards were irrevocably slipping. Indeed the level of recent Shakespeare work has been higher than for many years.

(4) The RSC's biggest mistake has been to compromise its identity by presenting too many musicals. The motive has been clear enough: to make money. But, with the exception of *Les Misérables*, none of them has turned into golden money-spinners. What they have done is to make people question the company's *raison d'être*. I believe passionately that the RSC should be concentrating on what it does best: classical work. I will go to the barricades for a company that presents

productions of the calibre of Adrian Noble's *The Master Builder* but not for one increasingly devoted to musicals. The one good thing to come out of the crisis may be the cancellation of *Blitz* and of *Children Of Eden* based, we are chillingly told, on the Book of Genesis. Musicals are not what the RSC is about; and if Adrian Noble and Michael Attenborough are to be the new artistic directors, I hope they will put the stoppers on these expensive behemoths.
(5) The Barbican. Everyone goes on about the supposed awfulness of the Barbican. I cannot comment on the backstage working conditions but, from the public's point of view, it is a valuable amenity. It is not pretty, but the main auditorium is preferable to most West End theatres with their atrocious sightlines and rotten facilities. I recently sat in row Q of the Barbican stalls from which I could see and hear perfectly: contrast the back stalls of the RSC's last London home, the Aldwych, with its over-hanging balcony cutting off the upper half of the stage. Front of house, much could be done to make the Barbican a more welcoming place, but most of the arguments about the building are based on snobbery and an old-fogeyish anti-modernism.
(6) What prescription can one offer for the future? A recognition by the Government that the National and the RSC are equally important companies demanding matching subsidies (and not at the expense of the rest of British theatre either). A rigorous self-appraisal by the RSC acknowledging that it is not part of the light-entertainment industry but exists to present Shakespeare, other classics and new work to the highest standard. A determination by the new managing director of the Barbican Centre to make it a friendlier place in order to capitalise on its splendid performance-spaces.

The projected closure of the two Barbican theatres next winter and the cancellation of the RSC's regional tour is a national scandal that will permanently damage the company and make Britain look even more penny-pinchingly foolish in its attitude to the arts than it does already. But if the Government or the City does come to the rescue, I hope it will be rewarded with a programme of classical and new work rather than trashy musicals.

Sunday In The Park With George

Lyttelton: 17 March 1990

Steven Pimlott's production of *Sunday In The Park With George* at the Lyttelton is startingly different from the version I saw at New York's

Booth Theatre five years ago: visually bolder, physically bigger, emotionally a little less charged. But Stephen Sondheim's music and lyrics and James Lapine's book retain their extraordinary wit and audacity: this is a genuine musical of ideas rather than simply a sumptuous *divertissement*.

It is built around the work of Seurat, a painter who applied rigorous analytical reason to art, and in particular his composition of *Sunday On The Island Of La Grande Jatte*. The first half shows the obsessive, pioneering Seurat working on separate figures in his canvas, sacrificing his mistress, Dot, to his work and finally bringing the elements in the picture together in a miracle of composition and design.

By the second act we have moved on a century. Seurat's great-grandson is also an artist but a corporation-pleasing technocrat who works with a machine called a Chromolume (Seurat originally called himself a 'chromo-luminarist'). But, revisiting La Grande Jatte, he encounters his great-grandfather's ghostly mistress and through her re-discovers the infinite joys and possibilities of art.

That is the broad outline of a musical that subordinates conventional narrative to teeming ideas; but three particular concepts thread their way through this amazingly rich work. One is the recurrent theme, explored by everyone from Ibsen and Chekhov to Ayckbourn, of art versus life. The point is not simply that George loses Dot to a compliant baker, but that personal relationships are suspended in the ecstasy of creation. The idea is articulated superbly in the number, 'Finishing The Hat', where George explains 'How you watch the rest of the world from a window' while losing your identity in the mastery of detail.

But this is also a musical about the changing role of the artist: while Seurat is a private, reclusive visionary, his great-grandson is a sponsor-seeking, hi-tech collaborator who puts the names of his contributors on the side of his Chromolume. I suspect the contrast is over-sharp (artists have always needed patrons) but Sondheim's big, second-act number, 'Putting It Together', is a classic and highly topical statement about the kow-towing process of fund-raising: as the younger George punningly puts it, 'First of all you need a good foundation. Otherwise it's risky from the start.'

The third and most profound theme is the Shakespearean one of nature versus nurture: the tension between the world as it is and our urge to re-order it. It comes out in 'Beautiful', a haunting song shared between Seurat and his mother that is the intellectual lynchpin of the show. She wistfully mourns transience and change: he tells her 'What the eye arranges *is* what is beautiful.' You realise the whole thrust of the first half comes from seeing Seurat re-order reality and finally arrange the Sunday idlers into an harmonious composition: a gesture cynically echoed in the second act when George is busy fixing introductions and supplying drinks.

But this is also a deeply personal show about the joys and the cost of creation; and what is startling about Sondheim's score is the way it corresponds to Seurat's own visual style. His pointilliste method is perfectly matched by the stabbing, jabbing, staccato music of 'Colour and Light'. But Sondheim also uses what he calls 'a rolling vamp' for *Sunday* which movingly echoes the finished picture's majesty of colour and design.

This is one point at which Mr Pimlott's production induces tears. But what is impressive is the way he and his partners, designer Tom Cairns and lighting-man Wolfgang Gobbel, have come up with a clean, clear visual concept different in many points from the New York original. The show begins and ends in a picture-framed, arctic-white box. By a dazzling trick of perspective, the second act starts with the figures of *La Grande Jatte* huddled together in an elevated, framed canvas. And where on Broadway the museum-scene was dominated by a laser-beam light-show it here becomes a satire on Robert Wilson-style performance-art: highly relevant since that too is about order, control and arranging bodies in space.

It is not a flawless show (thematic density cannot always make up for lack of narrative tension) but the two acts seem much more tightly integrated than they did in New York. The two lead roles are also superbly played. Philip Quast as the two Georges sharply contrasts the older one's monastic fervour with the younger one's gregarious emptiness and projects the words with clarity, elegance and style. Maria Friedman, as both Dot and her 98-year-old daughter Marie, also confirms she is an authentic star: she brings an earthy comedy to the chafing restrictions of Dot's existence, sings with note-true poignancy and has the gift of what Stanislavsky called 'public solitude'. In a large cast, Gary Raymond also shines out as both a velvet-smooth rival to Seurat and as a typical money-seeking modern museum-director. Jeremy Sams in the pit also ensures a balance between orchestral and vocal sound.

Sunday In The Park makes you work. But it demands and re-pays the closest attention since it is a genuine pathfinder that proves the musical can not only deal with ideas but illuminate the mystery of creation itself.

Someone Like You

Strand: 24 March 1990

Musicals have provided me with some of my most treasured theatrical memories. There was *Thomas And The King* in which Queen Eleanor, espying a copulating cleric, cried 'Seize that monk.' Or there was *Tom Brown's Schooldays* in which a thigh-brandishing, middle-European gypsy dance unaccountably erupted in the midst of Dr Arnold's Rugby. And I swear that in *Barnado* newsboys ran across the stage crying 'Mafeking Relieved.'

Someone Like You at the Strand may not achieve quite such rank awfulness but it confirms my thesis that history appears the first time round as tragedy and the second time as musical comedy.

The setting (book by Robin Midgley and Fay Weldon) is a hospital in battle-scarred West Virginia, the no-man's-land between North and South, at the end of the American Civil War. The land is ravaged. Men are dying from typhus-infested blankets and malfunctioning drugs. Racial bigotry is still alive. In this festering, disease-ridden, post-war world, we are asked to care about whether Petula Clark's English nurse will cast off her evil, profiteering husband and find true love with a Major who has healing hands.

It is perfectly possible, as *Miss Saigon* eloquently proves, for a musical to relate private emotion to public events. Here, however, the attempt is defeated by an illogical storyline and the insistent banality of Ms Clark's music and Dee Shipman's lyrics.

Ms Clark's Abigail, her elegant, ringleted coiffure untainted by war, rushes on to announce that she is a working nurse in desperate search of her preacher-husband. When he turns up, it transpires that he is a cynical exploiter touting dud medical supplies and leeringly inviting the Major's fiancée to be photographed in black lace. Since he is also symbolically called Kane, wears black, and as a figure of evil is somewhat to the right of Milton's Satan, you wonder why Abigail should have ever gone in search of this melodramatic villain.

But, even if judged as a Mills and Boon romance in which hero and heroine play doctors-and-nurses, the musical is sunk by the sheer inertia of the spoken dialogue and the lyrics. The show proves that what is too silly to be said ('Life is a spirit burning so bright' and 'Being burnt is being alive') is not improved by being sung. And though I looked forward to something more robust from a climactic number called 'The Women's Credo', its message that 'There is nothing we can't do' and 'Each of us is special' seemed unlikely to advance the cause of feminism.

Ms Clark's music, which has the mysterious quality of being played live but sounding taped, is an eclectic mixture of romantic ballads, gospel and blues without any definable character of its own. The one saving grace is that it is well sung. Ms Clark herself endows the nurse with her familiar vocal purity and winsome charm though I felt there might have been greater concessions to dramatic realism than a few dainty specks of blood on her forearm.

Dave Willetts, who has played Mr Lloyd Webber's Phantom and done time in *Les Mis*, emerges as a Donald Sutherland lookalike and, as the Major, projects a certain rugged integrity. But Clive Carter as Kane sweats nervously and suggests a nice chap from the shires erroneously cast as Elmer Gantry.

What is depressing, however, is the sheer dogged triteness of the evening. All the show says is that war is bad, love is good and liberty is fine; but it scarcely needs twenty songs, a picturesquely depleted set by Tim Goodchild and a competent production hauled up from Cambridge (where it began last October) by Robin Midgley to tell us that. Fleeing gratefully into the night, I found myself muttering 'Don't Take Me Back to Old Virginny.'

The Wild Duck

Phoenix: 19 May 1990

We have heard a lot about Peter Hall's intention of restoring the comedy to Ibsen's *The Wild Duck*. In fact, it has always been there. Shaw in 1897 famously referred to the audience 'shaking with laughter'. And I recall Michael Blakemore giving us a blackly funny version at the Lyric Hammersmith a decade ago.

Actually the greatness of Peter Hall's production at the Phoenix is that it puts the tragedy back into the play. As we sit spellbound watching the destruction of the Ekdal family by the meddling idealist, Gregers Werle, we feel we are watching something both particular and universal.

Particularity is shown by fanatical attention to detail, such as the fear everyone has of being touched: just as Gregers Werle shies away from contact with his father, so Gina Ekdal flinches at Gregers's touch as if she feared contamination. But the sense of cosmic tragedy is conveyed by the astonishing device of prefacing each act with the sound of a duck's wings vainly flapping: an aural extension of Ibsen's central symbol of wounded humanity's tendency to hide itself in illusion.

The real problem in *The Wild Duck*, in fact, lies in achieving the balance between Ibsen's realism and poetry. The tendency at the moment is to react against years of naturalistic clutter by pushing the play towards Expressionism. But Hall and designer, John Bury, brilliantly show the Ekdals living in a box-like attic, with the mini-menagerie off to the side and with a skylight periodically bathing the room in sun and shadow. Yet there is also pure stage-poetry in the use of an upstage door in which Gregers Werle appears framed like a neurotic Christ and his father like a bewhiskered Nemesis.

But Hall also intensifies the tragedy by casting the key roles much younger than usual. Alex Jennings plays Hjalmar Ekdal not as a dithery middle-aged buffoon but as a youngish man shrouded in self-pity and anger. With his languid manner and raffish saunter, Mr Jennings is not unamusing; but what you see, with blinding clarity, is the tragedy of a man who is prey both to Gregers's idealism and to doubts about his child's paternity. Mr Jennings doesn't just play the part: he illuminates it by suggesting that Hjalmar is cursed with the rage of the insecure.

Gregers is an even tougher part, which David Threlfall plays superbly as a soft-spoken zealot. He looks like an El Greco Christ in urgent need of psychiatric attention: everything he does has a terrifyingly quiet intensity, not least the obsessive way he quizzes Hedvig about the wild duck which has been down to 'the darkest depths of the sea'.

Nichola McAuliffe is also, for me, the definitive Gina Ekdal: a loving, malapropistic woman (she refers to the spare room as 'unused and vacuous') who yet has a sharper hold on reality than anyone in the play. She also sends a thrill down the spine at the moment when it is revealed that Werle's father, like Hedvig, is going blind: Ms McAuliffe, filled with prescient terror, allows the cup from which she is drinking suddenly to dangle in space.

Hall also gives us a supporting cast of National Theatre strength. Terence Rigby's grizzled, self-hating Doctor Relling is monumental in his lacerating attack on what the Hall and Inga-Stina Ewbank translation calls 'hyper-righteous fever'; Alan Dobie's Mr Werle exemplifies the hollow pillar of society; and Maria Miles's Hedvig (cannier than usual) and Lionel Jeffries's ghostly Old Ekdal are both touched with tragedy by their belief in the sanctity of their animal-filled loft.

We emerge shattered from a production that combines a hard-edged particularity with a universal, poetic applicability. After so many tame turkeys, it is inspiring to find a West End *Wild Duck* that captures all the play's polyphonic greatness.

Hidden Laughter

Vaudeville: 14 June 1990

The title of Simon Gray's new play, *Hidden Laughter* at the Vaudeville, comes from T. S. Eliot's *Burnt Norton*: a meditation on time and memory inspired by a visit to a Gloucestershire garden. And Mr Gray has here exchanged his familiar talent to abuse for a pensive, intelligent, serio-comic study of the changes wrought on an English family by ten years of escape to a Devon country-cottage: I like it as much as anything Mr Gray has written for the stage.

The novel-writing heroine at one point describes her work as 'Marriages, infidelity, children – the usual middle-class stuff.' And, on the surface, that is Mr Gray's theme. Harry is a literary agent, his wife Louise is a burgeoning novelist; and, accompanied by their two young children and Harry's old dad, they decide in 1980 to take a Devon weekend cottage to escape the London world of telephones and anger. Over five scenes spanning ten years we see how their lives are altered by Louise's thriving career, Harry's routine infidelities, the dad's decline into senility, a crippling accident to their son and the hurtful alienation of their daughter: the one constant factor in their lives is the loving friendship of the local vicar, Ronnie, which they take cruelly for granted.

In one sense, Mr Gray is demolishing the modern pastoral myth: the belief that if only you can find the right bijou rural property, your life will somehow be transformed. With steely wit, he shows how the Devonian bolt-hole is invaded not just by tellies and transistors but by an angry novelist demanding a bigger advance and by an importunate secretary offering advances of her own. Like Michael Frayn's novel, *The Trick Of It*, the play also deals with the painful sense of exclusion that the non-writer in a marriage feels at the woodpecker-like tapping of his partner's typewriter; though one wonders how much that is tied up with deflation of the male ego.

But what Mr Gray is really doing in this, for him, unusually compassionate play is exploring the idea behind the famous opening lines of *Burnt Norton*: 'Time present and time past are both perhaps present in time future.' Events in the play have a fascinating way of echoing down the years: thus the hidden laughter of children in the foliage, when their parents are scared stiff they have been gored by a neighbouring bull, becomes both a symbol of remembered joy and, more importantly, an ironic anticipation of their later misfortunes. Under the guise of domestic drama, Mr Gray has written a meditative, philosophical play about time, mortality, madness, decay, egoism and the bruising modern attitude towards friendship. Ayckbourn aside, it makes most contemporary plays in the West End look decidedly thin gruel.

There are occasional prolixities and contrivances but Mr Gray has directed his own play with a nice understanding of its comic melancholy. He has also got excellent performances from his cast and most especially Peter Barkworth as the local vicar.

We have all seen trimming clerics before but Mr Barkworth turns indecision into a style so that, when asked his views on God or abortion, he goes through exquisite moral contortions. Against that he conveys the power of constancy, in his love both for the garden and the family, in a world of temporary relationships. Mr Barkworth superbly combines professional dither and personal loyalty.

Felicity Kendal as Louise also has just the right quality of built-in obsessiveness so that a fusspot concern for her children gradually elides into a maternal tenacity towards her fiction: the suppressed rattiness Ms Kendal exhibits when someone pinches her typewriter is sheer joy. Her husband, Harry, is harshly dealt with by Mr Gray but Kevin McNally captures precisely the desperation of a man virtually cuckolded by his wife's creativity. And there are very good supporting performances from Richard Vernon as the child-like father, Samuel West as the death-haunted son and Sam Dastor as an eruptive novelist who looks as if he has put the grouch into Groucho's.

But what cheers me is that Mr Gray has got away from the device of a protagonist who compensates for his own failures through a whiplash tongue. Instead he has written a subtle and moving play about the disintegration of a family through what Eliot himself calls 'inoperancy of the world of spirit'.

King Lear

Royal Shakespeare Theatre: 13 July 1990

The year of the *Lear* starts officially with the unveiling of Nicholas Hytner's Stratford production starring John Wood. To cut the cackle and come to the 'osses, I would describe it as an immensely intelligent production with a brilliantly idiosyncratic performance from Mr Wood. Clearly there has been much throwing about of brains: all the evening lacks as yet is the ability to shatter one's emotional defences.

Confronted by this vast, unwieldy play, Mr Hytner is too wily to offer a confining concept. I do, however, see a consistent idea running through his production: an exploration of the insane contradictions of a world where the gods are seen as both just and wantonly cruel, where Nature is both purifying and destructive. The fashionable view is that *King Lear* is an essay in Beckettesque nihilism. Mr Hytner to his credit, treats it as a tragi-comedy full of turbulent paradox.

You see this in David Fielding's excellent set, reminiscent of that for ENO's *Masked Ball*: a revolving, open-sided cube that during the storm scene gives on to a dizzying skyscape. Order opens up to reveal chaos. And the same pattern is visible in erratic human behaviour. Lear, having cursed Goneril with sterility, rushes back to embrace her. Astonishingly, Regan first conspires in the blinding of Gloucester and then tenderly asks him, rather than her wounded husband, 'How dost my lord?' Mr Hytner ushers us into a morally topsy-turvy universe in which good and evil frequently cohabit within the same person.

I take this to be the clue to John Wood's ground-breaking Lear. He does not offer a simple linear reading in which folly leads to madness and thence to moral regeneration: Wood's Lear exists in a permanent state of spiritual schizophrenia. You see this in the brilliantly played first scene where he enters clutching the trisected map like a berserk geography master and then drifts into aphasia. Equally powerful is the way his rage against Cordelia is short-circuited by his love: 'Better thou hadst not been born,' he ferociously cries and then chokes, unable to finish the sentence.

As you would expect from Mr Wood, it is a highly original reading that notches up point after point. In the hovel scenes, he has a crazed sprightliness pursuing Poor Tom ('Thou art the thing itself') with the ecstasy of a scientist making a Eureka-like discovery. But perhaps his best moment comes when he promises the imprisoned Cordelia that they will take upon them 'the mystery of things'.

It is a performance that destroys the barrier between madness and sanity: this Lear occupies both territories at once. What for me excludes it, as yet, from the select club of great Lears is that it wants the gift of pathos. It is an intriguing, daring, pioneering performance but also one that is somewhat over-calculated. Mr Wood at the moment is superbly playing Lear. What he has to learn to do is to let Lear play him.

But this is anything but a one-man show. Amongst a host of good supporting performances, I was very taken with Norman Rodway's Gloucester: not the usual dour old duffer but a jokey, credulous sport who initially treats Edgar's fake letter as a lark and who gets his astrological opinions from the local paper. In a Lear that starts surprisingly light in tone, David Troughton's disguised Kent offers a very funny parody of the loyal old soldier marching up and down outside Albany's palace. But then the whole production is about contradictions: about the strange surreality of a world in which prankish jokers get blinded and old sweats shoved in the stocks. This element of paradox also applies to Estelle Kohler's Goneril and Sally Dexter's Regan who are less embodiments of evil than two neglected daughters (Alex Kingston's Cordelia is obviously dad's pet) who find themselves almost stumbling into gross cruelty.

The one dubious stroke is the casting of Linda Kerr Scott as the Fool, whom she plays as an asexual, black-capped figure reminiscent of the ventriloquist's dummy she played in *Ghetto*. Ms Scott is caperingly comic in a Scottish accent but you lose any sense of the Fool as simultaneously Lear's external critic and inner conscience.

But this is one of the few lapses in a richly intelligent production. It aims not at mythic grandeur but at absurd moral fluctuation. And in Mr Wood's Lear it sweeps away barnacled tradition to offer us not some Blakeian ancient but a man who is an anthology of warring emotions. It is such an immense play you cannot get it right in one go, but this RSC production offers an exhilarating, mind-expanding start to the Lear festivities.

Dancing At Lughnasa

Lyttelton: 17 October 1990

Is Brian Friel the Irish Chekhov? He certainly wrests poetry from everyday life and, since Friel's latest play, *Dancing At Lughanasa*, imported to the Lyttelton from Dublin's Abbey Theatre, features five unfulfilled sisters, comparisons with the great Russian are inevitable. But watching this strange, haunting, powerful play, another work altogether came to mind: the *Bacchae* of Euripides.

Like Euripides, Friel presents us with a conflict between reason and passion. His title, significantly, is a reference to the Irish harvest festival named after the pagan god Lugh. Friel's narrator/hero, Michael, in fact, takes us back to the warm harvest days of August 1936, when he was a seven-year-old child being brought up by his unmarried mother, Chris, and her four sisters in the family home in County Donegal. On one level, this is a touching memory-play about a group of Catholic women trapped by economic circumstance. On a much deeper level, it is about the undeniability of primitive, atavistic passion.

Dancing is throughout a key metaphor; and in the most extraordinary burst of ecstasy currently to be seen on the London stage, the five women at one point release their emotional and sexual repressions by dancing to a reel issuing from the radio. Kate, the prim, breadwinning teacher, the jokey man-hungry Maggie, the spinsterish knitters Agnes and Rose and the husband-less Chris all suddenly whirl and career round the stage like possessed dervishes. It is a brilliant and moving image that expresses Friel's point that there are emotions that lie far beyond words.

What might simply have been a nostalgia-play about growing up in rural Ireland becomes a study of the unquenchable passions that underlie Catholic propriety. Friel constantly reminds us that, beyond the sisters' kitchen, exists a world of pagan rituals. Underscoring the point is the malaria-ridden brother Jack, home after 25 years as a missionary in a Ugandan leper-colony, where he has enthusiastically worshipped strange gods.

Friel's strength as a writer is that his universal themes emerge from a precise evocation of family life. You learn, for instance, a vast amount about the sisters from their reactions to the arrival of Michael's father – a charming Welsh flanneller. Chris gently twirls with him in the garden to the strains of 'Dancing In The Dark', Maggie gazes wistfully out of the window at a world of lost romance, while Agnes (who clearly adores the fly-by-night Welshman) ferociously knits and Kate puritanically buries herself in the paper. It is pure stage poetry, deeply revealing of character.

All five sisters are so good that one must name them individually: Catherine Byrne as the beautiful Chris, Rosaleen Linehan as the purse-lipped Kate, Anita Reeves as the sex-starved Maggie, Brid Ni Neachtain as simple Rose and Brid Brennan as the shy Agnes.

Gerard McSorley as Michael steers us through the narration without seeming oppressively omniscient. And, joining the cast since Dublin, are Stephen Dillane, very good as the nimble-footed Welshman, and Alec McCowen, who is astonishing as Jack. What I shall long remember about Mr McCowen as the mufflered, dying priest, is his joy at learning that Chris has a love-child, which in Uganda was a sign of good fortune. That one moment epitomises the over-riding theme of Mr Friel's moving play: the wisdom of acknowledging the passions that lie beneath the hard crust of religious orthodoxy.

The Seagull

The Swan: 8 November 1990

I find myself staggered by the attitude of the Tory press to the current RSC crisis. The government reneges on an explicit commitment to implement the Priestley Report and it is the company which gets the raspberries. This is rather like attacking the homeless for their improvidence or the burgled for their fecklessness; which, come to think of it, is exactly what happens in the Alice in Wonderland world we currently inhabit.

The savage irony of all this is that, while the RSC is forced to vacate its London premises, it is enjoying a cracking year in Stratford: one that continues with Terry Hands's highly intelligent new production of *The Seagull* in The Swan. Thornton Wilder once wrote that in Chekhov's plays 'Nobody hears what anybody else says. Everybody walks in a self-centred dream.' But by highlighting the two-year time gap in *The Seagull* between the third and fourth acts, Mr Hands brings out a point I had never fully grasped before: that those characters who remain permanently locked inside their own ego are comic, while those who show any capacity for change are tragic.

Mr Hands and his designer, Johan Engels, remind us visually of the transformations achieved by time, but Chekhov's point emerges even more clearly through the performances. Thus Simon Russell Beale's superb Konstantin is at first a petulant, nervy figure desperate for affection and wracked by an Oedipal hatred of Trigorin. By the last act this Konstantin has changed into an obsessive solitary for whom suicide is a release. The moment I shall long remember is that in which Mr Russell Beale methodically tears up his stories and gazes silently at his desk in wan contemplation of the writer he might have been.

It is a performance devoid of false pathos which is also true of Amanda Root's sterling Nina. Initially, she is the epitome of provincial go-getting as she jumps with cat-like energy around the fit-up stage and instinctively primps her hair at Trigorin's approach: by the last act she has become a pale, ravaged figure acknowledging both her own second-rateness and the illusory nature of fame. The third figure in this tragic triptych is Katy Behean's self-hating Masha soured by a loathed marriage but still stealing hungry, devouring glances at Konstantin.

Mr Hands handles the tragic side of the play with scrupulous realism. My main doubt concerns Susan Fleetwood's interpretation of Arkadina as a monumental egotist who treats life as a walking melodrama. Ms Fleetwood is undeniably very funny as she makes *moues* at every passing male, admiringly inspects her elegant wrists and hurls herself at Trigorin with flailing desperation. But where in all this is the buried kindness of a woman who once looked after a battered washerwoman and bathed her children in a washtub? In conveying Arkadina's actressy self-love, Ms Fleetwood misses her internal contradictions.

Roger Allam, however, captures very well Trigorin's fretful obsessiveness. Even when he is falling for Nina, you feel he is checking his own reaction; and there is a delicious moment when he twigs Konstantin's suicide, from the torn-up manuscripts, and mentally stores it away as if it might be an idea for a novella. John Carlisle's Dorn, a crumpled-suited Don Juan wearily reconciling himself to age, and Alfred Burke's mischievous Sorin are also impeccably right.

It is hard, at this stage in history, to find a new angle on *The Seagull*. But, without wrenching the text or Michael Frayn's translation, Mr Hands questions the popular assumption that Chekhov's characters are all self-occupied soloists. The real tragedy of this play, he suggests, is that the hardened egoists survive while those who remain open to experience are patently doomed.

The Colour Of Saying

Multi-racial casting: 1 November 1990

When in Britain did you ever see a black Hamlet? Or for that matter, a black or Asian Lear, Vanya, Trigorin, Viola, Hedda Gabler or Saint Joan? The answer is almost certainly never. Casting in the British theatre has become marginally less colour conscious over the past decade: the National has recently given us Josette Simon as a sulphurous Maggie in *After The Fall* and an all-Asian production of *Tartuffe*, the RSC casts Rudolph Walker as Gower in *Pericles* (but nothing else), Paterson Joseph as Oswald and Clarence Smith as France in *King Lear*. One or two regional reps like Birmingham and Derby have also cast against tradition. But the blunt fact is that the British theatre has scarcely begun to represent the multi-racial diversity of our society. As Jatinder Verma, director of Tara Arts, puts it, 'British theatre is promoting a kind of myth that does not correspond to people's experience as they walk down the street.'

The whole subject is fraught with complexities. Does it make sense in realistic drama for families to embody colour contradictions? If black, brown or Oriental actors should be free to play anything, does that mean it's OK for Michael Gambon to play Othello or Jonathan Pryce the Engineer in *Miss Saigon*? Is positive discrimination a good or bad thing? Even the language one uses is open to question. Yvonne Brewster, director of the Talawa Theatre Company, jibs at my use of the term 'cross-cultural' on the grounds that British-based black actors eat fish and chips and go to the movies like everyone else. Josette Simon demurs at the term 'colour-blind casting' because 'it sounds as if you're pretending not to be black.' So maybe one should get the semantics sorted out first.

Four years ago American Actors' Equity held a two-day conference on this whole subject: 500 people came, speeches were made, scenes from plays (everything from Shakespeare and Chekhov to Neil Simon and David Mamet) were done with non-traditional casting. But the conference also came up with four categories that make rough sense. Firstly, societal casting: employing ethnic actors in roles that reflect the way they participate in society. Secondly, cross-cultural casting: the transposition of an entire play to an all-ethnic world. Thirdly, conceptual casting: the use of ethnic actors to make a specific point. Fourthly, colour-blind casting: casting without reference to the race or ethnicity of the characters.

It is fascinating when you start applying these categories to Britain. Societal casting, like hurricanes in Hertfordshire, hardly ever happens outside black or Asian companies. In the real world (thanks partly to Roy Jenkins's Race Relations Act and to social pressures) there are few jobs or professions that are exclusively white. But you would never guess this if you were a Martian visiting the British theatre. We pride ourselves on our drama of recognition; but you could comb the plays of Osborne, Wesker, Ayckbourn, Stoppard, Nichols (with the major exception of *The National Health*) Frayn, Gray, Hampton and numerous others without finding many indications that we inhabit a pluralistic, multi-racial society. The majority of these writers are liberal, even radical, figures; yet although they grapple with morality, ethics and the state of the nation, it is significant that they rarely venture beyond the perimeter of white experience (you could, of course, also ask how many black playwrights portray whites). There is no law that says they must or should: it just makes you wonder whether they are not perpetuating a social myth.

Cross-cultural casting has made greater strides. Michael Rudman once directed a Caribbean *Measure For Measure* at the Lyttelton. Tara Arts regularly transposes European classics to Asian settings: hilariously so in the case of an Indian-colonial *Government Inspector* (Jatinder Verma says that when they toured to Australia and New Zealand audiences were surprised and delighted to find 'a bunch of darkies, for want of a better word' representing a culturally-mixed Britain they knew about from TV.) Yvonne Brewster for Talawa recently directed an *Oedipus* set in Nigeria and an all-black *Importance Of Being Earnest*. It's a fine principle in that it banishes the ridiculous notion that classic plays are the exclusive property of any one race, class or colour.

Conceptual casting I find more problematic: the danger is that it subordinates art to political point-making and reinforces stereotypes. Jonathan Miller, for instance, in 1988 directed an intelligent, honourably-conceived *Tempest* that cast Rudolph Walker as Caliban and Cyril Nri as Ariel. Both actors were very good. But the unspoken implication was that black actors had access to a world of colonial oppression and non-human spirituality denied to whites. The truth is, of course, that black actors living in Britain today inhabit the same god-awful, materialist mess as everyone else.

But the real issue at stake is colour-blind casting. Should we simply cast actors regardless of race or skin-colour, historical accuracy or even internal consistency? The stock answer is that you can do almost anything in mythic or poetic drama (the Greeks or Shakespeare, for instance). Once you start dealing with post-nineteenth century naturalistic drama, however, the rules are supposedly different: a black Nora or an Asian Willy Loman in a basically white *Doll's House* or *Death Of A Salesman* would, so the theory runs, distort the meaning of the play. My own response is that all theatre is a precarious fiction and metaphor for life; that casting should depend on talent rather than skin-colour; and that, on logical grounds, white actors should not automatically be debarred from playing Othello, Aaron or even a Eurasian Engineer in *Miss Saigon*.

Not everyone, needless to say, agrees. A colleague recently argued on television: 'You can't have a black Hamlet – the character's Danish.' But anyone who went to *Hamlet* looking for a dissertation on Danish dynastic problems would be in trouble. More seriously, there is the question of internal consistency. Birmingham Rep recently staged Vanbrugh's *The Relapse* with a white actor and a black actor playing estranged brothers. Yvonne Brewster (who is shortly to direct *Abigail's Party* in Cambridge with a black actor, on grounds of social accuracy, playing a Yuppie house-salesman) pins her faith on logic. 'I don't like casting,' she says, 'that makes nonsense of life. In *The Relapse* you had one Indian and three black actors and there was no problem until you had the confrontation of the brothers. That's when the audience started to talk and me too. When you make nonsense of the possibilities I find it less than challenging. It becomes tokenistic.'

John Adams, whose production it was, denies tokenism. His policy at Birmingham is to reflect the multi-racial pluralism of the West Midlands. Thus recently he has had a black Banquo in *Macbeth*, a black Maria (so to speak) in *The School For Scandal*, and in Priestley's *When We Are Married* a black daughter of white parents. Audiences, he claims, have largely accepted this without demur. The real problem, he says, lies with the critics. 'That is sad for two reasons. It confirms the prejudices of diehard sections of the audience and it possibly deters potential black customers.'

But there seems to me a right way and a wrong way to break through tradition. The right way is to cast according to talent: the wrong way is to positively discriminate and cast an actor in a role he or she is not up to. At a stroke, that sets back the whole cause of non-traditional casting. Yvonne Brewster puts her finger on it when she says, 'I don't think positive discrimination is necessary because we have such a marvellous set of actors around. As a director, I don't want to be discriminated for or against. If I'm a load of rubbish I don't want people to employ me. I don't want to be patronised.'

Josette Simon, who resists being typed as a black actress, concurs. But although she resists being seen either as a role-model or a spokesperson, the blunt fact is she has gone further than any black performer in playing classical and contemporary roles at the RSC and the National. What exactly is her philosophy? 'I think more doors should be open to all. But you have to be clear about what you are doing. If the experiences the character goes through are related to colour, then it's difficult for someone who isn't that colour to play the part. If the primary thing is the kind of person they are, then anyone can play the role. But I still have a problem with white actors playing Othello. Regardless of the qualities that make up Othello's character, the colour of his skin is a primary part of him. What I find deeply uncomfortable is a white actor putting black stuff on his face. If I'd put white make-up on to play Isabella, I'd have felt a complete twit.'

I see that. I also understand the argument that white actors have long enjoyed an historical monopoly and that black actors should be given every opportunity to play the few roles (like Othello or the Emperor Jones) where colour seems a pre-requisite. But is *Othello* primarily about blackness or Moorishness? Isn't it also about the temperamental insecurity of an outsider and the credulity of a jealous nature? May not white actors understand that as well as black? On a lower level, the role of the Engineer in *Miss Saigon* is about rapacity more than it is about race which is why the brouhaha from American Equity, however comprehensible in human terms, seems somewhat misplaced.

Everyone agrees that casting has loosened up in Britain. Peter Plouviez, the General Secretary of Equity, reminds me that 25 years ago the union recommended 'the casting of artists, as far as possible, in accordance with their ability as performers regardless of racial origins.' In the last quarter-century things have marginally improved in that there is a large pool of black talent and a few attempts at imaginative casting. But are we going far enough fast enough? Two people who think not are Philip Hedley and Jatinder Verma. Philip Hedley runs the enormously buoyant Theatre Royal, Stratford East, which puts on a high proportion of black and Asian plays: a reflection of the fact that it is a community theatre in a 40 per cent Afro-Asian borough. What is equally remarkable is that, if first nights are anything to go by, it has also got the most integrated audiences I have ever seen in Britain.

But Hedley raises a number of vital questions. He suggests playwrights could do infinitely more to open up non-traditional casting: he cites the example of Barrie Keeffe handing him the script for *My Girl*, a Leytonstone love-story, and saying 'Either character could be either colour' (in the event the man was white, the woman was Asian). Hedley also thinks it a disgrace that there is not and never has been a black or Asian director running a building-based company in Britain (and when, he adds, did you ever see a non-white face in a West End orchestra-pit?)? More controversially he floats the idea of a quota system that would require all theatres, and the large national companies most especially, to reflect the racial diversity of Britain. The danger there is that you start playing a bureaucratic numbers game and that you impose change arbitrarily from without instead of allowing it to come voluntarily from within.

Jatinder Verma, however, interestingly wants to re-define the whole notion of 'integration'. On one level, it means providing a simulacrum of contemporary Britain. 'But,' he says, 'what fascinates me is the aesthetic consequence of putting a Yorkshireman next to a Scotsman next to an African next to an Asian on stage. The signs they represent by different ways of speaking English and different colours of skin suggest a possibility of cultural encounters, of different world views operating on the same text. That, in terms of its implications on the theatrical language, is immensely exciting.'

It is an idea Mr Verma hopes to pursue at the National Theatre Studio; and in a sense it is precisely what Peter Brook has done in Paris with his International Centre for Theatrical Research culminating in his productions of *The Mahabharata* and *The Tempest*. The result with Brook is not a bland internationalism but a sense that each actor brings his own cultural history on stage with him. I don't think even Brook has resolved all the questions this provokes. In *The Tempest*, for instance, I found that Sotigui Kouyate's Prospero had an austere spirituality but little of the character's emotional dynamic. But the miracle of Brook's production was the way it overturned stereotype and in the end made one colour-blind to the Franco-British-African-Oriental mix.

In Britain we are a long way off achieving that kind of harmonious integration. Indeed the whole debate about colour-blind casting takes place in an unfortunate context. We are living in a society where the theatre is being marginalised, undermined and even suppressed by the disastrous underfunding of the past decade: this government will be remembered as the one that helped to dismantle the British theatre. But even though survival is currently the name of the game, the theatre has to ask itself the key question: why does the work that takes place on our stages for the most part reflect a cultural apartheid (black plays for black audiences, white plays for white audiences) that is not that dissimilar to South Africa?

Josette Simon gets it right when she says, 'You really only change things by doing them.' Having been told at drama school that she would find it virtually impossible to do classical work and having been asked by some directors 'What does it mean to be black?' in the same way they'd ask 'What does it mean to have a wooden leg?' she has helped to make her own luck. The mere fact that she has played Shakespearean heroines and Miller's Maggie and has Hedda Gabler within her sights is worth a bevy of forums, discussion-papers and articles. But actors by themselves cannot change the system. The impetus for change has to come from the writers, directors and casting-directors who finally determine who does what. With a few honourable exceptions (including the RSC, the National, Stratford East, the Tricycle and the Birmingham Rep) our theatrical makers and shakers seem to be living in a white fantasy-land that bears no relation to modern Britain.

Thatcher's Downfall

26 November 1990

Spare a thought this morning for Ray Cooney. The premise of his West End farce, *Out Of Order*, is that a Tory junior minister is trying to get some nooky in a Westminster hotel while living in mortal terror of Mrs

Thatcher. It is hard to imagine the likes of Major, Hurd or Heseltine, one of whose names will have to be substituted, instilling sweaty panic or cramping Donald Sinden's libido. But that only highlights the extent to which the events of last week out-gunned anything on the West End stage in their unique blend of Shakespearean history, Greek tragedy and Whitehall farce.

It is ironic that everyone has dipped into the Bard to describe Thatcher's downfall: it was, after all, her shift from public subsidy to corporate sponsorship that helped to drive Shakespeare off all but a tiny handful of our stages. David Owen and others have also rather cornily looked to *Julius Caesar* for parallels with Mrs T's demise. True, Mrs Thatcher, like Shakespeare's Caesar, had a penchant for 'sleek-headed men' and I suppose it is just possible to see Howe as an agonising Brutus and Heseltine as a lean and hungry Cassius. But it is a bit difficult to cast Norman Tebbit in the role of the sexy hedonist, Mark Antony.

It is to the English history plays that one has to look for real parallels. Many would favour *Richard III*: the story of a man who, while apparently observing legitimacy of succession, hacks out a path to an increasingly isolated absolutism. But there is a demonic gaiety about Richard Crookback far removed from the hectoring style of Gladys Hacksaw.

No: a far better parallel can be found in *Richard II*. He is capricious, impetuous, authoritarian, surrounded by favourites and plagued by insoluble Irish problems. ('We will ourselves in person to this war' even has a vaguely Thatcherite ring.) Returning from Ireland, he also finds support slipping away towards the ambitious Heseltinian figure of Bolingbroke: as Richard says, 'All souls that will be safe fly from my side, For time hath set a blot upon my pride.' Wednesday night in Downing Street must have been exactly like the scene at Barkloughly Castle where a succession of messengers enter bearing news that makes the abdication of the king inevitable. In defeat Richard, like Mrs Thatcher, acquires a sympathy-vote he never achieved in power. But there is an even more serious parallel: the extent to which both, despite swingeing taxes, allowed the realm to fall into disrepair.

Think of the speech where an anonymous First Man compares the kingdom to a garden which 'Is full of weeds, her fairest flowers choked up, Her fruit trees all unpruned, her hedges ruined, Her knots disordered and her wholesome herbs Swarming with caterpillars.' Not too bad a description of the sleazy, polluted, crime-filled, traffic-ridden island we inhabit today.

But there is also more than a touch of Greek tragedy about Thatcher's fall. You find the right ingredients of hubris, hamartia (the fatal character-flaw), peripeteia (swift reversal of fortune) and, above all, dramatic irony. Oedipus seeks to cleanse Thebes of the plague which turns out to be himself: pure irony. The Downing Street propaganda-machine rubbishes Sir Geoffrey Howe thereby provoking his resignation and precipitating the leader's downfall.

But the political theatre of the past week has also had its necessary element of farce. There was the spectacle of Mrs Thatcher breathlessly running down the steps of the British Embassy Residence in Paris to announce her fatal second-ballot candidature (proving that those who live by television also die by it). There was the sight of her playing to the gallery at the Despatch Box on Thursday like the last of the Red Hot Mummers. Above all there were the laughably hypocritical affirmations of unswerving loyalty by ministers whom we now know were busy advising her on Wednesday night that the game was up, Carruthers.

Inevitably *The Thatcher Follies* had to come off (production-costs were mounting, box-office take was falling and the show was alienating the European audience) but one wonders whether the new production will be half as dramatic. I commend, in fact, to Messrs Major, Hurd and Heseltine the words of the Duke of York in *Richard II* who tells us that life is like a theatre where the eyes of men, 'After a well graced actor leaves the stage, Are idly bent on him that enters next Thinking his prattle to be tedious.' I wouldn't call Mrs Thatcher well graced but, if I were Major, I'd start dusting off the tightrope-walking act.

1991

The clouds began to lift. In the first PMT (post Margaret Thatcher) year in over a decade, one sensed a touch of hope. The recession still bit and Damoclean deficits hung in the air. But, after a parched six months, new plays on big issues began to pour in. And, at the year's end, Arts Minister Tim Renton was able to announce a 14% increase in government subsidy for the coming year: as Ned Sherrin sagely remarked, it made one wish that we had General Elections rather more often.

Opinions were mixed about many of the year's new plays, but at least no-one could say that that theatre was standing by on the sidelines. David Hare's

Murmuring Judges not only offered a devastating critique of the British legal system but was also flamboyantly and gloriously operatic in its structure. In an age obsessed with style and surface (a subject Hare himself addressed in a memorable TV interview on *The Late Show*) Timberlake Wertenbaker's *Three Birds Alighting On A Field* entered a passionate plea for the moral value of art and the transforming beauty of English landscape painting. Harold Pinter's *Party Time* pinned down, with cryptic precision, the danger of bourgeois indifference to society's cruelties. And from Chile (courtesy of the London International Festival of Theatre) came Ariel Dorfman's *Death And The Maiden* which asked a fundamental question: how the individual in an emergent democracy copes with past persecution.

One of my great fears as a critic has always been that the theatre would become irrelevant: an escapist pleasure-hatch, a sideshow operating at the margins of society, a quilted *divertissement* with music attached. In the West End, the ultimate exemplar of market-forces, it often does seem precisely that. But, as one nears the end of two decades, one can see the theatre beginning to recover some of its old moral and political ground. 1991 had its usual elements of bilious farce – not least the clumsily-handled choice of a successor to Max Stafford-Clark at the Royal Court – but at least there was a feeling of a theatre that intermittently reflected society rather than standing loftily apart.

Ken Campbell

10 January 1991

Ken Campbell is the British theatre's antic visionary. You don't find him much quoted in sobersided academic books on post-war drama, but underneath the anarchic actor-comedian lurks a shrewd impresario and unacknowledged pioneer. It was the Ken Campbell Roadshow that from 1971 to 1974 showcased such remarkable talents as Bob Hoskins and Sylvester McCoy (the ultimate Dr Who). And it was Campbell who in the eight-hour *Illuminatus*, which opened the Cottesloe, tapped a popular hunger for the inordinate and who in the 22-hour, *The Warp* patented promenade theatre ('the kind of thing Bill Bryden almost got knighted for,' he unrancorously points out). Campbell is both a genial nutter and a genuine pathfinder.

Two hours spent in his company is a roller-coaster ride through a series of subjects: the para-normal, British rep in the Sixties, Science Fiction, the dangers of TV addiction (Campbell has a new play on the subject called *Wogan's Potatoes*) and his new theory of acting, Phreno-logical Pphorming.

We met in the cafe at Riverside Studios (his more regular office is an outdoor picnic table on Walthamstow Marshes) where he is about to open a solo show cryptically entitled *Furtive Nudist*. Our conversation became a quasi-public entertainment as heads craned to catch some of Campbell's odd anecdotes and aperçus.

Ken Campbell might be described as the Acceptable Face of Essex Man. Born in Ilford in 1941, he soon revealed the only child's talent for insubordination and obsession. At school, he was instinctively sceptical: if a teacher said there had been no epic written in English since *Paradise Lost*, he would chirp up 'What about Hiawatha, Sir?'. On cross-country runs he and others would hide under the bushes to listen to fantastic tales spun by an older pupil whom Campbell mysteriously refers to as The Prophet (last sighted in Madagascar). And the rising Ken discovered a whole range of mind-bending books: *The Dawn Of Magic* by Puwels and Bergier and American Charles Fort's trilogy, *The Book Of The Damned*, *Lo*! and *Weird Talents*. 'I don't,' he says, 'believe in the para-normal. But I allow or enjoy it.'

Gnomes and fairies are among the things Campbell allows: not surprisingly since he himself, with his gleaming dome and outsize ears, could pass for Puck's Dad. But teleportation – the idea that people or things can be imaginatively transported – is what fascinates him. He outlines the case, expanded upon in *Furtive Nudist*, of a tubby Newfoundland actor called Andy Jones whom Campbell believes he unwittingly teleported in the early Seventies.

If anyone else told you such stories, you would scoff. But Campbell has the childlike innocence of the born yarn-spinner and the flickering mischief of the instinctive comic. He is not some psychic proselytiser but simply a recorder of bizarre phenomena who believes that imagination should be fun. And as he recounts, in that cawing Ilford voice, hilarious stories of his early days at RADA and in rep, you realise that he is a natural anarch and wrecker of pretension.

'I remember at Colchester they got in a Canadian who decided to do a Method production of *Macbeth*. He asked us all to go away and write essays on our characters and read them out one morning before coffee-break. I was playing Angus who comes on in Act One Scene Two with the stage-direction "Enter Ross and Angus". Nobody addresses him nor does he speak. So my essay asked whether they were pointedly ignoring him and if so why. Had they perhaps not seen him? Was he a dwarf? I followed these enquiries through the text and my essay made a bigger difference to the production than anything else. Whenever knots of thanes gathered together at court you could see them muttering, 'Aha, it's that smelly dwarf, Angus, again.'

Campbell was obviously a comic trapped inside an actor's skin. His particular forte, learned from Hugh Hastings, was stealing the show while playing third-act detectives in rep thrillers. The revolutionary technique was first to learn the lines (instead of reading them from a notebook) and then go round the stage looking for clues. Things reached such a pitch of hilarity in one production of *Signpost For Murder* that the lead actor first threw a fire bucket at Campbell's head and then threatened to kill him. A distraught Campbell asked the director what he should do.

'I was told there was only one sure way to stop an audience laughing. You've got to come on, deliver your first line, dry, and wait for an audible prompt. You won't get a laugh for the rest of the scene. Sure enough, it worked. At the end of the week, the leading lady came up and said she had been worried about my detective at first but now it was a performance of real strength.'

Under the jokes lies a serious point: Campbell's enemies were tat and pretension. But discovering that impersonation was not entirely his bag, he rapidly branched out into writing and direction. Typically, he started out as director of the shallow end, acting bits in an aqua-version of *Treasure Island* at Bournemouth Baths (The Blind Pew routine was apparently sensational with him running round the diving boards like Mr Magoo). At Stoke-on-Trent Campbell turned dramatist, producing scripts for commercial TV as well as for the resident company. What is striking is his lack of vanity. When he wrote a play about highway-man Jack Sheppard he turned up on the first day with bound scripts, told the actors 'It'll be a sorry day if we ever had to open these' and proceeded to re-write the show round the actors' personalities.

But it was the Ken Campbell Roadshow, initially a collection of bar-room tales, that tapped his gift for story-telling and discovering talent. The initial idea came from Simon Hoggart who suggested a show based on modern folk-myths such as The Vanishing Grandmother and The Ghostly Hitch-Hiker.

'The first series,' says Campbell, 'had Bob Hoskins who did The Man With An Earwig In His Brain. You could actually tell where the earwig had got to just by the look on Bob's face. But we discovered you can't do dramatic sketches in northern working men's clubs, so we came up with the stunt show featuring Sylvester McCoy.'

It was this that produced such legendary feats as the ferret down the trousers (Campbell's ferret, McCoy's trousers), the banging a nail into your head and the setting light to an object with the power of your mind. Without knowing it, Campbell, through the Roadshow, was fulfilling Peter Brook's ideal of Rough Theatre: popular, comic, full of oral myth and primitive magic.

But the striking thing about Campbell is that, working on hunch and instinct, he is a creator of prototypes. After working in rep for Richard Eyre at Nottingham, he created the Science Fiction Theatre of Liverpool in 1976. It was partly triggered off by a conversation with Brian Aldiss, who lamented the bifurcation of the novel that had taken place in 1939. Pre-1939, someone like H.G. Wells could write serious novels and fantasies: after that date, genres were hived off so that Sci Fi became a separate category in the wrong end of the bookshop. Campbell felt theatre had followed the path of the serious novel and so set about what he calls the de-furcation of drama.

The result was a series of epic spectaculars including *Illuminatus, The Warp* and *The Hitch-Hiker's Guide To The Galaxy*. Once again Campbell showed an impresario's nose for talent. Jim Broadbent and David Rappaport were in *Illuminatus*. Tim Albery organised the mammoth sets for Neil Oram's *The Warp*. How did Campbell fund it?

'By lying to the Arts Council. We told them it was going to be a modest little eight-hander. We ended up with a cast of 50.'

But perhaps the psychological clue to Campbell is that he is both prey to and recorder of ungovernable obsessions. At one point, for instance, he found he was becoming hopelessly addicted to TV news. 'I finally got cured,' he says 'in the Isle of Wight. I was sitting on the lav in a hotel in Ventnor looking at this old lino. It took me back to childhood when I was sent into the loo during an air-raid. I used literally to perform in there to creatures I could see in the lino. It was as if the TV addiction had stopped me talking to myself and it was remembering childhood experience that cured me.' But out of the addiction sprang a fascination with TV abolitionist movements and a play about a family destroyed by a manic preoccupation with the box.

Campbell, however, is no fanatic about TV. He profitably works for it. He also allows his 12-year-old daughter, Daisy, whom he amicably shares with her mother, Prunella Gee to watch it. He is a mixture of ingredients: populist and pioneer, clown and seer, sharp pragmatist and purveyor of the paranormal. Such dualities are also at the heart of his new theory of acting, Phrenological Pphorming, which involves the idea that the human face represents distinct halves of the personalities: acting is a matter of recognising and utilising this division. Pressed to explain his own twin profiles he describes himself as 'a mixture of inept housewife and spanking squire'. That ready self-analysis confirms my suspicion that Campbell has one of the shrewdest brains in British theatre.

The Homecoming

Comedy: 12 January 1991

Plays are not static objects. Their meaning is changed by time, place and the chemistry of casting. Twenty five years ago at the Aldwych, Harold Pinter's *The Homecoming* offered an image of a domestic jungle filled with ferocious predators. Watching Peter Hall's magically precise new production at the Comedy, it becomes much more a play about triumphant female assertiveness. The play has changed; but then so have we.

Even back in 1965 it was recognised that the homecoming referred to was that of Ruth: the wife of an expatriate academic, Teddy, who is brought home to meet his North London tribal brood and who is claimed by the family and set up in business as a whore. But what once seemed a Lorenz-like study in jungle law now becomes an image of self-fulfilment.

In this production Ruth seems to be escaping from a patronising academic chauvinist to rediscover her roots, her real identity and a world that allows her to be a manipulative queen-bee. To call Pinter a feminist would be pitching it strong; but he certainly presents us with a female victory over masculine arrogance and sterility.

This new vision of the play is the result both of social upheaval and subtle shifts of emphasis in Hall's direction. Greg Hicks here plays Teddy as an attenuated smoothie who has achieved intellectual equilibrium at the expense of his humanity and who treats his wife as part of his American academic doll's house ('You can help me with my lectures when we get back,' has a chilling Ibsenite ring). And Cherie Lunghi's marvellous Ruth has both the lacquered poise of a high-class lady of the night and a sense of effortless superiority to the brutish male clan by whom she is confronted. A smile of amusement constantly plays about her peach-coloured lips as if she sees through all the bull-swagger bravado.

But it is a sign of the richness of Pinter's play that it operates on several levels: as sexual myth, family drama and social comedy. By casting Warren Mitchell as Max, the patriarchal ex-butcher, Hall brings out particularly the play's Cockney-Jewish humour and Pinter's sharp awareness of the way sentimentality frequently dissolves into aggression.

Flat-capped and white-plimsolled, Mr Mitchell is at his funny-ferocious best at the start of the second act. One minute he is oozing unctuous family solicitude (as he cries 'What fun we used to have in the bath, eh boys?' his three sons raise their tea-cups in mutual astonishment); the next he is ranting about his bastard sons and his slutbitch of a wife. Mr Mitchell catches exactly the contradictions inside this ailing North London monster.

But, as always, Pinter also shows how language is used as an instrument of control. You see this most clearly in Nicholas Woodeson's Lenny, the pimp-son, who specialises in the Cockney piss-take and in employing graphic descriptions of his innate violence as a weapon of seduction. The least articulate characters are the ones most easily preyed upon: here John Normington as Max's chauffeur-brother, a beautiful study in ageing impotence, and Douglas McFerran as the failed pug, Joey, out of whom words are uneasily wrenched like money from a piggy-bank.

The scale of the Comedy Theatre means that John Bury's set, an essay in echoing grey-walled emptiness, doesn't quite have the monumentality it did at the Aldwych. But the heartening thing about the evening is that it is not a carbon copy of something that happened 25 years ago.

You are reminded once again of Pinter's iron verbal and visual control. But this time round, the family's crude, vituperative energy seems preferable to Teddy's philosophical detachment, and Ruth's final assumption of the roles of Madonna and Whore seems like a triumph of emancipation rather than a mark of captivity. The result is like seeing a familiar landmark in an exhilaratingly new light.

Shakespeare In Europe

18 April 1991

I take out my bankcard. In the bottom right-hand corner is a picture of Shakespeare over-printed with the words 'Cheque guarantee'. But hold the card up to the light and something strange happens. The colour, form and angle of Shakespeare's face alters: in profile he seems to be a beaming Bard, head-on he is a sombre sage. The picture is a kitsch symbol of a basic truth. Shakespeare stands for order, security, reliability. At the same time, he is shifting, elusive, infinitely variable. It is a duality which lies at the heart of the modern Shakespeare industry.

Others have written eloquently about Shakespeare's double role as national icon and pluralistic dramatist. Terence Hawkes in *That Shakespeherian Rag* shows how modern critics – Bradley, Raleigh,

Dover Wilson – all accommodated Shakespeare to their own world view. For the aptly-named Walter Raleigh in 1907 Shakespeare indeed became a symbol of maleness, Englishness and even linguistic imperialism. As Hawkes remarks, 'Shakespeare is always a powerful ideological weapon available in time of crisis.' For politicians he is constantly a handy source of quotation: on the day of the Gulf ceasefire, Sir Julian Amery remarked of Saddam Hussein, 'We have scotched the snake, not killed it,' (apparently forgetting these words are spoken by, and not about Macbeth). For business enterprises, Shakespeare is a potent commercial weapon. In a recent Stratford programme, British Telecom had an advert telling us that 'Poor communication was the death of those star-crossed lovers, Romeo and Juliet. While the speed and clarity of today's communications might well have saved them.' Though, personally, I wouldn't bank on it.

So, on the one hand, we have the Stratford lad as symbol of national pride and quality goods; and, before we sneer at cultural imperialism, I should add that there is something moving about watching British companies, as I can testify, playing Shakespeare to large, attentive, Bard-hungry throngs in places as diverse as Athens and Tbilisi.

But, on the other hand, there is the infinitely more mysterious Shakespeare: the dramatist of no fixed abode whose work takes on new resonances in different cultures. In Europe he seems European: in Asia, Asian. And of his booming popularity there is no doubt. The sold-out productions in Paris this spring have been Peter Zadek's *Mésure Pour Mésure* and Peter Brook's *La Tempête*. In Hamburg on a recent Sunday night, I found there was a choice at the two major theatres between Jürgen Flimm's *Was Ihr Wollt* (*Twelfth Night*) and Michael Bogdanov's *Romeo Und Julia*. No wonder the Germans call him 'unser Shakespeare'.

Sampling recent Euro-Shakespeare productions, I discovered several facts. One is that the current Bard-boom is not just a testament to his genius but a direct comment on the universal dearth of new dramatists. Another is that he reverses the old adage that poetry is what gets lost in translation: in fact, it is Shakespeare's prose that is curiously untranslatable. And, most crucially of all, that there is gain as well as loss in freeing Shakespeare from the rigorous explicitness of the English tongue. There is a mythical quality in his work which transcends language and may even be liberated by a foreign perspective.

As a classic example I would take Jürgen Flimm's stunning production of *Was Ihr Wollt* at Hamburg's Thalia Theater which I saw three days after Peter Hall's fine version at the Playhouse.

Like Hall, Flimm recognises that this is a play dominated by the sea: the Hamburg setting is a tilted circular greensward behind which is a cut-out cave leading on to a shimmering marine perspective. But Flimm enjoys certain practical advantages not found in England: one is the luxury of twelve weeks' rehearsal (Hall had six). Another is a continental philosophy of lighting which creates mystery by casting the forestage in shadow. What is most striking, however, is the way Teutonic intellectualism, which we casually deride, turns *Twelfth Night* into an exploration of the Platonic idea of love as a link between the sensible and the eternal world.

Eros is the guiding spirit of Flimm's production, which pushes the play's sexual confusion further than any version I have seen. Claudia Kaske's bosomy Olivia finds in Annette Paulmann's Cesario an image of perfection which leads her to unbutton her bodice and hitch up her skirts in a direct attempt at seduction. Jan Josef Liefers's self-loving. Orsino looks curiously like Cesario whom he clasps to his bosom and cradles lovingly in his lap. And Sebastian and Antonio embrace not only each other but the Platonic idea that truth and beauty may be achieved by mutual affection between persons of the same sex. Released from English inhibitions, the play becomes a study in the varieties of Platonic love.

What you lose in German even in Reinhard Palm's good, Schlegel-based translation is the pun-filled richness of the comedy. Feste, the emotional key to Hall's production, is here a mere cipher: it is fascinating to note that a line like 'I live by the church' loses its double-meaning in German. If the production is still very funny, it is because Flimm compensates physically for what is lost verbally. His Sir Toby, for instance, is a balletic, balloon-panted drunk who, at the prospect of Malvolio's yellow stockings, hurls himself thrice to the ground with a ferocity unseen since the heyday of Norman Wisdom. And Maria, at the same point, actually wets her knickers with excitement. But, for all the comic excess, the mythical power of the play still emerges and there are two moments of pure mastery: Viola vehemently stripping off her tunic on 'Disguise, I see thou art a wickedness' and the vengeful, anguished cries of Malvolio reverberating off-stage during Feste's plangent final song.

As Flimm's production shows, something strange happens when you lose the English language and context: you release the play's metaphorical power. It is an issue which directors Peter Brook and Peter Stein recently debated. Stein, who dispatched his Berlin actors to Warwickshire before even attempting *As You Like It*, believes you can research your way into Shakespeare's truth. Brook argued that you inevitably lose 70 per cent of Shakespeare in translation but that some mysterious quiddity remains. I would go even further and say that foreign Shakespeare, because it is a kind of analogue to the original, sometimes uncovers aspects of the work we have forgotten.

The case of Peter Zadek is especially fascinating. He was born in Berlin, came to England as a child in 1933 and returned to Germany in 1958 to become one of the country's most controversial directors. His two most recent Shakespeare productions – *Der Kaufman von Venedig* (*The Merchant Of Venice*) for the Vienna Burgtheater and *Mésure pour Mésure* for the Odéon in Paris – are particularly fascinating: both offer partial visions of the play concerned while, at the same time, forcing you to rethink its meaning.

Zadek's *Merchant* was certainly bold and radical in that it subordinated questions of anti-Semitism to an examination of capitalist morality. He set the action in contemporary Wall Street and cast as Shylock a blond, indisputably Aryan actor, Gert Voss, who could, as Zadek said, play Siegfried or an SS officer. This led to a totally assimilated Shylock whose hatred of Antonio was financial rather than racial. It also produced one richly comic moment when Eva Mattes's Portia, arriving in court, turned to the Homburg-hatted Antonio and asked 'Ist Ihr Name Shylock?' at which point Voss tetchily interposed, 'Shylock ist *mein* Name.'

By underplaying the racial aspect, Zadek reminded us that the real protagonist of *The Merchant* is money: money lent, borrowed, sought and invested. Solario and Solanio became a couple of small-time brokers busily reading the financial papers. Bassanio turned up in Belmont with his business cronies who offered shrewd market advice about which casket to plump for. And Shylock in the trial became less an heroic victim than a cool capitalist: advised to have a surgeon standing by, he spent a good couple of minutes scanning the contract and, at the end, far from being devastated by his losses he wrote out promissory-notes and made a dignified exit presumably to ring up his Swiss bank manager.

In one sense, Zadek's reading works against the text. If you deprive Shylock of any overt sense of alienation or persecution, you simply make him a bloodthirsty version of Michael Douglas's Gekko rather than an historically tormented figure seeking a legitimate revenge. But you also highlight another aspect of the play: the fact that Venice is, in Sigurd Burckhardt's words, 'a closed world, inherently conservative, because it knows that it stands or falls with the sacredness of contracts.' Just, in fact, like Wall Street.

I felt much the same ambivalence recently while watching Zadek's French production of *Mésure Pour Mésure* at the Odéon in Paris. What one gained, largely because of an astounding performance by Isabelle

Huppert, was fresh insight into the character of Isabella as well as into the cynicism of a Catholic culture about religious dissembling. What one lost was that pecularily Shakespearian juxtaposition of the earthy and the sublime, the prosaic and the poetic. Shakespeare's comedy simply doesn't travel well.

Huppert, however, reminded us that great acting is something that almost transcends language. In Britain the tendency is to play Isabella ('More than our brother is our chastity') as a figure of righteous moral fervour: Huppert made her a woman constantly torn between the call of the cloister and the demands of the flesh. Preparing to enter the order of St Clare, she was all tremulous uncertainty as she gazed wistfully in a vanity-mirror, while wiping off her lipstick. In her great confrontations with Angelo she was, to borrow a phase of Arnold Bennett's, 'flushed and thrilling with virginity': she also took seriously on board Angelo's arguments about female fragility, readily admitting 'nous sommes tendres comme l'est notre complexion.' But Huppert also made Isabella sufficiently worldly to whip off her wimple and share a glass of bubbly with the Duke, to win Mariana round to the bed-trick with insouciant gaiety and, at the last, nervously to slip her hand into the Duke's.

What you lose in French is the leprous comedy of the Viennese gaol-scenes here translated by Mr Zadek into a crude *Galgenhumor*. Pompey's great speech about the prison-inmates ('wild Halfcan that stabbed Pots') here became the excuse for him to enter with a female corpse whose leg he proceeded to saw off like a bungling conjurer. All this in spite of a superb translation by Jean-Michel Deprats that made one question Jean-Louis Barrault's assertion that Shakespeare's entry on the French stage begins with a crime in that 'in order to cross the Channel he has to be shorn of his poetic garb.'

Well does he? Deprats wrote a fascinating article in the Paris programme describing how the simplest phrases are often the most untranslatable. How, he asked, do you render Claudio's definition of death 'This sensible warm motion to become a kneaded clod.' In fact, he does it very well: '. . . Ce corps sensible, chaud, mobile devenir/Un motte de terre glaise.'

That at least has the right balance and sense of metamorphosing decay.

It also seems preferable to Jean-Claud Carrière's prose paraphrase for Peter Brook's 1978 Paris production, which renders the same passage as: '. . .cette chaleur sensible qui bouge devenir une pâte boueuse.' Carrière gives you the sense while Deprats gives you a hint of the Shakespearian rhythm.

But what are the lessons for us in Britain about Shakespeare's ability to change colours with the chameleon? Some would argue that we should enjoy the same freedom as foreign directors and treat the plays as myths to be plundered rather than texts to be minded. But if a British director gave us a Samurai *Macbeth* or a Noh-theatre *Tempest*, it would smack of tourist exoticism. Indeed the point is almost provable.

When Yuri Lyubimov directed *Hamlet* in Moscow with the folk-hero Visotski, and a mobile woollen curtain, the production seemed to evolve from a first-hand knowledge of Russian tyranny; when he recreated the same production with British actors, it never achieved the same impact because the style was imposed from without rather than growing from within.

My belief is that, in practice, there are two basic modern approaches to Shakespeare's multi-dimensionality. One is to anchor the plays in local experience in order to achieve universality: a classic example is Richard Eyre's *Richard III* which was filled with English iconography (khaki soldiery, Edwardian banquets, sun-dappled pastoral backcloths) but which reportedly achieved immediate resonance in East European countries. The other approach, adopted by Peter Brook in *La Tempête*, is to bring together actors of different colours, races and backgrounds and exploit their individuality: in Britain today, given the diversity of our society, we have a golden opportunity to attempt a multi-racial Shakespeare which still largely goes begging.

We cannot help but see Shakespeare in terms of our own language, history and culture; but we need urgently to widen that definition of culture not by doing ludicrous, down-market pop travesties of the plays but by working towards racially integrated productions.

Only then will we begin to reach the heart of the mysteriously shifting and elusive figure on the bank-card.

New Plays

4 May 1991

New writing for theatre is in a state of crisis. Of course, new plays are still written: around a hundred a year in the grant-aided theatre. Some are good. But for a variety of reasons – financial, political and cultural – new drama no longer occupies the central position it has in British theatre over the past 35 years.

The West End is drying up as a source of new material: the

unsatisfying *Silly Cow* and the genial *Jeffrey Bernard Is Unwell* (aside from long-runners like *Run For Your Wife* and *Mousetrap*) are currently the only plays that originated in the commercial heartland.

We have, of course, been spoilt. For more than three decades we have looked not just for regular supplies of new dramatists but for plays that put a large slice of the nation on stage. *Look Back In Anger* back in 1956 was, among many other things, a play about modern England: sex, politics, religion, the press were all in there. Peter Nichols's *The National Health* (1969) turned a decaying hospital ward into an epitome of the country at large; David Hare and Howard Brenton's *Brassneck* (1973) was a big family saga that caught the gamey aroma of municipal corruption; David Edgar's *Destiny* (1976) prophetically explored the rise of the National Front; and Ayckbourn's *A Small Family Business* (1987) was about the collapse of moral values in a society that sanctified greed.

All these plays took the moral temperature of society and stirred things up in a way I find increasingly rare. I don't want to sound too fell. Hare continues his analysis of British institutions with a play about the judiciary, *Murmuring Judges*, due at the Olivier in September. The Royal Court, Hampstead, the Bush and Stratford East keep up the quest for fresh voices. And new writing is, happily, becoming decentralised.

The West Yorkshire Playhouse has done a season of premieres. Ayckbourn's Scarborough venue has three new plays this summer. And Scotland boasts promising writers like Iain Heggie and Liz Lochhead. What troubles me is the small-scale nature of so much new writing and the way it increasingly privatises experience.

Money, as always, is at the root of the problem. The cutbacks of the past decade mean writers now instinctively think small: in the land of the deprived, the one-man show is king.

Jenny Topper, director of Hampstead Theatre, agonises over means of financing a new play by Jennifer Phillips that boasts a cast of ten: as she says, the optimum cast-size is now 'no more than six and preferably four'. But how can writers hope to deal with the broad range of human experience if they know in advance that they are doomed to shuffle round a pack of four?

Money is also a key factor in driving writers away from the theatre into television. A new play at a theatre like Hampstead will earn a writer a maximum of £5,000: a dramatist who knocked off seven segments of *EastEnders*, in less time than it takes to write a stage play, told me he earned £21,000. Writers are refreshingly honest about money. Peter Flannery told me that in 1982 he earned £2,000 for his three-hour social drama, *Our Friends In The North*, when it was staged in The Pit. More recently his superb TV series, *Blind Justice* – vintage political drama – earned him £90,000; and it might bring in more if BBC2 repeats it.

It's the old story: a playwright can make a killing in the theatre but he or she can't make a living. Only a tiny number makes more than £10,000 a year from the stage. So the temptation to write for TV is irresistible. That is fine if you are doing a Screen Two or a 4Play. But, as Flannery points out, the bread-and-butter writer on the soaps and long-running series is given stories and characters and is reduced to the status of a dialogue-writer. The symphonic skills needed to write a stage play are not called into being; and, as we know, organs atrophy through under-use.

What troubles me is that television uses theatre as a cheap recruitment facility without putting anything like enough back. Thames TV has an excellent scheme, with which I have long been involved, for offering bursaries to new writers. LWT also has a scheme for backing Plays on Stage. But these are the exceptions. A glance at the listings confirms that, without theatre, there would be virtually no TV drama at all.

In a recent week I noticed a 4Play by Daniel Mornin who, in 1987, wrote a promising play about Ulster, *Built On Sand* for the Theatre Upstairs. *Brookside*, that week, was the work of Peter Cox, who wrote a lovely play about the effects of the miner's strike on women, *The Garden Of England*, for 7:84. And don't I remember Don Webb, author of the sitcom *Joint Account*, as the man who once wrote a subversive comedy about colour-prejudice in business, *Black Ball Game*? Writers have to earn a living: TV has to be fed. But, at the moment, the economic blandishments of TV are so strong that writers are being snatched out of the nursery before they have had a chance to grow.

Television is having an aesthetic, as well as an economic, impact on the theatre. As Jenny Topper points out – and she should know since Hampstead Theatre still receives 1,200 scripts a year – 'there are fewer writers who know how to write for the stage. Plot development and structure have now become less formal and more casual because of TV. You feel a lot of dramatists simply haven't seen enough plays.'

In one way, theatre writing is bound to change under the influence of TV, film and pop video: Caryl Churchill has turned this to great advantage in plays like *Icecream* and *Mad Forest* by forging a new elliptical style in which the audience is obliged to make the connections between scenes. What makes the heart sink is the one-room, I'll-just-put-the-kettle-on kind of stage play, usually featuring a wrangle between mother and daughter or father and son, that seems no more than a slice of soap.

But new writing faces an even deeper problem, which is the inherent conservatism of a culture which prefers a sliced-up novel or a vapid musical to an original play.

Jenny Topper also suggests we explore the past at the expense of the present and mildly rebukes me for encouraging this tendency by my unremitting championship of European classics. But I have never suggested that researches in world drama should be conducted at the expense of the present: in a sane world, actors, writers, designers and directors would gain by moving effortlessly between the two.

This was the essence of Peter Hall's philosophy in opening up a London branch of the RSC in 1960. And it worries me more than somewhat that Adrian Noble's new-model RSC, while it has a number of writers under commission, vouchsafes no new work this season: the first time this has happened at Stratford, as someone pointed out, in 15 years.

But the new cultural conservatism goes deeper than that. It is only fair to point out that, under late Thatcherism, dramatists like Hare, Brenton and Ayckbourn formed a natural party of opposition by pointing up our moral decadence. At the same time, there has also been a palpable retreat from grappling directly with social realities.

Trevor Griffiths writes about the insidiousness of the class-system via the Chekhovian pastiche of *Piano*. Nick Dear and Howard Barker write about the patronage of the artists in *The Art Of Success* and *Scenes From An Execution* by going back to previous centuries. Timberlake Wertenbaker movingly demonstrates the power of drama in the historical *Our Country's Good* and the silencing of women in the mythical *The Love Of The Nightingale*. These are all fine plays and the past can be an effective metaphor for the present. But historical obliqueness can also turn into an evasion-tactic and a way of disguising the urgency of one's message.

The crisis in new writing, if there is one, is mainly to do with scale and connection: a manifest decline in big plays capable of addressing a large audience and tapping a vibrant communal response. Brian Friel's *Dancing At Lughnasa* does both things triumphantly; so too did Hare's *Racing Demon* and Flannery's *Singer*.

But too many plays today lack either emotional generosity or abundant theatricality. What is more the audiences are noticing: a West End producer told me recently the audience for most new plays evaporates after six months when the original star departs. There are no easy solutions to the current crisis except the obvious ones: more money for new writing, greater managerial courage in putting new plays onto main-house stages, a more ardent response by writers to the form and pressure of the times and possibly a statutory levy on the BBC licence-fee and Independent Television profits to repay the considerable debt to the theatre.

New British drama from the mid-Fifties to the mid-Eighties enjoyed a period of creativity unparalleled since the Elizabethan era. But, unless something is done soon, the Golden Age will have turned to lead and simply be a source of critical nostalgia and academic record.

Black Poppies

Theatre Royal Stratford East: 23 May 1991

Black Poppies at the Theatre Royal Stratford East, is an excellent piece of investigative theatre: a gripping 80-minute documentary about the experiences of black servicemen from the Forties to the present day. It also fascinatingly complements Fred D'Aguiar's recent Royal Court play, *A Jamaican Airman Foresees His Death*: where that was a poetic exploration of wartime racism, this offers a pungent panorama of post-war Britain. In researching the play, the actors set out with tape-recorders to interview black ex-servicemen: the pattern is one of progressive disillusionment. West Indian volunteers in the Forties, proud to fight for the mother-country, find themselves homeless and jobless in post-war Britain. An aircraftsman in the Fifties and a bugler in the Seventies discover promotion blocked because of their colour. A regular who has risked his life in Northern Ireland is picked up by the cops as a suspected criminal immediately upon returning to civilian life. A military policeman, testifying to the beating up of a black recruit, angrily announces: 'It's a dirty system.'

But the evening is far from being a sustained cry of rage: there is much wit, humour and resilience in these first-hand memories. What emerges is a complex picture in which racism within the services accurately reflects that in the society at large: this is a world in which career-advancement is blocked, in which conformist blacks are regarded as honorary whites and in which there are precisely defined no-go areas ('You'll never find one black guy in the Guards'). *Black Poppies* starts out as a survey of the entrenched racism of the armed forces over the past 50 years: it ends up as a portrait of modern Britain.

The standard arguments against docu-drama of this kind are that it depends on edited truth, that it pre-empts an imaginative response to life and that it can be done better by other media. But I see no reason why the theatre should not be a repository of oral history, or why it should be exclusively a house of fiction. My only reservation is that the final testament, in which a military policeman describes the actions of a psychopathic sergeant, is turned into a piece of such blistering rhetoric that you lose sight of the hideous reality.

But John Burgess stages the evening skilfully and simply, alternating between group testimony and monologues. The cast of twelve, who did all the research, are also indivisibly good: if I had to pick out anyone it would be Roger Griffiths who, as a raw army recruit in Royston, describes the horrors of being given lessons in how to commit suicide and of an entertainment in which anyone who failed to make his superiors laugh was forced to run through a bonfire. At moments like these the show goes beyond race to become a savage critique of the military ethos.

Henry IV

Royal Shakespeare Theatre: 1 June 1991

I hedged my bets when Adrian Noble's production of *Henry IV* Part One opened the new Stratford season. Now Part Two has joined the repertory and, after seeing both plays in a single day, I am prepared to leap off the fence: this has matured into a magnificently rich achievement and marks a radical new approach to the staging of Shakespeare's Histories.

Mr Noble and his designer, Bob Crowley, have adapted a style that is increasingly common in the opera house: a rejection of realistic clutter in favour of a spare, lean neo-Expressionism. In Part One this takes the form of a stark visual contrast between the grey court and the scarlet stew of Eastcheap. In Part Two, a very different play, the implication is that all England is afflicted by a creeping, melancholy sickness.

This sense of national decay is here caught in two arresting images. At the end of the Eastcheap tavern scene, with its talk of mortality, the sleepless, unshaven King Henry wanders into the action, instantly linking the high life with the low. And later, on his expiry, the King is borne out through Shallow's Gloucestershire orchard filled with white-masked bee-keepers who resemble deaths-heads. If Part One is about contrasting worlds, Part Two reminds us that England is unified by the spectacle of national decline.

But Noble's strength is that he combines visual stylisation with psychological realism. Back in April I found Michael Maloney's Hal a rather shadowy figure but he has now grown into a watchful princeling desperate to pierce his father's emotional defences. In Part One he addresses his father like a nervous schoolboy with hands behind his back. But the great moment of revelation comes in Part Two when he begins to understand the cost of kingship: Mr Maloney apostrophises the crown as if it were an enemy 'that had before my face murdered my father' uttering the last words with a heart-wrenching, accusatory cry.

Mr Noble, in fact, makes you realise that the two plays might be sub-titled, after Turgenev, *Fathers And Sons*. If Hal is a son desperately seeking a father, Falstaff, in Robert Stephens's breathtaking performance, becomes a man in search of a filial substitute. He grows superbly from the guileful charmer of Part One into a much more vicious, predatory figure in Part Two: Stephens unsentimentally becomes the sharp-toothed 'old pike' prepared to snap at and devour his former crony, Shallow. But when Stephens momentarily breaks down on 'If I had a thousand sons', you realise the old knight is forever haunted by his childlessness.

Julian Glover's Henry is the third side of this complex emotional triangle and again there is a sense of long-range character-development. Seeing both plays, you realise that the austere Gordonstoun headmaster-figure of Part One conceals a man racked by paternal and monarchial guilt: Mr Glover makes it blindingly clear that his deathbed anger at the prospect of a future England 'sick with civil blows' stems from the realisation that he is the ultimate cause. He precisely embodies Auden's point that 'the body politic of England catches an infection from its family physician.'

Not everything in Part Two is perfect. The eruption of Pistol into the tavern becomes an excuse for some protracted Keystone Coppery. But there is a sense of a complete world on stage and of a company that bats all the way down. David Bradley's Shallow wonderfully combines physical frailty with the finicky precision of a bossy local magistrate. Philip Voss's Lord Chief Justice is not the usual stiff-backed prune but a man who treats Falstaff with the right amused condenscension. And Joanne Pearce's Doll Tearsheet is a tart of unusual vigour.

It is, incredibly, 16 years since we saw these twin peaks of Shakespeare's genius on the main Stratford stage. In Mr Noble's fine production they become a deeply moving study of the inter-action between the demanding claims of kingship and the indissoluble ties of kinship.

Hedda Gabler

Playhouse: 5 September 1991

'*Hedda Gabler* again?' remarked my companion. And it is true that the play has lately become the theatrical equivalent of a Number 11 bus: miss one and there'll be another along in a minute. But Fiona Shaw's performance in Deborah Warner's production, imported from the Abbey Theatre Dublin to the Playhouse, is so mesmerising as to obliterate any sense of *déjà vu*: the word, I think, has to be mind-blowing.

One mark of great acting is that it tears up the rule book. And, just as John Wood this year seemed to be inventing Lear on the spot, so Ms Shaw defies all conventions: in particular, the notion that you can't start on a high emotional pitch because you'll have nowhere to go. We first see this Hedda, in fact, in a pre-textual scene prowling round the drawing-room in darkness, possibly after sex with Tesman, in a state of sighing desperation: the question becomes not whether she will kill herself but simply when and how.

By daylight, Ms Shaw shows us a Hedda who has returned from her excruciating six-month honeymoon a total nervous wreck. Her hands flutter in the air like doves when they are not restlessly tearing up flower petals. Her eyes are forever darting about the room as if looking for an escape-hatch. Her laughter is flecked with mania. But she is shrewd enough to cover her despair under a defensive irony: when she comes to the celebrated phrase about 'vine-leaves in his hair' she lapses into the mock-heroic gestures of 19th-century melodrama.

Great acting not only breaks rules. It is unafraid to go over the top. And throughout the evening Ms Shaw takes the most hair-raising risks. She beats her fists against the creaking up-stage double-doors at hints of her pregnancy. She kicks the furniture all over the room after Judge Brack has signalled his determination to be cock of the walk. And she sings a Brahms lullaby to Lovborg's manuscript which she cradles in her arms before consigning it to the flames.

But Ms Shaw's amazing performance is underpinned by a clear understanding of Hedda's predicament: that she is the victim of her character as well as her situation. When Lovborg accuses her of being a coward, at bottom, she closes her eyes hard against the sound of an unbearable truth.

For us, however, it is an eye-opening performance and one that totally transforms the play; instead of the usual stately pavane we get a frenzied gallop. And Deborah Warner, whose recent productions of

The Good Person Of Sichuan and *Lear* I found slow and heavy, responds magnificently. In place of the familiar heavy-handed point-scoring, with a lowering portrait of General Gabler and much phallic fingering of his pistols, we get a production that is fast, jagged and mercurial and yet capable of profound emotion: Lovborg's desperation at the destruction of his life and work has never seemed so powerful.

This is partly because Robert O'Mahoney plays him as a wild, almost Byronic romantic rather than the bourgeois scribbler he has lately become. And there is equally good work from Garret Keogh as a Tesman with sufficient balls to almost throttle Hedda for her destruction of Lovborg's book and from Doreen Hepburn as a clucking Aunt Julie.

My only quibble would be that Hugh Ross's Judge Brack is short on sexual menace and that Ingrid Craigie's Mrs Elvsted lacks that delight in her own power over Lovborg which sets Hedda's teeth on edge.

But this remains much the best *Hedda Gabler* I have ever seen. The tendency these days is to treat the play as a social tract about the spiritual suffocation of 19th-century women. In the quickening hands of Shaw and Warner, it becomes a study of a particular beleaguered ironist driven to madness and death by the sound of the escape-hatches being successively bolted down. A great evening.

Murmuring Judges

Olivier: 12 October 1991

'Let's kill all the lawyers,' cries Shakespeare's Jack Cade in *Henry VI*. But although David Hare's projected trilogy about British institutions – beginning with *Racing Demon* and now continuing with *Murmuring Judges* at the Olivier – was partly triggered by seeing *The Plantagenets*, his new play is no simple Cade-like crack at the law. It is, in fact, an immensely rich, subtle and complex play about the rigid compartmentalisation of the judiciary, the police and the prison system.

Hare's skill, however, lies on the way he dramatises his discovery. He presents us, initially, with three distinct worlds. In one we see an Ulster fall-guy, McKinnon, dispatched to a vilely overcrowded gaol for his part in a warehouse robbery. In the seductive world of chambers, a star QC washes his hands of the case though his inquisitive black junior, Irina Platt, scents an injustice. And in a busy South London cop-shop a young detective-constable preens himself on getting McKinnon and his partners convicted even when his girlfriend, WPC Sandra Bingham, starts asking awkward questions.

What is fascinating is the way Hare gradually breaks down the barriers separating these three worlds. And it is no accident that it is women, excluded from clannish male values, who act as the unremitting seekers after truth. One of Hare's key points, in fact, is that each area of the law subscribes to the team ethic. The judiciary, with its arcane collegiate rituals, is seen as an exclusive, mainly masculine club. The cops, too, have their own private code of loyalty. And even in prison, Hare shows McKinnon getting savagely beaten up for betraying the criminal freemasonry.

In short, Hare sees the law as a microcosm of British society: one still dominated by rigid hierarchical fraternities. But Hare's great theatrical virtue is that he doesn't just tell: he shows. It is hard, in fact, to imagine a more exhilarating first-act climax, beautifully staged by Richard Eyre, than the one here.

In a tremendous triptych, we simultaneously see McKinnon languishing in his prison-cell, the promoted, bent cop setting off for a celebratory game of snooker and the flash QC and Irina settling into a plush Covent Garden stall. It is typical of Hare's tight-knit structure that the opera in question is *The Magic Flute* which deals with trials, freemasonry and the final triumph of light over darkness.

No play is flawless: and once or twice I was reminded of Bagehot's description of Dickens as a 'sentimental radical'. Irina's crusading zeal is weakened, rather than strengthened, by her apparent sexual affection for the wronged McKinnon.

Hare's wit, at its best Wildean, also sometimes seems prejudiced. 'If you run the country,' asks Irina, 'is it compulsory to go to the opera in the evening?' Better, I would argue, an Establishment that goes to Mozart than not. But this is to cavil at a play that combines a savage indignation at the ineffectualness of our penal system with a surprising sympathy for the poor bloody infantry of police and prison-officers who have to make a collapsing system work.

I leave it to others to judge the play's legal accuracy: what impresses me is Hare's moral fervour and campaigning theatricality. Mr Eyre and his designer, Bob Crowley, have also brilliantly found a way of staging the play that echoes its main theme. The Olivier stage is dominated by giant triple screens on to which close-up images of prison, police station and barrister's chambers are projected. But, as connections are gradually forged, so the pictures acquire high-definition harmony as in a remarkable panorama of Crystal Palace. Eyre also directs the key confrontations with admirable stillness allowing the words to do the work.

In a 25-strong cast there are signally impressive contributions from Lesley Sharp as the inquisitive constable, Alphonsia Emmanuel as the unbudgeable lawyer, Richard Pasco as a paternalistic QC, Michael Bryant as a wickedly impish judge, Keith Allen as an unscrupulous copper and Paul Moriarty as a long-suffering desk-sergeant.

But what really cheers me is to find Hare chasing, with such stylish anger, after the big public issues and the National Theatre placing itself at the centre of the debate about law, order and the kind of society we inhabit.

A stirring evening.

Party Time *and* Mountain Language

Almeida: 7 November 1991

Political plays come in all shapes and sizes: polemical, dialectical, disquisitory. But Harold Pinter's double-bill of *Party Time* and *Mountain Language* at the Almeida belongs to the oblique, metaphorical, less-is-more school of drama. Running 75 minutes, the two plays together powerfully evoke the brutality and intolerance which Pinter sees as threatening all our lives.

Party Time, getting its world premiere, is set in smart, fashionable London. Gavin, a suave power-broker, is throwing a party at which his guests prattle of exclusive health-clubs, idyllic island retreats, past romantic liaisons. Meanwhile in the streets outside there is a violent disorder which is being savagely suppressed. Finally the external world intrudes in the shape of a burning white light and the vehement presence of Jimmy, brother of one of the guests, testifying to the merciless extinction of dissent.

So what is Pinter saying? Not, I think, that Britain is sliding into Fascism. What he offers is an image of a style-conscious, narcissistic, bourgeois society cut off from and culpably indifferent to the intolerance and squalor of the outside world. I was constantly reminded of those Buñuel films in which the privileged are sealed off from reality; and Pinter's point is surely that our lives are increasingly governed by an apolitical materialism in which it is uncool to get het up about injustice and corruption.

What is impressive is how much Pinter crams into a short space. For he also suggests that, under the drawing-room elegance, private relationships echo public brutality. Terry, a yuppified Cockney, verbally savages his wife for asking after the fate of her dissenting brother. And in a richly comic passage, Terry praises the harmony of the health club where people don't do offensive things adding 'and if they do we kick them in the balls and chuck them down the stairs with no trouble at all.' Pinter depicts a world of increasingly moral coarseness and spiritual barbarism where even the death of old friends is seen as a minor matter compared to expiration of beloved clubby institutions.

Pinter's deployment of language is as skilful as ever: at one point a svelte widow (Nicola Pagett) asks a trim ex-lover (Roger Lloyd Pack) 'What's your regime?' which could equally apply to his dietary habits or his political affinities. If I have any doubt about the play it is that Pinter never acknowledges something almost as worrying as moral indifference: the extent to which public events (the Gulf War, the Birmingham Six) are often reduced to between-courses dinner-party chat. But his play is a packed, swift indictment of blunted, modern sensitivities: and his production is sharply designed by Mark Thompson, whose set is all Venetian blinds and fake-Regency furniture, and excellently acted by Barry Foster as the brocade-waistcoated host, by Peter Howitt as Essex man in a kipper-tie and by Cordelia Roche as his browbeaten, mini-dressed wife.

But what the evening primarily proves is that it is nonsense to suggest that Pinter's recent political plays are dealing with some nebulous East European state. Much more than at the National, *Mountain Language* emerges as a deeply British play about the suppression of local differences in favour of a centralised culture. Peter Howitt's Officer has a clipped Sandhurst accent and Barry Foster's Sergeant is a recognisable regimental type. But, like *Party Time*, the play comes across as metaphor rather than literal truth. Pinter's point is not that we live in a police-state but simply that we invest increasing power in an officialdom that sees any non-conformity as a threat. In four short scenes, Pinter pins down superbly the closed, uniformed mind and, in this version, banishes the consoling myth that it couldn't happen here.

Damned For Despair

The Gate: 18 November 1991

Stephen Daldry, heir apparent at the Royal Court, has come up with another scorcher at The Gate: a production of Tirso de Molina's 1620

Spanish tragedy, *Damned For Despair*, that recalls, in its flamboyant theatricality, the young Peter Brook. Not only is the Court lucky to get Mr Daldry: talent-scouts from the RSC and the National should also be eagerly sniffing round the Gate.

Tirso's play, in fact, forms a fascinating companion-piece to his *Last Days Of Don Juan* which closed at The Pit on Saturday. There the hero is damned because he has excessive confidence in God's mercy: here because he has too little. We see Paulo, a saintly hermit, deluded by the Devil into believing that he has a spiritual twin in the shape of Enrico, son of a Neapolitan nobleman.

Discovering to his horror that Enrico is a murderous thug, Paulo concludes he might as well be hanged for a sheep as a lamb and turns marauding bandit. But Enrico has a redemptive love for his father and, at his dad's intercession, finally seeks God's mercy on his deathbed. In contrast, Paulo, convinced he has forfeited God's forgiveness, is damned for despair.

That bald summary does scant justice to a knotty theological masterpiece that, in Laurence Boswell's translation, makes Graham Greene look pallid. Tirso, a Mercedarian friar, is dramatising the age-old conflict between fate and free will. Paulo is damned not just for lack of trust but because he presumes to ask God to reveal his destiny: Enrico is saved because he is capable of spontaneous repentance.

We tend to associate Catholic drama with dogmatic certainty; but Tirso, a subversive enquirer, both asserts the importance of choice and suggests that the instinctive sinner may be closer to God than the willed saint planning for the after-life.

If this sounds dry stuff, get thee to the Gate. There Tim Hatley has designed an extraordinary set: a red, multi-panelled revolving wall that serves as mountain or prison and that spins round to become brothel or torture-chamber. In a series of visual coups, the panels also give way to reveal the awesome sight of a hanging child, an ascending angel or a musket-bearing army.

Deploying a cast of 30 with military skill, Mr Daldry also cunningly mixes historical reference with modern relevance. Timothy Walker, Cheek By Jowl's Hamlet, is an actor never afraid to go over the top and for my money makes Paulo so frenzied a saint he has few resources left when he turns vicious villain. But Lorcan Cranitch brilliantly turns Enrico into a black-leathered brute, ironically with a 'Jesus Saves' tee-shirt, attended by a gang of lager-swilling punks. And Saira Todd scores a notable treble as his butterfly-tattooed moll, a background bassoonist and one of the angelic voices in Stephen Warbeck's remarkable musical score.

In short, this is theatre at its most theatrical: a play that tests to the limits the meaning of the Christian belief in 'grace abounding to the worst of sinners' and a production of a visceral power scarcely matched in all London.

Dr Jekyll And Mr Hyde

Barbican: 29 November 1991

Scene: a murky pub near the Barbican. Dr Jekyll and Mr Hyde, two sides of the same critic, have just emerged from the first night of David Edgar's RSC adaptation of RLS's chilling novella. They compare notes over a vintage malt.

Dr J: My dear Hyde, a capital evening was it not?

Mr H: No sir, more like a capital offence.

Dr J: You astonish me. Has not Mr Edgar, an adaptor as cunning as Old Nick, fleshed out the somewhat bare bones of Mr Stevenson's Gothick thriller. He has given the good Jekyll a mysterious, one-eyed sister. He has suggested that the Jekylls were dominated, like RLS himself, by a fiendish father. He has given the old tale topical relevance by portraying a smugly hierarchical society tolerating homelessness, child abuse, the degradation of women. Above all, he has had the brilliant notion of splitting the central roles so that Jekyll can converse with his baser nature, even as I do now.

Mr H: Springes to catch woodcocks! What he has done is to ruin a rattling good yarn. Stevenson's genius was to make our flesh creep with implied horror and then provide a philosophical speculation about human duality. Egregious Edgar does exactly the reverse. He gives us acres of dry chat about Faustian contradictions, Himmel und Welt, two souls struggling in one bosom, the danger of repression, before anything of remotely dramatic interest happens. Even that doomsday stuff about millennial decline smacks less of the 1880s than the 1990s. Mr Edgar has turned a pungent fable into a Fabian pamphlet, a dolorous tale into dollarbook Freud.

Dr J: But you miss my central point. That Mr Edgar has dramatised the divided self by making Roger Allam's sober, Scottish Jekyll and Simon Russell Beale's snickering Hyde exquisitely antithetical. Is not this the ego and the id?

Mr H: No, sir, it is R.D. Laing and water. Mr Edgar has missed the point. Stevenson's Jekyll says of his contending natures that 'even if I could rightly be said to be either, it was only because I was radically both.' Stevenson's theme was that good itself gives form to the ecstasy of evil. Divide them into separate entities and you sacrifice the story's unitarian horror.

Dr J: But Peter Wood's production, aided by Carl Toms's revolving set, answers precisely that point. He uses many thrilling devices to show that Jekyll and Hyde are two sides of the same coin. Mr Allam sees Mr Beale's reflection emerging from his own mirror. Mr Beale later sneaks out of the shadows to accompany him on the piano. And, most startling, one actor changes into the other in a railway compartment. Did not these devices freeze your blood?

Mr H: Pure Maskelyne magic that would not frighten a rabbit. Sleight of hand that is slight of effect because you waste valuable time wondering how it is done. What, pray, is there to compare with the moment in the original when the hero wakes in the yellow light of a mid-London morning to discover his hand is 'lean, corded, knuckly, of a dusky pallor, and thickly shaded with a swart growth of hair. It was the hand of Edward Hyde.'

Dr J: Hammer horror we have seen a hundred times! I went expecting cheap thrills. I found instead a serious play about the divided soul, social decay, a creeping paranoia about 'the demons, lurking out there in the darkness'. A Victorian thriller has been turned into a metaphor for our own fear of other races, classes and cultures.

Mr H: Pious cant! Did you instantly come out and take a derelict into your home? Stevenson was not writing an anti-Thatcherite social tract. He created a powerful shocker that has endured for over a century because it preys on our own private fears and fantasies. By laboriously spelling out its implications, Mr Edgar leaves nothing to our own imaginations. He proves yet again that *le vice anglais* is adaptation.

Dr J: I protest. Is there not something here for both of us?

Mr H: Yes, but not enough for either of us.

They continue pouring doubles into the night. By the morning light of an impending deadline, a single body is discovered slumped over the table. It is the lifeless form of Mr Hyde from whose limp and withered hand sub-editors effortfully prise a notice steeped in blood.

Afterword

So where does British theatre stand as we lurch towards the end of the millennium? Like the lady in the Sondheim song, it's still here: it has survived a lean decade of miserly public funding, the collapse of the socialist dream that inspired many of its playwrights, and an entertainment-revolution that, with the rise of CDs, video, satellite and cable TV, has turned the domestic hearth into a miniaturised Cape Canaveral. It remains as gloriously anachronistic as a handmade carving in an age of machine-tooled trinkets.

And yet it seems poised to take totally divergent paths. The strength of our theatre over the past two decades – and even before – has been the existence of a continuum that mysteriously linked the Fringe, the regions, the West End and the big national companies. It was possible for a writer like Ayckbourn to float between Scarborough, Greenwich, the National and the gilt-edged vaults of Shaftesbury Avenue. It was equally possible for a director like Trevor Nunn, in the space of a single year, to feel no discrepancy about working on a West End musical, a Glyndebourne opera and an RSC small-scale tour. Not everyone has been as constantly mobile as these two but the British theatre has long been a loosely-knit federal state requiring neither passports nor visas.

What worries me about the theatre today – writing early in 1993 – is the growing gulf between the private and the public sector. Arthur Miller said recently, 'I think we are moving into an age of the end of commercial theatre as it was known.' That certainly seems true of the West End with its escalating ticket-prices, fickle audiences, environmental decay and terrifying dearth of new plays. In 1971 the West End boasted new work by Osborne, Nichols, Gray, Mortimer, Hampton, Bennett, Ayckbourn, Sartre and Anouilh. Scanning the lists as I write, I find nineteen musicals, a handful of estimable classics and an even tinier handful of new plays: not surprisingly when you consider that a one-set, small-cast play currently costs at least £200,000 to launch. Increasingly London's West End is coming to resemble New York's Broadway: a place of shows rather than plays that manages to combine insult to the intelligence with injury to the pocket.

Against that, we have a subsidised sector that is still nourishing and diverse. The regional theatre has been badly dented by a decade of scrape-and-save underfunding, but there is vital work being done in Glasgow (where the Citizens Theatre has added two studios to its main house), Scarborough, Manchester, Leicester and Leeds. A small-scale touring company like Cheek By Jowl criss-crosses the country and scoops up accolades at foreign festivals. New plays still appear at a network of London theatres including the Royal Court, the Bush, Hampstead Theatre, the Tricycle, the Theatre Royal Stratford East and Croydon Warehouse. And while the National Theatre prospers under Richard Eyre, the Royal Shakespeare Company has discovered a new sense of purpose – and stopped doing bad musicals – under its tow-haired maestro, Adrian Noble.

It is, of course, still possible for both individuals and productions to commute between the private and the public sector: the West End success of plays like *Dancing At Lughnasa* (from the Abbey Theatre, Dublin) and *No Man's Land* (from the Almeida) offers current proof. The real divorce is between the cost, quality and texture of the experience in the two different worlds. A West End night out has become an expensive excursion into a Dantëesque hell in search of mythical and often over-hyped Entertainment. A visit to the National, Greenwich Theatre, the West Yorkshire Playhouse or the Orange Tree at Richmond is still a moderately affordable event where, with any luck, the soul will be nourished and the body fed.

When I began, the British theatre operated on different levels, but there was still a qualitative link between a Michael Codron-produced new play or a Peter Bridge revival in the West End and the work in the subsidised sector. Now we increasingly have two theatres, two audiences, two levels of expectation almost as irrevocably sundered as the West and East Berlin of old. The future of the British theatre depends, as much as anything, on the state of the economy and the ability to keep ticket-prices down. But it also depends, I suspect, on our ability to restore unity and harmony to an art afflicted by an inglorious and destructive division.

Index